British TV Streaming Guide

US Edition: Spring 2021

Your guide to streaming roughly 2200 different British TV shows in the US

See more of our British TV books & news at

IHeartBritishTV.com

Shop.IHeartBritain.com

D0813623

Cover Art By: Tabitha Mary (River Dart, Devon)

Tabitha Mary designs prints inspired by the old railway posters. Her collection of over 200 prints spans the globe, there's bound to be something for everyone. See her full range of prints at www.tabithamary.co.uk

Published by IHeartBritishTV.com

Sacramento, California

ISBN:978-1-7332961-7-5

Welcome - and thank you for buying or borrowing this guide! We're a small business, and we genuinely appreciate your support.

Before we get any further, I just want to offer a few comments to help you get the most out of this book. We put hundreds of hours into researching, writing, and laying it out, and as far as we know, it's the only one of its kind in the world.

That doesn't mean it's perfect.

We've long resisted the idea of putting out a printed streaming guide, purely because the offerings on streaming services change very rapidly. It's literally impossible to put out a guide that will be 100% accurate by the time it goes through printing and shipping.

Though we've done our best to track down the new and leaving shows, even the streaming services themselves don't always know what's leaving in a month's time - and occasionally, premieres get pushed back.

That said, most services change no more than 3-5% of their offerings in any given month. This guide should still be mostly accurate for months to come.

There are a couple other quirks you should be aware of as you dig in:

- Few services offer a list of all their British programming. That means many of these lists were gathered through sheer force, spending hours upon hours clicking around and digging through thousands of shows and related shows to figure out what's British. It's possible we've missed a few.
- For Acorn TV and BritBox, we listed ALL programming - including movies. On other platforms, we stuck to television.
- Our primary focus was on British programming. We've included a handful of shows from Australia, New Zealand, Canada, and Europe, but those are just happy little extras. This guide is far from comprehensive when it comes to shows from those countries.

This is our third time publishing this quarterly guide, and we hope you like it. We've continued to make adjustments based on reader feedback, and this time around, we've added a set of movie recommendations, seasonal content for Autism Awareness Month, and underlines for titles that are new to a service.

We welcome your feedback at areyoufree@iheartbritishtv.com.

We hope we're adding something valuable to the British TV community, and we'll certainly put out future editions if it's well-received (and we'll be forever grateful if you share your book photos on social media and tell your British TV-loving friends about it).

Happy Watching!

Stefanie & David
IHeartBritishTV.com

TABLE OF CONTENTS

ACORN TV

Now Streaming
Mysteries & Crime Dramas

19-2 - *Canada* - 2014 to 2017 - This Canadian police drama follows two unwilling partners: Officers Nick Barron and Ben Chartier. Together, they patrol downtown Montreal's 19th precinct in cruiser number 2. Though they have wildly different backgrounds and outlooks on life, they eventually learn to work together.

Above Suspicion - 2009 to 2012 - DC Anna Travis is a rookie detective determined to prove herself. She finds herself quickly tossed into the deep end, working cases where a prime suspect is wealthy or prominent enough to be considered "above suspicion".

Acceptable Risk - 2017 to present – When Sarah's husband is murdered, she realises how little she knows about his past.

The Agatha Christie Hour - 1982 - This series is a collection of one-hour dramas based on Agatha Christie's short stories. Each of the adaptations feature talented casts with British actors like John Nettles (*Midsomer Murders*), Amanda Redman (*The Good Karma Hospital*), and Stephanie Cole (*Doc Martin*).

Agatha Christie's Marple - 2004 to 2013 - Julia McKenzie stars as the iconic sleuth of St. Mary Mead. At present, Acorn TV offers the three-episode Series 6.

Agatha Christie's Partners in Crime - 2015 - David Walliams (*Little Britain*) and Jessica Raine (*Call the Midwife*) star in this updated adaptation of Agatha Christie's Tommy and Tuppence Beresford stories. Together, they solve mysteries and search for enemy spies in Cold War Britain.

Agatha Christie's Poirot - 1989 to 2020 - David Suchet portrays the eccentric Belgian Detective Poirot in this long-running series of Agatha Christie mysteries. Acorn TV has seasons 7 and 8, while BritBox has all the others.

Agatha Christie's The Witness for the Prosecution - 2016 - In 1920s London, a handsome townhouse is the setting for the brutal murder of Emily French, a glamorous young socialite. Toby Jones (*Detectorists*) and Kim Cattrall (*Sex and the City*) are among the members of this feature film's all-star cast.

Agatha Raisin - 2016 to present - Based on the M.C. Beaton novels, Agatha Raisin leaves her high-flying London PR life for a peaceful existence in The Cotswolds - or so she thinks. Though originally cancelled after Series 1, Acorn TV brought this one back for another two seasons, and a fourth is planned.

Alibi - 2003 - Michael Kitchen (*Foyle's War*), Sophie Okonedo (*Hotel Rwanda*), and Phyllis Logan (*Downton Abbey*) star in this thriller about a man discovered with the dead body of his business partner. When a nearby witness helps him dispose of the body, the situation spirals out of control and she wonders what she's gotten herself into. This series is presented in three episodes.

A Model Daughter: The Killing of Caroline Byrne - 2009 - In 1995, model Caroline Byrne's body was recovered from a popular suicide spot in Sydney, Australia. Did she jump? Did someone push her? Though her boyfriend claimed she had been depressed, not everyone agreed. It was only through her father's unfailing determination that she finally got justice.

And Then There Were None - 2015 - Based on the Agatha Christie novel, this miniseries sees 10 strangers invited to an island, only to be killed off one by one.

Bäckström - *Sweden* - 2020 - This Swedish crime drama follows detective Evert Bäckström, a stand-out detective with a record of solving nearly every case he takes on. **Premieres April 26th.**

Balthazar - *France* - 2018 to present - This French crime drama revolves around Raphael Balthazar, a brilliant forensic pathologist who's haunted by the memory of his murdered wife. Highly unconventional in his approach, he frequently helps police commander Hélène Bach solve some of Paris' most baffling murder cases.

Blood - 2018 to 2020 - *Ireland* - Adrian Dunbar (*Line of Duty*) stars as a respected doctor and new widower in a small Irish town. Though everyone else believes his wife's death was an accident, his daughter has her doubts. Carolina Main (*Unforgotten*) stars alongside Dunbar as his daughter, Cat.

Bloodlands - 2020 - Produced by Jed Mercurio (*Line of Duty*), this series begins when an expensive car is pulled out of the water with a suicide note but no body. James Nesbitt (*Cold Feet*) stars as Northern Ireland police detective Tom Brannick, who instantly sees a connection to a cold case of personal significance.

Bloodlines - 2010 - It seems there will always be a few relatively smart people who think they're capable of committing the perfect murder – and this true crime movie tells the story of one of them. In November 1999, Dr. Colin Bouwer (Mark Mitchinson, *Mystery Road*), head of Psychiatry at Otago Hospital, decided to slowly kill his wife with insulin. It was only through the observant young consulting physician Andrew Bowers (Craig Hall, *A Place To Call Home*) that he was caught.

The Brokenwood Mysteries - 2014 to present - DI Mike Shepard arrives in the seemingly peaceful New Zealand town of Brokenwood with a classic car, country music, and a string of ex-wives. There, he quickly finds that all is not as it seems, and both secrets and animosities run deep in the local community. He's assisted in his crime-fighting efforts by the highly capable, by-the-books assistant DC Kristin Sims.

The Broker's Man - 1997 to 1998 - An ex-cop now puts his detective skills to work for insurance companies. Kevin Whately (*Lewis*) stars.

The Circuit - 2007 to 2010 - This drama follows a magistrate and an entourage of court officers and lawyers on a regular five-day 2000 kilometer round-trip to dispense justice to the remote communities of north Western Australia. It's a hard job for anyone, but for newly-hired Aboriginal lawyer Drew Ellis (Aaron Pedersen, *Mystery Road*) who had a white upbringing and has a white wife, it's a rude awakening as he gets a close-up view of the inequalities in the system.

Code of a Killer - 2015 - This criminal drama tells the story of the first time DNA fingerprinting was used to help solve a murder case. David Threlfall (*Shameless*) stars as DCS David Baker, who heads up the investigation. John Simm (*Life on Mars*) plays Dr. Alec Jeffreys, the scientist who invents the process for fingerprinting DNA.

The Commander - 2003 to 2008 - Amanda Burton (*Silent Witness*) stars in this thriller about the murder investigations of Commander Clare Blake, highest-ranking female officer at New Scotland Yard. The series was written by *Prime Suspect* creator Lynda La Plante.

The Cry - *Australia* – 2018 – Jenna Coleman stars in this miniseries about a young couple dealing with the abduction of their baby.

Darkness: Those Who Kill - 2019 - This Danish crime drama follows two investigators looking into a series of murders in hopes of rescuing the next victim in time. When a young woman disappears from the streets of Copenhagen, only Detective Jan Michelsen (Kenneth M. Christensen, The Legacy) believes she could still be alive. Joining forces with an expert profiler (played by Natalie Madueño, *Follow the Money*), they discover the disappearance is linked with another kidnapping and murder 10 years prior.

Dead Lucky - *Australian* - 2018 – When a dangerous armed robber resurfaces in Sydney, two very different detectives are forced to work together to catch him.

Deadwater Fell - 2019 - David Tennant stars in this dark miniseries about a Scottish family that's murdered one night, tearing apart their otherwise peaceful village and bringing secrets to the surface.

Deep Water - *Australian* - 2016 - Yael Stone (*Orange is the New Black*) and Noah Taylor (*Game of Thrones*) star as detectives investigating the vicious murder of a young man. As their investigation progresses, they discover connections to a string of unsolved cases involving gay men killed in the 80s and 90s.

A Difficult Woman – *Australia* – 1998 - A woman with a brilliant career and promising relationship sees everything derailed when a close friend is murdered. As she gets more information, it leads her well out of her comfort zone as she pursues the killer.

East West 101 - *Australian* - 2007 to 2011 - *Australia* - Malik and Crowley are a study in opposites as they investigate major crimes.

The Field of Blood - 2011 to 2013 - Set in early 1980s Glasgow, a young woman skillfully solves murders on a police force full of men. Unfortunately, her dedication to the truth also puts her in danger. The series stars BAFTA winner Jayd Johnson (*River City*) as Paddy Meehan, working alongside Peter Capaldi (*Doctor Who*) and David Morrissey (*The Missing*).

Foyle's War - 2002 to 2015 - DCS Foyle fights a war against crime in southern England as WWII goes on around him. Michael Kitchen (*The Life of Rock with Brian Pern*) and Honeysuckle Weeks (*The Five*) star.

George Gently - 2007 to 2017 - Loosely based on the Inspector Gently novels by Alan Hunter, this 1960s-based series follows Martin Shaw as Inspector George Gently, along with Lee Ingleby as DS John Bacchus. Together, they scour North East England's criminal underworld.

The Gulf - 2019 - This six-part New Zealand-based series follows Detective Jess Savage (Kate Elliott, *Wentworth*) as she investigates crimes in Waiheke Island. After losing her memory in the same car crash that killed her husband, she sets her sights on finding the killer and bringing him or her to justice. Unfortunately, her memory issues and increasing reliance on morphine make the investigation difficult, and she begins to become paranoid that someone is out to get her because of something she knows.

Hamish Macbeth - 1995 to 1997 - Hamish Macbeth (Robert Carlyle, *The Full Monty*) is a talented but unambitious Highlands constable who doesn't always follow the rules. The series was filmed in the lovely Highland village of Plockton on the shores of Loch Carron, and it's a great watch for those who enjoy good scenery.

Harry - *New Zealand* - 2013 - Detective Harry Anglesea returns to work just four weeks after his wife's suicide, and it may be too soon.

Hidden - 2011 - This four-part BBC conspiracy thriller stars Philip Glenister (*Life on Mars*) as Harry Venn, a high street solicitor who's unwittingly drawn into the investigation of his brothers murder 20 years prior. Thekla Reuten (*The American*) and David Suchet (*Poirot*) also appear.

Hidden - 2018 - When a young woman's body turns up with evidence that she was held prisoner prior to her death, the investigation leads DI Cadi John (Sian Reese-Williams, *Requiem*) to a string of disappearances in a beautiful but remote part of Wales. Only the first season is currently available on Acorn at time of print.

In Deep - 2001 to 2003 - Nick Berry (*Heartbeat*) and Stephen Tompkinson (*DCI Banks, Trollied*) star in this 2001 series about undercover detectives and the unique challenges they face while leading double lives.

Injustice - 2011 - A defense barrister has to deal with the consequences of defending an indefensible crime. *Foyle's War* and *Midsomer Murders* screenwriter Anthony Horowitz created the series, and it features an all-star cast with actors like James Purefoy (*Rome*), Dervla Kirwan (*Ballykissangel*), Charlie Creed-Miles (*The Fifth Element*), and Nathaniel Parker (*The Inspector Lynley Mysteries*).

Jack Taylor - *Ireland* - 2010 to 2016 - Resistant to rules, ex-cop Jack Taylor becomes a private investigator after losing his job with the Guard. Iain Glen (*Game of Thrones*) stars in this series set against the city of Galway. It's based on a series of novels written by Ken Bruen.

Jericho of Scotland Yard - 2005 - This period mystery gives us DI Michael Jericho, a WWII veteran who investigates murders while also seeking to figure out the circumstances surrounding his father's death.

Keeping Faith - 2017 to present - A Welsh lawyer cuts her maternity leave short when her husband goes missing. As she tries to solve the crime before she's arrested for it, she finds herself knee-deep in the criminal underworld of her small town. Eve Myles (*Torchwood*) stars, though some might argue her yellow anorak deserves a mention, too.

Killer Net - 1998 - A psychology student becomes obsessed with a computer game about murder, but it gets scary when it suddenly seems to be connected to real murders. Tam Williams (*Spectre*) and Paul Bettany (*The Avengers* films) star in this dark miniseries.

L'Accident - *France* - 2016 to 2017 - When police accuse his wife of drunk driving in the crash that killed her, Gabriel Cauvy (Bruno Solo, *Blood on the Docks*) sets out to clear her name. Unfortunately, the search proves more dangerous than he might have guessed.

Lawless - 1999 - This New Zealand TV movie sees undercover cop John Lawless wrongly accused of murder. To prove his innocence, he'll have to get help from friends on both sides of the law.

The Level - 2016 to 2017 - A detective is the missing witness in the murder of a drug trafficker. The police want her, and the killer wants her dead.

Line of Duty – 2012 to present - This suspenseful British police series is set in the fictional "anti-corruption unit" AC-12, where the police police the police. Yes, we know that sounds a bit odd. Lennie James, Vicky McClure, Martin Compston, and Adrian Dunbar all feature.

Liverpool 1 - 1998 to 1999 - This gritty, Liverpool-based police drama dives into the city's underworld. We follow the vice squad at Bridewell as they fight drug dealers, paeodophiles, pimps, and porn peddlers in this rough-around-the-edges port city. Samantha Womack stars as DC Isobel de Pauli.

Loch Ness - 2017 to present - Highlands Detective Annie Redford faces her first murder case when a human heart is found.

London Kills - 2019 - This Acorn TV Original follows a team of London's top detectives as they investigate homicides. Hugo Speer (*The Full Monty*) stars as DI David Bradford, the lead investigator whose talents seem to solve every case but the disappearance of his wife. Sharon Small (*The Inspector Lynley Mysteries*) and Bailey Patrick (*Bodyguard*) also star.

Lovejoy - 1986 to 1994 - Ian McShane (*Deadwood*) stars as Lovejoy, the slightly shady antiques dealer and part-time detective. *Downton Abbey* fans will be delighted to see a young Phyllis Logan (aka Mrs. Hughes) in this early role.

Manhunt - 2018 to present - Martin Clunes (*Doc Martin*) stars in this series based on the real investigation into the death of French student Amélie Delagrange. Clunes plays DCI Colin Sutton, the man who led the task force that ultimately brought her killer to justice. Though it feels very much like a miniseries, it's been confirmed that another series will be produced at some point in the future.

Mayday - 2013 - When the May Queen disappears just before May Day celebrations, a small town is thrown into chaos.

McCallum - 1995 to 1998 - Pathologist McCallum and his team help the dead tell their stories.

Midsomer Murders - 1998 to present - In Midsomer County, the landscapes are beautiful, the villagers all have secrets, and murder is rampant. This British mystery classic features John Nettles as DCI Tom Barnaby through the first 13 seasons, with Neil Dudgeon as DCI John Barnaby for the later seasons.

Midsomer Murders: 20th Anniversary Special - 2019 - John Nettles presents this look back at Midsomer Murders on its 20th anniversary. The hour-long special features appearances by Neil Dudgeon, Nick Hendrix, Daniel Casey, Jason Hughes, Jane Wymark, and more.

Midsomer Murders: Neil Dudgeon's Top 10 - This special collection doesn't include any new episodes of Midsomer Murders, but it does feature commentary and behind-the-scenes stories from Neil Dudgeon.

Mind Games - 2001 - Fiona Shaw (*Killing Eve*) stars in this television movie about a nun turned criminal profiler who's called in to investigate the deaths of two middle-aged women. She quickly realises that these aren't just home robberies gone wrong - they're the work of a serial killer.

Miss Fisher's Murder Mysteries - *Australian* -2012 to 2015 - In 1920s Melbourne, Miss Phryne Fisher works as a skilled private detective. Essie Davis and Nathan Page star.

Miss Fisher & The Crypt of Tears - *Australian* - 2020 - This movie is a continuation of the original Miss Fisher's Murder Mysteries stories, and it premiered in early 2020. In this one, Essie Davis returns to the role of Phyrne in 1929 Jerusalem. There, she rescues a young Bedouin girl and finds herself on a globe-trotting adventure with her favourite handsome detective, Jack Robinson (Nathan Page).

Mr. and Mrs. Murder - *Australian* - 2013 - A married couple runs a crime scene cleaning business while also helping to solve the murders they clean up.

Ms. Fisher's Modern Murder Mysteries - *Australian* - In this spin-off to the original *Miss Fisher's Murder Mysteries* series, Phryne Fisher's long-lost niece follows in her aunt's footsteps as a 1960s lady detective with her own handsome officer. Geraldine Hakewill stars as Peregrine Fisher, and Joel Jackson plays Detective James Steed.

Murder Investigation Team - 2003 to 2005 - A London-based team of elite investigators handles exceptionally challenging murders.

Murderland - 2009 - This miniseries looks at a murder from the perspectives of the daughter, the detective, and the murder victim.

Murdoch Mysteries - *Canada* - 2008 to present - Set in the 1890s, Murdoch uses early forensics to solve murders. Yannick Bisson stars as Detective William Murdoch, Helene Joy plays Dr. Julia Ogden, and Thomas Craig and Jonny Harris fill the roles of Inspector Thomas Brackenreid and Constable George Crabtree, respectively.

Murdoch Mysteries: The Movies - *Canada* - 2004 to 2005 - Before it was a hit television series, there were three Murdoch Mysteries movies. Also set in 1890s Canada, the movies feature Peter Outerbridge as Detective William Murdoch (as opposed to Yannick Bisson) and Keeley Hawes (*The Durrells, Bodyguard*) as Dr. Julia Ogden.

Murphy's Law - 2001 to 2007 - James Nesbitt (*Cold Feet*) stars as Tommy Murphy, a charming but tough Northern Irish cop with a tragic past.

My Life is Murder - *Australia* - 2019 - Lucy Lawless (*Xena: Warrior Princess*) stars as retired Melbourne cop Alexa Crowe. Alexa is a mystery, but we know she's tough, smart, hurting from a past trauma, and great at baking bread. She's also slowly warming up to the cat who's invited itself to live with her. In each episode, her old boss (played by Bernard Curry) requests her assistance on a tough case - and on each case, she seeks a bit of extra help from her protégé Madison (Ebony Vagulans).

The Mystery of a Hansom Cab - 2012 - Set in 1880s Melbourne, this period drama is based on the bestselling novel by Fergus Hume. It follows the murder of a man connected to a wealthy benefactor, along with an accused man unable to provide an alibi.

Mystery Road - *Australia* - 2018 to present - Detective Jay Swan investigates crimes in the Australian Outback.

No Offence - 2015 to 2018 - This gritty Manchester-based police drama showcases the work of some talented serious crimes investigators under the straight-talking DI Viv Deering. Sadly, one of the actors, Will Mellor, made an Instagram post letting people know that a fourth season won't be happening due to changes at the network (Channel 4). The writer, Paul Abbott (*Shameless*), had already been working on ideas for a new season, but unless the show is somehow saved, it looks like we may never see them brought to life.

The Oldenheim 12 - *The Netherlands* - 2017 - A traditional Dutch village is shaken to its core when multiple residents suddenly go missing without a trace.

One Lane Bridge - *New Zealand* - 2020 - While working a murder investigation, a young Maori detective accidentally awakens a spiritual gift that may harm the case. **Premieres April 26th.**

Pie in the Sky - 1994 to 1997 - When DI Crabbe leaves the police force to open a restaurant, they continue to pull him back in for part-time crime-solving. Richard Griffiths (Vernon Dursley in *Harry Potter*) stars, but you'll also spot guest appearances from actors like Phyllis Logan (*Downton Abbey*), Jim Carter (*Downton Abbey*), Jane Wymark (*Midsomer Murders*), Keeley Hawes (*Bodyguard*), Ian McNeice (*Doc Martin*), Michael Kitchen (*Foyle's War*), Derren Litten (*Benidorm*), Abigail Thaw (*Endeavour*), Nicola Walker (*Unforgotten*), and Joan Sims (*As Time Goes By*).

The Poison Tree - 2012 - Matthew Goode (*A Discovery of Witches*) stars in this psychological thriller about a man who returns home after being released from prison. Though his devoted wife (MyAnna Buring, *Ripper Street*) has always maintained his innocence, he comes to realise she may be hiding more than her fair share of dark secrets.

Prisoners' Wives - 2012 - Gemma thinks she has a perfect life until her husband is arrested for murder.

Queens of Mystery - 2019 - Young Matilda Stone is just beginning her career in law enforcement and she has not one, not two, but three crime-writing aunts. Her quirky aunts raised her after her mother's disappearance, and they always try to poke around in her cases. The series was created by *Doc Martin* writer Julian Unthank, with appearances by Olivia Vinall (*The Woman in White*), Julia Graham (*Bletchley Circle*), Siobhan Redmond (*Taggart*), and Sarah Woodward (*Gems*).

Rebecka Martinsson - 2017 to present - *Sweden* - This Swedish crime drama follows a young Stockholm lawyer as her life is turned upside down by the violent murder of a childhood friend. She quits her job and returns to her hometown to investigate a world that's not what it seems.

Rebus - 2000 to 2004 - Based on the novels of Scottish author Ian Rankin, Inspector Rebus is an old-fashioned detective in every sense of the word. He smokes, drinks, and doesn't have a lot of luck with his personal life. Set in Edinburgh, the series features John Hannah as DI John Rebus in early episodes, followed by Ken Stott in later episodes.

The Rivals of Sherlock Holmes - 1971 to 1973 - This vintage British mystery series offers up a variety of detective story adaptations from Sir Arthur Conan Doyle's contemporaries.

Rumpole of the Bailey - 1978 to 1992 - No British TV education is complete without watching this series about the cigar-puffing, cheap wine-drinking, incredibly eccentric defense barrister Horace Rumpole (played by Australian Leo McKern). This classic comedy features relatively early performances from Patricia Hodge (*Miranda*), Camilla Coduri (*Doctor Who*), and Brenda Blethyn (*Vera*).

The Schouwendam 12 - *Netherlands* - 2019 - Decades ago, teenagers Alice and Olaf disappeared from their Dutch village of Schouwendam without a trace. Now, an unknown man has arrived, strongly resembling Olaf but with no memories of his past. It's not long before more deaths start to occur, and the village is forced to confront not just the past, but the possibility there might be a killer in their midst.

The Silence - 2006 - Rake star Richard Roxburgh stars as Detective Richard Treloar, an officer under investigation for a fatal shooting. He's been re-assigned to a desk job at the Police Museum, and his new position draws him into an old mystery. While working on a photographic exhibition, he becomes obsessed with an archival image of a beautiful murder victim. Searching through more images, he looks for her face – seeing her first in the background of images, then in the company of criminals, and later, as the victim of an unsolved crime.

The Silence – 2010 - While struggling to integrate into the hearing world, a young girl with a new cochlear implant witnesses the murder of a police officer. Douglas Henshall (*Shetland*) is among the stars of this miniseries.

Single-Handed - 2007 to 2010 - *Ireland* - Jack Driscoll is transferred back to his hometown to take over the Garda Sergeant role his father left.

Sisters, aka Sorelle - 2017 - *Italy* - In this Italian-language mystery, a young lawyer returns to her Italian hometown to investigate the disappearance of her younger sister. As she's drawn further into the case, she realises the main suspect may be closer than she thinks.

The Sommerdahl Murders - *Denmark* - 2020 - In the beautiful Danish coastal town of Helsingør, Detective Chief Inspector Dan Sommerdahl (Peter Mygind, *Flame and Citron*) is the undisputed hero at North Sjælland Police. When the body of a young woman washes up on a beach, Dan and his best friend and colleague, Detective Flemming Torp (André Babikian, *The Protectors*), quickly determine this wasn't an accident, and they are in hot pursuit to find the murderer and the baby the female victim had just given birth to.

The Sounds - 2020 - A happily married Canadian couple moves to New Zealand to escape the husband's domineering family, but when he disappears soon after relocating, long-buried secrets come to light.

Still Life: A Three Pines Mystery - *Canada* - 2013 - In this television movie, Chief Inspector Armand Gamache (Nathaniel Parker) arrives in Three Pines to investigate a strange death in the sleepy village of Three Pines.

The Strange Calls - 2012 - This oddball comedy/mystery series follows a disgraced Australian cop, Toby Banks, after he's transferred to the seemingly idyllic coastal town of Coolum Beach. There, his job is to answer night calls from locals – calls that reveal bizarre truths about something sinister lurking beneath the town's cozy surface.

Supply and Demand - 1997 to 1998 - This crime drama features an elite team of detectives charged with investigating large-scale smugglers and importers.

Suspects - 2014 to 2016 - Three Greater London detectives investigate serious crimes in this heavily improvised series.

Thorne - 2010 - This collection of two Thorne movies includes *Scaredy Cat* and *Sleepyhead*. In *Sleepyhead*, DI Thorne (David Morrissey, *Men Behaving Badly*) is in a race against time to find a serial killer who enjoys making unusual attacks on young women. *Scaredy Cat* sees Thorne is working with a new team to tackle a tough double

murder case, but it's not long before he's hunting down two different serial killers.

Traffik - 1989 - This drama tells a story about the international drug trade through the lens of three different characters: Jack, the British government minister who sees heroin hurting his constituents; Helen, a woman whose husband has been arrested; and Fazal, a Pakistani man who works for a drug lord. The series was filmed on location in London, Hamburg, and Pakistan.

Trial & Retribution - 1997 to 2009 - DS Walker and his team follow criminals from their crime to the courts.

The Truth Will Out - 2018 to present - Detective Peter Wendel sets out to create an elite task force to help solve cold cases, but when he finally gets his chance, the only available officers seem to be some of Sweden's worst. Meanwhile, he's dealing with the possibility that a noted serial killer may not have killed all his victims - leaving another murderer, or even many murderers, running free.

Vera - 2011 to present - DCI Vera Stanhope investigates murders in the Northumberland countryside. Brenda Blethyn (*Chance in a Million*) stars in this long-running crime drama based on Ann Cleeves' *Vera* novels. This series is split between Acorn TV and BritBox, with Acorn having seasons 1, 2, 6, and 7.

Vexed – 2010 to 2012 - A young male and female detective team frustrate each other with their different attitudes and complicated personal lives.

Winter - 2015 - *Australia* - Eve Winter, a Sydney homicide detective, solves some of the most difficult cases while dealing with bureaucracy and the challenges of being a woman in her field. Rebecca Gibney (*Packed to the Rafters*) stars.

Wire in the Blood - 2002 to 2009 - An eccentric psychologist helps the police solve murders by getting inside the minds of the killers. Robson Green (*Grantchester*) stars.

Wisting - 2019 - This Norwegian drama follows homicide detective William Wisting as he investigates the possibility of an American serial killer living in Norway.

Dramas

800 Words - *New Zealand* - 2015 to 2018 - After the death of his wife, a man relocates his family from Sydney to a small coastal community in New Zealand.

A Dance to the Music of Time - 1997 - This miniseries adaptation of Anthony Powell's novel of the same name charts the lives of characters from the 1920s thru the 1960s.

The Advocates - 1991 to 1992 - This Scottish legal drama is set in the high-powered world of lawyers and advocates

A Place to Call Home - *Australia* - 2013 to 2018 - A mysterious woman begins a new life in Australia after World War II.

The Attaché - *France/Israel* - 2019 - Eli Ben David (Buba Shel-Medina) based this series on his own experiences of living in Paris as an Israeli Jewish man of Moroccan descent. He plays a successful musician who relocated to the city for his wife's new job as the attaché to the Israeli embassy in Paris, highlighting the troubles he experiences with his marriage, masculinity, and fatherhood.

A Voyage Round My Father - 1984 - Sir Laurence Olivier stars in this family drama based on the life of John Mortimer, creator of Rumpole of the Bailey.

Ackley Bridge - 2017 to present - Two struggling schools merge to form one, and it creates big problems for the headmistress.

Amnesia - 2004 - This miniseries tells the story of DS MacKenzie Stone, his tireless search for his wife who disappeared 5 years prior, and an amnesiac who factors into the case.

An Accidental Soldier - 2013 - In this acclaimed WW1 drama, a 35-year-old Australian soldier flees the Western Front and finds love and refuge with a French woman in a remote farmhouse. The film is based on the novel *Silent Parts* by John Charalambous, and it tells the story of two people who find passion at an age when they thought love had passed them by. *Editor's Note: Is anyone else laughing a bit at the thought of 35 being too old to find love?*

Anna Karenina - 2000 to 2001 - Helen McCrory plays the title role in this adaptation of Tolstoy's classic novel.

Anner House - 2007 - Based on one of Maeve Binchy's short stories, this film is a romantic drama about two Irish emigrants who begin new lives in Cape Town while struggling to deal with their pasts.

Anzac Girls - *Australia* - 2014 - Heroic women rise to the occasion during the war.

A Suitable Boy - 2020 - This Andrew Davies (*House of Cards*) adaptation of Vikram Seth's novel of the same name follows the story of a young woman coming of age in 1951 North India. The series filmed in India featuring Bollywood celebrities Ishaan Khatter and Tabu (*Life of Pi*) alongside rising star Tanya Maniktala in the central role of Lata.

B&B - 1992 - After getting fired from his architectural job, single dad Steve Shepherd (Keven Whately, *Inspector Morse*) opens his home to guests to help pay the bills. Not long after he loses his job, his former boss, Horace Gilbert (Ian McNeice, *Doc Martin*) learns that his former employee's home lies right in the middle of their intended development site for vacation homes.

Back Home - *Italy* - 2017 - After spending five years in a coma, an Italian man awakens to find that his wife is now with his best friend, his kids are grown up, and his business is all but ruined.

The Badness of King George IV - 2004 - Oliver Ford Davies (*Star Wars: Episodes 1 and 2*) plays the highly unpopular monarch in this film that explores his failings as a monarch.

Bang - 2017 to present - In this bilingual Welsh crime drama, a man comes into possession of a gun and his life is forever changed.

Bed of Roses - *Australia* - 2008 to 2011 - A mother and daughter struggle after the death of their husband and father.

Belonging - 2003 - Brenda Blethyn (*Vera*) and Kevin Whately (*Lewis*) star as a married couple who've been happily married for decades and now live with a number of extended family members. Jess (Blethyn) has given up her job to care for the older family members, and it's all going rather well until her husband disappears. **Premieres April 26th.**

The Black Velvet Gown - 1991 - Set in 1830s Northumberland, this two-part film explores what happens when a mother and daughter are set apart by their shared ability to read and write.

Black Widows - *Finland* - 2016 to 2017 - Three best friends are going through a mid-life crisis and think that life will be better if their husbands are dead. Unfortunately for them, it's not quite as simple as they had imagined.

The Blue Rose - New Zealand - 2013 - This investigative drama sees a group of law firm employees joining together to figure out what happened in the mysterious death of a co-worker.

Bodily Harm - 2002 - Timothy Spall (*Blandings*) stars as a suburban man whose life is changed forever after he loses his job, finds out his father is dying, and catches his wife cheating.

Bomb Girls - 2012 to 2013 - Set during World War II, BOMB GIRLS tells the stories of women who risked their lives in a munitions factory as they built bombs for the Allied Forces. The series stars Meg Tilly (*The Big Chill*), Jodi Balfour (*Quarry*), Charlotte Hegele (*When Calls the Heart*) and Ali Liebert (*Ten Days in the Valley*).

The Boy with the Topknot - 2017 - This film tells the story of Sathnam, young Indian raised in Britain, as he tries to adjust to his multicultural life.

Brief Encounters - 2016 - When a group of women start selling lingerie and other marital aids through at-home parties in the early 1980s, their lives are transformed.

Care - 2018 - Sheridan Smith (*Gavin & Stacey*) stars as a single mother struggling to raise her two children after a family tragedy. After her husband's departure, she's fully reliant on the childcare her mother Mary (Alison Steadman, also from *Gavin & Stacey*) provides. That all changes when Mary suffers a devastating stroke and develops dementia.

The Case - 2011 - This legal drama tells the story of a man put on trial for the murder of his terminally ill partner after he helped her commit suicide.

Cilla - 2014 - Cilla tells the story of British entertainer Cilla Black and her rise to fame in 1960s Liverpool.

Clean Break - 2015 - When a car dealer realises he's in trouble and about to lose everything, he sets out to fix his problems while also exacting revenge on those who have hurt him.

Close to the Enemy - 2016 - After WW2, a German engineer is taken to Britain in hopes of gaining his cooperation. Jim Sturgess (*Across the Universe*) and Charlotte Riley (*Press*) star.

Cloudstreet - *Australia* - 2011 - This period drama is set around Perth, Australia between 1943 and 1963, and it tells the story of two families thrown together in a large house after a series of catastrophes.

The Code - *Australia* - 2014 to 2016 - When two brothers, a hacker and a journalist, are facing the possibility of extradition to the US, the Australian National Security offers them a way out. They're taken to a government facility and told that if they help out, the slate will be wiped clean.

Cold Call - 2019 - When a single mum gets caught up in a cold call phone scam, her entire life is turned upside down.

The Crimson Petal & the White - 2011 - In late 1800s London, a prostitute finds her position greatly improved after becoming the mistress to a powerful man. Romola Garai (*The Hour*) stars as prostitute Sugar, with Chris O'Dowd (*The IT Crowd*) playing William Rackham, the perfume heir who becomes involved with her.

Danger UXB - 1979 - This vintage series was titled after the shorthand term for "danger, unexploded bomb", and it tells the story of the men who worked in bomb disposal during WWII. Each hour-long episode follows these brave young men as they carried out one of the most difficult and terrifying jobs in the war effort.

Dear Murderer - *New Zealand* - 2017 to present - This series tells the true story of Mike Bungay, one of New Zealand's most successful and controversial defense lawyers.

Delicious - 2016 to present - Two women in Cornwall try to get on somewhat peacefully after circumstances in their lives change dramatically.

Doctor Finlay - 1993 to 1996 - After WW2 and before the NHS is created, a doctor returns to his Scottish hometown.

Dominion Creek - *Ireland* - 2015 to present - Three Irish brothers dream of striking it rich in the Klondike Gold Rush.

East of Everything - *Australia* - 2008 to 2009 - When an Australian woman dies, she dictates in her will that her two estranged sons must reopen the family hostel in Broken Bay.

Family Business - *France* - 2017 - A mother-daughter lawyer pair juggle the ins and outs of running a family law practice, all while balancing and navigating their own issues away from the office.

Fanny Hill - 2007 - Based on the scandalous classic novel, orphaned Fanny Hill is a prostitute who falls in love with a handsome merchant's son who also happens to be her first customer.

Fingersmith - 2005 – In Victorian England, a young female thief hatches a plan to get close to an heiress and scam her. It doesn't go as planned.

Flame Trees of Thika - 1981 - Hayley Mills (*Wild at Heart*), David Robb (*I, Claudius*), and Holly Aird (*Waking the Dead*) star in this miniseries about a British family who relocate to British East Africa (now Kenya) to set up a coffee plantation.

The Fragile Heart - 1996 - Nigel Hawthorne (*The Madness of King George*) stars as a successful cardiac surgeon in the midst of a professional and personal crisis. He plays Edgar Pascoe, a man whose world begins to cataclysmically crumble during a visit to China. Confronted by an ethical dilemma over human rights abuses, he's forced into a painful moral awakening which seeps into every area of his life.

From Father to Daughter - *Italy* - 2017 - This Italian saga begins in 1958 and covers nearly 30 years in the lives of the Franza sisters. The three work hard to impress their father, take on the family distillery business, and find love.

Girlfriends - 2018 - A group of middle-aged women experience some strange and dramatic situations, but get through it together. Miranda Richardson (*Good Omens*) stars alongside Zoë Wanamaker (*Love Hurts*) and Phyllis Logan (*Lovejoy*).

The Gods of Wheat Street - *Australia* - 2014 - This Australian series gives us a closer look at the lives of the Freeburns, a rough-around-the-edges Aboriginal Australian family with a complicated and chaotic life.

Gold Digger - 2019 - Julia Ormond (*Sabrina*) stars as Julia Day, a wealthy 60-year-old woman who falls in love with a handsome man 26 years her junior. As secrets come to light, no one can be sure what's real and what's merely convenient.

The Good Karma Hospital - 2017 to present - After a relationship sours, a young British-Indian woman decides to move to India to work in an impoverished hospital. Little does she know, she's got a lot to learn. Amanda Redman stars alongside Amrita Acharia.

The Great Train Robbery - 2013 - This two-part series tells the story of 1963's Great Train Robbery from two perspectives - the side of the robbers, and the side of the cops. Martin Compston (*Line of Duty*), Luke Evans (*The Girl on the Train*), and Jim Broadbent (*Iris*) star.

The Heart Guy (aka Doctor Doctor) - *Australia* - 2016 to present - When a prominent heart surgeon falls from grace, he's forced to go work as a country GP in his former hometown. At his lowest moment, he'll have to face the people and places he's spent his life trying to get away from.

The Helen West Casebook - 2002 - Amanda Burton (Silent Witness) stars as crown prosecutor Helen West, a justice-driven woman who pursues tough cases even as her boss recommends dropping them.

The Hour - 2011 - This period drama takes us behind the scenes during the launch of a new London news programme during the mid-1950s. Ben Whishaw (*Spectre*), Romola Garai (*Emma*), Dominic West (*The Affair*), and Peter Capaldi (*Doctor Who*) are among the cast members.

I, Claudius - Sir Derek Jacobi (*Last Tango in Halifax*) and Sir Patrick Stewart (*Star Trek*) star in this BBC television adaptation of Robert Graves' 1934 novel of the same name (along with its sequel, *Claudius the God*). The series covers the early history of the Roman Empire, with an elderly Emperor Claudius narrating.

The Indian Doctor - 2010 to 2013 - An Indian doctor and his wife move to a small Welsh mining village during the 1960s. They have to adjust to culture shock, and Dr. Sharma must win the trust of the locals as their GP.

The Irish R.M. - *Ireland* - 1983 to 1985 - When an Englishman leaves home to become an Irish Resident Magistrate, he quickly learns the normal rules don't apply with his eccentric new neighbours.

The Invisibles - 2008 - A couple of retired master burglars tried living in Spain, but after a bout of homesickness, they returned to England with their wives to live in a Devon fishing village. It's not long before a return to familiar shores sees them taking up the same old bad habits.

Jack Irish - *Australia* - 2012 to 2018 - Guy Pearce (*Memento*) stars as Jack Irish, a talented PI and ex-lawyer with a checkered past. Marta Dusseldorp (*A Place to Call Home*) also appears as his occasional girlfriend and talented journalist helper.

Janet King - Australia - 2014 to 2017 - This spinoff from the legal drama *Crownies* follows Senior Crown Prosecutor Janet King as she returns from maternity leave and progresses through her career. Marta Dusseldorp (*A Place to Call Home*) stars.

Jennie: Lady Randolph Churchill - 1974 – This miniseries tells the story of American-born socialite and mother to Winston Churchill, Lady Randolph Churchill.

Jericho - 2016 - This Yorkshire-based 1870s period drama tells the story of a community dominated by the construction of a new viaduct. Jessica Raine (*Call the Midwife*) stars.

Just William - 2010 - This series follows the adventures of a mischievous 11-year-old boy, William Brown (Daniel Roche, *Outnumbered*), and his friends in 1950s England. The series takes us back to a fun, carefree time when kids could run off for the day and not return home until teatime. The series also includes appearances from Daniel Ryan (*Home Fires*), Caroline Quentin (*Jonathan Creek*), Lily James (*Cinderella*), and Warren Clark (*Poldark*).

Lady Chatterley - 1993 - Sean Bean and Judy Richardson star in this adaptation of the scandalous DH Lawrence novel.

Land Girls - 2009 to 2011 - Land Girls follows four women in the Women's Land Army during WW2.

Law & Order: UK - 2009 to 2014 - This adaptation of the successful American courtroom drama sees the format carried over to the British legal system. It's one-part law (investigative work) and one-part order (the court proceedings).

The Lilac Bus - *Ireland* - 1990 - This drama tells the story of seven people who share a bus from Rathdoon to Dublin each weekend. It's based on a collection of eight interconnected stories by Maeve Binchy, and the stories explore topics like alcoholism, sexuality, abortion, drug use, and infidelity.

Lorna Doone - 1976 - This miniseries tells the story of star-crossed lovers in 17th century Somerset and Devon.

Love Hurts - 1992 to 1994 - After a messy breakup, an ambitious woman leaves the rat race and finds herself pursued by a wealthy man who seems like trouble.

Love, Lies, & Records - 2017 - Ashley Jensen (*Agatha Raisin*) stars as Kate Dickinson, a woman constantly challenged in her efforts to balance a personal life with the stress of the records she oversees.

Love My Way - 2004 to 2007 - This Australian drama follows a thirtysomething woman as she attempts to juggle her desires for a rewarding career, a good relationship, and a healthy family life. Claudia Karvan (*Newton's Law*) stars.

Marvellous - 2014 - Toby Jones (*Detectorists*) stars in this drama about a man with learning disabilities who did better than anyone expected.

The Mayor of Casterbridge - 2003 - Ciarán Hinds (*Above Suspicion*) and James Purefoy (*Rome*) star in this adaptation of Thomas Hardy's novel of the same name. It tells the story of a drunken farmer who sells his family, only to realise the horror of what he's done and change his life.

McLeod's Daughters - 2002 to 2009 - Two sisters separated as children are reunited when they jointly inherit a ranch in the Australian bush: the independent Claire McLeod (Lisa Chappell, *Gloss*) and her estranged half-sister, Tess (Bridie Carter, *800 Words*), a stubborn city girl with a drive to change the world. Together, they build an all-female workforce and commit to life at Drovers Run. Nearby, the men of the Ryan family help keep things interesting.

Missing - 2006 - Joanne Froggatt (*Downton Abbey*) stars as a young runaway who scams men to survive. When one of them turns up dead, she becomes the main suspect in a string of murders.

Mrs. Biggs - 2012 - Sheridan Smith (*Gavin & Stacey*) stars as Mrs. Charmian Biggs, the unsuspecting wife of one of Great Britain's most notorious robbers.

The Nest - 2020 - Sophie Rundle (*Bodyguard*) and Martin Compston (*Line of Duty*) star in this Glasgow-based drama about a couple who would do almost anything to have a child. When they meet a troubled young woman, they make her an irresistible offer.

New Worlds - 2014 - Jamie Dornan (*50 Shades of Grey*) stars in this period drama set in the 1680s. The story takes place in both England and the new American colonies, and it focuses on love and conflict in the uncertain time period. It was produced as a follow-up to *The Devil's Whore* (aka *The Devil's Mistress* in North America).

Newton's Law - *Australia* - 2017 - Josephine Newton (Claudia Karvan, *Love My Way*) is a suburban solicitor whose life has hit a few bumps. When an old friend suggests she join Knox Chambers, she decides to take on a new challenge and return to her barrister's robe.

The Norman Conquests - 1977 - Based on a trilogy of Alan Ayckbourn plays, this miniseries depicts six characters over the same weekend, but in different parts of a house. Dames Penelope Keith and Penelope Wilton are among the cast, and both appeared in stage versions of the plays. The late Richard Briers (*The Good Life*) is also among the stars. **Premieres April 5th.**

No Tears - 2002 - This Irish legal drama is based on the true story of women who were infected with hepatitis C during childbirth in the 1990s. Brenda Fricker (*My Left Foot*) and Maria Doyle Kennedy (*The Tudors*) star.

Nothing Trivial - 2011 to 2014 - For one group of New Zealand-based friends, a weekly trivia night is the one constant in their lives. They're all in their thirties and forties and none of them have great luck with love, but they always meet up for the weekly pub quiz and some friendly banter.

Party Tricks - *Australia* - 2014 - This Australian series follows Kate Ballard (Asher Keddie, *X-Men Origins: Wolverine*), a woman facing her first election for State Premier. Victory seems guaranteed until the opposition brings in a new shock candidate – David McLeod (Rodger Corser, *The Heart Guy*). McLeod is a popular media

figure, but more concerning is the fact that she had a secret affair with him years earlier.

Pitching In - 2019 - Larry Lamb and Melanie Walters (both of *Gavin & Stacey*) reunite in this fun family drama about a North Wales holiday camp owner who contemplates selling up after his Welsh wife dies. Though the series has been criticised for inauthentic North Wales accents, it offers a feel-good viewing experience and scenery from a different part of the UK than we typically see in TV and film. Hayley Mills (*Wild at Heart*) also appears as Iona.

Place of Execution - 2008 - Based on the novel by Scottish novelist Val McDermid, this series follows a journalist making a film about the 1963 disappearance of a young schoolgirl.

Poldark - 1975 to 1977 - Based on the Poldark novels by Winston Graham, this series tells the story of a man who went off to fight a war and came back to find everything changed. Robin Ellis stars as Captain Ross Poldark in this older adaptation.

The Promised Life - *Italy* - 2018 - This eight episode series tells the epic tale of a Sicilian family's troubles and their eventual migration from Italy to New York.

Public Enemies - 2012 - This series tells the story of a young man recently released from prison after serving 10 years, and the parole officer working with him after returning from a professional suspension.

Rake - *Australia* - 2011 to 2018 - Defense lawyer Cleaver Greene makes a career out of hopeless cases, perhaps because his own personal life is troubled enough to help him relate.

Relative Strangers - *Ireland* - 1999 - This drama tells the story of an Irish nurse whose happy life comes to an end when her husband dies and she learns she was living a lie. He was deeply in debt and living a double life in Dublin. After meeting the other family, she learns the other wife's child has leukaemia and needs help from her own children to survive.

Restless – 2012 – This two-part TV movie is based on a bestselling spy novel by William Boyd. It focuses on a young woman who finds out her mother was a spy for British intelligence during WWII, and that she's been on the run ever since.

The Return - 2003 - Julie Walters (*Harry Potter*) stars in this film about a woman released from prison after serving time for killing her husband. Neil Dudgeon (*Midsomer Murders*) also appears.

Réunions - 2020 - This French drama follows two half-brothers who learn about each other's existence after their father dies and they inherit a hotel on the island of Réunion. With their newly-acquired hotel on the verge of bankruptcy, the two brothers and their families make big sacrifices and move to the beautiful island to help turn things around.

Run - 2013 - Olivia Colman and Lennie James star in this four-part miniseries about four seemingly unconnected people whose lives intersect after a random act of violence.

The Saint - 1962 to 1969 - Roger Moore stars as Simon Templar, a wealthy adventurer who travels the world solving crimes and engaging in all manner of secret agent hijinks. Though the settings are occasionally exotic, nearly every episode was filmed at a studio in Hertfordshire using "blue-screen" technology. The series was based on the Simon Templar novels by Leslie Charteris.

The Scapegoat - 2012 - Set in 1952, this period drama sees two men with similar faces switching places. The film is based on the novel by Daphne du Maurier, and Matthew Rhys (*The Americans*) stars.

The Scarlet Pimpernel - 1982 - Jane Seymour, Anthony Andrews, and Sir Ian McKellen star in this period drama set during the French Revolution. While many aristocrats are facing the guillotine, quite a few have escaped thanks to the efforts of a young Englishman known as the "Scarlet Pimpernel". The film is based on Baroness Orczy's 1905 novel by the same name.

Seachange - *Australia* - 1998 to 2000 - After her husband is arrested for fraud and has an affair with her sister, Laura Gibson decides to undergo a "seachange" with her children. They move to the coastal village of Pearl Bay and embark on a new kind of life.

Seachange: Paradise Reclaimed - 2019 - This 2019 reboot features original cast members Sigrid Thornton (*The Man from Snowy River*), Kerry Armstrong (*Lantana*) and John Howard (*All Saints*), and takes place 20 years after the final season. After divorce and job loss, Laura Gibson (Thornton) finds herself questioning her place in the world. But when she returns to the beachside paradise of Pearl Bay, she's able to start putting the pieces back together.

The Secret - 2016 - Based on a true story, this miniseries stars James Nesbitt (*Bloodlands*) as killer dentist Colin Howell, a man whose affair leads to deadly consequences.

Secret Daughter - *Australia* - 2016 to 2017 - When a wealthy man goes out looking for the daughter he never knew, a young singer pretends to be her.

Seesaw - 1998 - David Suchet (*Poirot*) and Geraldine James (*Back to Life*) star in this series about what happens in the aftermath of a kidnapping when ransom has been paid and the loved one is returned home.

Sensitive Skin - 2014 - Kim Cattrall (*Sex and the City*) stars in this dramedy about a mid-life couple who sell their family home and move to an urban condo. Unfortunately, their wish for more excitement brings a little too much of it.

The Slap - *Australia* - 2011 - This series explores how one brief event can create waves of repercussions within a group of friends and family. Essie Davis (*Miss Fisher's Murder Mysteries*) and Sophie Okonedo (*Hotel Rwanda*) star in this miniseries based on Christos Tsiolkas' 2008 novel.

Slings & Arrows - *Canada* - 2003 to 2006 - This Canadian dark comedy is set at a fictitious Shakespeare festival in Canada as they embark on a production of Hamlet. Paul Gross (*Due South*) stars as washed-up actor Geoffrey Tennant, along with Rachel McAdams (*Wedding Crashers, The Notebook*), Luke Kirby (*The Marvelous Ms. Maisel*), Stephen Ouimette (*Mentors*), and Mark McKinney (*Kids in the Hall, Superstore*), who is also the co-creator/co-writer.

The South Westerlies - 2020 - In this Irish six-part comedy-drama, Orla Brady (*Mistresses*) plays Kate, an environmental consultant for a Norwegian energy firm. She's asked to go undercover among Irish protestors and help eliminate their objections to a wind farm near their small coastal town. Her task's difficulty is compounded by the arrival of a surfer who bears a strong resemblance to her teenage son.

Straight Forward - *Denmark / New Zealand* - 2019 - After attempting to get revenge for her father's death, a Danish conwoman is forced to flee to New Zealand.

Striking Out - *Ireland* - This series stars Amy Huberman (*Finding Joy*) as Tara Rafferty, a Dublin lawyer who abandons her safe life after discovering that her fiancé is cheating on her. She cancels the wedding, quits her job, and begins a new and unconventional private practice. Neil Morrissey (*Men Behaving Badly*) and Rory Keenan (*War & Peace*) also star.

The Sum of Us - 1994 - Russell Crowe stars in this touching comedy about a father and gay son who are complete opposites but get on very well. Unfortunately, new relationships eventually put a strain on their bond.

The Syndicate: All or Nothing - 2013 - Each series of The Syndicate follows a different group of lottery winners as they grapple with personal dramas, newfound wealth, and temptation. Acorn has just one series, but there are two others (and another one recently announced).

Taken Down - *Ireland* - 2018 - When a Nigerian girl is killed in Dublin, Inspector Jen Rooney is drawn into a refugee community where some may know more than they're letting on.

Tales of the City - 1994 - This British-American miniseries is based on Armistead Maupin's book about colorful people living in San Francisco.

Terry Pratchett's Going Postal - 2010 - This adaptation of Pratchett's novel sees con man Moist von Lipwig (Richard Coyle, *Chilling Adventures of Sabrina*) caught by the law and given two choices: suffer a painful death, or take over a derelict post office. Also starring David Suchet (*Poirot*), Charles Dance (*Game of Thrones*), and Claire Foy (*The Crown*).

Terry Pratchett's The Colour of Magic - 2009 - This series is based on the *Discworld* series of novels by Terry Pratchett, and features Sean Astin as tourist Twoflower alongside Sir David Jason as wizard Rincewind. When a fire breaks out during Twoflower's holiday, the two flee the city together, beginning an interesting magical journey.

Therese Raquin - 1980 - Based on the novel by Emile Zola, this miniseries tells a tale of passion, obsession, and desperate acts. When first published, the novel was described as "putrid" by the newspaper *Le Figaro*, and it's not recommended for young audiences.

The Time of Our Lives - *Australia* - 2013 to 2014 - This drama follows the lives of an extended family in inner-city Melbourne as they build families, pursue careers, and work on their relationships.

Trust - 2000 - Caroline Goodall (*Schindler's List*) stars as Anne, a successful young woman in what seems like a happy marriage. Unfortunately, there's something quite dark on the horizon.

Turning Green - *Ireland* - 2005 - When a teenage boy's mother dies, he's forced to live with his three Irish aunts. He wants nothing more than to return to America, and in pursuit of the funds to do so, he starts a successful business selling illegal magazines.

United - 2011 - David Tennant (*Deadwater Fell*) stars in this film based on the true story of Manchester United's 1958 air crash that killed eight of their members.

Vidago Palace - *Portugal* - 2017 - Set in 1936, this Portuguese romance is set at the Vidago Palace hotel where Europe's elite flee from the Spanish Civil War.

War & Peace - 2007 - Based on the Tolstoy novel, this series follows four aristocratic families during the Napoleonic era. Malcolm McDowell (*A Clockwork Orange*), Brenda Blethyn (*Vera*), Clemence Poesy (*The Tunnel*), and Ken Duken (*Inglourious Basterds*) are among the stars.

The Way Back - 2010 - A group of prisoners escape from a Siberian gulag and trek across four thousand miles to reach freedom in India. Ed Harris, Colin Farrell, and Saoirse Ronan are among the stars.

Wide Sargasso Sea - 2006 - This prequel to Jane Eyre tells the story of the first Mrs. Rochester and how she ended up in the attic at Thornfield Hall. Rebecca Hall (*Parade's End*) and Rafe Spall (*The Big Short*) star.

Wild at Heart - 2006 to 2013 - Stephen Tompkinson (*DCI Banks*, *Ballykissangel*) stars in this series about a British veterinarian who takes his family along to South Africa to release an animal back into the wild. When he sees the area and meets pretty game reserve owner Caroline (Hayley Mills), he ultimately decides to stay.

The Wipers Times - 2013 - Ben Chaplin, Julian Rhind-Tutt, Michael Palin, and Steve Oram star in this dramedy about the publication of a satirical newspaper during WWI. Based on a true story, the film celebrates the resilience of the human spirit in the face of adversity.

What to Do When Someone Dies - 2011 - Anna Friel (*Marcella*) plays schoolteacher Ellie Manning, a woman trying to have a baby with her husband Greg (Marc Warren, *Jonathan Strange & Mr. Norrell*). One night, he doesn't return home from work. Ellie is horrified to learn he has been killed in a terrible car accident, and he wasn't alone – there was a woman in the passenger seat.

A tormented Ellie begins to question: who is the mystery woman and was Greg having a secret affair?

Wreckers - 2011 - Benedict Cumberbatch (*Sherlock*), Claire Foy (*The Crown*), and Shaun Evans (*Endeavour*) star in this film about a couple who move to an idyllic town to start a family, only to find new stress on their relationship when husband David's disturbed brother starts sharing old secrets.

Comedies

Ain't Misbehavin' - 1997 - Robson Green (*Grantchester*) and Jerome Flynn star as two bandsmen during 1940s London. Julia Sawalha (*Absolutely Fabulous, Press Gang*) stars as the lovely Dolly Nightingale, Green's character's love interest. *Downton Abbey*'s Jim Carter also appears.

All in Good Faith - 1985 to 1988 - Middle-aged Reverend Philip Lambe decides to relocate from rural Oxfordshire to an urban Midlands parish, inheriting a whole new set of issues. Richard Briers (*The Good Life, Monarch of the Glen*) stars.

Boomers - 2014 to 2016 - Retired friends make comedy of learning to deal with retirement.

Count Arthur Strong - 2013 to 2017 - A delusional former actor tries to put together his life story with the help of a partner's son.

Cradle to Grave - 2015 - Danny Baker and his friends grow up in 1970s South London.

Decline and Fall - 2017 - After a prank, an Oxford student is wrongly dismissed for indecent exposure, going to work at a sub-par private school in Wales. This series is an adaptation of Evelyn Waugh's novel of the same name.

Detectorists - 2014 to 2017 - Two quirky friends scan the fields of England with metal detectors, hoping for the big find that will finally let them do the gold dance.

The Delivery Man – 2015 - Former police officer Matthew begins work as a midwife. He's the first male midwife to hit the unit, and he hopes his new career will give him more satisfaction than his previous work.

Doc Martin - 2004 to present - Martin Clunes (*Men Behaving Badly*) stars in this comedy about a brilliant but grumpy London surgeon who suddenly develops a fear of blood. He leaves his high-flying career and takes a post in a Cornish fishing village where he spent holidays as a child with his Aunt Joan. His lack of social skills makes his new life difficult.

Executive Stress - 1986 to 1988 - Penelope Keith (*The Good Life, To the Manor Born*) stars in this sitcom about a couple forced to go undercover to work together, only to have the wife become the husband's boss.

Finding Joy - *Ireland* - 2018 to present - A young Irish woman named Joy struggles in the aftermath of a breakup, but not nearly as much as her dog (who becomes incontinent). At the same time, Joy is promoted to a position that takes her out of her comfort zone.

French Fields - 1989 to 1991 - A British couple moves to France and has difficulties adjusting to French culture. This series is a follow-up to *Fresh Fields*.

Fresh Fields - 1984 to 1986 - A suburban couple must find new hobbies and interests after their children leave the nest.

Golden Years - 2016 - This quirky film sees a couple of pensioners lose their hard-earned retirement funds in a financial crisis, only to turn to robbing banks to replenish the loss.

Henry IX - 2017 to present - King Henry has a mid-life crisis.

How to Murder Your Wife - 2015 - This dark comedy tells the true story of Alfred Benning, the mild-mannered animal welfare inspector who ended up becoming a famous murderer at the age of sixty-five. The unlikely murderer decided life is simply too short to live with a woman you can't stand – so the obvious solution is to hack her into bits.

It Takes a Worried Man - 1981 to 1983 - This retro, early 80s British comedy follows 35-year-old Philip Roath, a lazy, self-centered, and insecure man trying to come to terms with aging and a life that hasn't lived up to his lofty expectations. Constantly bothered by his overdraft, his boss (who wants him to work), his ex-wife (who wants to remind him how inadequate he is), and his analyst, actor and series writer Peter Tilbury manages to find humour in the mundane.

Kingdom - 2007 to 2009 - Stephen Fry (*QI*) stars as a country solicitor in the small town of Market Shipborough. Working with his trusty secretary Gloria and reasonably capable assistant Lyle, it should be a peaceful life. The only problem? He has a crazy sister and he recently lost his half-brother in mysterious circumstances. Hermione Norris (*Cold Feet*) and Celia Imrie (*Bergerac*) also star.

The Labours of Erica - 1989 to 1990 - Vera star Brenda Blethyn stars in this delightful retro comedy about a woman who has spent her whole life looking after everyone else. As her 40th birthday approaches, she revisits a list of all the things she wanted to accomplish by 40. In an instant, she gives up much of her current life in pursuit of something different and better.

Ladies of Letters - 2009 to 2010 - Two widows meet under a table at a wedding, then maintain a friendship via letters.

The Man Who Lost His Head - 2007 - Martin Clunes stars in this film about a curator at the British Museum who gets in over his head while returning an ancient Maori carving to New Zealand.

Monday, Monday - 2009 - Fans of *Lucifer* and *Miranda* will love this quirky 2009 series about a woman, Sally (Morven Christie, *Grantchester*), who relocates with her company in hopes of a fresh start after a breakup. Fay Ripley (*Cold Feet*) plays

Christine, her wildly incompetent boss, while Tom Ellis (*Miranda*) plays the role of Steven. He's the resident "charming fella", but their first meeting was less than ideal. He's also the boy-toy of the company's COO.

The Moodys - Australia - 2012 to 2014 - This Australian comedy follows a dysfunctional family over the course of several Christmas holidays. In the second season, it follows the family as they progress through significant events in their year.

Mount Pleasant - 2011 to 2017 - This dramedy dives into the lives of a tight-knit Manchester family, focusing on their everyday struggles and hurdles. The cast includes Pauline Collins (*Upstairs Downstairs*), Sally Lindsay (*Coronation Street, Scott & Bailey*), and Daniel Ryan (*Black Sea*). Robson Green (*Grantchester*) also appears in a handful of episodes.

The Other One - 2017 - After a man drops dead at his birthday party, his family learns he has another, entirely separate family they didn't know about - just 13 miles away. What else can they do but decide to make the best of it?

Over the Rainbow - 1993 - On his wedding day, Neil is arrested for robbery. A year later, he returns to his wife's flat only to learn she's living with his best mate.

Parents - 2012 - A businesswoman finds out her husband has lost their life savings on the day she loses her job, and they have to go live with her parents.

Raised by Wolves - 2013 to 2016 - A single mother raises her large family in a not-so-conventional way.

The Rebel - 2016 to 2017 - A grumpy retired man rebels against everything, leaving his friends and family to clean up whatever messes he makes. Simon Callow stars in this Brighton-based comedy.

Reggie Perrin - 2009 to 2010 - Martin Clunes stars in this remake of the classic Reginald Perrin stories.

Sando - 2018 to present - *Australia* - Sando is the queen of package furniture deals in Australia.

The Simple Heist - *Sweden* - 2017 - When two older women find themselves cash-strapped and overlooked, they decide to turn to crime.

Very Small Business - 2008 - This series follows two unlikely business partners. One, Don Angel, is a small businessman with a pile of failures behind him. The other, Ray Leonard, is a former noted feature writer returning to the workforce after six years off battling depression. Working together is a series of small but amusing disasters.

White Teeth - 2002 - Based on Zadie Smith's popular novel, this series tells the story of three families in Willesden, a neighbourhood in northwest London. The series takes places over three decades in the increasingly diverse modern Britain.

Stars include Om Puri (*The Hundred-Foot Journey*), Phil Davis (*Vera Drake*), Naomie Harris (*28 Days Later*) and Archie Panjabi (*The Good Wife*).

Worst Week of My Life - 2004 to 2007 - Ben Miller (*Death in Paradise*) stars with Sarah Alexander (*Coupling*) as the world's most disastrously awkward fiancé and husband.

You, Me, & Them - 2013 to 2015 - Anthony Head and Eve Myles star in this sitcom about an age gap romance. Acorn has Series 1, but you can find Series 2 on Amazon's Prime Video.

Documentary & Lifestyle

1900 Island - 2019 - On a deserted island in Wales, four modern families live as people would have lived more than 100 years ago. The series gives us a look at both the hardships and the joys of a simpler kind of life.

A Royal Tour of the 20th Century - 2019 - This docuseries takes a look at the royal tours and state visits of the British royal family over the last century.

A Stitch in Time – 2016 - Amber Butchart takes a look at historical figures through the clothing they wore.

Alexandria: The Greatest City - 2016 - Historian Bettany Hughes explores the once-grand city of Alexandria, founded by Alexander the Great and home to Cleopatra.

The Art Detectives - 2017 to present - Art experts track down previously-unknown masterpieces by some of the world's greatest artists.

At Home with the Georgians - 2010 - Over the course of three episodes, author Amanda Vickery unlocks the secrets of the Georgian home by looking at the people who lived in them. The series is based on her highly-acclaimed book "Behind Closed Doors – At Home in Georgian England".

The Ballroom Boys - 2016 - This short documentary follows a group of Welsh boys as they prepare for a ballroom dancing competition.

Baroque - 2015 - Noted art critic Waldemar Januszczak traces the history of the Baroque movement from its start as a Vatican-approved religious art style to a bigger global movement.

Barristers - 2014 - This groundbreaking series takes us behind the scenes to see the inner workings of the British courts.

The Big House Reborn - 2015 - This series follows National Trust conservators as they work on restoring The Mount Stewart House.

Blitzed: Nazis on Drugs - 2018 - This series takes a look at the possible influence the stimulant Pervitin may have had on Nazi Germany.

Bollywood: The World's Biggest Film Industry - 2018 - This two-part series examines the world's largest film industry, complete with access to stars and active productions.

The Bone Detectives - 2007 to 2008 - This docuseries follows a group of women who piece together the stories of bodies found via archaeological discoveries. From battles to disease to tragic accidents, they piece together the fascinating untold stories of Britain's past.

The Brilliant Brontë Sisters - 2013 - Sheila Hancock takes us on a journey through Yorkshire, looking at these incredible sisters who changed British literature forever.

Britain's Bloodiest Dynasty - 2014 - Historian Dan Jones tells the story of the Plantagenets, one of Britain's darkest and most brutal dynasties.

Britain's Bloody Crown - 2016 - Dan Jones presents this four-part documentary about the War of the Roses.

Caligula with Mary Beard - 2013 - Cambridge classicist Mary Beard takes a look at the life and times of the scandalous Roman emperor Caligula.

Can a Computer Write a Hit Musical - 2016 - As computers become more and more advanced, they get closer to taking over those creative tasks many of us assumed to be out of their capabilities. In this programme, a team of scientists and musical writers attempt to devise a recipe for a computer-generated musical.

Cat Hospital - 2019 - This reality series takes a look at daily life in Ireland's first veterinary hospital dedicated exclusively to our feline friends. We follow cat expert Clare Meade and the rest of her team at Cork Cat Hospital as they help with everything from grooming and checkups to life or death emergencies.

Churchill: Blood Sweat, & Oil Paint - 1970 - Hosted by Andrew Marr, this BBC special tells the fascinating story of Winston Churchill's lifelong love of painting. He meets Churchill's descendants and explores the connections between his private passion for painting and his public career as politician and statesman.

The Churchills - 2012 - David Starkey looks at the links between Winston Churchill and his ancestor John Churchill, a man who dared to go up against Louis XIV of France.

Civil War - 2002 - Dr. Tristram Hunt takes a look at the conflict that briefly toppled the English monarchy back in the 17th century.

Civil War: The Untold Story - 2014 - Elizabeth McGovern (*Downton Abbey*) hosts this documentary about the Civil War and the North/South divide in the United States.

Coast and Country Walks - 2008 - Keen rambler and host Julia Bradbury (*The Magicians, The Greek Islands with Julia Bradbury*) takes viewers on an adventure around historic railway lines in England, Scotland and Wales.

Coastal Railways with Julie Walters - 2017 - Julie Walters travels Britain's most scenic coastal railways, stopping off to visit the people and villages along the way.

David Jason's Secret Service - 2017 - Sir David Jason hosts this fascinating docuseries about Britain's history of espionage.

David Suchet's Being Poirot - 2015 - Generally regarded as the best Poirot of all time, David Suchet held the iconic role for roughly a quarter of a century. In this three-part series, he attempts to share some of his experiences and explain why people have loved Poirot for so long.

Digging for Britain - 2010 to 2016 - Professor Alice Roberts shares her passion for Britain's history as she takes us to a variety of exciting archaeological sites. From Roman burial sites to Viking treasures to history as recent as World War II, there's a bit of everything in this one, along with plenty of expert commentary to help add context.

Discovering Britain - 2018 - In this fun travel series, Maureen Lipman (*Metamorphosis*) and Larry Lamb (*Gavin & Stacey*) join a number of their fellow British actors as they travel the country exploring its heritage.

Edward & Mary: The Unknown Tudors – 2002 - This two-part special tells the story of King Edward and Queen (Bloody) Mary, eldest daughter of Henry VIII and first English queen since Matilda.

Elizabeth I & Her Enemies - 2017 - Presenters Dan Jones (*Britain's Bloody Crown*) and Suzannah Lipscomb (*Hidden Killers*) take a look at those who wanted to bring down the much-respected Queen Elizabeth I.

The Family Farm - 2018 - In this four-part docu-series, three UK families with no farming experience volunteer to spend a summer working on a farm in Wales. High in the Snowdonia mountains, they seek a simpler kind of life.

The Genius of Roald Dahl - 2012 - Comedian and bestselling author David Walliams delves into Roald Dahl's world, chatting with those who knew him best. He meets Dahl's widow at the family home, and chats with longtime illustrator Quentin Blake as he draws a Dahl villain.

Genius of the Ancient World – 2015 - Historian Bettany Hughes travels the world to study the lives and times of great philosophers like Socrates, Confucius, and Buddha.

Growing Up Gracefully - 2017 - Comedians Hannah and Eliza Reilly star in this humourous series about what it means to be a woman in the 21st century. The reality series follows the sisters as one follows a set of "the old rules" for women, while another follows the new.

Heavenly Gardens - 2020 - This two-part BBC One series follows garden lover Alexander Armstrong and garden designer Arit Anderson as they visit some of the loveliest sacred gardens around the UK. It includes visits to The Bishop's Palace in Somerset, Pluscarden Abbey in the Scottish Highlands, Cambridge University, and Alnwick Castle's unique gardens in Northumberland.

Hidden Britain by Drone - 2016 - Tony Robinson (*Time Team*) uses drones to snoop on parts of Britain not normally visible to those of us confined to the ground. The series includes a look at abandoned homes in the Outer Hebrides of Scotland, a WWII shipwreck along the Kent coast, and a peek at an abandoned theme park.

Joseph Campbell: Mythos 1 - 1999 - Watch this series of lectures on the "one great story", filmed shortly before Joseph Campbell's death in 1987.

Keeping the Castle - 2018 - Though it may sound wonderful, managing a stately home can be an enormous financial burden and family obligation. This series takes a look at the challenges of managing these enormous, sometimes crumbling homes.

The Life of Verdi - 1982 - This biographical miniseries tells the story of Giuseppe Verdi, composer of operas like Aida, Rigoletto, and La Traviata.l

Living in the Shadow of World War II - 2017 - World War II affected more than just the people on the battlefield. Back home, the war cast a shadow over nearly every aspect of day-to-day life. This series takes a look at the ways the war affected people on the homefront.

Magic Numbers: Hannah Fry's Mysterious World of Maths - 2018 - Hannah Fry examines where math came from.

Martin Clunes: Islands of America - 2019 - Martin Clunes travels the islands of the United States, stopping off in Hawaii, Alaska, Washington, California, Louisiana, Puerto Rico, Georgia, North Carolina, Virginia, New York, Massachusetts, and Maine.

Martin Clunes: Islands of Australia - 2016 - Martin Clunes explores some of the lesser-known islands off Australia's coast

Medieval Lives - 2013 - This series takes a look at how people handled life's three major rites of passage in the Middle Ages: birth, marriage, and death.

Monty Don's Paradise Gardens - 2018 - Gardening expert Monty Don takes us to the Middle East and beyond in search of some of the world's finest "paradise" gardens.

<u>**Muse of Fire: A Shakespearean Road Movie**</u> - 2013 - This documentary follows a couple of actors who once shied away from Shakespeare – until they became actors. Over four years, they journey around the world trying to get at what makes Shakespeare's work so great. The film includes appearances by Dame Judi Dench, Sir Ian McKellan, Ewan McGregor, Ralph Fiennes, and Jude Law.

A Music Lover's Guide to Murdoch Mysteries - 2020 - Since the pandemic delayed the new season of *Murdoch Mysteries* and there won't be new episodes on Christmas Eve this year, the producers decided to put together a special concert featuring Murdoch-era music. This behind-the-scenes special features Detective William Murdoch (Yannick Bisson) as host alongside a seven-piece ensemble from the Toronto Symphony Orchestra.

My Welsh Sheepdog - 2016 - BBC presenter Kate Humble travels around Wales with her dog Teg to learn more about the rare Welsh sheepdog breed.

Narnia's Lost Poet: The Secret Lives and Loves of C.S. Lewis - 2013 - C.S. Lewis biographer A.N. Wilson embarks on a journey to find the man behind Narnia. He was incredibly secretive about his private life, and even his best friend (J.R.R. Tolkien) was unaware of his late-in-life marriage to a divorced American woman.

The Nile: 5000 Years of History - 2018 - Historian Bettany Hughes takes us on a 900-mile adventure along the River Nile, sharing history and landmarks as she goes.

Off the Beaten Track - 2018 - BBC presenter Kate Humble is back with her Welsh sheepdog Teg, this time travelling through some of the wildest bits of Wales.

<u>**Only Foals & Horses**</u> - 2019 - This series follows horse vets Lisa Durham and

Philippa Hughes as they care for their four-legged clients. **Premieres April 5th.**

Penelope Keith's Hidden Coastal Villages - 2018 - Penelope Keith (*The Good Life*) travels the UK, visiting some of the most beautiful coastal villages.

Penelope Keith's Hidden Villages - 2014 to 2016 - Penelope Keith takes us on a tour of the UK's loveliest villages and quirkiest characters.

Penelope Keith's Village of the Year - 2018 - This delightful competition gives us a great deal of insight into what makes some of the UK's most beautiful villages tick. Rather than just looking at the scenery, we get to meet village inhabitants and find out what they love about the places they call home.

Poirot: Super Sleuths - 2006 - David Suchet takes us behind the scenes to look at the enduring appeal of Hercule Poirot. The programme features interviews with cast, crew, and a variety of Agatha Christie experts.

Pride & Prejudice: Having a Ball - 2013 - This BBC documentary was created to celebrate the 200th anniversary of Jane Austen's most popular novel. To reveal the hidden world behind the story, hosts Amanda Vickery and Alistair Sooke lead a team of experts in reconstructing a Regency-era ball at Chawton House, the grand estate of Jane Austen's brother.

Prince Charles: Inside the Duchy of Cornwall - 2019 - Back in 1337, the Duchy of Cornwall was established to provide income for heirs to the throne – and roughly 700 years later, it continues to do just that. The land and people associated with the Duchy of Cornwall currently generate more than £21 million in yearly income for the man lucky enough to have inherited it. This two-episode series offers exclusive access to Prince Charles, William, and Camilla to offer insight into this royal money machine.

The Real Prince Philip - 2019 - This documentary celebrates the life of Prince Philip, from his early years in Greece to his many years of service to the United Kingdom.

The Rise of the Nazi Party - 2014 - This 10-episode series takes a look at how Hitler and his inner circle used economic uncertainty to influence regular people into going along with their genocidal agenda.

Rococo Before Bedtime - 2014 - British art historian Waldemar Januszczak examines the history and grandeur of the Rococo period.

Rome: Empire Without Limit - 2016 - Historian Mary Beard takes a look at how a small city like Rome was able to capture an empire - and why it ultimately fell.

Savile Row - 2008 - This fascinating documentary series goes behind the scenes of the iconic Savile Row storefronts most of us will never visit. Here, skilled craftsmen apply their talents to make some of the finest suits in the entire world. Now threatened by chain stores and a decline in appreciation for fine handiwork, we see the shops struggling to stay relevant and pay rent in one of the world's most expensive cities and neighbourhoods.

Saving Britain's Worst Zoo - 2019 - When the Tweedy family bought a zoo in West Wales, they never could have imagined the troubles that would follow. With no experience and more than 300 exotic animals to care for, the situation quickly evolved into lawsuits, threats, and massive debts. This series tells the real, behind-the-scenes story.

The Secret History of the British Garden - 2015 - Gardening expert Monty Don takes a look at the stories behind four of Britain's most famous gardens, digging deep for the details that tell us how British gardens have changed in the last 400 years.

She-Wolves: England's Early Queens - 2012 - Presenter Helen Castor explores the lives of seven of England's early queens and how they managed to challenge male power and rule in a time where women had comparatively few rights.

Soundbreaking: Stories from the Cutting Edge of Recorded Music - 2016 - Using dozens of interviews and rare studio footage, this eight-part series takes a look at the impact of recorded music on our lives.

The Spy Who Went Into the Cold - 2013 - At the height of the Cold War in 1963, Kim Philby defected to Moscow after 30 years in senior positions in British intelligence offices. This documentary takes a look back at the scandal.

Tales of Irish Castles - 2014 - Actor Simon Delaney hosts this six-part series about the stories and legends associated with some of Ireland's most majestic and interesting castles. Visiting Dublin, Blarney, Limerick, Trim, Carrickfergus, Kilkenny, Birr, and more, this series takes us on a journey around the island where more castles were built than in the rest of the British Isles combined.

Theatreland - 2010 - This docuseries goes behind the scenes of the Haymarket's production of *Waiting for Godot*, giving us a look at what it takes to make a West End theatre survive and thrive.

Time Team - 1994 to 2014 - A group of archaeologists travel around Britain working on different excavation sites.

Treasure Houses of Britain – 2011 - This series travels around Britain, exploring the history and architecture of some of the island's greatest estates.

Victorian Farm - 2008 to 2009 - This BBC Two observational series sees historian Ruth Goodman and archaeologists Alex Langlands and Peter Ginn immersing themselves in the lifestyle of a Victorian farmer. They spend a full calendar year living on the Acton Scott Estate in Shropshire, working the land with antique tools and machinery.

Victorian House of Arts and Crafts - 2019 - Over the course of four episodes, we see a late 1800s Victorian Arts & Crafts commune in the Welsh hills painstakingly brought back to life as a group of six 21st century crafters – three men and three women move in to experience the highs and lows of living and working together as a creative commune. Over their month-long stay, the crafters are set to renovate four of the key spaces in the house.

Victoria Wood's A Nice Cup of Tea - 2013 - Comedian Victoria Wood travels the globe to investigate Britain's love of tea.

Vintage Roads: Great and Small - 2018 to present - Christopher Timothy and Peter Davison, stars of All Creatures Great & Small, host this entertaining travelogue about the golden age of motoring. Behind the wheel of a classic car, they explore beautiful backroads and the history of motoring in Britain.

Wainwright Walks - 2007 - Julia Bradbury stars in this outdoor series following some of guidebook author Alfred Wainwright's best walks.

Walks with My Dog - 2017 - British celebrities like John Nettles and Robert Lindsay explore the countryside with their dogs.

Wartime Farm - 2012 - Made by the producers of *Edwardian Farm* and *Victorian Farm*, this series sees Alex Langlands, Peter Ginn, and Ruth Goodman taking on the challenge of running a farm for an entire year – using only those tools and resources that would have been available during WWII.

The Yorkshire Vet - 2015 to present - This engaging series follows the staff of Skeldale Veterinary Centre as they work with the animals.

The Yorkshire Vet: Countryside Specials - 2020 - This set of four specials gives us even more insight into what goes on at the Skeldale Veterinary Centre, the practice founded by British veterinarian and author Alfred Wight. It's the true story behind the enormously popular series *All Creatures Great & Small*.

Young, Gifted, and Classical: The Making of a Maestro - 2017 - At 17, Sheku Kannah-Mason because the first black winner of the BBC Young Musician competition. This documentary looks at what drives him and his musically-talented family to succeed.

BRITBOX

Website: http://britbox.com

Description: A joint venture between the BBC and ITV, this service focuses exclusively on British programming. In addition to the standard categories, BritBox also offers several soaps, quiz shows, and panel shows, along with a number of live events throughout the year.

Available On: Roku, Fire TV, Apple TV, Apple iPhone & iPad, Chromecast, Android phones and tablets, and computer (via web browser). You can also subscribe via Amazon Prime Video.

Cost: $6.99/month, $69.99/year

Now Streaming

Mysteries & Crime Dramas

15 Days - 2019 - This crime thriller is a mystery told in reverse. It immediately flashes back to 15 days prior to the crime, allowing viewers to watch a family crisis as it festers and develops into something truly terrible. The series is a re-make of the Welsh series *35 Diwrnod*, and even includes some of the same actors.

35 Days - 2014 to 2019 - Each season of this Welsh mystery begins with a murder, then rolls the clock back 35 days to follow the events that led to the murderous conclusion.

A Confession - 2019 - Martin Freeman (*Sherlock*), Siobhan Finneran (*Downton Abbey*), and Imelda Staunton (*Cranford*) star in this drama based on a real-life tragedy. The series dramatises the search for Sian O'Callaghan, a young woman who went missing in Swindon, Wiltshire after a taxi ride.

A Touch of Frost - 1992 to 2010 - Rumpled and slovenly DI Jack Frost follows his instincts to find justice for the underdogs. The gritty series is set in the fictional South Midlands town of Denton, and Sir David Jason (*Only Fools and Horses*) stars.

Agatha Christie's Evil Under the Sun - 1982 - On the trail of a millionaire's fake diamond, Poirot finds himself at a resort full of rich and famous people – and a murderer. This film was Peter Ustinov's first outing as the Belgian detective, and you'll also see Dames Maggie Smith and Diana Rigg looking quite a bit younger.

Agatha Christie's Marple - 2004 to 2013 - BritBox offers Seasons 1-5 of this delightful mystery adaptation. In the first three, Geraldine McEwan portrays the iconic sleuth, with Julia McKenzie taking over after that.

Agatha Christie's Partners in Crime - 1983 to 1984 - Francesca Annis (*Bancroft*) and James Warwick (*Iron Man*) star as the famous crime-fighting duo, Tommy and Tuppence Beresford, as they solve mysteries and search for enemy spies in 1950's Britain. Our two sleuths, Tommy and Tuppence, are now married and well-established as secret agents working under the watchful eye of Scotland Yard.

Agatha Christie's Poirot - 1989 to 2020 - David Suchet portrays the eccentric Belgian Detective Poirot in this long-running series of Agatha Christie mysteries. Acorn TV has seasons 7 and 8, while BritBox has all the others.

Agatha Christie's Seven Dials Mystery - 1981 - Cheryl Campbell (*Breathless*) stars as Lady Eileen "Bundle" Brent, a young and glamorous aristocrat who insinuates herself into all sorts of unsavoury situations...including murder.

Agatha Christie's Sparkling Cyanide - 2003 - Pauline Collins (Dickensian) and Oliver Ford Davies (A Royal Scandal) star in this modern-day adaptation of Agatha Christie's classic. It sees an elderly husband and wife working as secret agents brought in to investigate the murder of a football club manager's trophy wife. As more secrets come to light, it becomes a race against time to find the killer before there's another victim.

Agatha Christie's The Mirror Crack'd - 1980 - This star-studded movie features Angela Lansbury (*Murder, She Wrote*) as Miss Marple, investigating a murder that takes place while a movie films in her quiet village (as if we needed any more evidence that murders follow Angela Lansbury). Supporting actors include Rock Hudson, Tony Curtis, Kim Novak, and Elizabeth Taylor.

Agatha Christie's The Murder of Roger Ackroyd (Radio Play) - 1939 - Orson Welles directs and plays Hercule Poirot in this radio dramatisation of the classic Agatha Christie story. When a woman is found dead of an overdose, a rumour links her to Roger Ackroyd, who is then also found dead. Hercule Poirot is left to unravel the mystery.

Agatha Christie's The Secret Adversary - 1983 - In this Tommy and Tuppence mystery, James Warwick (*Agatha Christie's Partners in Crime*) and Francesca Annis (also in *Agatha Christie's Partners in Crime*) star as two friends who decide to become investigators to get a bit of extra money. What seems like a simple idea quickly becomes quite dangerous. This production immediately preceded the related television series.

Agatha Christie's Why Didn't They Ask Evans? - 1981 - When Agatha Christie was alive, she allowed very few television adaptations of her work because she didn't care for the medium. After her death, daugher Rosalind Hicks relaxed the restrictions - and this was the first major production to move forward as a result. While golfing on the coast of Wales, Bobby Jones hits a stranger whose puzzling last words are, "Why didn't they ask Evans?"

An Inspector Calls - 2015 - Set in 1912, this mystery follows Inspector Goole as he investigates the wealthy Birling family in connection with the suicide of a young woman. Each family member has their own set of dark and intriguing secrets.

The Bay - 2019 to present - Morven Christie (*Grantchester*) plays DS Lisa Armstrong, a family liaison officer who discovers she has a personal connection to a missing persons case. Many have compared this series to *Broadchurch*, and it's been renewed for a second season.

Best in Paradise - 2020 - In this exclusive BritBox interview, cast members Kris Marshall (*Sanditon, Love Actually*), Josephine Jobert, Don Warrington (*Holby City*), and Tobi Bakare (*Kingsman, Silent Witness*) share anecdotes and insights about their favourite episodes of *Death in Paradise*.

The Bill, Series 25 & "The Best Of" - 1984 to 2010 - This long-running police series follows the lives of officers at the fictional Sun Hill Police station. BritBox currently offers Series 25 and a "best of" collection that includes appearances from stars like David Tennant (*Doctor Who*), Hugh Laurie (*A Bit of Fry & Laurie*), Craig Charles (*Red Dwarf*), and Keira Knightley (*Pride & Prejudice*).

The Blake Mysteries: Ghost Stories - 2018 - After her husband Lucien's disappearance, Jean Blake (formerly Beazley) struggles to adapt to life without him. She doesn't get much time to breathe, though, as she's pulled into a murder investigation just eight months after his disappearance.

The Bletchley Circle: San Francisco - 2018 to 2019 - This Bletchley Circle spin-off picks up in 1956 when former colleagues Millie and Jean learn of a set of murders in San Francisco that mimic a murder they saw during the war. They reach out to an American codebreaker they knew during the war, and before too long, they're all solving murders together in the Bay Area.

Blue Murder - 2003 to 2009 - DCI Janine Lewis struggles with the challenge of being a single mom to four kids while leading a team of homicide detectives. Caroline Quentin (*Jonathan Creek*) stars.

The Body Farm - 2011 to 2012 - This spin-off of Waking the Dead follows a team of forensic scientists who've left academia to work in the world of criminal forensics. They team up with a London cold case unit to do research on how people are killed and how criminals try to cover it up. The series includes Tara Fitzgerald (*Jane Eyre*), Wunmi Mosaku (*Vera*), Mark Bazeley (*Broadchurch*), and Finlay Robertson (*How Not to Live Your Life*).

Boon - 1986 to 1992 - After suffering permanent lung damage rescuing a child from a fire, a fireman retires and begins a new life of odd jobs and later, detective work.

Cadfael - 1994 to 1998 - In 12th century Shrewsbury, a monk solves mysteries. Derek Jacobi (*Last Tango in Halifax*) stars.

Campion - 1989 to 1990 - An aristocrat in the 1930s adopts a fake name and investigates mysteries with help from his servant. Peter Davison (*Doctor Who*) stars as Albert Campion, with Brian Glover (*Rumble*) as his manservant. The series was based on the Albert Campion mystery novels written by Margery Allingham.

The City & The City - 2018 - Inspector Borlú investigates a murder in the twin city, which occupies the same space differently. This unusual series blends mystery with science fiction.

Cold Blood - 2005 to 2008 - A notorious murderer is finally placed in prison, but they can't find his last victim. Now, he's playing a ruthless game with the detective who wants what he knows.

The Coroner - 2015 to 2016 - A solicitor returns to her coastal hometown, becomes coroner, and investigates suspicious deaths.

Cracker - 1993 to 2006 - Though he's obnoxious and anti-social, Fitz is a brilliant criminal psychologist and police consultant.

Dalziel & Pascoe - 1996 to 2007 - Two Yorkshire-based police partners with very different personalities find a way to bond as they solve crimes. This series was based on the Dalziel and Pascoe novels by Reginald Hill, and stars Warren Clarke (*Poldark*) and Colin Buchanan (*The Pale Horse*) in the title roles. Colin Buchanan has also narrated a number of Reginald Hill audiobooks.

Dark Heart - 2018 - DI Wagstaffe leads an investigation into a series of attacks on accused pedophiles.

Death in Paradise - 2011 to present - A British inspector who's fundamentally incompatible with island life is sent to investigate murders on a tropical island. This long-running series began with Ben Miller (*The Worst Week of My Life*) in the lead role, but the torch was later passed to Kris Marshall (*Love Actually*), Ardal O'Hanlon (*Father Ted*), and Ralf Little (*The Cafe*).

The Doctor Blake Mysteries - 2013 to 2018 - Dr. Lucien Blake left his Australian home in Ballarat as a young man. Now, he finds himself returning to take over not only his dead father's medical practice, but also his on-call role as the town's police surgeon. Craig McLachlan (*Packed to the Rafters*) stars as Dr. Blake.

Emerald Falls - 2008 - After her divorce, Joni Ferguson and her 15-year-old son move to the Blue Mountains in New South Wales, Australia to open a bed and breakfast. Just six months after starting her new life, the local doctor is found dead in his home. When Joni shows up on the list of suspects, her son Zac sets out to prove her innocence.

The Fall - 2013 to 2016 - Gillian Anderson (*The X-Files*) and Jamie Dornan (*50 Shades of Grey*) star in this series about a senior investigator who goes head-to-head with a serial killer who's attacking young professional women in Belfast.

Father Brown - 1974 - A Catholic priest dips his toe into mysteries in spite of the police warning him off. Kenneth More (*The Forsyte Saga*) stars as Father Brown in this early adaptation of G.K. Chesterson's *Father Brown* stories.

Father Brown - 2013 to present - Based on the mysteries of GK Chesterson, a Catholic priest solves mysteries in his small English village. Mark Williams (*Blandings*) stars as Father Brown in this long-running adaptation.

From Darkness - 2015 - In Greater Manchester, Officer Claire is disturbed by four bodies that seem linked to her past cases.

The Gil Mayo Mysteries (aka Mayo) - 2006 - Gil Mayo is an eccentric detective with a life full of complications and awkwardness. His ex-love interest is a colleague, and he's raising a teenage girl on his own. Alistair McGowan (*Leonardo*) stars in this light mystery.

Good Cop - 2012 - When his best friend is killed on duty, a good cop wants revenge. Warren Brown (*Luther*) stars as John Paul Rocksavage.

Grace - 2021 - *Endeavour* creator Russell Lewis is behind this new ITV drama starring John Simm (*Life on Mars*). He'll play detective Roy Grace (from Peter James' award-winning novels), a man who fights crime in the coastal city of Brighton, England. Grace is a talented but unorthodox detective who's haunted by the disappearance of his beloved wife. The series will begin with two feature-length episodes based on the first two stories in the Roy Grace series: *Dead Simple* and *Looking Good Dead*. **Premieres April 27th**.

Hetty Wainthropp Investigates - 1996 to 1998 - A tough old pensioner becomes a private detective and investigates crimes with the help of her husband and a teenage boy called Geoffrey. Dame Patricia Routledge (*Keeping Up Appearances*) stars in this cozy mystery.

Hound of the Baskervilles - 1982 - Tom Baker steps into the world of Sherlock Holmes in this faithful adaptation of the classic Sherlock Holmes story.

The Ice House - 1997 - The peaceful lives of three women are shattered when a corpse is discovered in the ice house on their property. Daniel Craig (*James Bond* series) stars.

In Plain Sight - 2016 - This series covers serial killer Peter Manuel's crimes in 1950s Lanarkshire, Scotland. Though it's a dramatisation, it's based on a true story.

In the Dark - 2017 - While dealing with an unexpected pregnancy, DI Weeks returns to her hometown to help a childhood friend after an abduction.

The Inspector Lynley Mysteries - 2001 to 2007 - An Oxford-educated detective pairs up with a working-class partner to investigate mysteries.

Inspector Morse - 1987 to 2000 - Grumpy, classical music-loving Inspector Morse investigates crimes around Oxford with his junior partner Sergeant Lewis. This much-loved British mystery series is based on the books of Colin Dexter, and it later spawned two additional television shows (*Inspector Lewis* and *Endeavour*).

Jonathan Creek - 1997 to 2016 - After meeting a pushy investigative journalist, an eccentric magic trick developer finds himself investigating murders.

The Lady Vanishes - 2013 - Based on the 1936 Ethel Lina White novel *The Wheel Spins*, this film follows a young English socialite on a train trip back to England from Croatia. When an English governess disappears, she enlists the aid of fellow passengers Max Hare and his former Oxford professor. Selina Cadell (*Doc Martin*) stars as the disappearing Miss Froy, while Tuppence Middleton (*The Imitation Game*) plays socialite Iris Carr.

The Last Detective - 2003 to 2007 - Because he's decent, old fashioned and a generally good guy, his fellow detectives and his boss don't like him much. Still, DC Davies proves that his style works by constantly solving cases no one else wants.

Life of Crime - 2013 - Hayley Atwell (*Agent Carter*) stars as Denise Woods, a bright WPC attempting to solve the murders of three possibly connected victims across three decades. Each episode of the series is filmed in a different decade, and she has a different rank in each.

Life on Mars - 2006 to 2007 - DCI Sam Tyler has a car accident in 2006 and wakes up in the 70s. John Simm (*White Dragon*) stars alongside Philip Glenister (*Living the Dream*) in this much-loved series. The series is often cited for its excellent classic rock soundtrack, and it was recently announced that after a long break, it will be coming back with a third season.

Line of Duty - 2012 to present - This series focuses on a group of officers in the ACU (Anti-Corruption Unit), a team that investigates the wrongdoings of its fellow officers.

Maigret - 1992 to 1993 - Michael Gambon stars as Georges Simenon's iconic French detective in this early-90s adaptation. Each of the 12 episodes is based on a single Maigret novel.

Maigret - 2016 to 2017 - Rowan Atkinson takes on a rare serious role as he fills the role of Maigret in this two series, four episode adaptation. Each of the four episodes are based on a single novel (*Maigret Sets a Trap, Maigret's Dead Man, Maigret at the Crossroads,* and *Inspector Maigret and the Strangled Stripper*).

The Mallorca Files - 2019 - This drama stars Elen Rhys (*Ordinary Lies*) and Julian Looman as a pair of international detectives who solve crimes on the Baleric island of Mallorca. It's a light, action-driven drama with a bit of British and German culture clash between the detectives.

McDonald & Dodds - 2020 - BAFTA-winner Jason Watkins (*The Crown, Trollied*) stars alongside newcomer Tala Gouveia in this fun detective drama that's not quite cozy, but still far from gritty. The series is set in Bath, England and it follows an incredibly mismatched but competent pair as they learn to work together to solve difficult cases.

Midsomer Murders - 1998 to present - In Midsomer County, the landscapes are beautiful, the villagers all have secrets, and murder is rampant. This British mystery classic features John Nettles as DCI Tom Barnaby through the first 13 seasons, with Neil Dudgeon as DCI John Barnaby for the later seasons.

Midsomer Murders: 20th Anniversary Documentary - 2019 - John Nettles presents this look back at Midsomer Murders on its 20th anniversary. The hour-long special features appearances by Neil Dudgeon, Nick Hendrix, Daniel Casey, Jason Hughes, Jane Wymark, and more.

Midsomer Murders Favourites - 1998 to 2018 - This collection rounds up the favourite episodes of several Midsomer Murders cast members - Neil Dudgeon, John Nettles, Annette Badland, and Nick Hendrix. Each episode includes commentary from the actor in question.

Miss Marple - 1984 to 1992 - In the small village of St. Mary Mead, Miss Marple helps her community by solving murders. In this collection of Christie tales, Joan Hickson takes the title role.

The Moonstone - 1972 to 1973 - In this Hugh Leonard adaptation, a man goes on a quest to find a stolen but cursed stone that's said to bring ill fortune to all who possess it. This series is based on the Wilkie Collins novel of the same name.

The Moonstone - 2016 - This updated adaptation of the Wilkie Collins novel stars Joshua Silver as Franklin Blake alongside Terenia Edwards (*On Chesil Beach*) as Rachel Verinder.

The Mrs. Bradley Mysteries - 1998 - Diana Rigg (*The Avengers*) stars as Mrs. Bradley, a sort of edgy Miss Marple who solves mysteries with the assistance of her devoted chauffeur George Moody (Neil Dudgeon, *Midsomer Murders*).

New Blood - 2016 - Two young investigators are brought together by cases that initially appear unrelated.

New Tricks - 2003 to 2015 - This long-running series stars Amanda Redman as a disgraced detective chosen to head up a group of retired detectives recruited to investigate unsolved cases. Along with the challenges of tracking down old evidence and witnesses, they'll also have to come to terms with the fact that the "old ways" aren't always welcome in modern policing.

The Pembrokeshire Murders - 2021 - The true crime cold case drama follows the investigation into the most notorious serial killer in Welsh history. In 2006, newly-promoted DS Steve Wilkins decided to re-open an unsolved double murder from the 1980s. Using the latest forensic techniques, he and his team were able to connect the murders to a string of burglaries.

Prime Suspect - 1991 to 2006 - Helen Mirren stars as Detective Jane Tennison, battling crime as well as sexism on the job.

Quirke - 2014 - Gabe Byrne plays a pathologist in 1950s Dublin.

Rebus - 2000 to 2004 - Based on the novels of Scottish author Ian Rankin, Inspector Rebus is an old-fashioned detective in every sense of the word. He smokes, drinks, and doesn't have a lot of luck with his personal life.

River - 2015 - Stellan Skarsgård, Nicola Walker, and Lesley Manville star in this series about a brilliant police officer haunted by guilt.

Rosemary & Thyme - 2003 to 2008 - Former policewoman Laura and a horticulture professor Rosemary are brought together by a love of gardening, but murder seems to follow them. Felicity Kendal (*The Good Life*) and Pam Ferris (*Call the Midwife*) star in this quaint mystery series.

The Ruth Rendell Mysteries: Next Chapters (aka Ruth Rendell Mysteries) - 1994 to 2000 - This collection includes a variety of suspenseful tales adapted from the novels of author Ruth Rendell.

Sally Lockhart Mysteries - 2006 to 2007 - Two of the four Sally Lockhart novels were adapted into these two television movies starring Billie Piper.

Scott & Bailey - 2011 to 2016 - Two very different female police detectives enjoy a close friendship and productive partnership.

Shakespeare & Hathaway - 2018 to present - In beautiful Stratford-Upon-Avon, an unlikely pair of private investigators solves crimes together.

Sherlock Holmes - 1984 to 1994 - Jeremy Brett and David Burke star in this set of Sherlock Holmes adventures.

Sherlock Holmes & the Case of the Silk Stocking - 2004 - Rupert Everett (*An Ideal Husband*) stars as Sherlock Holmes in this TV movie in which a serial killer stalks and kills young daughters of the aristocracy. The disappearances bring Sherlock Holmes and Watson out of retirement to seek the perpetrator. Neil Dudgeon (*Midsomer Murders*) plays Lestrade, and Ian Hart (*The Last Kingdom*) plays Dr. Watson.

Shetland - 2013 to present - In the remote island community of Shetland, DI Jimmy Perez and his team investigate threats to the peace of their village. This series is based on the Shetland novels by Ann Cleeves.

Silent Witness - 1996 to present - A team of pathologists investigates crimes based on evidence gleaned from autopsies.

Stonemouth - 2015 - A man returns to his small Scottish hometown in hopes of finding out the truth about his friend's murder.

The Suspicions of Mr. Whicher: Beyond the Pale - 2014 - Whicher is hired to investigate threats made to the son of an important government employee, leading him to some of the most dangerous parts of Victorian London. Paddy Considine (*Informer*) stars.

The Suspicions of Mr. Whicher: The Murder at Road Hill House - 2011 - Based on Kate Summerscale's best-selling novel, this series sees DI Whicher pursuing the murderer of a three-year-old boy. Paddy Considine (*Informer*) stars.

The Suspicions of Mr. Whicher: The Murder in Angel Lane - 2013 - Whicher investigates the death of a young girl, pitting him against some of London's wealthiest and most powerful individuals. Paddy Considine (*Informer*) stars.

The Suspicions of Mr. Whicher: The Ties That Bind - 2014 - This entry sees Whicher taking on what appears to be a simple infidelity case, but it soon turns much darker. Paddy Considine (*Informer*) stars.

Taggart - 1983 to 2010 - This long-running crime series revolves around a group of detectives in Scotland. Initially set in the Maryhill CID of Strathclyde Police, many later storylines were set and shot in other parts of Greater Glasgow and other areas of Scotland.

Thorne: Scaredy Cat - 2010 - Thorne is working with a new team to tackle a tough double murder case, but it's not long before he's hunting down two different serial killers.

Thorne: Sleepyhead - 2010 - DI Thorne (David Morrissey, *Men Behaving Badly*) is in a race against time to find a serial killer who enjoys making unusual attacks on young women.

Traces - 2019 to present - New chemistry graduate Emma Hodges begins work at The Scottish Institute of Forensic Science and Anatomy, but when she joins an online course to build professional skills, she notices the case is eerily familiar. It's the case of how her mother's body was found eighteen years earlier.

Unforgiven - 2009 - Peter Davison (*The Last Detective*) and Suranne Jones (*Scott & Bailey*) star in this series about a woman released from prison after serving 15 years for the murder of two police officers. Having spent half her life in jail, Ruth must build a new life for herself in spite of the damage she's done.

Vera - 2011 to present - DCI Vera Stanhope investigates murders in the Northumberland countryside. Brenda Blethyn (*Chance in a Million*) stars in this long-running crime drama based on Ann Cleeves' *Vera* novels. This series is split between Acorn TV and BritBox, with BritBox having seasons 3, 4, 5, 8, 9, and 10.

Vera Postmortem - 2018 - This BritBox exclusive includes interviews with Brenda Blethyn (Vera herself) and author Ann Cleeves. They discuss what it's like making the series, along with some of their favourite moments.

Waking the Dead - 2000 to 2011 - Using new forensic technology, DS Boyd and his team open unsolved cases.

Wallander - 2008 to 2016 - This English-language, Sweden-based mystery series is an adaptation of Henning Mankell's novels about Kurt Wallander, a highly empathetic detective.

What Remains - 2013 - When a young couple moves into an apartment, they find a dead body and it kicks off an investigation into a young woman's disappearance two years prior.

Without Motive - 2000 to 2001 - A detective attempts to solve a series of murders that seemingly lack motive.

Wycliffe - 1993 to 1998 - Based on W.J. Burley's novels, this Cornwall-based series features DS Charles Wycliffe, a man who investigates murders with a unique level of determination and accuracy.

Zen - 2011 - A handsome detective works to bring integrity and justice to Roman streets.

BRITBOX

Dramas

A Christmas Carol - 1977 - Michael Hordern (*The Wind in the Willows*) stars as Ebenezer Scrooge in this adaptation of Dickens' classic Christmas story of greed and redemption.

The Alchemists - 1999 - Grant Show (*Melrose Place*) stars in this thriller set in the world of genetic engineering. The series was based on Peter James' 1996 novel, *Alchemist*.

A Royal Scandal - 1996 - Richard E. Grant (*Gosford Park*), Susan Lynch (*From Hell*), Michael Kitchen (*Foyle's War*), and Frances Barber (*Silk*) are among the cast members of this period drama about the troubled marriage of King George and Caroline of Brunswick.

A Song for Jenny - 2015 - Based on real events, this film tells the story of a mother struggling after her daughter was killed in the 2005 London bombings.

Against the Law - 2017 - When Peter Wildeblood and Edward McNally fell in love in 1952, it was still a crime in Britain. This film takes a look at the devastating consequences for each of the two men.

Age Before Beauty - 2018 - This contemporary drama is set in a struggling family-owned beauty salon in Manchester.

An Adventure in Space & Time - 2013 - This television movie is a dramatisation of how Doctor Who was brought to our televisions back in 1963.

Anna of the Five Towns - 1985 - Adapted from Arnold Bennett's 1902 novel of the same title, this series follows a young and strictly-controlled Methodist woman living in Staffordshire around the turn of the century. It follows her struggles for freedom and independence against a dictatorial father and the church.

Aristocrats - 1999 - This miniseries follows the lives of four aristocratic sisters through 1700s England.

Armadillo - 2001 - When loss adjuster Lorimer Black goes out on a routine appointment, he finds a hanged man. This three-part miniseries is based on William Boyd's 1998 novel of the same name.

A Tale of Two Cities - 1980 - This eight-part adaptation of the Dickens classic sees Paul Shelley (*Doctors*) in the roles of Sydney Carton and Charles Darnay, along with Sally Osborne (*King's Royal*) as Lucie Manette. Set against the backdrop of the French Revolution, it follows French Dr. Manette as he is released from an 18-year imprisonment in the Bastille and goes to meet his daughter Lucie in London.

Ballykissangel - *Ireland* - 1996 to 2001 - A young English priest adjusts to the pace of life in a small Irish village. Stephen Tompkinson (*DCI Banks*) stars as Father Peter Clifford.

Bancroft - 2017 to present - DS Elizabeth Bancroft is a brilliant officer, but the questionable tactics she employed in the past are coming back to haunt her.

Banished - 2015 - When British convicts are sent to Australia to pay for their crimes, they and the soldiers who guard them have to adapt to the new world.

The Baron - 1966 to 1967 - American Steve Forrest (*S.W.A.T.*) plays John Mannering, an antiques dealer who also dabbles in undercover work for the British Diplomatic Intelligence. It was the first ITC Entertainment programme made in full colour but without marionettes, and it was based on the Baron series by Anthony Morton.

Bleak House - 1985 - This eight-part miniseries starred Dame Diana Rigg (*Detectorists*) in the role of Lady Dedlock and Denholm Elliott (*Raiders of the Lost Ark*) as John Jarndyce. It was based on the Dickens novel of the same name that centers around the *Jarndyce and Jarndyce* legal case regarding a number of conflicting wills (with numerous subplots).

Bleak House - 2005 - This classic BBC adaptation is based on the Dickens legal drama of the same name. The miniseries features an all-star cast that includes Gillian Anderson (*The Fall*), Timothy West (*Great Canal Journeys*), Carey Mulligan (*Collateral*), Alun Armstrong (*New Tricks*), Sheila Hancock (*Edie*), Catherine Tate (*Doctor Who*), and Hugo Speer (*The Full Monty*).

Bleak Old Shop of Stuff - 2011 - This Dickens parody stars Robert Webb (*Peep Show*) and Katherine Parkinson (*The IT Crowd*) alongside numerous celebrity guest appearances from actors like David Mitchell (*Peep Show*), Stephen Fry (*Kingdom*), Sarah Hadland (*Miranda*), and Phyllida Law (*Kingdom*). The story follows Jedrington Secret-Past (Webb) and his family as evil lawyer Maxifax Skulkingworm (Fry) terrorises them just before Christmas.

Bramwell - 1995 to 1998 - Set in 1895, Eleanor Bramwell works first under a doctor's supervision and then opens her own infirmary.

Brideshead Revisited - 1981 - Jeremy Irons and Anthony Andrews star in this adaptation of Evelyn Waugh's novel by the same name. *The Telegraph* awarded it the top position in its list of greatest television adaptations of all time.

Broken - 2017 - Sean Bean stars as Father Michael, a flawed but good-hearted Catholic priest in Northern England.

The Buccaneers - 1980 - We weren't able to locate a description for this one. There's a 1980 show called *Buccaneer* (about an air freight company) and a later series called *The Buccaneers*, but no perfect fit for the year BritBox provided. If it IS the 1995

version, that series follows four American women who secure wealthy British husbands, only to find it's not all it's cracked up to be.

Casualty - 1986 to present - This *Holby City* spinoff takes place in the A&E (Accidents and Emergency) department of the fictional Holby City Hospital.

Casualty 1900s: London Hospital - 2006 to 2009 - This medical period drama was inspired by the *Holby City* spinoff *Casualty*, but is otherwise unrelated. It takes place in the receiving room of the London Hospital in London's East End, and each case is based on the writings and memoirs of real doctors and nurses from the time period.

Catherine Cookson's The Cinder Path - 1994 - This three-part series follows a prosperous middle-class famer's son, Charlie MacFell, as he navigates a variety of challenges while attempting to keep a dark secret hidden. Lloyd Owen (*Monarch of the Glen*) stars alongside Catherine Zeta-Jones (*The Darling Buds of May*).

Catherine Cookson's Colour Blind - 1998 - In England's industrial north during WWI, a family is turned upside down when their daughter Bridget comes home with a black husband. Niamh Cusack (*Heartbeat*) stars.

Catherine Cookson's A Dinner of Herbs - 2000 - After a man is killed, friend Kate Makepeace (Billie Whitelaw, *Hot Fuzz*) agrees to raise his surviving children. As time goes on, painful secrets from the past begin to emerge.

Catherine Cookson's The Dwelling Place - 1994 - Tracy Whitwell (*The Accidental Medium*) stars as 16-year-old Cissie Brodie, a young woman forced to care for her younger siblings after the death of her parents and the repossession of the family home.

Catherine Cookson's The Fifteen Streets - 1989 - In turn-of-the-century northern England, the impoverished John O'Brien falls in love with his sister's teacher, the daughter of a wealthy family. She's determined not to let issues of class stand in the way of their relationship. Owen Teale (*Game of Thrones*) and Sean Bean (*Game of Thrones*) are among the stars.

Catherine Cookson's The Gambling Man - 1995 - Robson Green (*Grantchester*) stars in this three-part miniseries about Rory Connor, a Tyneside rent collector with a taste for high-stakes poker. Some suspect the source novel to have been autobiographical, given that Catherine Cookson's own father was a bigamist and gambler.

Catherine Cookson's The Girl - 1996 - In mid-19th century England, young Hannah Boyle is left with the family of Matthew Thornton, the man who supposedly fathered her. She's treated terribly and ultimately pushed out into an unhappy marriage with the village butcher. *Shakespeare & Hathaway* fans will spot Mark Benton in the role of Fred Loam.

Catherine Cookson's The Glass Virgin - 1995 - This three-part serial stars Emily Mortimer (*The Newsroom*) and Brendan Coyle (*Downton Abbey*). Mortimer plays Annabella Grange, a wealthy young woman who runs away from home after discovering a terrible secret. Coyle plays Mendoza, the young Irish traveller she joins on a lengthy roam around the Northumberland countryside. One reviewer said the series "might have been sponsored by the Northumbrian tourist board" in reference to the number of sunny shots of the local scenery.

Catherine Cookson's The Man Who Cried - 1993 - Ciarán Hinds (*Above Suspicion*) stars as Abel Mason, a man trapped in a bad marriage with a woman who belittles him and beats their son. When his true love is killed by her husband after his evil wife sends him a letter exposing the affair, Abel grabs his son and leaves.

Catherine Cookson's The Moth - 1987 - In 1913 Northumbria, a young shipyard worker arrives home one day to find his father has died. At the funeral, he meets his father's estranged brother and starts fresh with his newly-discovered family. It's all going rather well until his cousin turns up pregnant and everyone thinks he's the father. Jack Davenport (*Coupling*) stars.

Catherine Cookson's The Rag Nymph - 1997 - *Foyle's War* fans will enjoy seeing a young Honeysuckle Weeks acting alongside her sister Perdita in this three-part miniseries. Young Millie is separated from her prostitute mother as she flees from the police in 19th century Newcastle. From there, she meets rag lady Aggie who helps protect her from a local pimp who wants to add her to his business.

Catherine Cookson's The Round Tower - 1998 - Emilia Fox (*Delicious*) stars as Vanessa Ratcliffe, a young woman who feels slighted by her parents' attention to her eldest sister's upcoming nuptials. When a family friend seduces and impregnates her, her life begins a downward spiral.

Catherine Cookson's The Secret - 2000 - Colin Buchanan (*Dalziel & Pascoe*) stars as Freddie Musgrave, a reformed smuggler who tries to go straight, but gets dragged back into his old ways when a face from the past shows up. Unlike most of Cookson's work, this miniseries is a thriller.

Catherine Cookson's The Tide of Life - 1996 - This three-part miniseries follows housekeeper Emily Kennedy as she learns about life and love through relationships with three different men. Gillian Kearney (*The Forsyte Saga*) stars.

Catherine Cookson's Tilly Trotter - 1999 - This four-part serial follows Tilly Trotter, a beautiful young woman in rural England in the 1830s. Envied by women and desired by men, she's accused of witchcraft before being saved by a married farmer.

Catherine Cookson's The Wingless Bird - 1997 - Claire Skinner (*Outnumbered*) stars as Agnes Conway in this WWI-era period drama. The twentysomething finds herself managing not only her father's shops, but also the seemingly endless problems of her family. The real question is whether she'll be able to navigate those troubles and carve out a bit of happiness for herself.

The Cazalets - 2001 - This six-part miniseries follows the life of a wealthy Sussex family between the chaotic years of 1937 to 1947. It's based on *The Cazalet Chronicles* by Elizabeth Jane Howard.

The Champions - 1968 to 1969 - After a plane crash in the Himalayas, three secret agents are rescued by members of an advanced civilisation living secretly in the mountains. In the course of the rescue, they grant the three agents a set of supernatural abilities. Now, they use those special talents in service of a mysterious international agency called Nemesis.

Charles II: The Power and the Passion - 2003 - Rufus Sewell (*The Pale Horse*) stars in this four-part drama about the life of Charles II.

Christopher and His Kind - 2011 - This BBC television film tells the story of novelist Christopher Isherwood's youthful experiences as a young gay man living in

Berlin in the 1930s. Matt Smith (*Doctor Who*) and Toby Jones (*Detectorists*) star.

Churchill: The Darkest Hour - 2013 - This docu-drama takes a look at Winston Churchill's experiences during World War I.

Coalition - 2015 - This tense political TV movie follows David Cameron, Nick Clegg, and Gordon Brown in the aftermath of the 2010 UK general election.

Cold Feet - 1998 to 2003 - This long-running dramedy follows the lives of six thirtysomething friends living in Manchester, England as they do their best to get their lives sorted.

Cold Feet: The New Years - 2016 to 2020 - Nearly 15 years after the original series ended, it returned for another set of episodes focusing on the Manchester-based friends, now in their 50s. Though 2020 marked the last set of episodes for this run, there's been talk of an additional series when the group is facing the next big phase of life.

Coronation Street - 1960 to present - Running since 1960, and there are more than 9400 episodes of this daytime drama classic. The show is set in the fictional area of Wetherfield, where residents walk cobbled streets among terraced houses and the ever-present Rovers Return pub. No service currently offers all 9000+ episodes, but BritBox maintains a running set of the most recent episodes.

Cranford - 2007 to 2009 - *Cranford* tells the story of women in a small, fictional market town at the dawn of the Industrial Revolution. Dame Judi Dench (*As Time Goes By*) stars in this modern adaptation of Elizabeth Gaskell's novellas.

Crime Story - 1992 to 1993 - This series features dramatic reenactments of some of Britain's most heinous and notorious crimes. Among them are the tale of Erwin van Haarlem, the story of Graham Young, and a case in which a young man's body was found by divers in a Lancashire quarry.

Daleks' Invasion Earth 2150 A.D. - 1966 - This theatrical adaptation of "The Dalek Invasion of Earth" sees Peter Cushing reprising his role as Doctor Who, an inventor who created the TARDIS.

Dandelion Dead - 1994 - Michael Kitchen (*Foyle's War*) stars in this true crime period drama about Herbert Rowse Armstrong, a Hay-on-Wye solicitor who was convicted

and hanged for the murder of his wife and attempted murder of fellow solicitor, Oswald Martin.

Daniel Deronda - 2002 - This four-part adaptation of George Eliot's final novel focuses on a Victorian man torn between the love of two women. Hugh Dancy (*The Jane Austen Book Club*) stars as Daniel.

David Copperfield - 1986 - Simon Callow makes an appearance in this adaptation of the classic Dickens novel.

David Copperfield - 1999 - Daniel Radcliffe (*Harry Potter*) stars as young David in this adaptation of the Dickens novel.

Desperate Romantics – 2009 - In 1851 London, a group of artists lead colorful lives amidst the chaos of the Industrial Revolution.

Dickensian - 2015 to 2016 - This ambitious miniseries is set in the world of Charles Dickens's novels, bringing together a variety of characters in 19th century London.

Dirk Gently - 2010 to 2012 - An unusual detective looks to the universe for holistic solutions to mysteries. Stephen Mangan (*Bliss*) stars in this adaptation of the popular Douglas Adams novels.

Classic Doctor Who - 1963 to 1989 - *Doctor Who* originally ran for 26 seasons between 1963 and 1989. Though some episodes of the British sci-fi classic no longer exist, those that are available are included on BritBox.

Doctor Who Specials - 1991 to 2013 - This collection features some of the less common *Classic Doctor Who* specials, including the un-aired pilot and reunion episode.

Doctor Who: The Doctors Revisited - 2013 - This series introduces the first seven doctors from Doctor Who. It includes classic footage and interviews from cast and crew members.

Doctor Zhivago - 2002 - Kiera Knightley (*Pride and Prejudice*) and Hans Matheson (*The Tudors*) star in this miniseries adaptation of Boris Pasternak's classic 1957 novel.

Dombey and Son - 1983 - This 1983 Charles Dickens adaptation reminds us that money can't protect you from the heartbreak of life. Julian Glover (*Game of Thrones*) stars as Paul Dombey Sr.

Downton Abbey - 2010 to 2015 - This popular period drama follows the lives of the Crawley family and their servants during the early 1900s.

Drovers' Gold - 1997 - In 1843 Wales, an English drover refuses to give a widow a fair price for her cattle, so she sends her son to take the herd to market in London.

Dr. Who and the Daleks - 1965 - This feature length adaptation of "The Daleks" stars Peter Cushing as Dr. Who, a man who invented a device to travel across time and space with his granddaughters.

The Duchess of Duke Street - 1976 - Gemma Jones (*Bridget Jones's Diary*) starred in this series about a woman who worked her way up from servant to cook to owner of an upper-class hotel on Duke Street in London. The story is loosely based on the real life of Rosa Lewis, who ran the Cavendish Hotel. Keep an eye out for an appearance from Julian Fellowes (*Downton Abbey*).

Dunkirk - 2004 - Benedict Cumberbatch (*Sherlock*) stars in this docudrama about the Dunkirk evacuation during World War II. The series uses a mixture of eyewitness accounts, archive footage, and newly-dramatised sequences to bring the story to life.

EastEnders - 1985 to present - Known for its diversity and modern storylines, EastEnders is set in the fictional London borough of Walford around a Victorian square that includes a pub (The Queen Vic), a market, a launderette, and a cafe. As with a number of British soaps, BritBox typically keeps a running set of the most recent episodes.

Elizabeth R - 1971 - Brenda Jackson (*Women in Love*) stars as Elizabeth I in this series about the "Virgin Queen". She won two Emmys for the performance.

Emma - 1972 - Doran Godwin and John Carson star in this six-part adaptation of Jane Austen's classic novel. Set in the fictional country village of Highbury, it follows would-be matchmaker Emma as she meddles in the affairs of those around her.

Emma - 2009 - Romola Garai (*The Hour*) stars as Emma Woodhouse in this four-part adaptation of Jane Austen's classic novel. Jonny Lee Miller (*Elementary*) plays her dear friend Mr. Knightley.

Emmerdale - 1972 to present - Originally known as *Emmerdale Farm*, this series was originally set in a village called Beckindale. In the 90s, the show rebranded and began to focus on the entire village of Emmerdale. Now, storylines are bigger, sexier, and more dramatic than ever.

Extremely Dangerous - 1999 - Sean Bean (*Game of Thrones*) stars as a former MI-5 agent seeking vengeance after being wrongfully convicted of his family's murder.

Fanny by Gaslight - 1981 - This four-part miniseries is an adaptation of Michael Sadleir's novel of the same name. It follows Fanny Hooper, a young woman who's fallen on hard times as an orphan in Victorian London. This adaptation sees Chloe Salaman in the role of Fanny.

Father and Son - 2009 - Michael O'Connor may have been one of the toughest gangsters around, but he thinks he's left that behind when he moves to Ireland to start over. When his son Séan is accused of a murder he didn't commit, Michael must return to Manchester and face his past.

Fields of Gold - 2002 - Benedict Cumberbatch (*Sherlock*) and Anna Friel (*Marcella*) star in this two-part thriller about genetically modified food.

Five by Five - 2017 - Idris Elba (*Luther*) stars in this series of five intertwining short films about random encounters in London.

Florence Nightingale - 2008 - This hour-long film tells the story of Florence Nightingale's defining moments after the Crimean War, and how those moment would shape the impact she would come to have on medicine.

Frankie - 2013 - Eve Myles (*Keeping Faith*) stars as the head nurse on a traveling nursing team.

Gideon's Daughter - 2006 - Emily Blunt (*The Devil Wears Prada*), Tom Hardy (*The Dark Night Rises*), and Bill Nighy (*Love Actually*) star in this film about a public relations guru who rethinks his life as his daughter goes off to study at the University of Edinburgh and he goes through a series of personal changes. The series is set in the late 90s against the backdrop of Princess Diana's death and the development of the Millennium Dome.

Great Expectations - 1981 - Joan Hickson (*Miss Marple*) stars as Miss Havisham alongside Gerry Sundquist (*The Last Days of*

Pompeii) as Pip in this 1981 adaptation of the Dickens classic. Set in Kent and London, it follows the coming of age of an orphan nicknamed Pip.

Great Expectations - 1999 - Ioan Gruffudd (*Harrow*) stars as Pip in this dark and unsentimental retelling of Dickens' classic novel.

Great Expectations - 2011 - This star-studded adaptation of the Dickens classic sees Gillian Anderson (*The Fall*) playing Miss Havisham, Douglas Booth (*Worried About the Boy*) as Pip, Vanessa Kirby (*The Crown*) as Estella, and David Suchet (*Poirot*) as Jaggers. Though many criticised the fact that Anderson was just 43 when playing Miss Havisham, reception was generally positive.

Hard Times - 1994 - Thomas Gradgrind is a wealthy merchant who's raised his children to be rational, self-interest, and above imaginative pursuits. Over the course of the film, we see those methods tested. The film is based on the Dickens novel of the same name. *Hard Times* was the shortest of all the Dickens novels, and the only one not to include scenes in London.

Heading Home - 1991 - Gary Oldman (*Bram Stoker's Dracula*) and Joely Richardson (*Nip/Tuck*) star in this film about a young woman who moves to London to start a new life after WWII. She soon finds herself torn between two men and tangled up with both the literary scene and a more criminal element.

Heartbeat - 1992 to 2010 - This Yorkshire-based period crime drama ran for 18 seasons and 372 episodes, focusing on the lives of characters in a small village. Initially, it focused on a central couple, PC Nick Rowan and Dr. Kate Rowan, but as time went on, it branched out to include storylines all over the village. The series is based on the "Constable" novels written by Peter N. Walker under the pseudonym Nicholas Rhea.

Hearts of Gold - 2003 - Doctor Andrew John has always found his girlfriend to be lacking in spirit, but when he meets vibrant miner's daughter Bethan Powell, he falls madly in love in spite of their different social classes.

The Heist at Hatton Garden - 2019 - Also known as The Heist at Hatton Garden, this series is based on the true story of a spectacular diamond heist carried out in London by a group of elderly criminals. The all-star cast includes Timothy Spall (*Blandings*), Alex Norton (*Taggart*), David Hayman (*The Paradise*), and Kenneth Cranham (*The White Princess*).

Him - 2016 - Fionn Whitehead (*Dunkirk*) stars as a character known only as HIM. Set in suburban London, the series follows as he struggles to adjust to telekinetic powers inherited from his grandfather.

Holby City - 1999 to present - This medical soap follows the lives of those working on the wards of Holby City Hospital. This series is a spin-off from *Casualty*, and it's set in the same hospital with occasional cross-over characters and plots. It was designed to offer a look at what happened to people taken from the A&E (emergency room) to the other departments within the hospital.

Homefront - 2012 to 2014 - This six-episode miniseries follows the lives of four army wives in the UK while their husbands are serving in Afghanistan.

Honour -

The House of Eliott - 1991 - Stella Gonet (*Breeders*) and Louise Lombard (*CSI: Crime Scene Investigation*) star in this series about two sisters who start a dressmaking business in 1920s London.

Isolation Stories - 2020 - Filmed remotely during the COVID-19 pandemic of 2020, this limited dramatic series taps into the feelings different people experience during lockdown.

Jane Eyre - 1983 - This adaptation of Brontë's classic stars Timothy Dalton and Zelah Clarke as Jane and Mr. Rochester.

Jane Eyre - 2006 - Ruth Wilson (*Luther*) stars as Jane Eyre in this mildly steamy adaptation of Charlotte Brontë's classic novel.

Jekyll & Hyde - 1990 - Michael Caine (*The Dark Knight*) stars as Dr. Henry Jekyll (and Mr. Edward Hyde) in this chilling feature-length adaptation of the classic Victorian horror story.

The Jury - 2002 to 2011 - When the killing of a 15-year-old boy rocks the nation, 12 jurors find themselves under intense pressure to make the right decision. The second season is entirely unconnected to the first, and sees a set of jurors called up to handle the controversial retrial of a convicted murderer.

Justice - 2011 - Robert Pugh (*Game of Thrones*) and Jodie Comer (*Killing Eve*) star in this short-lived dramatic series about a judge sworking in the Public Justice Centre in Dovefield, Liverpool. It's a rough area, and it's no easy task bringing a bit of law and order to the area.

K9 & Company: A Girl's Best Friend - 1981 - This single-episode television pilot was intended as a spin-off of Doctor Who, featuring series regular Sarah Jane Smith (Elisabeth Sladen) and K9, a dog robot voiced by John Leeson. It sees Sarah Jane searching for her missing aunt in a quiet Gloucestershire village.

Kat & Alfie: Redwater - 2017 - 32 years after giving her son up for adoption, Kat moves to the town of Redwater in an attempt to find him.

Kavanagh QC - 1995 to 2001 - John Thaw (*Inspector Morse*) stars as James Kavanagh QC, a barrister with a working-class background and a strong sense of right and wrong. It was one of Thaw's final roles before he died of cancer at the age of 60. Pay close attention to the guest stars in this one, as it's loaded with actors who went on to well-known roles, including Lesley Manville (*Mum*), Larry Lamb (*Gavin & Stacey*), Barry Jackson (*Midsomer Murders*), Phyllis Logan (*Downton Abbey*), Bill Night (*Love Actually*), and Julian Fellowes (*Downton Abbey*).

Killed By My Debt - 2018 - This programme tells the story of Jerome, a young man whose small debt and poor prospects led him to kill himself. Chance Perdomo (*Chilling Adventures of Sabrina*) stars.

Lady Chatterley's Lover - 2015 - Holliday Grainger (*Strike*), Richard Madden (*Bodyguard*), and James Norton (*Grantchester*) star in this film adaptation of DH Lawrence's classically scandalous 1928 novel by the same name. The film follows Lady Chatterley, a women who's happily married to an aristocrat until injuries from WWI leave him impotent and confined to a wheelchair. Unable to get her "marital needs" fulfilled, she finds comfort in the arms of their dark and brooding gamekeeper.

Theatre Night: Lady Windermere's Fan - 1985 - Based on Oscar Wilde's play of the same name, this comedy follows Lady Windermere, a woman who suspects her husband of being unfaithful. Though he denies it when confronted, he still invites the other woman to his wife's birthday ball, where things quickly get a bit ridiculous.

Lark Rise to Candleford - 2008 to 2011 - Set in the late 19th century in the small Oxfordshire hamlet of Lark Rise and the nearby market town of Candleford, this period drama follows a young woman who moves towns to work in a post office. The series is based on Flora Thompson's semi-autobiographical novels about living in the English countryside.

Life in Squares - 2015 - This series dramatizes the lives of those in the Bloomsbury group, a set of influential artists, writers, and intellectuals in England.

Little Boy Blue - 2017 - This ITV series is a dramatisation of the real-life murder of 11-year-old Rhys Jones during a wave of gang violence in Liverpool in 2007.

Little Dorrit - 2008 - Claire Foy (*The Crown*) and Matthew Macfayden (*Ripper Street*) star in this adaptation of Dickens' story of struggle in 1820s London. Andrew Davies (*Pride & Prejudice*) wrote the screenplay for this adaptation.

Little Women - 1970 - Poorly received by critics, this low-budget adaptation of the Louisa May Alcott classic features inauthentic American accents and a cast of actresses noticeably older than their ages in the novel. Patrick Troughton (*Doctor Who*) played the role of Mr. March.

London Road - 2015 - Olivia Colman (*Broadchurch*) and Tom Hardy (*Peaky Blinders*) star in this film adaptation of the musical of the same name (which is based on a series of interviews about the Suffolk Strangler).

Lorna Doone - 2000 - When a man falls in love with a woman from the same clan that killed his father, he's horrified. This adaptation is based on the 1869 Richard Doddridge Blackmore novel of the same name, and it includes appearances from Anton Lesser (*Endeavour*), Richard Coyle (*Coupling*), Honeysuckle Weeks (*Foyle's War*), Martin Clunes (*Doc Martin*), James McAvoy (*Shameless*), Michael Kitchen (*Foyle's War*), and Joanne Froggatt (*Downton Abbey*).

Lost in Austen - 2008 - A bored young *Pride and Prejudice* fan is changed forever when Elizabeth Bennet stumbles into her modern bathroom. This miniseries includes Hugh Bonneville (*Downton Abbey*) as Mr. Bennet, Morven Christie (*Grantchester*) as

Jane Bennet, and Jemima Rooper (*Gold Digger*) as lead Amanda Price.

Love in a Cold Climate - 2001 - Between 1929 and 1940, three young women search for love.

Madame Bovary - 1975 - Francesca Annis (*Home Fires*) stars as Emma Bovary in this classic adaptation of Flaubert's novel about the frustrated, unfaithful wife of a French country doctor. Tom Conti (*Parents*) plays Charles Bovary.

Madame Bovary - 2000 - In Flaubert's classic, a woman marries a doctor in hopes of escaping a boring provincial life. It doesn't work. This adaptation features Frances O'Connor (*Mansfield Park*) as Emma Bovary, with Hugh Bonneville (*Downton Abbey*) in the role of Charles Bovary.

Mansfield Park - 1983 - Sylvestra Le Touzel stars as Fanny Price in this miniseries adaptation of Jane Austen's third novel. It's about a young woman sent to live with wealthier relatives, who later falls in love with her sensitive cousin.

Margaret - 2009 - Lindsay Duncan (*Rome*) stars as Margaret Thatcher in this drama about her fall from power.

Martin Chuzzlewit - 1994 - When a wealthy old man nears death, everyone comes out of the woodwork to try to get their piece of his riches. This miniseries is based on the Dickens novel of the same name.

MI-5 (aka Spooks) - 2002 to 2011 - This dramatic series follows top secret missions of the MI-5, the UK's elite domestic security and counter-intelligence agency. Matthew Macfadyen (*Pride & Prejudice*), Keeley Hawes (*Bodyguard*), Hermione Norris (*Cold Feet*), and Richard Armitage (*North & South*) are among the stars.

Middlemarch - 1994 - Robert Hardy, Rufus Sewell, Pam Ferris, Patrick Malahide, and Dame Judi Dench all appear in this adaptation of the classic George Eliot novel. It sees Dorothea Brooke marrying a much older man in an attempt to grow intellectually, only to find he has no interest in involving her in his intellectual pursuits. After his death, she meets his much younger cousin, a man who is interested in her despite the fact that she's oblivious to his intentions.

Miss Austen Regrets - 2008 - This feature-length drama is based on Jane Austen's life and collected letters. Olivia Williams (*An Education*) plays Jane Austen.

Mo - 2010 - Julie Walters (*Dinnerladies*) stars in this biopic about the life of Mo Mowlam, a controversial Labour Party politician in Northern Ireland.

The Moorside - 2017 - This two-part television drama is based on the 2008 disappearance of 9-year-old Shannon Matthews in Dewsbury, West Yorkshire. The cast includes Sheridan Smith (*Gavin & Stacey*), Gemma Whelan (*Game of Thrones*), Sian Brooke (*Doctor Foster*), and Sibhan Finneran (*Downton Abbey*).

Mother's Day - 2018 - Based on a true story, this film follows two mothers, one English and one Irish, as they pave the way for peace in the aftermath of an IRA attack in Warrington, England.

Moving On – 2009 to 2016 - This anthology series gives us stories of people preparing to move on to something new in their lives.

Mrs. Brown - 1997 - Dame Judi Dench stars in this film about Queen Victoria and her unusual friendship with servant John Brown (Billy Connolly). Her portrayal of the scandalous relationship earned an Academy Award nomination.

Murdered by My Boyfriend - 2014 - This dramatisation of a true story tells of a young woman who falls in love with the wrong man. The adaptation was commissioned to help educate young viewers about the dangers of relationship abuse.

Murdered by My Father - 2016 - This one-off drama tells the story of a young British Asian Muslim girl who was killed by her father for loving the wrong man.

Murdered for Being Different - 2017 - Based on the real 2007 murder of Sophie Lancaster, this film sees two young goths attacked for being different.

My Boy Jack - 2007 - Daniel Radcliffe (*Harry Potter*), Carey Mulligan (*Pride and Prejudice*), and Kim Cattrall (*Sex and the City*) star in this WWI drama about Rudyard Kipling and his son John. The name of the film is taken from Kipling's poem, "My Boy Jack".

My Family and Other Animals - 2005 - Fans of *The Durrells in Corfu* will enjoy this television film based on Gerald Durrell's autobiographical book about his family's stay on Corfu. The source material was part of the trilogy that ultimately turned into the television series, and this take on it includes Eugene Simon (*Game of Thrones*), Imelda Staunton (*Flesh & Blood*), Matthew Goode (*A Discovery of Witches*), and Russell Tovey (*Flesh & Blood*) among the cast members.

The Mystery of Edwin Drood - 2012 - Matthew Rhys (*Perry Mason*) stars as John Jasper in this adaptation of the unfinished 1870 novel by Charles Dickens.

North & South - 2004 - Based on the 1855 Victorian novel of the same name by Elizabeth Gaskell, this series follows Margaret Hale, a young woman from southern England who's forced to move north after her father leaves the clergy. The series is a study in class and gender issues of the time, and we see Margaret torn between sympathy for the northern mill workers and increasing attraction to wealthy John Thornton.

Northanger Abbey - 1987 - Katharine Schlesinger (*Doctor Who*) stars in this adaptation of Jane Austen's classic parody of Gothic fiction. She plays seventeen-year-old tomboy Catherine Morland, a young woman with a wild imagination and love of Gothic novels. Robert Hardy (*All Creatures Great & Small*) and Peter Firth (*Spooks*) are also among the cast members.

NW - 2016 - Based on Zadie Smith's award-winning novel, this series follows two friends from a northwest London housing estate as they reunite during a challenging time.

Oliver Twist - 1985 - This is the 1985 BBC adaptation of the classic Dickens tale with Ben Rodska as Oliver Twist. Keep an eye out for Frank Middlemaas (*As Time Goes By*) and Miriam Margolyes (*Miss Fisher's Murder Mysteries*) as Mr. Brownlow and Mrs. Bumble.

Oliver Twist - 2007 - Morven Christie (*Grantchester*), Tom Hardy (*Peaky Blinders*), and Sarah Lancashire (*Happy Valley*) all appear in this star-studded adaptation of the Dickens classic.

One Night - 2012 - In one night, the lives of four people are linked by a single event.

Ordinary Lies - 2015 to 2016 - Each series of this show is set in a perfectly ordinary location, but the people have dark secrets. Series 1 takes place at a car dealership in Warrington, while Series 2 is set in a sporting goods company.

The Other Boleyn Girl - 2003 - Based on Philippa Gregory's novel of the same name, this film follows Mary Boleyn, sister to Anne and George Boleyn. She's recently gotten married to William Carey, but because Henry VIII favours her, she's also his mistress. Natascha McElhone (*Californication*) stars as Mary Boleyn, with Jodhi May (*A Quiet Passion*) as Anne.

Our Friends in the North - 1996 - This series follows a group of four friends from Newcastle as their lives unfold over a period of 31 years. Daniel Craig (*Quantum of Solace*) and Christopher Eccleston (*Doctor Who*) are among the stars.

Our Girl - 2013 to present - This series follows a young woman from East London as she embarks on her career as an army medic. Lacey Turner (*EastEnders*) stars as Molly Dawes, with Michelle Keegan (*Brassic*) entering later as Georgie Lane.

Our Mutual Friend - 1998 - This adaptation of Dickens's last completed novel contrasts money and poverty in Victorian London. The adaptation features a number of familiar faces, including Paul McGann (*Luther*), Anna Friel (*Marcella*), Pam Ferris (*Rosemary & Thyme*), Peter Vaughan (*Game of Thrones*), and Keeley Hawes (*The Durrells*).

The Paradise - 2012 - In this period drama, a young and ambitious woman heads to the city to make her way working in a department store.

The Passing Bells - 2014 - This British-Polish drama tells the story of two teens, one British and one German, who sign up to fight in WWI.

Persuasion - 2007 - Sally Hawkins (*Tipping the Velvet*) and Rupert Penry-Jones (*Whitechapel*) star in this film adaptation of Jane Austen's 1817 novel. Eight years before the story begins, Anne (Hawkins) rejected Wentworth's (Penry-Jones) proposal of marriage. Now, he's made his fortune and he's looking for a wife, so long as it's not Anne.

The Pickwick Papers - 1985 - Nigel Stock and Clive Swift star in this adaptation of Dickens' great comic masterpiece.

Pride and Prejudice - 1980 - Elizabeth Garvie and David Rintoul star in this five-part television adaptation of Austen's classic. *Grantchester* fans may also notice Tessa Peake-Jones (Mrs. Maguire) in the role of Mary Bennet. The series follows

Mrs. Bennet's efforts to secure good husbands for her five daughters.

Pride & Prejudice - 1995 - Jennifer Ehle and Colin Firth star in this much-loved adaptation of Jane Austen's classic novel that starts with "a single man in possession of a good fortune". ***Digitally remastered.***

The Quatermass Experiment - 2005 - Based on the 1950s sci-fi classic, this film focuses on the sole survivor of a rocket crash, and the Professor who must stop him. David Tennant (*Doctor Who*) appears as Dr. Gordon Briscoe.

Reg - 2016 - Tim Roth (*Reservoir Dogs*) stars as Reg Keys in this political drama about a bereaved military father who took on Tony Blair in the 2005 elections.

Room at the Top - 2012 - This two-part television adaptation is based on John Braine's 1957 novel of the same name, with a cast that includes Matthew McNulty (*Misfits*), Maxine Peake (*Shameless*), and Jenna Coleman (*Doctor Who*). It tells the story of one ambitious young man's rise in post-war Britain.

The Royal - 2003 to 2011 - This *Heartbeat* spinoff is set in the 1960s and focuses on an NHS hospital serving the seaside Yorkshire town of Elsinby.

Royal Celebration - 1993 - Keira Knightley (*Pride & Prejudice*) and Minnie Driver (*Good Will Hunting*) star in this drama about the wedding of Prince Charles and Lady Diana.

The Royal Today - 2008 - This follow-up to *The Royal* takes place in the same Yorkshire hospital, but 40 years later.

The Sandbaggers - 1978 to 1980 - This spy drama follows the men and woman on the front lines of the Cold War. Based in Leeds and produced by Yorkshire Television, it starred Roy Marsden (Adam Dalgliesh in the P.D. James adaptations), Director of Operations in Britain's Secret Intelligence Service.

Sense and Sensibility - 1981 - This seven-part adaptation of Jane Austen's 1811 novel follows the newly widowed and destitute Mrs. Dashwood as she attempts to survive and marry off her three daughters. This adaptation is unique in that it omits the character of Margaret Dashwood.

Sense and Sensibility - 2008 - This Andrew Davies adaptation of Austen's 1811 novel featured Mark Gatiss (Sherlock) as John Dashwood, a young man whose nasty wife Fanny (Claire Skinner, *Outnumbered*) convinces him to reduce the amount of money he provides to his widowed stepmother and half siblings. Newly widowed and destitute with three unmarried daughters, Mary Dashwood (Janet McTeer, *Tumbleweeds*) downsizes and attempts to find good husbands for her daughters.

Servants - 2003 - Written and created by Lucy Gannon, this series followed the lives of a group of servants in an 1850s English country house.

Sharpe - 1993 to 2010 - Sean Bean (*Game of Thrones*) stars in this 19th century period drama set during the Napoleonic Wars in Spain. It's based on the *Sharpe* novels by Bernard Cornwell.

Single Father - 2010 - David Tennant stars in this drama about a regular guy trying to raise his family after the death of his wife.

The Six Wives of Henry VIII - 1971 - This collection of television plays focuses on the wives of Henry VIII, with each play telling the story of one woman. Second Doctor Patrick Troughton (*Doctor Who*) is among the stars.

Small Island - 2009 - Based on the 2004 novel of the same title by Andrea Levy, this film sees Naomie Harris (*28 Days Later*) and Ruth Wilson (*Mrs. Wilson*) playing two women who struggle to achieve their dreams in World War II London. Benedict Cumberbatch (*Sherlock*) and David Oyelowo (*Spooks/MI-5*) also appear.

Sticks and Stones - 2019 - After a sales pitch goes terribly wrong, Thomas Benson begins to feel his colleagues have turned against him. Desperate to fix things, he resorts to extreme measures to get back on top. Ben Miller (*Death in Paradise*) is among the stars of this psychological thriller.

The Street - 2006 to 2009 - Each episode takes a look at what's going on with a different family who lives on the same street.

The Sweeney - 1975 to 1978 - Before John Thaw played Inspector Morse, and before Dennis Waterman appeared on *New Tricks*, they co-starred in The Sweeney. Groundbreaking at the time, this was one of the first TV portrayals to show British police as ruthless, rule-bending, and fallible. Thaw and Waterman play two members of the Flying Squad, a branch of police that handle armed robbery and violent crimes in London.

The Tenant of Wildfell Hall - 1996 - In a remote Yorkshire village, a widow and her son move into the creepy, crumbling Wildfell Hall. Based on the classic story by Anne Brontë.

Tess of the D'Urbervilles - 2008 - In this miniseries based on the Thomas Hardy work, Gemma Arterton (*Lost in Austen*) stars as Tess Durbeyfield, the poor country girl with connections to nobility.

That Day We Sang - 2014 - Based on the Victoria Wood musical of the same name, this television adaptation starring Imelda Staunton (*A Confession*) is based in 1969 with flashbacks to 1929. It tells the story of a middle-aged couple that finds love when they meet on a television programme about a choir they were once in.

Three Girls - 2017 - Authorities ignore the trafficking of young girls by British Pakistani men.

Tina & Bobby - 2017 - This miniseries follows the relationship of Tina Dean and her West Ham United footballer husband, Bobby Moore.

Tipping the Velvet - 2002 - This period drama tells the story of a love affair between two music hall women in the 1890s. Rachael Stirling (*Detectorists*) and Keeley Hawes (*Bodyguard*) star. The series is based on Sarah Waters' best-selling 1998 debut novel of the same name.

Trauma - 2018 - This thriller shows how two fathers' lives collide when one man's son dies at the hands of the other.

The Turn of the Screw - 1999 - This TV movie adaptation of The Turn of the Screw stars Colin Firth and Johdi May. Pam Ferris *(Rosemary & Thyme)* also appears.

Tutankhamun - 2016 - This adventure miniseries is based on Howard Carter's discovery of King Tut's tomb.

Under the Greenwood Tree - 2005 - Keeley Hawes (*Bodyguard*) and James Murray (*Age Before Beauty*) star in this ITV adaptation of Thomas Hardy's first *Wessex* novel. It follows members of the Mellstock parish choir, including two (Hawes and Murray as Fancy Day and Dick Dewy) who become romantically entangled.

Upstairs Downstairs - 1971 to 1977 - This drama follows the aristocratic Bellamy family and the servants who live downstairs. The series is set between the years of 1903 and 1930, showing the gradual decline of the aristocratic class in Britain.

Upstairs Downstairs - 2010 to 2012 - This series picks up the Upstairs Downstairs saga shortly after the period covered by the original series. Covering 1936 to 1939, it tells the story of the new owners of 165 Eaton Place, ending with the outbreak of World War II. Ed Stoppard (*Home Fires*) and Keeley Hawes (*Bodyguard*) play new owners Sir Hallam Holland and Lady Agnes Holland.

Vanity Fair - 1987 - This adaptation of Thackeray's Napoleonic War-era tale starred Eve Matheson, Rebecca Saire, James Saxon, and Simon Dormandy in the lead roles.

Vanity Fair - 1998 - This BBC adaptation of Thackeray's novel featured a screenplay by Andrew Davies (*Pride & Prejudice*), with Natasha Little in the role of Becky Sharp.

The Victim - 2019 - This four-part Scottish miniseries tells the story of Anna Dean (Kelly MacDonald, *Boardwalk Empire*), a mother whose young son was murdered more than a decade prior. She's been accused of sharing information about the man she believes to be guilty, damaging his reputation and causing him to be attacked. The series focuses on the trial and a mother's unrelenting search for the truth.

The Village - 2013 to 2014 - Written by Peter Moffat (*Cambridge Spies*), this series is set in a Derbyshire village between 1914 and the mid-1920s. Though originally envisioned as a 42-hour epic televised drama, it lasted just two seasons. It tells the story of life and history through the eyes of Bert Middleton and his fellow villagers.

The Way We Live Now - 2001 - Adapted from Anthony Trollope's 1875 novel of the same name, this series was written by Andrew Davies (*Pride & Prejudice*) and features a cast of British acting favourites like David Suchet (*Poirot*), Shirley Henderson (*Hamish Macbeth*), Matthew Macfadyen (Ripper Street), Cillian Murphy (*Peaky Blinders*), and Miranda Otto (*Homeland*). The series follows Augustus Melmotte, a mysterious foreign financier who becomes the talk of the town when he arrives on the scene in London.

White Heat - 2012 - Claire Foy (*The Crown*) stars in this epic drama about the lives of seven students who meet in a London flatshare during the 1960s. Some have compared it to a more female-friendly version of *Our Friends in the North*. Each of the six episodes take place in a different year: 1965, 1967, 1973, 1979, 1982, and 1990.

Wild Bill - 2019 - Rob Lowe stars as Chief Constable Bill Hixon in this comedy-drama about a widowed American police chief who moves to Lincolnshire with his teenage daughter after he's sacked for assaulting a boy who shared inappropriate images of his daughter online. Rachael Stirling (*The Bletchley Circle, Detectorists*) stars as Lady Mary Harborough, a local judge who becomes well-acquainted with Hixon.

The Woman in White - 1981 - Based on the Wilkie Collins novel of the same name, this series sees two Victorian sisters caught up in a mystery that involves a mysterious doppelganger dressed all in white.

Women in Love - 2011 - Rosamund Pike and Rachael Stirling star in this adaptation of DH Lawrence's classic novel. It was originally written as a sequel to *The Rainbow*.

WPC 56 - 2013 to 2015 - This period crime drama follows Gina Dawson, the first woman police constable in her West Midlands hometown. The first two seasons focus on Gina's struggles to gain acceptance in a male-dominated work environment, while the third season follows her successor at the station.

Wuthering Heights - 1978 - Widely considered to be one of the most faithful adaptations of Emily Brontë's 1847 novel, this five-part miniseries stars Ken Hutchison (*The Bill*) as Heathcliff, with Kay Adshead (*Family Affairs*) filling the role of Cathy.

The Shakespeare Collection

This collection was added to BritBox in early 2020.

A Midsummer Night's Dream (1981)

A Midsummer Night's Dream (2016)

A Winter's Tale (1981)

All's Well That Ends Well (1981)

Antony and Cleopatra (1981)

As You Like It (1978)

The Comedy of Errors (1983)

Cymbeline (1982)

Hamlet, Prince of Denmark (1980)

Henry IV: Parts 1 and 2 (1979)

Henry V (1979)

Henry VI: Parts 1-3 (1983)

Henry VIII (1979)

Julius Caesar (1979)

King Lear (1982)

The Life and Death of King John (1984)

Love's Labour's Lost (1985)

Macbeth (1983)

Measure for Measure (1979)

The Merchant of Venice (1980)

The Merry Wives of Windsor (1982)

Much Ado About Nothing (1984)

Othello (1981)

Pericles, Prince of Tyre (1984)

Richard II (1979)

Romeo and Juliet (1978)

The Taming of the Shrew (1980)

The Tempest (1980)

Timon of Athens (1981)

Titus Andronicus (1985)

The Tragedy of Coriolanus (1984)

The Tragedy of Richard III (1983)

Troilus and Cressida (1981)

Twelfth Night (1980)

The Two Gentlemen of Verona (1983)

Play for Today Collection

BRITBOX

This classic anthology series ran from 1970 to 1984, and brings a collection of adaptations of plays and novels. It includes a number of performances from British acting greats, including Helen Mirren, Nigel Hawthorne, and Alison Steadman.

Abigail's Party

A Cotswold Death

All Good Men

A Passage to England

A Photograph

Back of Beyond

Bar Mitzvah Boy

The Bevellers

The Black Stuff

Coming Out

Country

The Elephants' Graveyard

The Executioner

The Fishing Party

Funny Farm

The Hallelujah Handshake

Hard Labour

Home Sweet Home

Jessie

Just Another Saturday

Just A Boy's Game

King

Kisses at 50

Leeds United!

Nuts in May

The Other Woman

Penda's Fen

Rainy Day Women

The Slab Boys

Soft Targets

Still Waters

Who's Who

Comedies

'Allo 'Allo - 1982 to 1992 - This classic British comedy follows René, a cafe owner in Nouvion with German soldiers in residence, even as he does his best to aid the Resistance. He's hiding two British airmen and a radio transmitter upstairs, and he's hidden a priceless painting (Fallen Madonna with the Big Boobies) in a large sausage. At the same time, he's having affairs with two sexy waitresses – right under the nose of his suspicious wife.

300 Years of French and Saunders - 2017 - This special brings much-loved comedy team Jennifer Saunders and Dawn French back together for another set of hilarious sketches.

8 Out of 10 Cats - 2019 - This quirky panel show comes up with unusual questions and then polls the general public to get their take on the issues.

8 Out of 10 Cats Does Countdown - 2012 to present - This show is a mash-up of *8 Out of 10 Cats* and the more intellectually-challenging *Countdown*. Initially created as a special, it proved quite popular and it's now been running since 2012.

A Bit of Fry & Laurie - 1987 to 1989 - This sketch show is an important piece of British comedy history, and it was responsible for turning Stephen Fry (*Kingdom*) and Hugh Laurie (*House*) into household names.

A Child's Christmases in Wales - 2009 - Michael Sheen narrates this nostalgic comedy about a series of Christmases in the life of a South Wales family during the 1980s.

Absolutely Fabulous - 1992 to 2012 - In this groundbreaking classic, two wild women do everything but act their age. The series was based on a sketch comedy called "Modern Mother and Daughter" by Dawn French (*Vicar of Dibley*) and Jennifer Saunders (Edina Monsoon in *Absolutely Fabulous*). Joanna Lumley stars alongside Saunders as Patsy Stone, and Julia Sawalha plays Edina's daughter Saffron.

Alan Davies: As Yet Untitled - 2014 to 2015 - Alan Davies (*Jonathan Creek*) hosts this discussion show featuring a mix of famous and soon-to-be famous faces. Topics of discussion include everything from the US military to giant rabbits to Bob Mortimer's unusually high backside.

Alfresco - 1983 to 1984 - This early-80s variety show is packed with now-famous actors like Emma Thompson, Robbie Coltrane, Hugh Laurie, and Stephen Fry.

All Creatures Great and Small - 1978 to 1980 - Set in the lovely Yorkshire Dales, this classic comedy is based on the books of James Herriot (pen name to James Alfred Wight). It follows the adventures of a country veterinarian in 1930s England.

Are You Being Served? - 1972 to 1985 - At the Grace Brothers Department Store, fine fashions are served with a healthy side of mischief.

Are You Being Served? - 2016 - In this one-off reboot of the original series, a young Mr. Grace is determined to bring the store into the 1980s...in 1988. It was poorly reviewed, and no further episodes were made.

Are You Being Served? Again! - 1982 to 1993 - When the Grace Brothers store is closed, the staff takes over managing a manor house in the countryside.

As Time Goes By - 1992 to 2002 - Separated by a lost letter during the war, lovers Lionel and Jean are reunited by chance many years later. Dame Judi Dench stars opposite Geoffrey Palmer in this charming light comedy.

At Last the 1948 Show - 1967 - A must for *Monty Python* fans, this quirky 1967 comedy sketch series features future MP collaborators John Cleese and Graham Chapman.

BBC's Lost Sitcoms - 2016 - This collection features re-enactments of three lost sitcom episodes from iconic BBC sitcoms: *Steptoe & Son, Hancock's Half Hour,* and *Till Death Us Do Part.*

Benidorm - 2007 to 2018 - In this delightfully tacky comedy, a parade of British holidaymakers try to get their money's worth at an all-inclusive resort in Benidorm. If you enjoy spotting well-known British actors in guest roles, this is a great one to check out. It includes guest appearances from Mark Heap (*Friday Night Dinner*), Nigel Havers (*Coronation Street*), Una Stubbs (*Sherlock*), Wendy Richard (*Are You Being Served?*), and Kate O'Mara (*Doctor Who*), among others.

Bill - 2015 - This quirky take on Shakespeare's rise to fame comes to us from the same folks who made Horrible Histories. Mathew Baynton (aka Deano in *Gavin & Stacey*) portrays Shakespeare as a hopeless young lute player heading to London with big dreams.

Billionaire Boy - 2016 - When Joe's father Len invents a new sort of toilet roll, they become overnight billionaires. Now, Joe can have anything money can buy - but he soon learns it can't buy everything.

Blackadder - 1983 to 1989 - Rowan Atkinson stars as antihero Edmund Blackadder, accompanied by Sir Tony Robinson as his sidekick Baldrick. Each series of this quirky comedy is set in a different period within British history, and Edmund carries different titles throughout. The "essence" of each character remains largely the same in each series, though.

Blandings - 2013 to 2014 - A nobleman struggles to keep his stately home and strange family in line so he can spend more time with his beloved pig. The series was based on P.G. Wodehouse's *Blandings Castle* stories, and it's one of a relatively small number of scripted programmes filmed on location in Northern Ireland (mostly at Crom Castle in County Fermanagh).

Bliss - 2018 - Stephen Mangan plays a man living an exhausting double life in this family sitcom.

Boy Meets Girl - 2015 to 2016 - This romantic comedy combines a transgender romance with age gap love, pairing a 40-something transgender woman with a 26-year-old man.

Bucket - 2017 - When free-spirited Mim tells her daughter she's dying, they go on a road trip together. Miriam Margolyes (*Miss Fisher's Murder Mysteries*) stars alongside Frog Stone (*No Offence*).

Rowan Atkinson Presents: Canned Laughter - 1979 - This short comedy tells the story of a dinner date gone terribly wrong. It's often considered an early inspiration for Atkinson's Mr. Bean character.

Chef! - 1993 to 1996 - Lenny Henry (*Broadchurch*) stars as a touchy chef with incredible culinary skills...and little in the way of interpersonal abilities. Though he works hard to keep standards high, his staff cuts corners whenever possible, his wife is bored, and his customers still have the gall to ask for salt.

Clash of the Santas - 2008 - This follow-up to Northern Lights sees Robson Green

(*Grantchester*) and Mark Benton (*Shakespeare & Hathaway*) reprising their roles as bickering friends Colin and Howie. In this outing, they're off to the World Santa Championships in Lithuania.

Click and Collect - 2018 - Stephen Merchant (*Hello Ladies*) stars as Andrew, a man on a desperate Christmas mission to purchase the elusive Sparklehoof the Unicorn Princess for his daughter.

Cruise of the Gods - 2002 - Steve Coogan, David Walliams, and Rob Brydon star in this feature-length comedy about a group of 1980s sci-fi programme actors reuniting to attend a cruise arranged by the show's fan club.

Dad's Army - 1968 to 1977 - One of the most-loved British sitcoms of all time, *Dad's Army* follows the challenges facing a Home Guard platoon during World War II. Under constant threat of invasion by Nazi Germany, the Home Guard was made up of men not able to join the regular army (often older men who wanted to take a more active role in the war effort). Because so many were older, it was often referred to as "Dad's Army".

Damned - 2016 to 2018 - Alan Davies (*Jonathan Creek*) and Jo Brand (*Getting On*) star in this series about workers dealing with endless bureaucracy in a social services department.

The Darling Buds of May - 1991 to 1993 - Based on the 1958 H.E. Bates novel of the same name, this series is set in rural 1950s Kent and follows the Larkin family as they go about their daily lives. This early 90s dramedy was a breakout role for Welsh actress Catherine Zeta-Jones.

Do Not Adjust Your Set - 1967 to 1969 - This innovative British comedy classic was an early evening sketch show featuring a number of actors who would go on to become massively famous. It was written by Michael Palin (*Ripping Yarns*), Terry Jones (*The Meaning of Life*), and Eric Idle (*At Last the 1948 Show*), and it includes some great performances by David Jason (*A Touch of Frost*) and Denise Coffey (*Sir Henry at Rawlinson End*).

Don't Forget the Driver - 2019 - Toby Jones (*Detectorists*) takes on another comedy role in this series about a depressed single dad who works as a coach driver. His mundane existence is shaken up when he takes a group across the English Channel and finds a migrant stowed away in his wheel arch. Jones co-wrote the series with playwright Tim Crouch.

Edge of Heaven - 2014 - In the seaside town of Margate, a close-knit but quirky family runs a 1980s-themed guest house.

Fawlty Towers - 1975 to 1979 - John Cleese and Prunella Scales star in this classic British comedy about a very poorly managed hotel. Though it only lasted 12 episodes, it's considered one of the great British comedy classics.

Gavin & Stacey - 2007 to 2019 - After months of chatting, Gavin and Stacey leave their homes in Essex and Wales to meet for the first time in London. This much-loved comedy classic features a number of British acting favourites including Larry Lamb, Ruth Jones, Alison Steadman, Rob Brydon, and James Corden.

Good Neighbors (aka The Good Life) - 1975 to 1978 - *The Good Life* sees Tom Good (Richard Briers) turning 40 and deciding to quit his job designing cereal box toys in favour of "living off the land" at the suburban home he shares with his wife Barbara (Felicity Kendal). Next door, snooty neighbour Margo Leadbetter (Penelope Keith) is rather displeased with the development – while her husband (Paul Eddington) just thinks poor Tom has lost his mind.

The Hitchhiker's Guide to the Galaxy - 1981 - Arthur Dent is one of the last surviving members of the human race. Still in his dressing gown, he's dragged through an intergalactic portal and sent on an adventure through the universe. The series is based on Douglas Adams' novel of the same name, and he also wrote the TV adaptation.

Hold the Sunset - 2018 to 2019 - Two mature neighbors are anxious to start a new life together, but they're interrupted when Edith's adult son arrives on her doorstep. Alison Steadman (*Gavin & Stacey*) and John Cleese (*Fawlty Towers*) star, and Jason Watkins (*The Crown*) plays Edith's adult son Roger.

Horrible Histories: Formidable Florence Nightingale - 2018 - Florence Nightingale gets the *Horrible Histories* treatment, and we follow her as she embarks on her journey to help soldiers during the Crimean War.

Insert Name Here - 2017 to 2018 - This comedy panel show focuses on people with one thing in common. They all have the same name. Sue Perkins hosts, and Josh Widdecombe and Richard Osman act as team captains.

Inside No. 9 - 2014 to 2020 - Dark humor, crime, drama, and horror are showcased in this anthology series. Every episode incorporates the number nine in some way, so keep an eye out as you watch.

The Job Lot - 2013 to 2016 - In a Midlands job centre, it's hard to tell if anyone actually works. Sarah Hadland (*Miranda*) stars.

Kate & Koji - 2020 - Brenda Blethyn (*Vera*) stars as struggling café owner Kate. Jimmy Akingbola (*Rev*) is an African asylum seeker who's also a qualified doctor - but since he's waiting to be granted asylum, he can't work. Neither of them like each other all that much, but they find an arrangement that works. **Premieres April 13th.**

Keeping Up Appearances - 1990 to 2002 - Dame Patricia Routledge stars as Hyacinth Bucket, a woman in perpetual denial of her working-class roots.

Last of the Summer Wine - 1973 to 2010 - The world's longest-running sitcom features grandpas gone wild in rural Yorkshire. It was created and written by Roy Clarke (*Keeping Up Appearances*).

The League of Gentlemen - 1999 to 2002 - In the fictional Northern England town of Royston Vasey, strange characters exist with interweaving storylines.

Living the Dream - 2017 to present - When a Yorkshire family buys an RV park in Florida and moves to pursue the American dream, they end up with a serious case of culture shock.

Mapp and Lucia - 1985 to 1986 - Based on E.F. Benson's novels, this series is set in the fictional coastal Sussex town of Tilling-on-Sea during the 1920s and 30s. Prunella Scales (*Fawlty Towers*) and Geraldine McEwan (*Marple*) star.

Mapp and Lucia - 2014 - Steve Pemberton (*Inside No. 9*) wrote this later adaptation of E.F. Benson's novels, with Miranda Richardson (*Blackadder*) and Anna Chancellor (*Spooks*, aka *MI-5*) starring. Like the first adaptation, this one was also filmed largely in Rye, East Sussex.

Marley's Ghosts - 2015 to 2016 - After an accident, Marley (Sarah Alexander, *Coupling*) is haunted by the ghosts of her husband, her lover, and a local vicar.

Mock the Week - 2005 to present - This satirical celebrity panel show is hosted by Dara Ó Briain and sees two temas of comedians tackling news and world events, often with improvised funny answers.

Mr. Stink - 2012 - This hour-long television adaptation is based on David Walliams' novel of the same name. It follows 12-year-old Chloe Crumb as she befriends an unusual homeless man named Mr. Stink.

Mr. Bean - 1992 to 1995 - Bumbling Mr. Bean rarely speaks and has some very peculiar ways of doing things, but it usually works out for him. Rowan Atkinson (*Maigret*) stars as the iconic British character.

Mrs. Brown's Boys - 2011 to 2020 - Brendan O'Carroll stars as Agnes Brown (in drag), powerful Irish matriarch. She's loud, nosy, and fiercely proud of her substantial brood.

Mum - 2016 to 2019 - After her husband dies, a woman tries to rebuild her life amidst all manner of problems from family and friends.

The New Statesman - 1987 to 1994 - This Yorkshire Television classic was written by Laurence Marks and Maurice Gran (*Birds of a Feather, Goodnight Sweetheart, Love Hurts*) and stars Rik Mayall (*The Young Ones*) as Alan B'stard, a Conservative MP who gets elected purely because there are no opposing candidates. He has an unquenchable thirst for power, and he'll stop at nothing to get to the top.

Newzoids - 2015 to 2016 - This unusual sketch show features animated puppets tackling current events and pop culture. Often compared to *Spitting Image*, the series has poked fun at public figures like Nigel Farage, Prince George, Donald Trump, and Boris Johnson.

Northern Lights - 2006 to 2007 - Robson Green and Mark Benton are Colin and Howie, best friends with a deep affection for one another...and an intense rivalry. The two work at the same transport depot, they're married to sisters, and they live on the same street.

Not Safe for Work - 2015 - When budget cuts move Katherine's civil servant job to Northampton, she reluctantly goes along with the relocation.

Not the Nine O'Clock News - 1995 - This vintage sketch news comedy features Mel Smith (*Alas Smith and Jones*) and Rowan Atkinson (*Mr. Bean*).

The Office - 2001 to 2003 - Before there was Michael Scott in the US, there was David Brent in Slough, England. Written by Ricky Gervais (*After Life*) and Stephen Merchant (*Hello Ladies*), this mockumentary-style programme takes place in the office of the fictional Wernham Hogg paper company. Mackenzie Crook (*Detectorists*) and Martin Freeman (*Sherlock*) are also among the stars.

One Foot in the Grave - 1990 to 1992 - Victor Meldrew (Richard Wilson, *Merlin*) may be a pensioner, but he still has plenty to say about what goes on in the world. The series follows his misadventures - mostly of his own creation - as he attempts to keep himself busy in retirement. It was created and written by David Renwick, also known for *Jonathan Creek*.

Only Fools and Horses - 1981 to 2003 - This classic comedy follows a couple of dodgy brothers always out for the big score.

Open All Hours - 1973 to 1985 - Penny-pinching Arkwright (Ronnie Barker, *Porridge*) runs a corner shop, spending much of his time separating customers from their money and keeping his wayward nephew Granville (David Jason, *A Touch of Frost*) in line. He also finds plenty of time to pursue the lovely nurse Gladys (Lynda Barron, *Fat Friends*).

Pointless - 2009 to present - This quiz series challenges its contestants to score as few points as possible by guessing unpopular but correct answers to general knowledge questions.

Porridge - 1974 to 1977 - This prison comedy features a man trying to do his time honestly and stay out of trouble. Ronnie Barker (*Open All Hours*) stars as habitual criminal Fletch, and Richard Beckinsale (*The Lovers*) stars as Lennie Godber, the new cellmate he decides to mentor.

Porridge - 2016 to 2017 - This modern reboot sees Fletch's grandson Nigel Fletcher navigating his way through Wakeley Prison.

Psychoville - 2009 to 2011 - This award-winning comedy is a mash-up of everything from horror to thriller to mystery to black comedy, and it sees Reece Shearsmith and Steve Pemberton (both of *Inside No. 9*) playing a number of characters. In the series, five different characters around England have received threatening letters stating, "I know what you did..."

Puppy Love - 2014 - This heartwarming sitcom sees two women doing their best to handle cute dogs and challenging families. Joanna Scanlan (*No Offence*) and Vicki Pepperdine (*Getting On*) star.

QI - Stephen Fry and Sandi Toksvig star in this entertaining quiz show where contestants are more amply rewarded for interesting answers.

Red Dwarf - 1988 to 2020 - In the far future, the last human lives aboard a spaceship with a highly evolved cat-man. **Remastered**.

Rev. - 2010 to 2014 - This smart sitcom follows the adventures of an Anglican vicar, his wife, and his run-down inner-city parish. Olivia Colman (*Broadchurch*) and Tom Hollander (*Baptiste*) star.

Ripping Yarns - 1976 to 1979 - Monty Python comedians Michael Palin and Terry Jones star in this anthology series that both parodied and celebrated pre-WWII schoolboy literature. Early episodes were directed by Terry Hughes, a BAFTA-winner who would later go on to direct *The Golden Girls* and *3rd Rock from the Sun*.

Rising Damp - 1974 to 1978 - Rupert Rigby runs the most dilapidated, seediest boarding house in all of England. This classic Britcom follows him and his unfortunate tenants – university administrator Ruth Jones, med student Alan, and town and country planning student Phillip.

Scarborough - 2019 - In the coastal town of Scarborough, North Yorkshire, a group of locals live, work, and love, punctuated by frequent trips to the pub for karaoke. The series was written by *Benidorm* writer Darren Litten, but it was not commissioned for a second series.

Spitting Image - 1984 to 1988 - Major public figures are turned into puppets to satirize British life.

There She Goes - 2018 to present - David Tennant (*Doctor Who*) stars in this dramedy about a family dealing with the challenges of their daughter's chromosomal disorder. The series was based on the real-life experiences of writer and creator Shaun Pye. Miley Locke plays Rosie Yates.

The Thick of It - 2005 to 2012 - This political satire follows government officials who lie, cheat, and generally do whatever it takes to keep their jobs.

The Thin Blue Line - 1995 to 1996 - Rowan Atkinson (*Mr. Bean*) stars as Inspector Fowler, an arrogant but ethical uniformed cop who's constantly being shown up by the plain-clothes detectives. This comedy is set in the fictional English town of Gasforth.

To the Manor Born - 1979 to 1980, 2007 - After her husband dies, Audrey fforbes-Hamilton (Penelope Keith, *The Good Life*) finds out they're broke. Forced to sell the family home, Grantleigh Manor, she takes up residence in the lodge on the property to spy on the new owner. That new owner happens to be Richard DeVere, a handsome nouveau riche supermarket owner who proves difficult to hate forever.

Up the Women - 2013 to 2015 - Set in 1910, this comedy takes place among the women of the Banbury Intricate Craft Circle as they participate in the women's suffrage movement. To support their efforts, they form a league called Banbury Intricate Craft Circle Politely Requests Women's Suffrage (BICCPRWS).

Upstart Crow - 2016 to 2018 - This sitcom gives us William Shakespeare, before he was famous.

The Vicar of Dibley - 1994 to 2015 - When the 100-year-old Vicar of Dibley is replaced by a woman, some villagers are less than pleased. Dawn French (*The Trouble With Maggie Cole*) stars.

Waiting for God - 1990 to 1992 - Two grumpy pensioners fall in love while biding their time in a retirement home.

Would I Lie to You? - This comedy panel show sees contestants bluffing about their deepest and darkest secrets whilst the other team attempts to figure out what's true.

Yes, Minister - 1980 to 1984 - James is a Cabinet Minister who thinks he's finally in a position to get things done.

Yes, Prime Minister - 1986 to 1988 - This follow-up to Yes Minister continues with the same cast but a new address on Downing Street.

Young Hyacinth - 2016 - *Keeping Up Appearances* writer Roy Clarke returned to create this prequel to the original series. Kerry Howard (*Him & Her*) stars as young Hyacinth Bucket (then Walton) in this 1950s-based period comedy.

Documentary & Lifestyle

24 Hours in Police Custody - 2014 to 2019 - This dramatic docu-series follows police detectives around the clock as they work to build cases against suspects in custody before running out of time.

7 Up & Me - 2019 - This special takes a look at how "The Up Series" has impacted popular culture.

70 Glorious Years - 1996 - Take a look back on Queen Elizabeth II's life as she celebrates her 70th birthday.

A History of Ancient Britain - 2011 to 2012 - Scottish archaeologist Neil Oliver looks back at thousands of years of ancient history to tell the story of how Britain came to be.

A Queen is Crowned - 1953 - This feature-length documentary is narrated by Sir Laurence Olivier and offers a Technicolor look at Queen Elizabeth II's 1953 coronation.

A Very British Murder with Lucy Worsley - 2013 - Historian Lucy Worsley takes a look at the British fascination with murder and mystery, along with some of the famous murders of 19th century Britain.

Africa & Britain: A Forgotten History - 2016 - Historian David Olusoga takes a look at the enduring and occasionally difficult relationship between Great Britain and Africa.

All Aboard! - 2015 to 2016 - This series takes us on several slow, uninterrupted journeys around Britain. Whether moving by bus, canal boat, or sled, there are no interruptions for talking, just the scenery of the journey with a few facts imposed over parts of the landscape.

Ancient Rome: The Rise and Fall of an Empire - 2006 - This dramatised documentary gives us greater insight into how the Roman Empire was built and destroyed by excessive greed, lust, and ambition.

Anthem for Doomed Youth: The War Poets - 2015 - Poet Wilfred Owen was killed in action in France during World War I. Using his diaries, letters, and poems, Peter Florence tells his story.

Antiques Roadshow - 1979 to present - Filmed at a variety of stately homes around the country, this series allows members of the public to bring in cherished items for expert appraisal.

The Aristocrats - 2011 to 2012 - This series takes a look at four of the families that make up modern-day British high society. These are the individuals who, through no skill, talent, or hard work of their own, have been fortunate enough to inherit titles and grand estates.

Around the World in 80 Faiths - 2009 - Pete Owen Jones takes us on a journey around the world, taking a look at how people worship in six continents.

Autumnwatch - 2019 - This edition of the popular nature series takes us to the Cairngorms in Scotland to see how autumn is unfolding out in the wild.

The BBC at War - 2015 - Presenter Jonathan Dimbleby shows us how the BBC helped out in the fight against Hitler and fascism, and how it's helped to shape the British government over time.

Beechgrove Garden - 1978 to present - This popular Scottish gardening series offers practical advice on making the most of your garden – even in some of Scotland's most challenging conditions.

Britain's Biggest Adventures with Bear Grylls - 2015 - Bear Grylls combines history and adrenaline as he visits North Wales, the Yorkshire Dales, and the Scottish Highlands in search of Britain's biggest adventures.

Britain's Royal Weddings - 2011 - This series takes a look back at some of the grandest royal weddings in Britain's history.

Britain's Secret Treasures - 2012 to 2013 - Presenter Michael Buerk and historian Bettany Hughes take a look at 50 of the greatest treasures ever discovered by members of the public in the UK.

Britain's Tudor Treasure - 2015 - Historian Lucy Worsley celebrates the 500th anniversary of one of the finest surviving Tudor structures, Hampton Court.

The Britannia Awards - 2018 to 2019 - This Los Angeles-based British award show is presented by BAFTA. In this particular round of awards, honorees included Emilia Clarke, Cate Blanchett, and Jim Carrey.

Cameraman to the Queen - 2015 - For nearly 20 years, Peter Wilkinson has enjoyed a high level of royal access as he captured both state events and personal moments. This short documentary is a tribute to the effort, discretion, and loyalty involved in his work.

Caroline Quentin's National Parks - 2013 - Caroline Quentin takes us on trips to three of Great Britain's most beautiful national parks - the New Forest, Local Lomond, and Snowdonia.

Carols from King's 2020 - 2020 - Each year, the King's College Chapel Choir performs a carol service from the medieval chapel of King's College. It begins with "Once in Royal David's City" and always includes a newly-commissioned carol for each year.

Charles & Diana: Wedding of the Century - 2011 - This documentary takes a look back at the wedding of Prince Charles and Lady Diana Spencer, examining its impact on both participants and viewers.

Civilisation - 1969 - Art historian Sir Kenneth Clark offers his thoughts on the ideas and values that have influenced the evolution of western civilisation over the years. Though more than 50 years old, many continue to count the series among the greatest documentaries in existence.

Classic Doctor Who Comic Con Panel - 2017 - Colin Baker, Peter Davison, and Sophie Aldred come together to discuss fan questions during Comic Con 2017.

Coast - 2005 to present - This series mixes history, nature, and great scenery as they travel around the coastline of the UK and surrounding areas.

Code Blue: Murder - 2019 - Detectives from the South Wales Police Major Crime team investigate murders and seek justice for those who are grieving.

Codebreakers: The Secret Geniuses of World War II - 2011 - This documentary takes a look at how two men hacked into Hitler's super-code machine, ultimately turning the Battle of Kursk and powering the D-Day landings.

The Coronavirus Newscast - 2020 - The *Brexitcast* team takes on COVID-19 and post-Brexit politics.

Countryfile - 2021 - This factual series documents modern country life around the UK.

Countryfile Autumn Diaries - 2019 - Enjoy the countryside around Oxford, England as autumn sets in. You can almost feel the cool, crisp air through the screen.

Countryfile Spring Diaries - 2019 - Few things are more beautiful than the British countryside coming back to life after a long, cold winter. This series takes a look at the flora and fauna as spring arrives in the country.

David Suchet on the Orient Express - 2010 - The quintessential Poirot, David Suchet, sets off on a journey to find out why the Orient Express is so famous around the world.

Days of Majesty - 1993 - This film was made to mark the 40th anniversary of Queen Elizabeth II's coronation, and it offers a look back at a variety of royal celebrations over the years.

Dead Good Job - 2012 - This series takes a look at the different ways Brits choose to say their final goodbyes to friends and loved ones.

Diana: The Interview that Shook the World - 2020 - In 1995, Diana sat down for a gossip-filled interview with Martin Bashir, spilling all the private details of her marriage with Prince Charles. Twenty-five years later, this documentary takes a look back at what the interview revealed about society, royal life, and her psychological troubles.

Downton Abbey Extras - 2020 - This web series goes behind the scenes with the cast of *Downton Abbey*, sharing stories of their days on set together.

Edible Gardens - 2020 - *Gardeners' World* presenter Alys Fowler shows us how cooking your own fruit and veg can be both rewarding and cost-effective, even in relatively small garden spaces.

Escape to the Country - 2002 to present - Each episode follows a different set of homebuyers looking to leave crowded areas and find new homes in the British countryside.

Funny is Funny: A Conversation with Normal Lear - 2018 - Emmy award-winning television pioneer Norman Lear sits down to reflect on his lengthy career.

Gardeners' World - 1968 to present - This long-running gardening series offers ideas, expert advice, and lovely scenery.

Gentlemen, The Queen - 1953 - This vintage film provides an up-close look at the early years of Queen Elizabeth II's life, including King George VI's coronation, her first broadcast, the war years, and her engagement.

Girls with Autism - 2015 - Because autistic girls and women are often better at masking their unique traits, they've gone largely overlooked in studies of autism. At the Limpsfield Grange boarding school, they're doing their best to change perceptions and help autistic girls lead better lives.

Good Morning Britain - 2020 - Each day, Susanna Reid and Pierce Morgan share the latest in news, pop culture, sports, and weather.

Grand Designs - 1999 to present - Kevin McCloud follows people as they attempt to build their dream homes. As the long and complicated projects wear on, the early optimism and enthusiasm is often replaced by relationship and budgetary problems.

The Great British Countryside - 2012 - Hugh Dennis (*Outnumbered*) and Julia Bradbury (*Countryfile*) take us on adventures in four very different but equally stunning British landscapes. The series visits Cornwall and Devon, Yorkshire, the South Downs, and the Highlands.

The Great Chelsea Garden Challenge - 2015 - Six amateurs compete for a change to design and build a garden for display on Man Avenue at the 2015 RHS Chelsea Flower Show.

Great Escape: The Untold Story - 2001 - During World War II, 76 men attempted escape from the Stalag Luft III prisoner of war camp in Germany. Of those men, 3 made it home, 73 were captured, and 50 were shot on Hitler's instruction. This documentary tells their story.

Hairy Bikers' Bakeation - 2012 - Hairy Bikers Si and Dave take a 5000-mile road trip around Europe, sampling the best baked goods on the continent.

Hairy Bikers' Christmas Party - 2011 - Hairy Bikers Dave Myers and Si King show us how to make the perfect festive finger foods for a Christmas party with friends.

Hairy Bikers' Everyday Gourmets - 2013 - The Hairy Bikers show us how to prepare impressive feasts on very average budgets.

Hidden: World's Best Monster Mystery - Loch Ness - 2001 - For centuries, there's been rumour of a monster hiding in the murky depths of Scotland's Loch Ness. This programme takes a look at those who claim to have seen it, and those who spend their lives looking for it. **Fun fact**: Naturalist and Nessie expert Adrian Shine (along with his lovely wife Maralyn) helped IHeartBritishTV.com's co-editors get engaged in Drumnadrochit last year.

Home Away from Home - 2014 - This series sees families swapping homes for a change of pace. On each swap, homeowners leave packets of information and activities for the new inhabitants of their homes.

Inside Claridge's - 2012 - Over the course of three episodes, we go behind the scenes at one of Britain's poshest hotels, looking at what it takes to deliver five-star service with an emphasis on tradition.

The Instant Gardener - 2015 - Danny Clark, garden designer extraordinaire, renovates the gardens of deserving members of the public.

Kirstie's Vintage Home - 2012 - Kirstie Allsopp helps viewers learn to add stylish vintage touches to their homes. This show blends DIY, upcycling, and bit of mid-century inspiration.

Last Night of the Proms - 2020 - For those not familiar with the BBC Proms, it's an eight-week series of classical concerts held annually in London. In 2020, the Proms is turning 125 – but due to the current situation, this year is being celebrated with six weeks of concerts from previous seasons and a final two weeks of live performances from the Royal Albert Hall in London.

The "Last Night of the Proms" is quite different from the other nights, taking place on the second Saturday in September with widespread broadcast. The concert usually features some lighter classics and then a second half consisting of patriotic British pieces (like Henry Wood's Fantasia on British Sea Songs" and Thomas Arne's "Rule, Britannia!").

Lennon's Last Weekend - 2020 - Recognising the 40th anniversary of John Lennon's passing, this documentary shares the last in-person interview with John Lennon. In it, he spoke about topics including solo albums and The Beatles breakup. Interviewer Andy Peebles travels to New York City to revisit some of the iconic locations of Lennon's life and final days there.

Licence to Thrill: Paul Hollywood Meets Aston Martin - 2015 - Though better known for his baking skills, this series sees Paul Hollywood exploring the world of Aston Martin cars. In addition to meeting with the latest company boss, he also trains up to race.

Life in a Cottage Garden - 2011 to 2013 - *Gardeners' World* veteran Carol Klein takes us through a year of life in her garden at Glebe Cottage in Devon. It's a lovely walk through all four seasons and their unique challenges in southern England.

The Lights Before Christmas - 2019 to 2020 - Enjoy 90 minutes of unhurried footage of some of Britain's best Christmas lights.

The Lights Before Christmas: Luminous London - 2018 - Follow a hop-on, hop-off tour of London's best Christmas lights.

Looking for Victoria - 2003 - Prunella Scales (*Fawlty Towers*) takes a look back at Queen Victoria, the monarch she's been portraying in a one-woman show for roughly 20 years.

Louis Theroux - 2007 to 2016 - This series sees British documentarian Louis Theroux tackling a variety of controversial topics including American religious extremists, Miami prisons, and an American school for autistic individuals.

Marco's Great British Feast - 2008 - Chef Marco Pierre White travels around Britain sourcing some of the best and most unique local ingredients.

Mary Berry's Absolute Favourites - 2014 to 2015 - Britain's favourite home cook shares some of her absolute favourite recipes from a lifetime of cooking.

Mary Berry's Country House Secrets - 2017 - In this series, Mary Berry travels to some of the grandest homes in Great Britain to see what goes on in their kitchen. It includes visits to Highclere Castle, Scone Palace, Powderham Castle, and Goodwood House.

The Monarchy - 1992 - This early 90s series takes a closer look at the British monarchy - the allure, their purpose, and how much they cost the British taxpayer.

Monumental Challenge - 2010 - Visit some of the world's greatest landmarks and learn about the specialist teams that maintain, repair, and expand them. The series visits the Eiffel Tower, the Sydney Harbour Bridge, Big Ben, Santiago Di Compostela, the Taj Mahal, and The Bund (China's Wall Street).

Murder, Mystery, and My Family - 2018 to present - This true crime series pairs the relatives of convicted killers with talented criminal barristers, allowing for a new examination of evidence using modern forensic techniques.

My Family Secrets Revealed - 2018 - This innovative factual series uses family trees, DNA, and historic records to discover long-hidden family stories and secrets. Always entertaining, episodes uncover stories of scandal, loss, heroic acts, and forbidden love.

The Mystery of Mary Magdalene - 2013 - Melvyn Bragg takes a closer look at the questions surrounding Mary Magdalene, a highly controversial biblical figure.

Nigellissima - 2012 - Nigella Lawson shows viewers how to bring a bit of Italy into their kitchens, even without access to specialty Italian grocery stores.

Our Cops in the North - 2019 - Meet the detectives, emergency response officers, and command centres of the Northumbrian Police Force as they struggle to maintain the peace and catch the guilty in their little corner of the world.

Panorama: Fighting Coronavirus - The Scientific Battle - 2020 - This series offers reports from the scientific frontline, offering insights into what experts are doing to combat the virus that's gripped the world.

Paul O'Grady: For the Love of Dogs - 2012 - Comedian Paul O'Grady explores the bond between man and dog, Much of the series takes place at the Battersea Dogs & Cats Home.

Pompeii: The Last Day - 2003 - In AD79. Mount Vesuvius erupted, obliterating a number of Roman cities (including Pompeii). It's said to have released 100,000 times the thermal energy of the Hiroshima-Nagasaki bombings. This documentary attempts to dramatise that last day, giving us a better idea of what happened before the eruption.

Prime Minister's Questions - 2013 to present - In the House of Commons, MPs put their questions to Prime Minister Boris Johnson.

Question Time - 2019 to 2020 - This debate show sees politicians and media figures answering questions from the general public.

Rachel Khoo's Kitchen Notebook: London - 2014 - London-born chef Rachel Khoo goes back to London to explore the food scene and offer tips on how to create great British meals at home.

Rachel's Coastal Cooking - 2015 - Chef Rachel Allen hits the road to track down local food and ingredients around the Irish coast.

Secrets from the Sky - 2014 - Using drones, historian Bettany Hughes takes a look at Britain's historic sites from the air.

Seven Wonders of the Commonwealth - 2014 - Several presenters travel the globe to see the people and the natural wonders of nations in the Commonwealth.

Shakespeare in Italy - 2012 - Shakespeare placed a number of his most famous plays in cities around Italy. This series sees Francesco da Mosto and a variety of special guests (including Emma Thompson) travelling around the country and visiting Shakespearean locations like Padua, Verona, and Venice.

The Shard: Hotel in the Clouds - 2014 - The Shard is a London hotel that promises the ultimate in luxury. This documentary takes a look at what goes on behind the scenes.

Springwatch - 2005 to present - Along with *Autumnwatch* and *Winterwatch*, this series follows British flora and fauna through the changing of the seasons each year.

The Story of Luxury - 2011 - This two-part docuseries takes a look at the things we've valued over the years, with a particular emphasis on luxury in the Classical and Medieval time periods.

Suffragettes - 2018 - Lucy Worsley presents this documentary about a group of working-class women working towards the right to vote.

Supermarket Secrets - 2013 to 2014 - Go behind the scenes of some of Britain's biggest supermarket chains to learn how they bring us fresh food on a truly massive scale. Learn how they forecast demand, develop new products, and automate increasingly large portions of what they do.

Swingin' Christmas - 2010 - Michael Parkinson hosts this festive, musical Christmas special. The programme features special guest Seth MacFarlane and music led by conductor John Wilson.

Tales from the Coast with Robson Green - 2017 - Follow Robson Green on a trip around the British coast, visiting North Devon, Wales, the Outer Hebrides, Essex, and Suffolk.

This Farming Life - 2016 to 2019 - This dramatic docuseries gives us an often unromantic look at the highs and lows of modern farm life in Britain.

Unfinished Portrait: The Life of Agatha Christie - 1990 - Based on the notoriously private Christie's personal correspondence, this biographical programme takes a look at why a proper English lady might spend so much time imagining grisly murders.

The Up Series - 1964 to 2020 - This series represents the world's longest-running documentary, following a group of Britons as they pass through life's stages. The series began with 14 individuals back in 1964, and they do follow-up interviews every seven years.

Vincent Van Gogh: Painted with Words - 2010 - Benedict Cumberbatch (*Sherlock*) takes on the role of the iconic Dutch post-impressionist. Though dramatised, the dialogue is sourced from Van Gogh's own words.

Virgin Atlantic: Up in the Air - 2015 - Virgin Atlantic may be hip (as airlines go), but that hasn't translated to a stable financial situation. This programme follows CEO Craig Keeger as he attempts to turn things around.

Winterwatch - 2005 to present - It may be dark and cold, but there's still plenty to see out in nature. Broadcasting from the Scottish Highlands, the *Winterwatch* team looks at what's going on with the local wildlife, along with a bit on how all of Britain's wildlife is doing.

The Women of World War One - 2014 - Kate Adie takes a look at the impact women had on the outcome of WWI. Though not on the front lines, women contributed to the war effort in many ways.

PBS MASTERPIECE

Website: http://amazon.com/channels/masterpiece

Description: Only available via Amazon, this PBS channel offers a wide variety of British programmes, particularly period dramas and mysteries. It also offers a number of foreign-language "Walter Presents" shows.

Available On: Roku, Amazon Fire TV, Android devices, iPad, desktop, Chromecast, and most smart TVs.

Cost: $5.99/month

Now Streaming

All Creatures Great and Small - 2020 - This remake of the much-loved classic Yorkshire veterinary series is expected to hit screens in January 2021. It's based on the books by James Herriot.

Anne of Green Gables: Fire and Dew - *Canada* - 2018 - This adaptation of L.M. Montgomery's Anne of Green Gables world has Anne growing up and heading off to college in the city.

Apple Tree Yard – 2017 - This miniseries is based on Louise Doughty's novel by the same name, and it's a suspenseful combination of sex and murder. When a woman gets an intriguing proposition, it excites her – until she realizes it may not be quite what it seemed. Emily Watson and Ben Chaplin star.

A Room with a View - 2007 - Elaine Cassidy (*No Offence*) stars alongside Rafe Spall (*Desperate Romantics*) in this story about a young Englishwoman in 1912 who finds love on a trip to Italy.

Arthur and George - 2015 - Martin Clunes (*Doc Martin*) stars as Sir Arthur Conan Doyle. When he finds himself outraged at an injustice against an Anglo-Indian solicitor, he uses his own fictional detective's methods to get justice.

Baptiste - 2019 - This spinoff from the series *The Missing* sees Tchéky Karyo returning as Julien Baptiste, a clever detective who agrees to help the Dutch police look for a missing sex worker in Amsterdam. Tom Hollander (*Rev*) and Jessica Raine (*Call the Midwife*) also appear.

Beecham House - 2019 - Set in 1795, this period drama depicts the lives of a former East India Company soldier who's determined to create a safe home in Delhi for his family. Critics have dubbed it "The Dehli Downton". Tom Bateman (*Vanity Fair*) and Lesley Nicol (*Downton Abbey*) star.

The Bletchley Circle - 2012 to 2014 - In 1952, four former Bletchley Park codebreakers from WWII come together to track a killer.

Breathless - 2013 - Set in early 1960s England, this series looks at the lives of hospital staff who perform illegal off-site abortions in their spare time.

The Child in Time - 2018 - Benedict Cumberbatch (*Sherlock*) stars in this film about a man struggling to find purpose after the disappearance of his daughter. It's based on a novel by Ian McEwan.

Churchill's Secret - 2016 - Set during the summer of 1953, this film sees Michael Gambon (*Maigret*) portraying Winston Churchill as he recovered from a life-threatening stroke.

Cobra - 2020 - This political drama sees Robert Carlyle (*Hamish MacBeth*) playing the role of British Prime Minister Robert Sutherland as he deals with a national emergency and the impossible decisions that go along with such a situation. Victoria Hamilton (*The Crown*) plays his Chief of Staff.

The Crimson Field - 2014 to 2015 - At a busy WWI hospital, Kitty tries to escape her past.

Death Comes to Pemberley – 2014 - Three episodes pay homage to Jane Austen's *Pride and Prejudice*, bringing us into the home of Elizabeth and Darcy after six years of marriage. As they prepare for their annual ball, tragedy brings the festivities to a halt.

Deep Water - 2019 - Anna Friel (*Marcella*) stars in this miniseries about three mothers struggling with challenging moral and ethical problems.

Elizabeth I: The Virgin Queen – 2005 - Anne-Marie Duff stars in this fascinating miniseries about Queen Elizabeth I, the enigmatic and long-reigning queen who never took a husband. Tom Hardy stars as her dear friend and possible lover Robert Dudley, 1st Earl of Leicester, and Emilia Fox takes on the role of Dudley's wife.

Elizabeth is Missing - 2019 - Glenda Jackson stars as a woman trying to solve two mysteries while suffering from dementia. Her only friend has gone missing, and she's not sure what information she can trust.

Endeavour – 2012 to present - In this prequel to Inspector Morse, a young Endeavour works with Sergeant Thursday to develop his investigative skills. Shaun Evans stars as Morse during this 1960s period mystery.

Excalibur: Behind the Movie - 2020 - The 1981 film Excalibur is still considered by some to be one of the finest adaptations of the Arthurian legend. It also launched the careers of several well-known Irish and British actors including Ciarán Hinds, Liam Neeson, Sir Patrick Stewart, Helen Mirren, and Gabriel Byrne. This documentary takes a look back at the masterpiece.

Exile – 2011 - John Simm (*Life on Mars*) stars in this mystery-thriller about a man who returns home after his life falls apart – only to find a different kind of trouble there.

Far From the Madding Crowd - 1998 - This television movie is an adaptation of Thomas Hardy's novel of the same name, this time starring Paloma Baeza (*A Touch of Frost*) and Nathaniel Parker (*Inspector Lynley Mysteries*). Set against the backdrop of rural southwest England during Victorian times, it follows the life of Bathsheba Everdene and the people she knows in her small farming community.

Flesh & Blood - 2020 - When a widow finds unexpected romance with a retired surgeon, her family's reactions are mixed. A web of lies and secrets brings chaos and eventually, murder. This one's full of crazy relatives, dark secrets, and for good measure, a nosy neighbor played by Imelda Staunton.

The Forsyte Saga – This 2002 adaptation of John Galsworthy's novel follows the life of an English family over 34 years stretching from Victorian England to WWI.

Frankie Drake Mysteries – *Canada* - 2018 to present - Set in 1920s Toronto, Frankie Drake is a great series for anyone who loved Miss Fisher's Murder Mysteries. Ms. Drake is a female detective whose Drake Detective Agency takes on the cases police don't want. Along with her trusty partner Trudy, they get into all manner of trouble.

Grantchester – 2014 to present - In the village of Grantchester, a clever vicar assists a local police detective with his investigations. James Norton (*Happy Valley*) stars as vicar Sidney Chambers, and Robson Green (*Wire in the Blood*) plays DI Geordie Keating. Later in the series, Tom Brittany takes over for him in the role of Reverend Will Davenport, a former inner-city chaplain.

The Great Fire - 2015 - This four-part series is a dramatisation of 1666's Great Fire of London. The fire went on for four days, leaving nearly 90% of the city's population homeless.

Great Houses with Julian Fellowes - 2015 - This two-part series sees Julian Fellowes (*Downton Abbey*) guide us on a tour of two of Britain's great homes, Burghley House and Goodwood House.

Great Performances: Macbeth - 2010 - Sir Patrick Stewart stars in this acclaimed adaptation of Shakespeare's "Scottish Play".

Henry and Anne: The Lovers Who Changed History - 2014 - Historian Dr. Suzannah Lipscomb tells the story of the love affair between Henry VIII and Anne Boleyn.

Henry IX: Lost King - 2017 - Many have called Henry Frederick, Prince of Wales the best king England never had. Though bright and promising, he died at the age of 18 from typhoid fever. This documentary looks at the achievements in his short life, along with what might of been, had he lived.

Inside the Court of Henry VIII - 2015 - This documentary takes a look at why things were so terribly chaotic and brutal inside the court of Henry VIII.

Inspector Lewis - 2006 to 2015 - Inspector Lewis was a lovely parting gift after the departure of Inspector Morse. In Lewis, Kevin Whately returns to play Morse's former sidekick once more – except this time, he's the DI and his sidekick is DS James Hathaway.

Jamestown – 2017 to 2019 - This series goes 400 years back in time to follow a group of English settlers in 1619 Virginia. When it opens, it's a little more than a decade since a group of men settled Virginia, and a group of woman is arriving to marry the men who settled the area and paid their way over.

Jekyll & Hyde - 2015 - Set in 1930s London, this variation of the classic story sees Robert Jekyll living in London, a sensitive young man trying to find his way independent of his foster family. Unfortunately, be begins to feel the influence of a powerful darkness that's outside his control – and he realises his parents had been trying to protect him all along. Young Robert has inherited his grandfather's curse, and he's soon drawn into Hyde's dark and unsavoury world. Tom Bateman stars as Dr. Robert Jekyll.

The Jewel in the Crown - 1984 - This award-winning television serial is set during the final days of the British Raj in India during and after World War II. The series is based on Paul Scott's *Raj Quartet* novels.

Les Misérables – 2018 - Victor Hugo's epic tale of love and poverty in war-torn France returns to the screen in this 2018 adaptation starring Olivia Colman, Dominic West, and Lily Collins. The 6-episode miniseries takes a deeper dive into some characters who have traditionally gotten a bit less screentime (like Fantine), making the progression slower and more grueling – but also much more dramatic.

The Long Song - 2018 - Based on Andrea Levy's 2010 novel about the end of slavery in Jamaica, this miniseries sees Tamara Lawrance playing a slave and Hayley Atwell playing the plantation owner.

Lovejoy - 1986 to 1994 - Ian McShane (*Deadwood*) stars as Lovejoy, the slightly shady antiques dealer and part-time detective. *Downton Abbey* fans will be delighted to see a young Phyllis Logan (aka Mrs. Hughes) in this early role.

Lucy Worsley's Royal Myths and Secrets - 2020 - This three-part series sees historian Lucy Worsley travelling across Europe in search of places central to royal history.

Lucy Worsley's 12 Days of Tudor Christmas - 2019 - Lucy Worsley takes us on a fun and educational stroll through Tudor Christmas festivities.

Man in an Orange Shirt - 2018 - This two-part series tells two separate love stories set 60 years apart. One, a forbidden relationship, takes place during WWII, while the other is modern.

Mansfield Park - 2007 - Billie Piper (*Doctor Who*) stars in this television movie adaptation of Jane Austen's third novel. It's about a young woman sent to live with wealthier relatives, who later falls in love with her sensitive cousin.

Margaret: The Rebel Princess - 2019 - A controversial figure in her time, Princess Margaret was a reflection of many of the societal changes going on during her time. This series takes a look at her life.

Masterpiece: The Chaperone - 2018 - With a screenplay by Julian Fellowes (*Downton Abbey*), this period drama focuses on Norma Carlisle, a middle-aged woman charged with chaperoning the teenage Louise Brooks, not yet a flapper icon and sex symbol.

Masterpiece: Wind in the Willows - 2007 - Matt Lucas (*Little Britain*) stars as Mr. Toad in this feature-length adaptation of Kenneth Grahame's classic tale.

The Miniaturist – This 2017 BBC miniseries is an adaptation of Jessie Burton's novel by the same name. In 17th century Amsterdam, a woman moves in with her new husband and his sister. Oddly, the husband gives her a mysterious dollhouse to occupy her time.

Miss Scarlet and the Duke - 2020 - When Eliza Scarlet is left destitute after her father's death, she can either get married or take over his detective agency. Because she's living in the 1880s and it's deemed inappropriate for a woman to take part in the trade, she gets a partner - Scotland Yard's Detective Inspector William Wellington, "The Duke".

Mr. Selfridge - 2013 to 2016 - Jeremy Piven (*Entourage*) stars as the American Harry Gordon Selfridge, a man who revolutionised British retail.

Mrs. Wilson – 2018 - Mrs. Wilson is fascinating because it's not just a true story, it's a true story about the grandmother of Ruth Wilson (*Luther*), the actress playing the title role. Alison Wilson was widowed in 1963, only to realize her husband had been leading a secret life. Iain Glen (*Jack Taylor*) plays her departed husband, a foreign intelligence officer with more than one "Mrs. Wilson" in his life.

Murder on the Homefront - 2014 - This crime drama is set during the London Blitz of 1940, where the worst criminals could use blackouts and destruction to hide their terrible crimes.

Nicholas and Alexandra: The Letters - 2019 - Dr. Suzannah Lipscomb presents this two-part docudrama about the love story between Tsar Nicholas II and his wife Alexandra.

Northanger Abbey - 2007 - Felicity Jones (*Brideshead Revisited*) stars in this adaptation of Jane Austen's classic parody of Gothic fiction. She plays seventeen-year-old tomboy Catherine Morland, a young woman with a wild imagination and love of Gothic novels.

Pie in the Sky - 1994 to 1997 - When DI Crabbe leaves the police force to open a restaurant, they continue to pull him back in for part-time crime-solving.

Pollyanna - 2003 - Pam Ferris (*Rosemary & Thyme*), Kenneth Cranham, and Tom Ellis (*Miranda*) are among the stars of this television movie based on the Pollyanna novels of American author Eleanor H. Porter. Georgina Terry (*William and Mary*) stars as Pollyanna.

Poldark Revealed - 2016 - This programme goes on set to get a look at what makes Poldark such an enduring favourite.

Press - 2019 - This series follows the rivalry between two major newspapers, taking a hard look at some of the awful things they do to get a scoop. David Suchet (*Poirot*) appears.

Prince Charles at 70 - 2019 - This documentary takes a look at Prince Charles' ongoing charity work and his likely future role as monarch of the United Kingdom.

Prince Philip: The Plot to Make a King - 2016 - This one-episode special tells the story of what went on behind the scenes when Queen Elizabeth II fell in love with Prince Philip. Royal courtiers felt Philip was rough, poorly educated, and unlikely to make a good or faithful husband. Many disapproved of his German roots and ambitious family. The film takes a look at maneuvers for the marriage that took places as early as 1939-40, when the future queen was just 13.

Queen and Country - 2012 - Trevor McDonald walks us through some of the British monarchy's greatest traditions and institutions.

The Queen at War - 2020 - This documentary takes a look at how Queen Elizabeth II served her country during WWII, and how the war shaped her.

Queen Elizabeth's Secret Agents - 2018 - This docuseries takes a look at the incredible father-and-son team that kept Queen Elizabeth I safe during her reign.

Rebecca – 1997 - Emilia Fox and Charles Dance star as the new Mr. and Mrs. Maxim de Winter in this adaptation of Daphne du Maurier's classic gothic suspense novel. Diana Rigg plays Mrs. Danvers, the housekeeper still loyal to her dead mistress, Rebecca.

Reilly, Ace of Spies – 1983 - In this series, we get a glimpse at the life of Sidney Reilly, the spy who inspired James Bond.

Remember Me – 2014 - Michael Palin (*Monty Python, Great Railway Journeys*), Jodie Comer (*Killing Eve*), and Mark Addy (*The Syndicate*) star in this sublimely creepy three-part mystery about a series of unfortunate events that unfold around an unhappy pensioner who fakes a fall in order to be moved to a care home.

Roadkill - 2020 - Hugh Laurie (*House*) and Helen McCrory (*Peaky Blinders*) star in this four-part political thriller about a charismatic politician whose personal life is in shambles thanks to the enemies he's made. Now, he's in a race against time to do the things he wants to do before the problems of his past bring him down. Laurie stars as politician Peter Laurence.

Royal Paintbox - 2014 - Hosted by Prince Charles himself, this documentary takes a look at rarely seen art created by British royals from the past and present.

Royal Wives at War - 2016 - This documentary uses dramatised monologues to give us a closer look at the 1936 abdication crisis through the eyes of the two women most deeply involved - Elizabeth the Queen Mother and American Wallis Simpson.

Rumpole of the Bailey – 1978 to 1992 – Leo McKern starred as Horace Rumpole, a defense barrister who often took on underdog clients.

Sanditon - 2019 - Prior to her early death at the age of 41, Jane Austen began a new and different sort of work. It was the story of Sanditon, a fledgling seaside resort town along the southern coast of England. It was never finished. In this miniseries, screenwriter Andrew Davies (*Mr. Selfridge, Pride & Prejudice*) finishes her final masterpiece. Rose Williams (*Curfew*) stars as Charlotte Heywood, and Theo James plays the outrageous Sidney Parker. Anne Reid (*Last Tango in Halifax*) and Kris Marshall (*Death in Paradise*) also appear.

Secrets of Britain - 2014 - This series takes a look at the secrets behind some of Britain's most notable landmarks and institutions. It covers the Tower of London, Selfridges, Scotland Yard, the London Underground, Her Majesty's Secret Service, and Westminster.

Secrets of Britain's Great Cathedrals - 2019 - Though many travel shows visit the great cathedrals, few of them offer as much detail as this eight-part series. It covers York Minster, Canterbury Cathedral, St. Paul's Cathedral, Westminster Abbey, Salisbury Cathedral, Wells Cathedral, Bath Abbey, Gloucester Cathedral, Durham Cathedral, Lincoln Cathedral, Worcester Cathedral, Tewkesbury Abbey, St. David's, Brecon, St. Asaph, Bangor Cathedral, Ely Cathedral, Peterborough Cathedral, and King's College Cambridge.

Secrets of Highclere Castle - 2013 - This hour-long documentary takes a look at the stately home made famous by *Downton Abbey*.

Secrets of Iconic British Estates - 2013 - This lovely British tour series takes us to Hampton Court, Althorp, and Chatsworth.

Secrets of the Manor House - 2012 - While life may have seemed glamorous in Britain's stately homes, this series looks at the real challenges faced by owners of these massive estates.

Secrets of the Six Wives - 2017 - Historian Dr. Lucy Worsley hosts this series about the most dramatic moments in the lives of Henry VIII and his many wives.

Spying on the Royals - 2018 - In the late 1930s, King Edward VIII and his American lover were considered a significant security risk to the country. This documentary looks at the controversial espionage operation that kept tabs on the pair.

Tales from the Royal Bedchamber - 2014 - Historian Dr. Lucy Worsley examines our lengthy fascination with what goes on inside the royal bedchambers.

Tales from the Royal Wardrobe - 2015 - Historian Dr. Lucy Worsley takes a look at the phenomenon of watching royal attire, offering evidence that it's not just a modern behaviour.

Talking Heads - 2020 - This newly-rebooted series features talented British actors performing a variety of Alan Bennett monologues. Ten are remakes of the original monologues, but Bennett also wrote two new episodes in 2019: The Hand of God (read by Kristin Scott Thomas), and A Chip in the Sugar (read by Martin Freeman). Expected in Spring 2021.

Three Sovereigns for Sarah - 1986 - Vanessa Redgrave (*Mrs. Dalloway*) stars in this historic drama about the Salem witch trials.

The Trouble with Maggie Cole - 2020 - Dawn French brings us this new comedy-drama about the dangers of gossip. She plays Maggie Connors, a seaside village busybody who likes to ignore the saying that "those who live in glass houses shouldn't throw stones."

Unforgotten – 2015 to present - Cassie and Sunny use modern technology to get to the bottom of very cold cases. This recent crime drama is based in London and stars Nicola Walker and Sanjeev Bhaskar as Cassie and Sunny.

Van der Valk - 2020 - This reboot of the 1970s series will see Marc Warren (Beecham House) as Commissaris Piet Van der Valk. Set in modern Amsterdam, it's a major departure from the original Nick Freeling novels.

Victoria and Albert: The Wedding - 2019 - Historian Lucy Worsley re-stages the wedding of Queen Victoria and Prince Albert, using historic documents, diary entries, and archives to pull together all the necessary details. More than just a re-enactment, she also talks about how the wedding changed history and created new traditions.

Vienna Blood - 2019 - Set in 1900s Vienna, this three-part drama follows brilliant English doctor Max Liebermann as he studies under Sigmund Freud. When Liebermann encounters Austrian detective Oskar Rheinhardt, they forge a partnership to take on some of Vienna's most deadly and disturbing cases.

What the Durrells Did Next - 2019 - Hosted by Durrells star Keeley Hawes, this special takes a look at what happened to the real-life Durrell family after they left Corfu.

The Widower - 2015 - Reece Shearsmith (*Inside No. 9*) and Sheridan Smith (*Gavin & Stacey*) star in this miniseries about Malcolm Webster, a man who worked as a nurse and also happened to be a serial killer.

The Windermere Children - 2020 - This movie tells the true story of child survivors of the Holocaust and their rehabilitation in the Lake District in England.

The Windermere Children: In Their Own Words - 2020 - This documentary talks with some of the children whose new, post-Holocaust lives began along the shore of Lake Windermere in England.

The Windsors: A Royal Family - 2018 - This four-part documentary offers an in-depth look at Britain's current royal family, including interviews with friends, aides, and family members.

Wolf Hall - 2015 - This historical drama charts Thomas Cromwell's rise in the Tudor Court as he moved from a poor blacksmith's son to the closest advisor of Henry VIII. The series is based on Hilary Mantel's award-winning novel of the same name.

The Woman in White – 2018 - This BBC miniseries adaptation of Wilkie Collins' famous book of the same name includes Jessie Buckley, Ben Hardy, and Olivia Vinall. This classic gothic tale begins when a man meets a mysterious woman in white before heading to Limmeridge House to tutor his nieces. He's told its a woman who escaped from an asylum, but already, a mystery has begun to unfold around him...

World on Fire - 2019 - This miniseries shines a light on the lives of ordinary people from Poland, France, Germany, and the United Kingdom during the early years of World War II. The large and talented cast includes Helen Hunt (*Mad About You*), Lesley Manville (*Mum*), and Sean Bean (*Game of Thrones*)

The Worricker Trilogy - 2014 - An analyst in the British intelligence forces want to find out why the PM had his friend killed. Bill Night (*Love Actually*) stars.

Wuthering Heights - 2009 - Charlotte Riley (*Press*) and Andrew Lincoln (*The Walking Dead*) star in this two-part adaptation of Emily Brontë's classic novel.

BBC SELECT

Website: https://bbcselect.com

Description: BBC Select offers an eclectic variety of non-fiction programming from the BBC's own archives. NPR fans will likely enjoy this channel's mix of political and social documentaries, as well as it's history and travel shows.

Available On: Apple TV and Amazon Prime Video Channels

Cost: $4.99/month

Now Streaming

100 Vaginas - 2019 - This documentary follows Laura Dodsworth's project to photograph 100 vulvas.

9/11: Truth, Lies, and Conspiracies - 2016 - Roughly half of all Americans believe there's something they aren't being told about 9/11. This documentary explores what happened, and why so many people think the full story may never come out.

A Black and White Killing - 2019 - This two-part documentary takes a look at the increasing racial tensions in America, including interviews with some of those trying to change it.

Addicted to Pleasure - 2012 - Actor Brian Cox explores the origin stories of four of the world's most addictive substances - sugar, opium, tobacco, and whisky.

Africa & Britain: A Forgotten History - 2016 - Historian David Olusoga takes a look at the occasionally difficult relationship between Great Britain and Africa.

All Watched Over by Machines of Loving Grace - 2011 - In this series, Adam Curtis takes us on a journey through the dream of technology - and the reality.

Amazing Hotels: Life Beyond the Lobby - 2017 - Food critic Giles Coren and chef Monica Galetti take a look behind the scenes at some of the world's most extraordinary hotels. The series includes visits to Marina Bay Sands in Singapore, Giraffe Manor in Kenya, Mashpi Lodge in Ecuador, and Icehotels in Sweden.

American History's Biggest Fibs - 2019 - British historian Lucy Worsley digs deep into America's history to find out the truth.

Amish: A Secret Life - 2012 - This groundbreaking documentary sees an Old Order Amish couple who have taken the great risk of allowing cameras into their home.

A Nation Divided: The Charlie Hebdo Aftermath - 2015 - In 2015, Muslim extremists opened fire on the employees of the Charlie Hebdo magazine, angered by caricatures of Muhammad published by the magazine. Comedian Shaista Aziz visits Paris to take a closer look at the incident, a growing far right movement, and the debate over free speech.

Archaeology: A Secret History - 2013 - This series sees archaeologist Richard Miles battling heat, ticks, and leeches as he goes out in search of ancient secrets.

Ariana Grande: Live in London - 2018 - Pop star Ariana Grande performs in London and discusses the Manchester Arena Bombing.

Art of China - 2014 - Historian Andrew Graham-Dixon takes us on a journey through 3000 years of Chinese art.

Art of France - 2017 - Over the course of three episodes, Andrew Graham-Dixon walks us through the rich history of French art.

Art of Russia - 2009 - Art expert Andrew Graham-Dixon takes a closer look at Russian art and its preoccupation with icons.

Art of Scandinavia - 2016 - Though it's a region where darkness reigns for months on end, art expert Andrew Graham-Dixon discovers surprising creativity, playfulness, and eroticism in Scandinavian art.

Art of Spain - 2008 - Critic and historian Andrew Graham-Dixon goes out on the road to reveal some of Spain's greatest artistic treasures.

Aung San Suu Kyi: The Fall of an Icon - 2020 - Though once hailed as an icon of resistance, this Nobel Prize winner has more recently faced allegations of mass murder and rape of Rohingya Muslims. This documentary takes a look at Aung San Suu Kyi and whether anyone really understood her.

Auschwitz: The Nazis and the Final Solution - 2005 - Using computer graphics, reconstructions, and interviews, this docu-series attempts to offer insight into the full scale of the atrocities that took place at Auschwitz.

The Beauty of Anatomy - 2014 - Dr. Adam Rutherford takes a look at the close relationship between art and anatomy over the years.

The Birth of Empire: The East India Company - 2014 - This documentary takes a look at how the East India Company became the world's first multinational, as well as a massively corrupt imperial power.

Borderlands: Life on the Line - 2017 - This documentary takes a look at the individuals who spend time around the US-Mexico border - from the criminal vigilantes to the border patrol officers to the humanitarian groups trying to aid those attempting to cross.

Brainwashing Stacey - 2016 - British reporter Stacey Dooley immerses herself in anti-abortion and big game hunting groups to see if their extremist mindsets will sway her.

Brazil with Michael Palin - 2012 - In spite of its size and population, Brazil is a destination that eluded Michael Palin for decades. In this series, he visits the country, exploring everything from the cities to the most remote areas.

Bright Lights Brilliant Minds: A Tale of Three Cities - 2014 - Art expert James Fox takes a look at the underbelly of three cities - Paris, Vienna, and New York - at important moments in their cultural histories.

Britain's Forgotten Slave Owners - 2015 - This two-part series takes a look at who owned slaves in Britain, and the country's unusual decision to compensate slave owners for "loss of property" when slavery was outlawed in 1834.

Celebs, Brands, and Fake Fans - 2013 - This undercover sting takes a look at some of the less-than-honest things marketers do to promote their clients in the new world of online influence.

Charles and Di: The Truth Behind Their Wedding - 2019 - Prince Charles proposed to Diana after just twelve meetings, and the two would walk down the aisle together just five months later. This documentary takes a look at what was really going on behind the fairy tale.

China: A New World Order - 2019 - Since Xi Jinping came to power, Communist power has increased and more dissent has been quieted. This series take a look at the causes and implications of these changes.

China on Four Wheels - 2012 - British journalists Anita Rani and Justin Rowlatt embark on two very different car journeys across China - one seeing the cities in luxury and style, the other travelling rural areas where life is simpler.

China: Triumph and Turmoil - 2012 - Professor Niall Ferguson talks with Chinese citizens about living in a Communist country with a capitalist economy, and looks at how a system seemingly designed to fail has endured for 2000 years.

Chopin Saved My Life - 2013 - This documentary from James Kent takes a look at how Chopin's Ballade Number 1 has affected the lives of two young men.

Civilization: Is the West History? - 2011 - Historian Niall Ferguson takes a look at whether the West's power is coming to an end.

Click to Change Your Life: Secrets of a Global Craze - 2019 - British reporter Ellis Flynn goes undercover to get a closer look at internet-based multi-level marketing and the sub-culture of deeply-indebted influencers who target other vulnerable women.

Confessions of a Serial Killer - 2019 - This documentary takes a look at how Samuel Little got away with murdering as many as 93 women over the course of 40 years.

Conspiracy Files: George Soros - The Billionaire Global Mastermind? - 2019 - This documentary explores how George Soros became the world's favourite billionaire boogeyman.

Conspiracy Files: Vaccine Wars - 2019 - This documentary takes a look at how one man - the disgraced former doctor Andrew Wakefield - kicked off a dangerous anti-vax movement with his fraudulent data.

Couples on the Couch - 2019 - In a specially-constructed clinic, couples hash out their most intimate arguments and misunderstandings.

Cuba with Simon Reeve - 2012 - Journalist and adventurer Simon Reeve heads to Cuba to find out what modern Cuba is really like.

The Dark Charisma of Adolf Hitler - 2012 - Why did millions support this hateful man, ultimately destroying their own country by following him? This compelling docu-series takes a look at how regular people can become devoted to a horrible person.

Design for Life - 2009 - Designer Phillippe Starck sets out to find one worthy designer in a crowd of twelve hopefuls.

Diana: 7 Days That Shook the World - 2017 - This documentary takes a look at the public reaction after Diana's death, along with her death's impact on the royal family.

Dictatorland - 2017 - Journalist Benjamin Zand heads for the portion of central Asia which has the highest concentration of dictators in the world.

Did Darwin Kill God? - 2009 - Theologist Conor Cunningham takes a look at the often strained relationship between science and religion.

Don't Panic: How to End Poverty in 15 Years - 2015 - Swedish statistician Professor Hans Rosling uses data to show us how allowing poverty to exist is a choice, not a given.

Don't Panic: The Truth About Population - 2013 - Swedish statistician Professor Hans Rosling uses data to demonstrate that the population crisis isn't what it's been made out to be, and that human population is on track to stabilise by the end of the 21st century.

Drowning in Plastic - 2018 - Wildlife biologist Liz Bonnin talks with scientists who are trying to get the plastic problem under control before it ruins our planet.

Eat to Live Forever with Giles Coren - 2015 - Food writer Giles Coren tries three extreme diets to figure out what's best. Should we embrace unusual diets or accept a shorter life that includes cake?

Ed Balls: Trump's America - 2016 - As a puzzled world looks on at the US, British former politician Ed Balls travels to the "MAGA heartland" to meet and listen to some of the people who love Trump.

Extraordinary Places to Eat - 2018 - Accomplished London maître d' Fred Sirieix travels to some of the world's finest restaurants in its finest cities.

Extreme Combat: The Dancer and the Fighter - 2020 - Dancer Akram Khan takes a look at the rise of MMA and what draws people to its spectacle.

Fake News: A True History - 2019 - This documentary takes a look at the history and consequences of "alternative facts".

Feasts - 2009 - Gastro-adventurer Stefan Gates travels the world to explore some of the most decadent and unusual food-related festivals.

The Flu That Killed 50 Million - 2018 - This documentary takes a look at the Spanish Flu and the lessons we can learn from it.

Frankenstein and the Vampire: A Dark and Stormy Night - 2014 - This documentary takes us back to an important moment in gothic history, a night where Mary Shelley, Lord Byron, and a number of their contemporaries gathered to share ghost stories.

Frat Boys - 2016 - While movies portray fraternities as harmless fun, this documentary takes a look at what happens when fraternities cross the line, giving safe harbour to things like hazing, brutality, and sexual assault.

Gandhi - 2009 - Journalist Mishal Husain takes a look at Mahatma Gandhi's complicated legacy and impact on India.

Genderquake - 2018 - This two-part series puts 11 people of differing gender identities in a house together in hopes of promoting discussion and understanding.

The Genius of Carl Faberge - 2013 - Originally made for the Russian Tsars as Easter gifts, these expensive eggs have a fascinating history. Stephen Smith goes on a hunt to uncover their secrets.

Genius of the Ancient World – 2015 - Historian Bettany Hughes travels the world to study the lives of great philosophers like Socrates, Confucius, and Buddha.

Genius of the Modern World – 2016 - Historian Bettany Hughes looks at the world that helped shape intellectual greats like Friedrich Nietzsche, Sigmung Freud, and Karl Marx.

Germany's New Nazis - 2016 - In Germany, right-wing extremism is reaching its highest levels since the Third Reich. This film looks at what we can learn about the conditions that allow extremist views to flourish.

Gorbachev: The Man Who Changed the World - 1996 - This documentary takes a look at how the son of a peasant family grew up to become the last leader of the Soviet Union, ushering in a new era of change and collaboration.

Grayson Perry: All Man - 2016 - Dress-wearing artist Grayson Perry takes a look at what really constitutes manhood in our modern age.

Grayson Perry: Big American Road Trip - 2020 - Artist Grayson Perry travels the US to get a closer look at the increasingly deep lines between people of different races, classes, and political leanings.

Grayson Perry's Art Club - 2020 - Throughout the lockdown, artist Grayson Perry offered artistic expression and escapism through his art club.

Grayson Perry: Who Are You? - 2014 - Artist Grayson Perry explores the concept of identity in a world where we're constantly bombarded by our own curated image of ourselves.

Greek Myths: True Stories - 2015 - Robin Lane Fox takes a look at how Greek myths have crossed over into our modern stories.

Harry Potter: A History of Magic - 2017 - JK Rowling invites us into her private archive to learn more about what inspired the enchanting world she created.

Harry Styles Live in Manchester - 2017 - Former One Direction member Harry Styles performs for a live audience.

Her Story: The Female Revolution - 2016 - This series takes a look at some of the women who bravely fight against men who'd rather they didn't.

The High Art of the Low Countries - 2015 - Andrew Graham-Dixon explores the region that gave us Vermeer, Rembrandt, Mondrian, Magritte, and Van Gogh.

Hiroshima: The Real History - 2015 - This documentary takes a closer look at what we know about the bombing of Hiroshima and the new age it ushered in.

Hotel Secrets with Richard E. Grant - 2012 - Oscar-nominated Richard E. Grant gives us unprecedented access to some of the world's most luxurious hotels.

House of Saud - 2018 - This documentary takes a closer look at both the wealth and the challenges faced by Saudia Arabia's new Crown Prince Mohammad bin Salman.

How to Go Viral - 2019 - Digital culture expert Richard Clay meets modern meme designers and internet trolls to find out how memes influence us.

In and Out of Hell: The Meat Loaf Story - 2015 - This hour-long documentary takes a look at Meat Loaf, the world-famous musician who helped shape the power ballad as we know it.

In Louboutin's Shoes - 2015 - For years, Louboutin shoes were known only among the fashion elite and extremely wealthy. This documentary looks at how the shoe became such a common status symbol.

In Search of Frida Kahlo - 2014 - This documentary heads to Mexico City to learn more about artist Frida Kahlo's difficult life and work.

Inside the Billionaire's Wardrobe - 2016 - Reggie Yates traces the path from animal to closet, investigating whether "sustainable killing" can clear a buyer's conscience.

Isis: The Origins of Violence - 2017 - English historian Tom Holland explores the tensions between Islam and the Western world, asking difficult questions about the origins of violent Islamist terrorism.

It Was 50 Years Ago Today - 2007 - Fifty years after its release, documentarian Alan G. Parker takes a look back at the Beatles' legendary Sgt. Pepper's Lonely Hearts Club Band album.

I Was Once a Beauty Queen - 2012 - Beauty contests were popular on British TV in the 1970s and 80s, but what happened to the women once it was all over?

Japan with Sue Perkins - 2019 - Comedian Sue Perkins travels Japan to immerse herself in some of their strangest cultural offerings.

Joanna Lumley's Japan - 2016 - Actress and activist Joanna Lumley (*Absolutely Fabulous*) explores some of Japan's biggest cities and most remote islands.

Joanna Lumley's Trans-Siberian Adventure - 2015 - Actress Joanna Lumley takes a 6000-mile rail trip from Hong Kong to Moscow via China and Mongolia.

The Joy of Winning - 2018 - Mathematician Dr. Hannah Fry takes a look at how you can apply game theory to your daily life to improve your odds of success.

The Killer Years - 2012 - This two-part series takes a look at the fight of F1 drivers to improve safety in their sport.

Kolkata with Sue Perkins - 2015 - *Great British Bake Off* presenter Sue Perkins travels to the Indian city of Kolkata to offer up an interesting look at modern India.

Kylie's Secret Night - 2019 - Comedian Alan Carr hosts a show in which some of Kylie Minogue's most dedicated fans are brought together to enjoy a night with her.

Leaving Amish Paradise - 2011 - This documentary follows two Amish families as they struggle to adapt to the modern world.

Louis Theroux: A Different Brain - 2016 - Documentarian Louis Theroux takes a look at how patients and families cope with life-changing brain injuries that come with little to no outward physical signs.

Louis Theroux: Altered States - Choosing Death - 2018 - Louis Theroux looks at the growing movement urging governments to allow euthanasia for the terminally ill.

Louis Theroux: Altered States - Love Without Limits - 2018 - Louis Theroux visits Portland, the US capital of polyamory, to learn more about couples who've opened up their relationships.

Louis Theroux: Altered States - Take My Baby - 2018 - In this hour-long documentary, Louis heads to the open adoption state of California, where he talks with women handing over their babies to families paying tens of thousands of dollars.

Louis Theroux: Beware of the Tiger - 2011 - The United States has more captive tigers than the total number of wild tigers in the rest of the world. British filmmaker Louis Theroux visits breeder and collector Joe Exotic at his Oklahoma zoo to investigate why people collect rare and dangerous animals.

Louis Theroux: Drinking to Oblivion - 2016 - Louis Theroux spends time at King's College in London as liver specialists try to help alcoholics who can't seem to help themselves.

Louis Theroux: Extreme Love - Autism - 2012 - British filmmaker Louis Theroux looks at how autistic children perceive the world around them, and the impact it can have on their families.

Louis Theroux: Extreme Love - Dementia - 2012 - Filmmaker Louis Theroux visits Phoenix, dementia capital of America, to see how it affects patients and their loved ones.

Louis Theroux: LA Stories - City of Dogs - 2014 - Louis Theroux travels to LA to learn about the city's vast dog population - from weaponised dogs in downtrodden areas to the pampered pooches of Beverly Hills.

Louis Theroux: LA Stories - Edge of Life - 2014 - Louis Theroux visits America to take a look at the country's for-profit healthcare system and how its extremely high costs can impact end-of-life decisions for patients and their families.

Louis Theroux: Law and Disorder in Johannesburg - 2008 - Louis Theroux takes a look at the lengths wealthy South Africans go to in order to stay safe in the often dangerous city of Johannesburg.

Louis Theroux: Law and Disorder in Lagos - 2010 - British filmmaker Louis Theroux spends time with some of Nigeria's paramilitary state groups and youth gangs to help make sense of a city that can at times seem both lawless and orderly.

Louis Theroux: Miami Mega Jail - 2011 - The United States incarcerates an enormous percentage of its people, and it's brought about the need for mega jails where inmates can await sentencing. Louis Theroux visits one of those facilities to meet men awaiting their day in court.

Louis Theroux: Most Hated Family in America - 2007 - In this documentary, Louis Theroux spends time with Christian extremists from the Westboro Baptist Church hate group.

Louis Theroux: Mothers on the Edge - 2019 - This documentary takes a look at what happens when new mothers experience postpartum psychosis.

Louis Theroux: Selling Sex - 2020 - In the era of online ordering, it's become increasingly easy to market and sell sex. Should it be as easy as hailing an Uber? Louis Theroux examines the issue.

Louis Theroux: Surviving America's Most Hated Family - 2019 - Thirteen years after he first encountered them, Louis Theroux returns to the extremists of the Westboro Baptist Church to see what happens after a hate group loses its patriarch.

Louis Theroux: Talking to Anorexia - 2017 - Louis Theroux visits two of London's biggest adult eating disorder clinics to find out why anorexia is so deadly and difficult to treat.

Louis Theroux: The Night in Question - 2019 - Louis Theroux visits American universities to meet students whose universities have found them guilty of sexual assault under stricter new policies.

Louis Theroux: The Return of America's Most Hated Family - 2011 - A few years after his initial visit with the Westboro Baptist hate group, Louis Theroux returned to the US to accompany the Phelps family as they travelled the country.

Louis Theroux: The Ultra Zionists - 2011 - British documentarian Louis Theroux travels to Israel's West Bank to meet the extreme Jewish nationalists who consider it their obligation to populate its most contested and sensitive areas.

Louis Theroux: Under the Knife - 2007 - Filmmaker Louis Theroux travels to Beverly Hills, meeting some of its plastic surgery-obsessed residents and joining them on consultations as they attempt to stay eternally youthful.

Mad Dog: Inside the Secret World of Muammar Gaddafi - 2014 - This documentary takes a look at the evil reign of Libyan leader Colonel Gaddafi - from his billion-dollar weekly oil income to the tactics he used to silence his opposition.

The Making of Merkel - 2013 - Andrew Marr takes a look back at Angela Merkel's life and rise to power in Germany.

The Man Who Shot Vietnam - 2016 - Welsh photographer Philip Jones risked his life to bring the world incredible images of the Vietnam War's victims. This documentary takes a look at the man and humanitarian behind the camera.

Mark Zuckerberg: Inside Facebook - 2012 - In 2012, British reporter Emily Maitlis was given exclusive access to Mark Zuckerberg and other senior executives at Facebook. She tackles the question of how a company can grow while also keeping both investors and users happy.

Meet the Young Americans - 2014 - British investigative journalist Stacey Dooley travels to the US to find out more about the challenges facing young Americans today.

Me, My Selfie, and I - 2019 - Many of us have more images of ourselves in our phones than we have from our entire childhoods. This documentary takes a look at whether selfies are a modern phenomenon, and how they impact our well-being.

Me and My Penis - 2020 - This show marked the first time an erect penis was seen on UK television, and it follows artist and sex activist Ajamu as he explores the relationship between men and one of their most beloved parts.

The Mekong River with Sue Perkins - 2014 - British presenter and comedienne Sue Perkins travels along the Mekong River, telling the story of this important river and the people who rely on it.

Meet the Trumps: From Immigrant to President - 2017 - This documentary looks at the Trump family's immigrant history.

Million Dollar Wedding Planner - 2019 - This documentary follows wedding planner Lelian Chew to learn more about the increasingly lavish weddings thrown by Asia's new billionaire class.

Murder 24/7: True Crime/Real Time - 2020 - This docu-series follows the team of experts who work non-stop to solve violent and deadly crimes.

The Murder Detectives - 2015 - This three-part documentary follows a real-life murder case from the initial call through the arrest and process of building a case.

Muslim Beauty Pageants and Me - 2015 - Dina Torkia is Britain's top Muslim fashion blogger, and this documentary sees her heading to Indonesia as a finalist in the World Muslimah pageant.

Mystery of the Missing Princess - 2018 - In 2018, Princess Latifa of Dubai fled to India, hoping to escape her life. Unfortunately, she was captured, and it wasn't long before a video detailing her repression and abuse was released. She'd arranged for it to be released if her escape failed.

Obsessed with My Body - 2016 - This series explores the increasing body pressures on men and the rise in male eating disorders.

One Deadly Weekend in America: A Killing at the Carwash - 2017 - In May 2015, an autistic teenager was murdered for wearing the wrong colour of shoes. Through his story, we get a look at what life is like in LA's gangland.

The Plastic Surgery Capital of the World - 2018 - With 60% of Korean women in their 20s having had plastic surgery, it's the plastic surgery capital of the world. This documentary takes a look at the cost of the pressure to be perfect.

Power and the World's Women - 2015 - Three of the world's most powerful women - Hillary Clinton, Condoleezza Rice, and Madeleine Albright - discuss the way women's power has evolved, and the work that's still to be done.

The Pregnant Man - 2008 - Trans man Thomas Beatie and his wife Nancy want to have a family together, but it's Thomas who gets pregnant. This documentary takes a look at the legal and medical issues that arise with their unusual situation.

Putin: A Russian Spy Story - 2015 - After the chance viewing of a Russian spy drama, young Vladimir Putin was inspired to sign up for the KGB, ultimately going on to become the leader of Russia. This documentary interviews members of his inner circle, along with his opponents and victims.

Putin's Russia - 2018 - British journalist David Dimbleby attempts to gain some insight into Russia's long-time, notoriously secretive leader.

Rallying: The Killer Years - 2016 - In the 1980s, rallying was immensely popular and incredibly dangerous. This series takes a look at how increasingly powerful cars led to a series of tragedies that would ultimately bring about greater regulation.

Rat Pack: A Conference of Cool - 1999 - For a few short years, Frank Sinatra and his friends were the epitome of cool. This documentary tells the story of their influence.

Reagan - 2011 - This documentary explores how the first "make America great again" president shaped the last 40 years in US politics.

Reggie Yates in China - 2019 - Presenter Reggie Yates takes a look at the latest generation of Chinese young people, and how they're transforming both their country and the world.

Rembrandt - 2014 - Simon Schama takes a look at Rembrandt's final, scandal-plagued years.

The Rise of Female Violence - 2015 - From drunken partygoers to female gangs, this series sets out to explore the causes of increasing violence by women.

The Rise of the Murdoch Dynasty - 2020 - Rupert Murdoch owns the biggest media operation in the planet, and it's given him unprecedented levels of influence. This three-part documentary looks at how it happened.

Rock 'n' Roll Guns for Hire: The Story of the Sidemen - 2016 - This documentary shines a light on the side artists who helped make some of the world's most iconic acts look good.

Royal Cousins at War - 2014 - At the beginning of the 20th century, three cousins ruled Britain, Russia, and Germany. This documentary takes a look at how their chaotic relationships had a devastating impact on Europe.

Russia 1917: Countdown to Revolution - 2017 - In just a few months, Stalin, Lenin, and Trotsky went from troublemakers to world leaders. This documentary takes a look at how it happened so quickly.

Secret Rules of Modern Living: Algorithm - 2015 - Algorithms power everything from search engines to dating apps, and mathematician Marcus du Sautoy attempts to demystify them.

Secrets of Silicon Valley - 2015 - Silicon Valley entrepreneurs set out to change the world, but those changes haven't always been for the best. This series examines whether we're all heading for a tech-led disaster - or whether technology might genuinely improve the human condition.

Secrets of South America - 2014 - Reporter Billie JD Porter dives into the darker side of South American life.

Secrets of Sugar Baby Dating - 2019 - High university tuition and soaring housing costs have led some young women to become "sugar babies". This series meets women whose lives are funded by wealthy older men.

Sex and the Church - 2015 - Professor Diarmaid MacCulloch looks at how Western attitudes on sex and gender have been shaped by Christian influence.

The Sex Changes That Made History - 2015 - When the "sci-fi surgery" of gender reassignment became available in the 1940s, it was a media sensation. This documentary takes a look back at some of the earliest people to make that choice.

Sex, Death, and the Meaning of Life - 2015 - Richard Dawkins explores the way man's thoughts on sin, gods, and the afterlife have shaped our world.

Shock of the Nude - 2020 - Classicist Mary Beard takes a closer look at what drives our obsession with the body in art.

Simon Schama's Power of Art - 2006 - This eight-part series sees art historian Simon Schama attempting to illustrate the power of art through in-depth looks at eight iconic masterpieces.

Simon Schama's Shakespeare and Us - 2012 - Historian Simon Schama takes a look at what made Shakespeare's plays so groundbreaking and enduring.

Smartphones: The Dark Side - 2018 - More than half of us look at our smartphones immediately upon waking up, and we pick them up an average of 58 times in a day. This series looks at how the constant pings diminish our attention spans, and how we've become addicted to the dopamine rush they offer.

Soup Cans and Superstars: How Pop Art Changed the World - 2015 - Art historian

Alistair Sooke takes a look at how the works of artists like Andy Warhol and Roy Lichtenstein defined their eras.

Stalin: Inside the Terror - 2003 - At the end of WWII, Stalin gained a vast empire in the East. This documentary looks at how a once-principled man transformed into an evil and controlling despot.

Steve Jobs: Billion Dollar Hippy - 2011 - Insiders tell the story of Apple and its unusual founder.

The Story of Women and Art - 2014 - This three-part series takes a look at some of the largely overlooked women of art history.

Suffragettes - 2018 - In celebration of 100 years of the female vote in Britain, Lucy Worsley takes a look back at the brave women who helped bring about that change.

Tamara Rojo's Swan Lake - 2014 - World-famous dancer Tamara Rojo takes a look at why Swan Lake has enjoyed such enduring fame.

Touched by Auschwitz - 2016 - Six Auschwitz survivors share their experiences to help us understand the human cost of the Holocaust's atrocities.

TV's Black Renaissance: Reggie Yates in Hollywood - 2019 - Actor Reggie Yates travels to LA to explore some of the majority-black television shows of recent years.

U2 Live in London - 2017 - This programme sees U2 performing live from Abbey Road Studios in London.

Ugly Beauty - 2009 - Art critic Waldemar Januszczak shows us how to look at modern art in a new way.

Vienna: Empire, Dynasty, and Dream - 2016 - From its Roman origins onward, Vienna has been a pivotal city in the history of Europe. This series sees historian Simon Sebag Montefiore sharing that history.

Vincent Van Gogh: Painted with Words - 2010 - Benedict Cumberbatch (*Sherlock*) takes on the role of the iconic Dutch post-impressionist. Though dramatised, the dialogue is sourced from Van Gogh's own words.

Virtual Adultery and Cyberspace Love - 2008 - This documentary attempts to figure out why some people become so involved in virtual worlds, even to the point of taking on a virtual lovers and leaving their real families.

The Wild West - 2018 - This docu-series blends tales of the Wild West with modern archaeological and forensic research.

The Women of World War One - 2014 - War reporter Kate Adie takes a look at the impact of the work women did on the homefront during WWII.

The World's First Computer - 2014 - The Antikythera Mechanism was discovered on an ancient shipwreck, and it's thought to be one of the world's first computers. This documentary tells the story of the mysterious object thought to have been used to predict solar eclipses and time the Olympics.

World's Weirdest Homes - 2014 - This programme takes a look at some of the strangest homes the world has to offer, including a toilet house.

World War Three: Inside the War Room - 2016 - This documentary offers a look behind the scenes at those who are monitoring the world's greatest threats and creating strategies to help avoid nuclear attack.

BBC SELECT

INSIDE OUTSIDE

Website: https://www.inside-outside.tv/

Description: This subscription service offers a selection of the best British home and garden television shows. Though the total amount of programming is relatively low, you may still feel it's worth it to subscribe occasionally.

Available On: Roku, Amazon Fire TV, Apple TV, Apple iPhone & iPad, Android TV, Android phones and tablets, computer (via web browser). You can also subscribe via Amazon Prime Video.

Cost: $5.99/month

Now Streaming

The Autistic Gardener - 2015 to 2017 - This fun series sees a team of autistic gardeners - led by an award-winning autistic gardener - as they remodel garden spaces for a variety of individuals around the UK.

Big Dreams Small Spaces, Series 1-3 - Monty Don joins amateur gardeners to help them realise the big dreams they have for their small gardens.

Clarissa & the King's Cookbook - 2008 - This brief documentary sees medieval foodie Clarissa Dickson Wright tracking down Britain's oldest-known cookbook, The Forme of Cury. Though brief, it's fascinating to see her recreate recipes from the 700-year-old scroll.

Damned Designs: Don't Demolish My Home - 2015 - In this series, we see individuals whose building projects have somehow broken local rules that put their project at risk. They'll fight to get on the good side of local authorities so they can save their homes.

Discovering Korean Food with Gizzi Erskine - 2016 - Gizze Erskine is a food writer for The Independent, and this series has her leading us around Korea in search of the best Korean food.

Food Glorious Food - 2013 - This series travels around the UK, checking out some of the best food on offer in different regions.

Areas visited include Malvern, Harrogate, Brighton, and Yorkshire.

Gardeners' World - 1968 to present - This long-running series offers support, ideas, and guidance for gardeners all over the UK - and the world.

The Garden Pantry - 2012 - This New Zealand-based series focuses on edible gardening, with loads of great scenery from around the country. Some episodes also get into food prep and preserving.

Garden Rescue - 2016 to present - Charlie Dimmock and the Rich brothers compete to design garden spaces for people around Great Britain.

Get Growing - 2014 - In this series, the Get Growing team travels to different locations around the British countryside, helping families solve their toughest backyard gardening problems.

Greatest Gardens - 2015 - This series seeks out the best private gardens in Northern Ireland.

Great Interior Design Challenge - 2014 to 2017 - Amateur designers attempt to transform inside spaces.

Hoarders, Get Your House in Order - This is another show that takes a look at Brits whose collections and obsessions have gotten a bit out of control.

Hoarder SOS - This series sees professional organizers helping people living in extreme clutter. With a bit of help, they're able to get a new start on life without all the baggage.

Homes Under the Hammer, Series 4 & 5 - This long-running British auction series follows property auctions that frequently require a large amount of refurbishment or development. The series follows properties from auction to refurbishment, though not every project is seen through to completion.

House Swap - 2009 - This four-part series follows people who've decided they would rather trade houses than attempt to buy and sell them.

How to Haggle for a House - 2012 - In this series, financial expert George Harrigan-Brown goes face-to-face to negotiate with property vendors to help buyers get better deals. He doesn't reveal the deal until after they've seen the house. Episodes featured include Eastbourne, London, Bath, Edinburgh, and Kendal/Lake District.

Jimmy Doherty's Escape to the Wild, Series 2 - This series follows British families who've given up on the rat race and relocated to remote parts of the world. Locations covered in this series include Indonesia, Uganda, and the Yukon.

Kevin McCloud's Escape to the Wild, Series 1 - 2015 - In this series, Kevin McCloud travels all over the globe to meet people who've moved to surprisingly remote and challenging places. From the Arctic Circle to the jungles of Central America, this is a show about people in search of a simpler kind of life.

Kitchen Criminals - 2007 - This amusing series sees top chefs John Burton Race and Angela Hartnett traveling around the US looking for its absolute worst cooks. They visit every region of the UK, from England to Wales to Scotland and Northern Ireland.

Love Your Garden, Series 1 & 3 - Alan Titchmarsh and his team travel around the country, educating viewers and helping guests find ways to get more from their gardens.

Market Kitchen - 2009 - This fun British series focuses on using local markets to get seasonal produce - then preparing dishes based on those finds.

Operation Homefront - 2013 - This series sees ex-British soldiers putting their skills to work in a variety of community projects around the UK. Among the projects are an Oxfordshire Scout Hut, a Glasgow community centre, and a Southampton Boathouse.

Paul Hollywood's Pies & Puds - This series features mostly savoury dishes by Paul Hollywood (of the *Great British Bake Off*). Dishes include Corned Beef Hash Pie, Paul's Cream Tea Pudding, Meat & Two Potato Pie, Thai Chicken Pie, Paul's Luxury Fish Pie, Traditional Mutton Scotch Pies, Goats Herd Pie, and more.

Royal Upstairs Downstairs - This 20-episode series travels in the footsteps of Queen Victoria, visiting and exploring the stately homes she visited during her reign. The series begins with Chatsworth, moving on to Shugborough, Harewood, Holkham, Brighton, Scone, Walmer, Wimpole, Belvoir, Blair, Burghley, Hatfield, Castle Howard, Stoneleigh, Warwick, Penryhn, Floors Castle, Hughenden, and Waddesdon.

The Secret History of the British Garden - 2015 - Monty Don takes us through the history and evolution of the British garden. The series is made up of four hour-long episodes, each one covering a century of gardening history (17th, 18th, 19th, and 20th).

Secret Removers - 2012 - This series follows individuals as they arrange secret moves for friends and family members. It sounds like an absolute nightmare to me, but presumably the people volunteering know their friends and family well enough to make it work.

When Patrick Met Kylie: A Love of Food Story - 2013 - Lawyer Patrick Drake and journalist Kylie Flavell join together for a whirlwind food trip around Italy.

Wine Oh TV - 2014 - This short series visits some of the world's great wine regions, sampling as it goes.

You Deserve This House - 2012 - This heartwarming series seeks out deserving homeowners in desperate need of renovation. From a retired nurse to a speech therapist to an ex-firefighter, you'll see good people getting some much-needed kindness from their fellow Brits.

PRIME VIDEO

Website: http://amazon.com

Description: As part of their Amazon Prime membership, Amazon offers thousands of shows and movies you can view at no additional cost. It's also possible to purchase a Prime Video membership without the free shipping benefits (at a slightly lower monthly cost).

Available On: Roku, Amazon Fire TV, Android devices, iPad, desktop, Chromecast, and most smart TVs.

Cost: $12.99/month or $119/year for Prime, $8.99/month for just Prime Video

Now Streaming

Mysteries & Crime Dramas

Accused - 2010 to 2012 - This drama follows people who've been accused of crimes as they await their day in court.

Agatha Christie's Ordeal by Innocence – 2018 - When a wealthy woman is murdered, her adopted son is arrested in spite of his claims of innocence. Later, his guilt is thrown into doubt and the family scrambles to figure out who killed her.

Bedlam – 2011 to 2012 - When a haunted former asylum is turned into a high-end apartment building, it has unexpected consequences for the building's new tenants.

The Bench – 2001 to 2002 - This legal drama takes place in a busy magistrates court in Wales. It follows the challenges they face in court, along with the general pressures of working on a high-profile legal team.

Black Widows - *Finland* - 2016 to 2017 - Three best friends are going through a mid-life crisis and think that life will be better if their husbands are dead. Unfortunately for them, it's not quite as simple as they had imagined.

The Bletchley Circle - 2012 to 2014 - In 1952, four former Bletchley Park codebreakers from WWII come together to track a killer.

Blood Ties - *Canada* - 2007 - When a Toronto detective begins losing her eyesight, she becomes a PI and teams up with a 470-year-old vampire (who is also the illegitimate son of Henry VIII). The series is an adaptation of author Tanya Huff's *Blood* novels.

Bounty Hunters – 2019 - Jack Whitehall and Rosie Perez star in this series about a sheltered Brit and a tough Brooklynite who must work together to help save his family's business after a dodgy antiques deal involving looted treasures.

Collision – 2009 - After a multi-car accident, a group of relative strangers see their secrets unfold around that single event that ties them together. This short series was written by Anthony Horowitz of Midsomer Murders fame, and Shetland fans will immediately notice Douglas Henshall as DI John Tolin.

Crownies – *Australia* – 2011 - Marta Dusseldorp (*A Place to Call Home*) stars in this series about young solicitors who act as primary points of contact for police, witnesses, and victims.

Cuffs – 2015 - In quirky coastal Brighton, police officers are over-stretched and under-resourced, but they do the best they can with what they've got.

Dead Lucky - *Australian* - 2018 – When a dangerous armed robber resurfaces in Sydney, two very different detectives are forced to work together to catch him.

DCI Banks – 2010 to 2016 - Stephen Tomkinson (*Ballykissangel, Wild at Heart*) stars as DCI Alan Banks, a skilled but stubborn Yorkshire-based investigator.

A Difficult Woman – *Australia* – 1998 - A woman with a brilliant career and promising relationship sees everything derailed when a close friend is murdered. As she gets more information, it leads her well out of her comfort zone as she pursues the killer.

Donovan – 2004 - This psychological thriller follows Joe Donovan, a forensics expert turned author who investigates some of the most evil crimes. Some of them hit a little too close to home.

Endeavour – 2012 to present - In this prequel to Inspector Morse, a young Endeavour works with Sergeant Thursday to develop his investigative skills. Shaun Evans stars as Morse during this 1960s period mystery.

The Fall - 2013 to 2016 - Gillian Anderson (*The X-Files*) and Jamie Dornan (*50 Shades of Grey*) star in this series about a senior investigator who goes head-to-head with a serial killer who's attacking young professional women in Belfast.

The Ghost Squad - 2005 - Similar to *Line of Duty*, this series follows an Internal Affairs division designed to help find and fix corruption within the police. Elaine Cassidy (*No Offence*) stars.

Gracepoint – 2014 - David Tennant stars in this American remake of *Broadchurch*.

Grantchester – 2014 to present - In the village of Grantchester, a clever vicar assists a local police detective with his investigations. James Norton (*Happy Valley*) stars as vicar Sidney Chambers, and Robson Green (*Wire in the Blood*) plays DI Geordie Keating. Later in the series, Tom Brittany takes over for him in the role of Reverend Will Davenport, a former inner-city chaplain.

Half Moon Investigations – 2009 - This comedy-mystery series for kids was filmed in North Lanarkshire, Scotland, and follows young investigator Fletcher Moon as he goes on stakeouts and undercover operations with his partner, Red Sharkey.

Hamish Macbeth - 1995 to 1997 - Hamish Macbeth (Robert Carlyle, *The Full Monty*) is a talented but unambitious Highlands constable who doesn't always follow the rules. The series was filmed in the lovely Highland village of Plockton on the shores of Loch Carron, and it's a great watch for those who enjoy good scenery.

Injustice - 2011 - A defense barrister has to deal with the consequences of defending an indefensible crime. *Foyle's War* and *Midsomer Murders* screenwriter Anthony Horowitz created the series, and it features an all-star cast with actors like James Purefoy (*Rome*), Dervla Kirwan (*Ballykissangel*), Charlie Creed-Miles (*The Fifth Element*), and Nathaniel Parker (*The Inspector Lynley Mysteries*).

Intruders – 2014 - John Simm (*Life on Mars*) stars as an ex-cop whose wife goes missing. The ensuing investigation leads him to Seattle, and a secret society dedicated to chasing immortality by hiding in the bodies of others. Based on Michael Marshall Smith's novel.

Lanester - *France* - 2018 - In France, three strange murders have been committed, each left with a strange display. Detective Eric Lanester loses his sight during the investigation, but carries on.

Line of Duty – 2012 to present - This suspenseful British police series is set in the fictional "anti-corruption unit" AC-12, where the police police the police. Yes, we know that sentence is a bit weird. The series is great, though. Lennie James, Vicky McClure, Martin Compston, and Adrian Dunbar all feature.

Liverpool 1 - 1998 to 1999 - This gritty, Liverpool-based police drama dives into the city's underworld. We follow the vice squad at Bridewell as they fight drug dealers, paeodophiles, pimps, and porn peddlers in this rough-around-the-edges port city. Samantha Womack stars as DC Isobel de Pauli.

The Living & the Dead – 2016 - When a man inherits his family estate in Somerset, strange things begin to happen.

Mayday - 2013 - When the May Queen disappears just before May Day celebrations, a small town is thrown into chaos.

McCallum - 1995 to 1998 - Pathologist McCallum and his team help the dead tell their stories.

The Missing – 2014 to 2017 - James Nesbitt (*Cold Feet*) stars in this drama about the disappearance of a 5-year-old and the manhunt that follows.

Murder City - 2004 to 2006 - DI Susan Alembic (Amanda Donohoe) and DS Luke Stone (Kris Marshall) are opposites, but they're very effective at working together to solve tough crimes.

Murphy's Law – 2003 to 2007 - James Nesbitt stars as DS Tommy Murphy, a maverick cop with a dark personal history. When given a final chance to prove his suitability for duty, he takes on a dangerous undercover assignment.

New Tricks – 2003 to 2015 - This long-running series focuses on a group of police who come out of retirement to work unsolved cases.

The Night Manager – 2016 - Based on John le Carre's novel focuses on an ex-British soldier recruited to join MI-6 and infiltrate a group of arms dealers.

The Pale Horse - 2020 - This two-part adaptation of Agatha Christie's story by the same name was written and executive produced by Sarah Phelps. Written in 1961, the original story is a creepy tale about what happens after a list of names is found in the shoe of a dead woman.

Paradox – 2009 - This sci-fi police drama focuses on a group of investigators who seek out evidence for crimes that haven't yet occurred.

Picnic at Hanging Rock – *Australia* – 2018 - In the year 1900, three schoolgirls and their governess disappeared. From there, the mystery deepens.

Prey – 2014 to 2015 - Manchester detective Marcus Farrow (played by John Simm) is on the run, accused of a crime and desperate to prove his innocence. All the while, his former friends and colleagues do their best to hunt him down. This series reunites

Philip Glenister and John Simm, who also appeared together in *Life on Mars*.

Prime Suspect: Tennison – 2017 - Set in the 1970s, this series is a prequel to the Helen Mirren classic, Prime Suspect.

River - 2015 - Stellan Skarsgård, Nicola Walker, and Lesley Manville star in this series about a brilliant police officer haunted by guilt.

Rose & Maloney - 2002 to 2005 - Sarah Lancashire and Phil Davis star in this series about two investigators at the fictional Criminal Justice Review Agency. Together, they take on claims of miscarriage of justice, deciding whether old cases should be re-opened.

Scott & Bailey - 2011 to 2016 - Two very different female police detectives enjoy a close friendship and productive partnership.

Second Sight – 2001 - Clive Owen (*Chancer*) stars in this series about an ambitious detective who is slowly but surely losing his sight.

The Secret of Crickley Hall – 2012 - Suranne Jones and Tom Ellis star in this supernatural miniseries about a family that relocates to a grand old estate up north after the disappearance of their young son.

Sherlock Holmes: Incident at Victoria Falls – 1992 - Sherlock Holmes steps out of retirement to help transport a valuable diamond from Africa to London.

Sherlock Holmes and the Leading Lady – 1991 - Sherlock Holmes pauses his retirement to help track down a stolen prototype for a bomb detonator.

Silent Witness - 1996 to present - A team of pathologists investigates crimes based on evidence gleaned from autopsies.

Sirens - 2002 - This two-part miniseries follows DC Jay Pearson (Daniela Nardini) and DI Clive Wilson (Robert Glenister) investigating a serial rapist attacking young women around Islington.

State of Mind - 2003 - After discovering her husband has been unfaithful, Grace takes her son Adam and moves back home with her mother, a busy GP. Niamh Cusack, Rowena Cooper, and Andrew Lincoln star.

Thirteen – 2016 - This BBC Three series centers around a 26-year-old woman who manages to escape from a cellar she's been trapped in for 13 years.

PRIME VIDEO

Tin Star – 2017 to 2019 - A former British detective moves to the Canadian Rockies and fights crime near a massive new oil refinery.

The Tunnel – 2016 to 2018 - This British-French show focuses on two teams of detectives who work together on cross-channel investigations.

Undercover – 2016 - This series tells the story of Maya, a barrister about to become the first black director of public prosecutions as her personal life falls apart.

Unforgotten – 2015 to present - Cassie and Sunny use modern technology to get to the bottom of very cold cases. This recent crime drama is based in London and stars Nicola Walker and Sanjeev Bhaskar as Cassie and Sunny.

Whitechapel - 2009 to 2013 - An inspector, a detective sergeant, and a historical homicide expert look at crimes that may have connections to the Whitechapel district.

White Dragon – 2019 - John Simm stars in this tense mystery about a man who starts to notice highly suspicious things after his wife is killed in a car accident in Hong Kong.

The Widow - 2019 - Kate Beckinsale stars in this drama about a woman who believes herself to be a widow, only to find that her husband did not actually die in a plane crash. While watching a news story on unrest in the Congo, she sees a man who looks like her husband and sets off to figure out what happened.

WPC 56 - 2013 to 2015 - This period crime drama follows Gina Dawson, the first woman police constable in her West Midlands hometown. The first two seasons focus on Gina's struggles to gain acceptance in a male-dominated work environment, while the third season follows her successor at the station.

Young Lions – *Australia* – 2002 - This Australian police drama follows the personal and professional lives of a group of young detective senior constables.

Period Dramas

The A Word - 2016 to present - This drama follows the Hughes family through their son's autism diagnosis and the events that follow it. Christopher Ecclestone (*Doctor Who*) and Morven Christie (*Grantchester*) star alongside child actor Max Vento.

Act of Will - 1989 - This miniseries is based on the Barbara Taylor Bradford novel of the same name, and it's one of Elizabeth Hurley's earliest starring roles. The story follows three generations of women from 1926 up to the 1980s.

Anzac Girls - *Australia* - 2014 - Heroic women rise to the occasion during the World War I.

The Aristocrats – 1999 - This 18th century period drama follows the lives of the Lennox sisters, four aristocratic women hoping to find happiness.

Banished – 2015 - In 1787, Britain sent its unwanted citizens to Australia. This series is about that new society.

Beau Geste – 1982 - Three British brothers join the French Foreign Legion in this 1982 miniseries. Based on the 1924 novel by PC Wren.

Bleak House – 1985 - This adaptation of the classic Dickens novel features Diana Rigg as Lady Honoria Dedlock.

Bramwell – 1995 to 1998 - In 1895, Dr. Eleanor Bramwell does her best to improve public health in Victorian London.

Britannia – 2018 - This US-UK co-production shows the Roman invasion in 43AD Britannia.

The Buccaneers – 1995 - Four American women secure wealthy British husbands, only to find it's not all it's cracked up to be.

Byron - 2003 - Jonny Lee Miller (*Elementary*) stars in this period drama about the life of Lord Byron.

Casualty 1900s: London Hospital - 2006 to 2009 - This medical period drama was inspired by the *Holby City* spinoff *Casualty*, but is otherwise unrelated. It takes place in the receiving room of the London Hospital in London's East End, and each case is based on the writings and memoirs of real doctors and nurses from the time period.

Crime and Punishment – 2002 - John Simm (*Life on Mars*) stars as Raskolnikov in this BBC production of the classic novel.

Daniel Deronda – 2002 - This adaptation of George Eliot's final novel focuses on a Victorian man torn between the love of two women.

Dark Angel – 2017 - Downton Abbey's Joanne Froggatt plays the Victorian poisoner Mary Ann Cotton, a woman who murdered a number of her husbands and children.

David Copperfield – 1986 - Simon Callow makes an appearance in this adaptation of the classic Dickens novel.

David Copperfield – 1999 - Daniel Radcliffe (*Harry Potter*) stars as young David in this adaptation of the Dickens novel.

Desperate Romantics – 2009 - In 1851 London, a group of artists lead colorful lives amidst the chaos of the Industrial Revolution.

Dickensian – 2015 to 2016 - This ambitious miniseries is set in the world of Charles Dickens' novels, bringing together a variety of characters in 19th century London.

Doctor Thorne – 2016 - This series tells the story of penniless Mary Thorne and her relationship with a wealthy family nearby.

Dombey and Son – 1983 - This 1983 Charles Dickens adaptation reminds us that money can't protect you from the heartbreak of life.

Dombey and Son – 2015 - This 2015 miniseries chronicles the life of a man who desperately wants a son.

Downton Abbey - 2010 to 2015 - This period drama follows the lives of the Crawley family and their servants during the early 1900s.

Drovers' Gold – 1997 - In 1843 Wales, an English drover refuses to give a widow a fair price for her cattle, so she sends her son to take the herd to market in London.

The Duchess of Duke Street - 1976 to 1977 - In Victorian London, a young woman learns to cook under a pompous French chef.

The Durrells in Corfu – 2016 to 2019 - This popular British series tells the story of a widow who moves her family out of 1930s England in search of a better life.

Elizabeth I – 2014 - This two-part series focuses on the controversial scandals surrounding Elizabeth I, including alleged lovers and espionage.

Fanny by Gaslight – 1981 - This BBC miniseries is an adaptation of Michael Sadleir's novel of the same name. It tells the story of a young woman who is orphaned in Victorian London, facing great hardship. The story has romance, scandal, prostitution, perversion, and blackmail.

From There to Here – 2014 - In 1996, England took on Scotland at the European Championship. At the same time, three men are caught up in an IRA explosion at a local pub, changing their lives forever.

Great Expectations – 1981 - This is the 1981 BBC adaptation of the classic Dickens novel.

Great Expectations - 1999 - Clive Russell and Charlotte Rampling star in this adaptation of the Dickens classic.

The Great Train Robbery - 2013 - This two-part series tells the story of 1963's Great Train Robbery from two perspectives - the side of the robbers, and the side of the cops. Martin Compston (*Line of Duty*), Luke Evans (*The Girl on the Train*), and Jim Broadbent (*Iris*) star.

Hard Times – 1977 - This adaptation of the Dickens novel contrasts seriousness and materialism against the magic of life.

Hold the Dream - 1986 - This two-part serial is based on Barbara Taylor Bradford's novel of the same name. The story picks up where *A Woman of Substance* left off, with Paula Fairley now in charge of the Harte chain of department stores. Sadly, *A Woman of Substance* is not currently available on any US-based streaming service, but you could always buy the DVD or read the book if you wanted to get everything in order. See also: *To Be the Best*

Home Fires – 2015 to 2017 - In WWII-era Britain, a group of women get by in a small village.

Howards End – 2018 - This miniseries is based on the E.M. Forster novel, and it examines class differences in 1900s England through the lens of three families.

Ivanhoe – 1997 - This is the BBC adaptation of the classic Sir Walter Scott novel.

Jane Eyre – 1983 - This adaptation of Brontë's classic stars Timothy Dalton and Zelah Clarke as Jane and Mr. Rochester.

Jane Eyre – 2006 - Anne Reid, Aidan McArdle, and Andrew Buchan star in this

BBC adaptation of the Charlotte Brontë classic.

King Lear – 2018 - This Prime Original stars Anthony Hopkins as King Lear.

Labyrinth - *Germany/South Africa* - 2012 - This international co-production jumps between modern and medieval France, and includes a cast of mostly British and Irish actors. It follows two women across time in their searches for the Holy Grail.

The Last Post – 2017 - In 1965, British soldiers fight a Yemeni insurgency in British-controlled Aden. This series focuses heavily on the women and children who came with them.

Life in Squares – 2015 - This series dramatizes the lives of those in the Bloomsbury group, a set of influential artists, writers, and intellectuals in England.

Little Dorrit – 2008 - Claire Foy and Matthew Macfayden star in this adaptation of Dickens's story of struggle in 1820s London.

Lorna Doone – 2000 - When a man falls in love with a woman from the same clan that killed his father, he's horrified.

Love in a Cold Climate – 2001 - Between 1929 and 1940, three young women search for love.

Madame Bovary – 2000 - In Flaubert's classic, a woman marries a doctor in hopes of escaping a boring provincial life. It doesn't work.

Mansfield Park - 1983 - Sylvestra Le Touzel stars as Fanny Price in this miniseries adaptation of Jane Austen's third novel. It's about a young woman sent to live with wealthier relatives, who later falls in love with her sensitive cousin.

Martin Chuzzlewit - 1994 - When a wealthy old man nears death, everyone comes out of the woodwork to try to get their piece of his riches. This miniseries is based on the Dickens novel of the same name.

Masterpiece: Indian Summers – 2015 - This drama dives into live in a social club during the final years of British colonial rule of India.

Merlin - 2009 to 2013 - Colin Morgan (*The Fall*) stars as a young Merlin in his days as a mere servant to Prince Arthur of Camelot. In this version, magic is banned and Merlin is forced to keep his talent hidden away.

Middlemarch – 1994 - Robert Hardy, Rufus Sewell, Pam Ferris, and Dame Judi Dench all appear in this adaptation of the classic George Eliot novel.

The Mill - 2013 to 2014 - This period drama is based on the real stories of textile mill workers in 1830s England. Set in Cheshire, it depicts the harsh realities of the Industrial Revolution.

Miss Austen Regrets - 2008 - This feature-length drama is based on Jane Austen's life and collected letters. Olivia Williams (*An Education*) plays Jane Austen.

Moby Dick - 1998 - Sir Patrick Stewart stars as Captain Ahab in this adaptation of Herman Melville's novel.

Moby Dick – 2011 - This British, Australian, and American co-production tells Herman Melville's story of Captain Ahab and the great white whale, Moby Dick.

The Moonstone - 2016 - This updated adaptation of the Wilkie Collins novel stars Joshua Silver as Franklin Blake alongside Terenia Edwards (*On Chesil Beach*) as Rachel Verinder.

My Mother & Other Strangers – 2017 - This period drama is set in 1940s Northern Ireland, documenting the culture clash that occurred when American servicemen were stationed along the Ards Peninsula.

The Nativity - 2010 - Writer Tony Jordan adapts the classic tale of Mary and Joseph and baby Jesus. Peter Capaldi (*Doctor Who*) and Tatiana Maslany (*Orphan Black*) are among the stars.

Neverland – 2011 - In turn-of-the-century London, a couple of pickpockets discover a portal to Neverland.

Oliver Twist – 1985 - This is the 1985 BBC adaptation of the classic Dickens tale with Ben Rodska as Oliver Twist. Keep an eye out for Frank Middlemaas (*As Time Goes By*) and Miriam Margolyes (*Miss Fisher's Murder Mysteries*) as Mr. Brownlow and Mrs. Bumble.

Oliver Twist – 2007 - In this 2007 adaptation of the Dickens classic, we see appearances from Morven Christie, Tom Hardy, and Sarah Lancashire, among others. The story focuses on the difficult life of a young orphan after he's sold into an apprenticeship with an undertaker.

Our Mutual Friend – 1998 - This adaptation of Dickens's last completed novel contrasts money and poverty in Victorian London.

The Paradise - 2012 to 2013 - In this period drama, a young and ambitious woman heads to the city to make her way working in a department store

The Passing Bells – 2014 - This BBC period drama takes place between 1914 and 1918, following two young men, one British and one German, as World War I takes a heavy toll on their lives.

The Pickwick Papers – 1985 - Nigel Stock and Clive Swift star in this adaptation of Dickens' great comic masterpiece.

Pinocchio – 2008 - Robbie Kay plays Pinocchio alongside Bob Hoskins as Geppetto.

Poldark - 1996 - John Bowe (*Prime Suspect*) and Ioan Gruffudd (*Harrow*) star in this feature-length adaptation of the Poldark story.

Poldark – 2015 to 2019 - Ross Poldark returns home to Cornwall after fighting in the American Revolution, only to find his fortune in ruins and the woman he loves promised to another man. Aidan Turner stars in this adaptation of the classic story.

Pride and Prejudice - 1980 - Elizabeth Garvie and David Rintoul star in this television adaptation of Austen's classic.

The Prisoner of Zenda – 1984 - An Englishman poses as Ruritania's monarch when the real king is abducted.

The Rainbow - 1988 - This three-part series is an adaptation of D.H. Lawrence's novel about a young woman emerging into adulthood. The story's frank treatment of sexual desire and same-sex relations caused it to be banned in Britain for 11 years.

Robin Hood – 2006 - After fighting in the Crusades, Robin Hood returns home to find a corrupt, changed Nottingham.

Robin of Sherwood - 1984 to 1986 - This period adventure has been described by historian Stephen Knight as "the most innovative and influential version of the myth in recent times". Though originally advertised as "family friendly", some conservative groups argued that there was too much violence for children.

Room at the Top - 2012 - Taking the BAFTA award for best miniseries in 2013, this series is an adaptation of John Braine's

1957 novel of the same name. It follows a young man making his way in post-WWII England, forced to choose between stability and true love.

Sense and Sensibility – 2008 - This BBC production is based on the Jane Austen novel of the same name.

Sense and Sensibility – 1981 - This BBC production is based on the Jane Austen novel of the same name.

Sinbad – 2012 - This BBC production tells the story of Sinbad, a man whose life falls apart after he unintentionally kills a man.

Small Axe - 2020 - This period drama is set in London's West Indian community between the 1960s and '80s, telling five stories in a six-part anthology format. It starts in 1968 with the story of a small restaurant, The Mangrove, opening in Ladbroke Grove. Over time, it becomes an epicenter of resistance in the community.

Spies of Warsaw - 2013 - David Tennant stars in this story set across three European cities ahead of World War II. The series is based on Alan Furst's spy novel of the same name.

A Tale of Two Cities - 1980 - Paul Shelley and Ralph Michael star in this classic Dickens story of love and sacrifice amidst the French Revolution.

The Talisman – 1980 - Based on the story by Sir Walter Scott, this miniseries tells the story of a brave Scottish knight who foils Richard the Lionheart's assassins during the Crusades.

The Tenant of Wildfell Hall – 1996 - In a remote Yorkshire village, a widow and her son move into the creepy, crumbling Wildfell Hall. Based on the classic story by Anne Brontë.

Tess of the D'Urbervilles - 2008 - In this miniseries based on the Thomas Hardy work, Tess Durbeyfield is a poor country girl with connections to nobility.

To Be the Best - 1992 - This is the third and final entry into the Barbara Taylor Bradford trilogy that begins with *A Woman of Substance* and *Hold the Dream*. It follows Paula O'Neill as she fights with her family in hopes of saving her grandmother's business and legacy.

Tom Jones – 1997 - In Georgian England, Tom Jones finds no shortage of trouble or romance.

United – 2011 - David Tennant stars in this sports period drama about the 1958 Munich air crash that claimed 8 of Manchester United's members.

Vanity Fair – 1987 - This adaptation of Thackeray's Napoleonic War-era tale starred Eve Matheson, Rebecca Saire, James Saxon, and Simon Dormandy in the lead roles.

Vanity Fair – 1998 - This BBC adaptation of Thackeray's novel featured a screenplay by Andrew Davies, with Natasha Little in the role of Becky Sharp.

Vanity Fair – 2018 - This ITV production of Thackeray's classic includes performances by Michael Palin, Olivia Cooke, Tom Bateman, Suranne Jones, and Martin Clunes.

A Very English Scandal – 2018 - Hugh Grant stars as the first British politician to stand trial for conspiracy to murder.

Victoria - 2016 to present - This series stars Jenna Coleman (Doctor Who) as Victoria and Tom Hughes (*The Game*) as Prince Albert, along with Peter Bowles (*To the Manor Born, Executive Stress*) as the Duke of Wellington. Much like *The Crown* is to Queen Elizabeth II, *Victoria* follows Queen Victoria as she progresses through her lengthy reign.

The Way We Live Now - 2001 - Based on Anthony Trollope's novel, this miniseries tells a Victorian tale of power, corruption, love, greed, and progress. It features appearances by Matthew Macfadyen, Cillian Murphy, Rob Brydon, Jim Carter, David Suchet, and more.

Women in Love – 2011 - Rosamund Pike and Rachael Stirling star in this adaptation of DH Lawrence's classic novel. It was originally written as a sequel to *The Rainbow*.

Other Dramas

Always Greener – *Australia* – 2001 to 2003 - This dramedy tells the story of two families who joke about swapping places, then actually do it. The series takes place in rural Inverness and suburban Sydney.

The Ambassador - 1998 - Pauline Collins stars as Ambassador Harriet Smith, British ambassador to Ireland. She's under constant pressure from all angles, and she struggles with guilt about her husband's death from a car bomb meant for her.

Banana – 2015 - This Channel 4 miniseries follows eight gay couples through a variety of relationship dramas.

Bed of Roses - *Australia* - 2008 to 2011 - A mother and daughter struggle after the death of their husband and father.

Being Erica – *Canada* – 2009 to 2011 - A young woman participates in a strange form of therapy that involves time travel.

Big Sky – *Australia* – 1997 to 1999 - This soap-y drama follows the employees at Big Sky Aviation as they form friendships and fly high over the Australian landscape.

Bodies - 2004 to 2006 - Created by Jed Mercurio (*Line of Duty*), this medical drama draws on his experiences in medicine, offering a more gritty and realistic portrayal than many hospital dramas.

Care - 2018 - Sheridan Smith (*Gavin & Stacey*) stars as a single mother struggling to raise her two children. After her husband's departure, she's fully reliant on the childcare her mother Mary (Alison Steadman, also from *Gavin & Stacey*) provides. That all changes when Mary has a stroke and develops dementia.

Clink - 2019 - This drama is set in the fictional BPS Bridewell women's prison, and focuses on the women who live there, and the woman who runs the place. Many have compared it to British prison series Bad Girls, and at least one cast member, Alicya Eyo (who plays new Governor Dominique Darby), was also in Bad Girls.

Cucumber - 2015 - This series offers a peek inside the lives of gay men in modern Manchester.

The Deep - 2010 - James Nesbitt (*Cold Feet*) and Minnie Driver (*Good Will Hunting*) star in this series about oceanographers who become stranded in the Arctic while looking for new forms of life below the ice.

Doctor Finlay - 1993 to 1996 - After WW2 and before the NHS is created, a doctor returns to his Scottish hometown.

The Driver - 2015 - This Manchester-based crime drama sees a man's life turned upside-down after he agrees to an illegal driving job. David Morrissey (*Thorne*) stars.

The Fades – 2011 - A young man is haunted by dreams he can't explain, and he begins to see spirits around him – some of them malicious.

Flack - 2019 to Present - A PR executive specializes in cleaning up after her selfish clients in London. Anna Paquin stars.

Foreign Exchange – *Australia/Ireland* – 2004 - When two children from Ireland and Australia discover a portal between the two countries, they're able to travel between the two countries.

Fortitude - 2015 - At the edge of the Arctic Circle, Fortitude has never had a history of violent crime - until a member of the community is found eviscerated in his home. Richard Dormer (*Rellik*), Michael Gambon (*Maigret*), and Ken Stott (*Rebus*) are among the cast.

The Fragile Heart - 1996 - Nigel Hawthorne (*Yes Minister*) stars as a brilliant and successful surgeon whose work heading a medical delegation in China forces him into a serious ethical dilemma.

Good Omens – 2019 - David Tennant and Michael Sheen star in this adaptation of Neil Gaiman and Terry Pratchett's novel by the same name. In it, two angels have grown quite fond of the human world, and they plan to do everything in their power to stop it from ending.

The Hitchhiker's Guide to the Galaxy - 1981 - Arthur Dent is one of the last surviving members of the human race. Still in his dressing gown, he's dragged through an intergalactic portal and sent on an adventure through the universe. Based on the Douglas Adams novel.

Home & Away – *Australia* – 1988 to 1989 - This soap opera follows the residents of Summer Bay, a coastal town near Sydney in Australia.

Humans – 2015 to 2018 - In a parallel modern world, everyone has a robotic servant.

Honest - 2008 - This short-lived family drama follows a woman who tries to turn her criminal family straight after her husband is sent down for robbery. Amanda Redman (*Good Karma Hospital*) stars.

Hustle - 2004 to 2012 - This series follows a group of talented con artists who prefer to operate long cons on the greedy and corrupt of London.

The Indian Doctor - 2010 to 2013 - An Indian doctor and his wife move to a small Welsh mining village during the 1960s. They have to adjust to culture shock, and Dr. Sharma must win the trust of the locals.

In the Flesh – 2013 to 2014 - After a zombie war, scientists work to cure and rehabilitate ex-zombies.

The Invisibles - 2008 - A couple of retired master burglars tried living in Spain, but after a bout of homesickness, they returned to England with their wives to live in a Devon fishing village. It's not long before a return to familiar shores sees them taking up the same old bad habits.

Jim Henson's The Storyteller - 1987 to 1988 - This British live-action and puppet series re-told a number of European fairy tales using actors and puppets. Sir John Hurt acted as the old storyteller.

Murder Call – *Australia* – 1997 to 2000 - This fun late 90s mystery series mixes action, suspense, mystery, comedy, and a bit of romance.

NY-LON - 2004 - This drama follows a transatlantic romance between New York record shop worker Edie (Rashida Jones) and London stock broker Michael (Stephen Moyer). Filming took place in both cities.

Our Girl – 2014 to 2020 - This series follows a girl who gets drunk on her 18th birthday, vomiting in the doorway of an army recruitment office. Drawn to the office, she joins up as an army medic.

The Prisoner –1967 - Patrick McGoohan stars in this surprisingly well-aged series about a secret agent who's abducted and taken to a mysterious prison dressed up as an idyllic seaside village.

Prisoners' Wives – 2012 to 2013 - This series takes a look at the women involved with men who've been sent to prison.

Proof - *Ireland* - 2004 to 2005 - Orla Brady (*The South Westerlies*) stars alongside Finbar Lynch (*Mind Games*) in this thriller about human smuggling and corrupt European politicians and financiers.

Public Enemies – 2012 - Released from prison after a 10-year sentence for murder, a man attempts to adjust to life on the outside. Anna Friel and Daniel Mays star.

QB VII - 1974 - Sir Anthony Hopkins stars as a physician who sues a novelist for implying he was a doctor involved in Nazi war crimes.

Queer as Folk - 1999 to 2000 - This groundbreaking British series follows a group of young gay men in Manchester.

Rake - *Australia* - 2011 to 2018 - Defense lawyer Cleaver Greene makes a career out of hopeless cases, perhaps because his own personal life is troubled enough to help him relate.

Red Rock – *Ireland* – 2015 to 2020 - Two feuding families battle it out in this Irish soap.

Republic of Doyle – *Canada* – 2010 to 2014 - Jake Doyle and his father Malachy work together as private investigators with a lot of rough edges. Even if it doesn't sound like your kind of show, you might love it for the scenery.

The Royals - *United States* - 2015 to 2108 - Though American, this prime-time soap stars Elizabeth Hurley and a largely British cast. It tells the story of a fictional British royal family and their power struggles.

Run - 2013 - Olivia Colman and Lennie James star in this four-part miniseries about four seemingly unconnected people whose lives intersect after a random act of violence.

The Secret Life of Michael Fry - 2000 - This quirky drama takes place in a Welsh seaside town, and it sees a new councilman getting mixed up in corruption and strange internet sex things.

The Secret Life of Us – *Australia* – 2001 to 2006 - In an apartment block near Melbourne, residents navigate life's challenges with the help of their friends.

Secret State – 2012 – In a miniseries that will reassure you that the US isn't the only place where government and big business are way too close, Secret State shows a Deputy Prime Minister entangled in an international conspiracy.

Seesaw - 1998 - David Suchet (*Poirot*) and Geraldine James (*Back to Life*) star in this series about what happens in the aftermath of a kidnapping when ransom has been paid and the loved one is returned home.

Silk – 2011 to 2014 - This series focuses on the challenges modern-day barristers face in their careers.

The Smoke – 2014 - When a fire fighter is badly injured on the job, he spends nearly a year in recovery. On return, he realises he may not be quite as ready as he thinks.

Spirit Breaker - 2018 - Dave (Liam Noble, *Peep Show*) wants nothing more than to spend all his time in the pub, and he's not going to let anyone get in the way of his goal. Produced by Dan Summers (*MumDem*), this series never made it beyond the pilot.

Spirited - *Australia* - 2010 to 2011 - This supernatural dramedy stars Claudia Karvan (*Love My Way*) as dentist Suzy, a woman who leaves a loveless marriage and moves into an apartment inhabited by Henry, the ghost of an English rock star from the 1980s.

The Time of Our Lives - *Australia* - 2013 to 2014 - This drama follows the lives of an extended family in inner-city Melbourne as they build families, pursue careers, and work on their relationships.

Train 48 – *Canada* – 2003 to 2005 - This Canadian drama takes place on a Toronto commuter train, and the format was based on a similar Australian series called *Going Home*.

Undeniable - 2014 - This two-part thriller follows the story of a murderer brought to justice by the woman who saw him killing her mother many years earlier.

Comedies

Absolutely Fabulous - 1992 to 2012 - In this groundbreaking classic, two wild women do everything but act their age. The series was based on a sketch comedy called "Modern Mother and Daughter" by Dawn French (*Vicar of Dibley*) and Jennifer Saunders (Edina Monsoon in *Absolutely Fabulous*). Joanna Lumley stars alongside Saunders as Patsy Stone, and Julia Sawalha plays Edina's daughter Saffron.

After Hours – 2019 - Ardal O'Hanlon appears in this family comedy about a young man named Willow living in Northern England and feeling pretty low about his achievement level in comparison to his friends. Meanwhile, his dad is struggling to find work. Life changes when he meets two new friends who host a popular internet radio show.

'Allo 'Allo - 1982 to 1992 - This classic British comedy is set in a French café during WWII.

A Touch of Cloth - 2012 to 2014 - This series is part mystery, part comedy, and definitely not for the faint of heart or easily offended. John Hannah and Suranne Jones play two detectives in a very unusual police department. The name of the series is based on the euphemism "touching cloth". It is a state of needing to defecate so badly that one's feces begins to protrude and "touch cloth".

A Bit of Fry & Laurie - 1987 to 1989 - This sketch show is an important piece of British comedy history, and it was responsible for turning Stephen Fry (*Kingdom*) and Hugh Laurie (*House*) into household names.

A Very British Coup - 1988 - When a radical Labour Party politician becomes Prime Minister, he quickly finds he has a lot of enemies.

Blackadder - 1983 to 1989 - Rowan Atkinson stars as antihero Edmund Blackadder, accompanied by Sir Tony Robinson as his sidekick Baldrick. Each series of this quirky comedy is set in a different period within British history, and Edmund carries different titles throughout. The "essence" of each character remains largely the same in each series, though.

The Bleak Old Shop of Stuff - 2012 - As proprietor of The Old Shop of Stuff, Jedrington Secret-Past sells all manner of unusual items. Unfortunately, Malifax Skulkingworm wants to make his life miserable. Robert Webb (*Peep Show*), Stephen Fry (*Kingdom*), and Katherine Parkison (*The IT Crowd*) star.

The Book Group - 2002 to 2003 - When an American woman moves to Glasgow, she starts a book group to make friends.

Bottom - 1991 to 1995 - Adrian Edmondson and Rik Mayall (both of The Young Ones) star in this quirky sitcom about a couple of largely unpleasant flatmates in Hammersmith, London. They spend much of their time pretending to be aristocrats and trying to get women to go to bed with them.

Catastophe – 2015 to present - This Prime Original tells the story of an unintended pregnancy between an American ad man and a British teacher.

Coupling – 2000 to 2004 - Six young adults in London navigate the work, love, and the transition into responsible adulthood. Many have called this "the British Friends".

Crackanory - 2013 to 2017 - Inspired by the children's series Jackanory, this series brings the same quirky style of storytelling to adults. Episodes include performances from popular British comedians like Sally Phillips (*Miranda*), Stephen Mangan (*Hang Ups*), Ben Miller (*Death in Paradise*), Sharon Horgan (*Catastrophe*), and Katherine Parkinson (*Doc Martin*).

Dead Boss – 2012 - Helen Stephens has been wrongly convicted of killing her boss, and while she hopes she'll be cleared soon, everyone she knows wants her in prison.

Fix Her Up – *Australia* – 2018 - In an all-female office, four women work towards love, happiness, and career success.

Fleabag – 2016 to 2019 - Phoebe Waller-Bridge stars as Fleabag, a comically troubled young woman who's experienced a great personal tragedy.

Fresh Meat – 2011 to 2016 - Six young friends go off to university.

Friday Night Dinner – 2001 to present - Each Friday night, a Jewish British family meets for dinner. It never goes smoothly (and it always includes a visit from eccentric neighbour Jim).

Fungus the Bogeyman - 2015 - Based on the 1977 Raymond Briggs picture book, this series follows Fungus, a working class bogeyman whose job is to scare humans.

Gavin & Stacey - 2007 to 2019 - After months of chatting, Gavin and Stacey leave their homes in Essex and Wales to meet for the first time in London. This much-loved comedy classic features a number of British acting favourites including Larry Lamb, Ruth Jones, Alison Steadman, Rob Brydon, and James Corden.

Getting On - 2009 to 2012 - This dark comedy follows the residents and staff in a geriatric ward.

PRIME VIDEO

The Goes Wrong Show - 2019 - This sitcom follows an amateur dramatic society as they perform a variety of short plays in which everything that can go wrong, does go wrong.

High Times - 2008 - Set in a Glasgow tower block, this sitcom follows Rab and Jake and their oddball neighbours. Be warned, Amazon only has the second series.

The House of Cards Trilogy - 1990 to 1995 - This sitcom is Andrew Davies' adaptation of Michael Dobbs' novels about greed, ambition, and British politics. It follows Frances Urquhart, an evil but charismatic man who will stop at nothing in the pursuit of power. An American adaptation was later made under the same name.

Hunderby – 2012 to 2015 - Julia Davis stars in this dark period comedy about a woman who washes ashore after a shipwreck off the English coast.

Hyperdrive - 2006 to 2007 - Nick Frost and Miranda Hart are among the stars of this sci-fi sitcom about the crew of HMS Camden Lock as they attempt to protect Britain's interests throughout the galaxy.

The Inbetweeners – 2008 to 2010 - This raunchy teen comedy focuses on a group of young men who aren't quite as cool as they'd like to be.

I've Got a Job for You Gav - 2020 - Gav is a middle-aged taxi driver from Newcastle whose life is going nowhere - but at least his passengers are interesting. Comedian Gavin Webster stars.

The Kennedys – 2015 - Katherine Parkinson (*The IT Crowd*) stars in this comedy about a family moving from a housing estate to a home, eager to move up the social ladder.

Kingdom - 2007 to 2009 - Stephen Fry (*QI*) stars as a country solicitor in the small town of Market Shipborough. Working with his trusty secretary Gloria and reasonably capable assistant Lyle, it should be a peaceful life. The only problem? He has a crazy sister and he recently lost his half-brother in mysterious circumstances. Hermione Norris (*Cold Feet*) and Celia Imrie (*Bergerac*) also star.

King Gary - 2020 - Gary and Terri King are childhood sweethearts living in suburban East London. Though he's a grown man with his own family, Gary is constantly trying to get out of his father's shadow.

Last Contact – 2014 - This low budget Sussex-based production concerns a team of university researchers seeking out novel ways to communicate with aliens.

Little Devil - 2007 - When his parents won't stop arguing, a little boy decides to try being as good as possible. When that doesn't work, he takes a different approach.

Love & Marriage - 2013 - Alison Steadman (*Gavin & Stacey*) stars in this series about a woman who's had enough of her own family and moves in with her unconventional sister.

The Mighty Boosh – 2003 to 2007 - Two young musicians work for a madman at a zoo.

Moone Boy – 2012 to 2014 - A young boy copes with life in a small Irish town, thanks to his imaginary friend.

Mr. Bean - 1992 to 1995 - Bumbling Mr. Bean rarely speaks and has some very peculiar ways of doing things, but it usually works out for him. Rowan Atkinson (*Maigret*) stars as the iconic character.

The Office - 2001 to 2003 - Before there was Michael Scott in the US, there was David Brent in Slough, England. Written by Ricky Gervais (*After Life*) and Stephen Merchant (*Hello Ladies*), this mockumentary-style programme takes place in the office of the fictional Wernham Hogg paper company. Mackenzie Crook (*Detectorists*) and Martin Freeman (*Sherlock*) are also among the stars.

Outnumbered - 2007 to 2014 - Hugh Dennis and Claire Skinner star in this sitcom about a couple who are outnumbered by their three children.

Pramface – 2012 to 2013 - In Edinburgh, a young woman sleeps with an even younger man and finds herself pregnant.

Peep Show – 2003 to 2015 - Two dysfunctional and very different friends share a flat in London and attempt (rather poorly) to grow up.

People Like Us - 1999 - Chris Langham stars as Roy Mallard, a fictional interviewer who probably shouldn't be allowed out of the house.

Plus One - 2009 - When a man is invited to his ex-girlfriend's wedding to a pop star, he needs a plus one. Miranda Raison (*Silks*) and Daniel Mays (*Good Omens*) star.

Pompidou – 2015 - This unusual Matt Lucas comedy sees a down-on-his-luck aristocrat living in a caravan outside his crumbling estate, with only his faithful butler and dog to keep him company.

Porterhouse Blue - 1987 - This British comedy classic takes place at the fictional Porterhouse College at Cambridge, where everyone is rich and male and stuck in the past. When the old headmaster dies and a new one comes to power, he attempts to make changes.

Reggie Perrin - 2009 to 2010 - Martin Clunes stars in this remake of the classic Reginald Perrin stories.

The Royle Family - 1998 to 2012 - This sitcom features a scruffy, argumentative, telly-obsessed family in Manchester. Ralf Little (*Death in Paradise*) is among its stars.

Some Girls - 2012 to 2014 - This sitcom follows a group of teenage girls who live on the same inner city housing estate.

Spitting Image - 2020 - Based on the 1984 series of the same name, this controversial series revives the old format by creating puppet caricatures of contemporary celebrities and public figures.

Still Standing – *Canada* – Comedian Jonny Harris embarks on a road trip around Canada, finding the humor in small and remote towns.

Terry Pratchett's Going Postal - 2010 - This adaptation of Pratchett's novel sees con man Moist von Lipwig (Richard Coyle, *Chilling Adventures of Sabrina*) caught by the law and given two choices: suffer a painful death, or take over a derelict post office. Also starring David Suchet (*Poirot*), Charles Dance (*Game of Thrones*), and Claire Foy (*The Crown*).

The Thick of It – 2005 to 2012 - This political satire takes place among the team at the Department of Social Affairs and Citizenship, where everything seems to be one giant farce.

Threesome – 2011 - A straight couple and their gay friend live together happily until one sordid night changes their lives forever. Amy Huberman (*Finding Joy*) stars.

Trivia - *Ireland* - 2011 to 2012 - A highly-dedicated quiz team leader in Ireland knows everything but how to deal with other people.

Truth Seekers - 2020 - Simon Pegg (*Shaun of the Dead*) and Nick Frost (*Hot Fuzz*) star in this comedy series about internet installers who moonlight as part-time paranormal investigators. Using homemade gadgets to track ghosts, their haunted adventures get increasingly terrifying as they're drawn further into the supernatural world.

Uncle - 2014 to 2017 - Nick Helm stars as Andy, a 30-something slacker who's left to care for his nephew in spite of the fact that he's utterly unsuited to the task.

Warren – 2019 - In this offbeat Lancashire-based comedy, Martin Clunes (*Doc Martin*) stars as an impatient and unsuccessful driving instructor who has recently moved in with his partner and her teenage sons. Unfortunately, it wasn't renewed for a second series.

Westside – *New Zealand* – 2015 to 2017 - This prequel to Outrageous Fortune is set between 1974 and 1979, and it recounts stories of crime and passion in Auckland.

Would I Lie to You? - 2007 to present - Rob Brydon (*Gavin & Stacey*) hosts this game show in which he and team captains David Mitchell and Lee Mack must figure out whether the celebrity guests are lying to them.

You, Me, & Them - 2013 to 2015 - Anthony Head and Eve Myles star in this sitcom about an age gap romance.

British History & Culture

Alexandria: The Greatest City - 2016 - Historian Bettany Hughes explores the one-grand city of Alexandria, founded by Alexander the Great and home to Cleopatra.

Ancient Egypt - Life and Death in the Valley of the Kings - 2013 - This documentary tells the story of the everyday lives of ancient Egyptians.

The Auction House – 2014 - Roger Allam appears in this docu-series about the eccentrics that populate the world of British auction houses.

A World Without Down's Syndrome - 2016 - British comedian Sally Phillips (*Miranda*) presents this series about the emotionally-charged debate surrounding Down's Syndrome and pregnancy termination.

Battle Castle - 2012 - Historian Dan Snow tells the stories of six famous castles with military significance.

Bear Grylls: Survival School - 2016 - Adventurer Bear Grylls takes a group of kids out to test their outdoor skills and teach them more about survival.

Bomber Boys – 2005 - This PBS-aired documentary series intersperses modern upcoming "bomber boys" with World War II history and footage.

Britain AD: King Arthur's Britain - 2004 - Francis Pryor takes a look at British history including Roman times, the Dark Ages, and the invasion of the Anglo-Saxons.

Britain's Real Monarch - 2003 - Sir Tony Robinson takes a look at compelling new evidence that Kind Edward IV may have been illegitimate - and what that would mean for today's monarchy.

British Bouncers – 2013 - This isn't quite a travel show, but if you want to shatter all your posh illusions about Britain, this show about drunken Brits going up against bouncers might be just the thing.

Castle Builders – 2015 - This series takes a look at what was involved in building the great castles of Europe.

Castles and Palaces of Europe - 2013 - Take a closer look at castles in Italy, France, Germany, Portugal, and Southern England.

Chatsworth – 2008 - Explore this stately home in a one-hour video tour.

Civil War - 2002 - Dr. Tristram Hunt takes a look at the conflict that briefly toppled the English monarchy back in the 17th century.

The Cops - 2018 - Follow British cops equipped with body cams as they keep peace in Great Britain.

Cut from a Different Cloth – 2019 - This series takes a look behind the scenes at British fashion company Superdry as they attempt to launch a high-end men's collection with Idris Elba.

Dangerous Roads - 2011 to 2012 - This BBC series takes a look at some of the most challenging and dangerous roads in the world.

David Jason's Secret Service - 2017 - Sir David Jason hosts this fascinating docuseries about Britain's history of espionage.

David Suchet: In the Footsteps of St. Peter - 2014 - David Suchet (Poirot) hosts this series in which he attempts to learn more about the life of St. Peter. It's divided into two parts, with both available on Amazon Prime at time of print.

Dinosaur Britain - 2015 - Presenter Ellie Harrison and archaeologist Dean Lomax share information about the dinosaurs that once roamed Great Britain.

The Doctors - 2020 - This series offers hours of interviews with people involved in the making of *Doctor Who*.

Doctor Who: Tales Lost in Time - 2011 - Cast and crew members take a look back at the Doctor Who series and some of its untold stories. The programme includes interviews with David Tennant, Peter Davison, Russell T. Davies, and many more.

Emergency Firefighters – 2005 - This series takes a look at the intense, demanding situations encountered by the Avon Fire and Rescue Service.

Empire: The Soul of Britannia - 2012 - Jeremy Paxman hosts this BBC series about the worldwide cultural impact of the British Empire.

Feathers & Toast - 2014 to 2018 - This comedy cooking show sees Mhairi

Morrison playing the quirky, slightly delusional chef Tallulah Grace.

The First Silent Night – 2014 - Actor Simon Callow uncovers the origins of the song Silent Night.

The Force: Manchester - 2015 - This reality series gives us a look inside the work being done by the Greater Manchester Police.

Gadget Man - 2012 to 2015 - Actors Stephen Fry (Series 1) and Richard Ayoade (Series 2-4) take a look at innovative products designed to make our lives easier. Note that Series 1 is listed entirely separate from Series 2-4, but at time of print, both are available on Prime Video.

The Grand Tour – 2017 to 2019 - Jeremy Clarkson, Richard Hammond, and James May roam around and drive unique, luxurious, and exotic automobiles.

The Great British Benefits Handout – 2016 to 2017 - One of the problems with benefits systems is that they pay out tiny amounts over a long time, making it hard for recipients to get ahead or invest in themselves to get out of the mess. As a social experiment, this show offers benefits recipients the opportunity to quit benefits and receive a year's worth of payments in one lump sum. It follows as they invest in themselves and their new businesses.

Great Cars: British Elegance - 2018 - Each episode of this series focuses on a different British car - Aston Martin, Bentley, Jaguar, Land Rover, Lotus, MG, Mini, Morgan, and Rolls Royce.

The Green Park - 2015 - Learn the story behind the glamorous kosher hotel opened in 1943 on the British Riviera.

The Gypsy Matchmaker - 2014 - Follow two British Roma families as they continue in the tradition of early teenage marriage.

Hadrian's Wall: Antonine Wall - 2006 - Take a look at Rome's northernmost borders from their time in Britain.

The Harbour: Aberdeen – 2013 to 2015 - This documentary-style show explores the history and modern reality of Aberdeen Harbour, a busy industrial harbour along the Northeastern coast of Scotland.

Helicopter ER - 2017 - This series follows the doctors and paramedics of the Yorkshire Air Ambulance.

Helicopter Search & Rescue – *Ireland* – 2016 - Watch real-life rescues by some of Ireland's most important rescue services – the Irish Coast Guard, the RNLI, Mountain Rescue Teams, Cork Fire Brigade, and the Irish Naval Services.

Horrible Histories – 2009 to present - While designed for children, this amusing educational program is every bit as entertaining for adults. The sketches cover different parts of history, but always with a dramatic or funny take on the event.

The Hotel Fixers – *Ireland* – 2017 - Hotel experts travel around Ireland and help struggling establishments.

Huge Moves - 2005 - This reality series shows us how truly enormous moves are handled. From moving fleets of mega yachts to Egyptian temples, the stakes are high and the risks are as big as the items being transported.

Inside the Merchant – 2016 - This series takes a behind-the-scenes look at the Merchant Hotel in Belfast, Northern Ireland.

In Toni's Footsteps: The Channel Islands Occupation - 2002 - This documentary takes a look at life in the Channel Islands during the Nazi occupation of WWII.

Iron Men - 2017 - This football documentary follows West Ham United as they bid farewell to Boleyn Ground after 112 years.

The Island with Bear Grylls - 2014 - Adventurer Bear Grylls puts 13 British men and women on an island to see if they can survive for 6 weeks.

James May: Oh Cook - 2020 - Non-chef James May gives cooking a try, learning to cook dishes that relatively normal people can replicate.

James May's Cars of the People - 2014 to 2016 - James May takes a look at different cars and the roles they've played in the lives of ordinary people.

James May's Man Lab – 2010 to 2013 - James May sets out to teach modern men a few useful skills.

James May's Toy Stories – 2009 to 2014 - James May sets out on a mission to get kids away from screens and back to classic toys.

Keys to the Castle - 2014 - After four decades in their beloved Scottish castle, a couple prepares to downsize.

Know the British - 1973 - This hilarious short film was meant to educate American businessmen on the unusual habits and customs of the Brits.

Living in the Shadow of World War II - 2017 - World War II affected more than just the people on the battlefield. Back home, the war cast a shadow over nearly every aspect of day-to-day life. This series takes a look at the ways the war affected people on the homefront.

The Machine That Made Us - 2008 - Stephen Fry takes us along as he learns more about the printing press at its inventor, Johann Gutenberg.

Magic Numbers: Hannah Fry's Mysterious World of Maths - 2018 - Hannah Fry examines where math came from.

Most Haunted - 2002 to present - Yvette Fielding leads this paranormal investigation series set in the British Isles.

Mysteries of Stonehenge - 2002 - Given recent discoveries, this will surely seem a bit dated - but it offers some lovely footage and history about Stonehenge.

The Nile: 5000 Years of History - 2018 - Historian Bettany Hughes takes us on a 900-mile adventure along the River Nile, sharing history and landmarks as she goes.

The Nurse – 2013 - This series takes a look at district nurses who travel around the UK, caring for patients at home.

The Only Way is Essex – 2010 to present - This reality series follows a group of young and "socially ambitious" individuals living in Essex.

Pawnbrokers - 2010 - Take a look inside Uncles, a crazy British pawn shop that's been in business for three generations.

The Petrol Age - 2012 - Actor Paul McGann takes a look at the history of Britain's classic cars.

Rachel Allen: All Things Sweet - *Ireland* - 2017 - Irish celebrity chef conquers the perfect desserts for a variety of everyday occasions.

Rachel Allen's Cake Diaries - 2012 - Chef Rachel Allen offers tips for cakes of all types.

Rachel Allen's Easy Meals - 2011 - *Ireland* - 2011 - Irish chef Rachel Allen focuses on meals anyone can replicate in their homes.

Rachel Allen's Everyday Kitchen - 2013 - Rachel Allen conquers simple but delicious meals that are perfect for normal daily life.

Return of the Black Death - 2014 - In this BBC documentary, scientists take a look at skeletons recently unearthed in a long-lost plague cemetery below London.

Roman Britain: From the Air - 2014 - Christine Bleakley and Dr. Michael Scott check out remnants of Roman Britain that can be seen more clearly from the air than the ground.

Rome: Empire Without Limit - 2016 - Professor Mary Beard offers her take on the Roman Empire.

A Royal Hangover – 2015 - This series takes a look at British drinking culture and binge drinking.

Salt Beef and Rye – 2016 - This fun documentary looks at the characters who frequent London's Brick Lane.

Scotch! The Story of Whisky – 2015 - This short series takes a look at the history and science of the Scottish whisky industry.

Sean Bean on Waterloo - 2015 - On the 200th anniversary of Waterloo, actor Sean Bean shares the story of one of history's bloodiest battles.

Secrets of the Castle - 2014 - Historians and archaeologists learn how to build a castle using medieval-era techniques and tools. Their building experiment is meant to take 25 years to complete.

Secrets of the Magna Carta - 2017 - Hugh Bonneville (*Downton Abbey*) narrates this look at the history of the Magna Carta.

Sex Pistols: Agents of Anarchy - 2019 - This documentary traces the path the Sex Pistols took to go from agents of anarchy to national treasures.

Sharon Horgan's Women - 2012 - Sharon Horgan (*Catastrophe*) takes a look at what it takes to be a good mum, handle a midlife crisis, and maintain a solid marriage in the 21st century.

The Spy Who Went Into the Cold - 2013 - At the height of the Cold War in 1963, Kim Philby defected to Moscow after 30 years in senior positions in British intelligence offices. This documentary looks back at the scandal.

The Story of Europe - 2017 - Cambridge historian Sir Christopher Clark takes us on an engaging walk through the history of Europe.

The Story of the Mini - 2004 - Take a look at the history of the Mini, and how it came to be one of the most-loved cars ever made.

The Story of Women and Power - 2015 - Historian Amanda Vickery takes us on a tour of the 300-year battle for women's equality in Britain.

The Scottish Covenanters – 1998 - If you enjoy 17th century Scottish history, you'll love this 54-minute program.

Scottish Myths and Legends - 2007 - From the Loch Ness monster to the shape-shifting kelpies, this programme takes a look at the legends of Scotland.

Stephen Fry: More Fool Me - 2014 - After the publication of his book More Fool Me, Stephen Fry spoke to a sold-out audience at London's Royal Festival Hall. Here, you can watch him recount tales of his younger, wilder years.

A Stitch in Time – 2016 - Amber Butchart takes a look at historical figures through the clothing they wore.

Surgeons: At the Edge of Life - 2018 to 2020 - Using behind-the-scenes access at the Queen Elizabeth Hospital Birmingham, this series takes a look at the incredible work being done by some of the UK's finest surgeons.

Time Team - 1994 to 2014 - A group of archaeologists travel around Britain working on different excavation sites.

Treasure Houses of Britain – 2011 - This series travels around Britain, exploring the history and architecture of some of the island's greatest estates.

Tudor Monastery Farm at Christmas – 2013 - Historians and archaeologists look at how the Tudors celebrated the 12 days of Christmas. See also: *Tudor Monastery Farm Christmas*

Art & Art History

Churchill: Blood Sweat, & Oil Paint - 1970 - Hosted by Andrew Marr, this BBC special tells the fascinating story of Winston Churchill's lifelong love of painting. He meets Churchill's descendants and explores the connections between his private passion for painting and his public career as politician and statesman.

Dark Ages: An Age of Light - 2012 - Art historian Waldemar Januszczak travels the world to show us art that proves the Dark Ages were a time of great creative achievement.

Exhibition on Screen: History's Greatest Painters – 2013 to 2016 - British documentarian Phil Grabsky produces cinematic immersions in great works of art, many filmed in conjunction with galleries like London's National Gallery and the Royal Academy of Arts.

Gauguin: The Full Story - 2003 - British art historian Waldemar Januszczak takes a look at the life and work of Paul Gauguin.

Great Artists with Tim Marlow – 2001 to 2003 - British art historian Tim Marlow travels around the world, taking a closer look at some of its greatest artworks.

Holbein: Eye of the Tudors – 2015 - British art historian Waldemar Januszczak looks at how Hans Holbein recorded the most notorious period in British history.

The Impressionists - 2015 - British art critic Waldemar Januszczak explores the work of the most significant Impressionist artists: Monet, Cezanne, Degas, Renoir, and more.

The Impressionists with Tim Marlow - 1999 - British art historian Tim Marlow takes us on a journey through the Impressionist artwork of the nineteenth century.

The Nude in Art - 2015 - British art historian Tim Marlow takes a look at how the naked body has been portrayed throughout various art movements.

Paul Gauguin: Paradise Beyond the Horizon - 2017 - This documentary looks at how Gauguin integrated cultures he encountered into his work.

Scarlet Woman: The True Story of Mary Magdalene - 2017 - British art historian Waldemar Januszczak takes a look at how faith and art come together in portrayals of Mary Magdalene.

William Dobson: The Lost Genius of Baroque - 2012 - British art critic Waldemar Januszczak takes a look at the little we know about William Dobson and his all-too-short career.

Home Buying & Renovation

Building Dream Homes - 2014 - This BBC series follows some of the country's top architects as they make housing dreams come true.

Double Your House for Half the Money - 2012 - British families see their homes transformed.

Half-Built House – 2012 - Property guru Sian Astley helps people who've started home renovations and gotten stuck.

The Home Show - 2008 - Architect George Clarke helps turn current homes into dream homes.

The House that 100k (GBP) Built – 2016 - Homes are expensive in the UK, but this series takes a look at people building homes from scratch – and on a budget.

Make My Home Bigger – 2015 - Jonnie Irwin follows along as people seek to enlarge their homes.

My Dream Derelict Home – 2014 - This series follows homeowners putting everything that have on the line to save and restore dilapidated properties around the UK.

Posh Neighbours at War – 2016 - This series takes a look at the multi-million pound disputes between London neighbours as they embark on messy and noisy building projects in cramped quarters.

Project Restoration – 2016 - Historical building surveyor Marianne Suhr travels the UK helping out on challenging restoration projects.

Animals

Addicted to Sheep - 2017 - In Northeast England, Tom and Kay Hutchison attempt to breed the perfect Swaledale Sheep.

Animal Squad – 2010 - This show follows RSPCA officers are they work to protect animals.

Man & Beast with Martin Clunes – 2012 - Animal lover and actor Martin Clunes sets out to explore the relationship between man and beast.

Martin Clunes: Man to Manta - 2013 - Martin Clunes (*Doc Martin*) scuba dives in the Maldives to see some of the region's most elusive creatures.

Pet School – 2012 - In this series, children are taught what's really involved in providing proper care for the pets they'd love to have. If they're good students, they might just get the chance to bring a new animal companion into their homes.

Small Animal Hospital - 2014 - This series follows the action at the Small Animal Hospital at the University of Glasgow.

The Tigers of Scotland - 2018 - Iain Glen (*Jack Taylor*) narrates this documentary about the extreme threats to Scotland's wildcats and what's being done to protect them.

Walks With My Dog - 2017 - British celebrities like John Nettles and Robert Lindsay explore the countryside with their dogs.

Year of the Hedgehog - 2009 - This nature documentary follows hedgehogs as they awaken from their winter slumber.

Literary History

Brontë Country: The Life and Times of Three Famous Sisters - 2002 - This programme takes a look at the area of Yorkshire where the Brontë sisters lived. Though the quality of footage could be better, the scenery is still lovely.

The Brontë Sisters – 2006 - This series charts the lives of the Brontë sisters.

Charles Dickens: The Man That Asked for More - 2006 - This series offers an in-depth biography of author Charles Dickens.

Cracking the Shakespeare Code – 2017 - Codebreaker Petter Amundsen and historian Dr. Robert Crumpton investigate possible secrets buried in Shakespeare's first folio, also looking at a coded map.

Jane Austen Country: The Life and Times of Jane Austen - 2002 - This hour-long documentary offers background on Jane Austen and the times that shaped her writing.

Jane Austen: Life – 2005 - This program takes a look at what author Jane Austen may have really been like, visiting places she lived and examining her correspondence.

The Mystery of Agatha Christie with David Suchet - 2014 - David Suchet (*Poirot*) embarks on a journey to learn more about Agatha Christie.

Narnia's Lost Poet: The Secret Lives and Loves of C.S. Lewis - 2013 - C.S. Lewis biographer A.N. Wilson embarks on a journey to find the man behind Narnia. He was incredibly secretive about his private life, and even his best friend (J.R.R. Tolkien) was unaware of his late-in-life marriage to a divorced American woman.

Rural Britain: A Novel Approach - 2008 - One part travel series, one part history lesson, this series walks you through Britain's most beautiful landscapes and talks about the authors who drew inspiration from them. The series looks at Jane Austen, Charles Dickens, the Brontë Sisters, George Eliot, Thomas Hardy, and D.H. Lawrence.

Shakespeare's Stratford - 2008 - This three-hour tour takes us all over Stratford to see the city that shaped William Shakespeare.

Sherlock Holmes Against Conan Doyle – 2017 - This series takes a look at the enormous success of Sherlock Holmes – success that prompted some of the people of his time to contact Sir Arthur Conan Doyle in hopes that Holmes might help them.

To Walk Invisible: The Brontë Sisters – 2017 - This two-part series takes a look at the incredible Brontë sisters and their unexpected success in light of their male-dominated time period.

Royals & Nobility

British Royal Heritage: The Royal Kingdom - 2004 - This series looks at the historic relationships between the British royals and the ancient kingdoms of Sussex, East Anglia, Wessex, and Kent.

Charles I: Downfall of a King - 2019 - Historian Lisa Hilton takes a closer look at King Charles I's downfall and the political climate that led to it.

Crown and Country – 1998 to 2007 - HRH Prince Edward hosts this series that tours some of England's greatest landmarks.

Diana & Sarah: The Royal Wives of Windsor - 2017 - From toe-sucking and affairs to tell-all interviews and scandals, this programme takes a look at two royal wives who became outcasts.

Edward & Mary: The Unknown Tudors – 2002 - This two-part special tells the story of King Edward and Queen (Bloody) Mary, eldest daughter of Henry VIII and first English queen since Matilda.

Edward VIII: The King Who Threw Away His Crown - 2011 - This documentary takes a look back at the (other) royal who traded title and duty for a life of money and celebrity with an American divorcée.

Elizabeth I: Killer Queen - 2016 - Did Queen Elizabeth I really have a woman killed so she could continue sleeping with her husband? This documentary takes a look at the evidence.

Elizabeth I: War on Terror - 2014 - This documentary takes a look at Sir Francis Walsingham and how his work for Queen Elizabeth I protected her and kept her on the throne.

Henry VII: Winter King – 2013 - Author Thomas Penn dives into the world of the first Tudor King, Henry VII.

How to Get Ahead - 2013 - Presenter Stephen Smith takes a look at what it took to survive and do well in a variety of historic royal courts.

Kate: The Making of a Modern Queen - 2018 - This documentary looks at how Kate Middleton rose from her well-above-average-but-not-noble circumstances to become a much-loved member of the British royal family.

King Arthur's Lost Kingdom - 2019 - Professor Alice Roberts takes us inside a stone palace excavation in Cornwall, the supposed birthplace of King Arthur.

King of Scots – 2007 - This documentary looks a the life and times of Robert the Bruce.

Legends of Power with Tony Robinson – 2003 - Tony Robinson dives into the lives of some of the world's most powerful leaders.

Lives in the House of Windsor - 2013 - This series attempts to offer insights into the lives of the Windsor family, from Queen Elizabeth II to Princess Diana to future king Prince William.

Lord Montagu – 2015 - *Upstairs, Downstairs* and *Downton Abbey* fans will enjoy this documentary on one of 20th century England's most controversial aristocrats.

Minding Our Manors - 2018 - This brief documentary sees Viscount John Crichton travel to meet his cousins Lord and Lady Dunleath, owners of Ballywalter Park in Northern Ireland. Together, they take us behind the scenes to see what goes into running a grand, stately home.

Prince Charles: The Royal Restoration - 2013 - This factual programme takes a look at Princes Charles' efforts to preserve Dumfries House in Scotland.

Princess Margaret: Her Real Life Story - 2007 - Born in 1930, Princess Margaret spent her years living in the shadow of her sister. This programme takes a look back at her life.

The Private Lives of the Tudors - 2016 - This series takes a very personal look at one of Britain's most celebrated dynasties.

Queen Victoria's Letters: A Monarch Unveiled – 2014 - This series takes a look at Queen Victoria through her correspondence and writings.

Royal Britain: An Aerial History of the Monarchy - 2013 - Learn a bit of history while getting aerial views of the places the British royals have called home.

Royals & Animals: 'Til Death Do Us Part - 2013 - This documentary takes a look at Queen Elizabeth's passion for animals, particularly horses and dogs.

Serving the Royals: Inside the Firm - 2015 - This documentary looks at the roughly 1200 servants and employees working for the House of Windsor.

Wallis Simpson: The Secret Letters - 2016 - This series takes a look at the private correspondence of Wallis Simpson and what it says about the scandalous relationship that saw a king leave his throne.

William the Conqueror - 2015 - This documentary tells the story of William the Conqueror, a man who became ruler at eight and led his country to victory at the Battle of Hastings.

Windsor Castle: After the Fire – 2006 - This one-hour program goes into the aftermath of the fire at Windsor Castle.

True Crime & Dark History

Ancient Ghosts in England - 2018 - This paranormal documentary explores locations like a haunted village in Hertfordshire and Borley Church of Essex. While it does have some "night vision" scenes, it also includes quite a bit of regular daytime footage of the locations.

Britain's Outlaws: Highwaymen, Pirates, and Rogues – 2015 - This series looks at some of the outlaws who ran wild in 17th and 18th century Britain.

Broadmoor: A History of the Criminally Insane – 2016 - This documentary sees criminology professor David Wilson using interviews and archives to look back at Britain's most dreadful criminals and the asylum that held them.

Crime & Violence in England – 2012 - This series takes you into the world of the people who work to combat gangs and street violence in England.

Fred Dinenage Murder Casebook – 2010 to 2013 - Fred Dinenage takes a modern forensic look at various murders that shocked the UK over the 20th century.

Halloween: Feast of the Dying Sun – 2010 - This documentary explores the Celtic origins of Halloween.

Historic Hauntings (aka Castle Ghosts of England) - 1995 - Robert Hardy (*All Creatures Great & Small*) narrates this set of spooky stories about British ghosts.

Inside Broadmoor - 2014 - Previous patients at Broadmoor have included Ronnie Kray and Peter Sutcliffe, the Yorkshire Ripper. This film takes a look at how the facility handles the criminally insane.

Jack the Ripper – 2017 - UK murder squad detective Trevor Marriott builds a team in an effort to unveil the identity of the infamous killer.

Jack the Ripper: The Definitive Story – 2012 - This documentary attempts to dispel myths and misconceptions surrounding the Jack the Ripper case, offering what they believe to be the real truth.

The Lost Village - 2018 - Haunted history lovers will enjoy this visit to an abandoned 15th century church village.

Medieval Paranormal Activity - 2018 - This documentary visits haunted castles and churches, offering insights into the potentially haunted history of the locations. The series is primarily filmed during the day, so it's a good one for those who like creepy history but not shaky night vision footage.

The Moors Murders – 2009 - Back in the mid-1960s, Ian Brady and Myra Hindley abducted, tortured, and murdered children and young teenagers, horrifying the British public. This documentary looks back at archival footage, creates dramatic reconstructions, and talks with some of those involved in the case.

Murderers & Their Mothers - 2016 - Irish investigative journalist Donal MacIntyre takes a look at the childhood experiences of ten convicted killers, examining whether childhood experiences might have played a role in their actions.

Murdertown - 2018 to 2019 - This series tells the stories of shocking and true murders around the UK. The stories are grisly, but they show a fair bit of scenery around the cities and towns in question, so many will enjoy it on that alone.

Neighbourhood Blues – 2011 - This series takes a look at police operations in Avon and Somerset as they deal with typical, day-to-day crimes.

The Secret Identity of Jack the Ripper – 1988 - Actor Peter Ustinov stars in this 1988 documentary which saw many of the world's best forensic scientists and criminologists reexamining the infamous case.

The Witches of Essex - 2018 - Though reviewers are quick to call this one boring, history buffs may enjoy this film about the history of witches and witchcraft in Essex.

Gardening

Big Dreams, Small Spaces - 2014 - Monty Don joins amateur gardeners to help them realise the big dreams they have for their small gardens.

Brilliant Gardens - 2012 - This programme features some of the loveliest gardens in Great Britain.

Gardeners' World - 1968 to present - This long-running series offers support, ideas, and guidance for gardeners all over the UK - and the world.

Gardens of the National Trust – 2007 - Four episodes take you to some of England's finest gardens.

Get Growing – New Zealand – 2014 to 2017 - Hosts Lynda Hallinan and Justin Newcombe encourage viewers to transform their outdoor living spaces.

Glorious Gardens from Above – 2014 - Horticulturist Christine Walkden explores some of Britain's loveliest gardens from a hot air balloon.

The Great Gardens of England – 2007 - Alan Titchmarsh takes us on a tour of some of the finest gardens in England.

Ground Force - 2005 - Professional gardeners and landscapers help transform unattractive gardens.

Ground Force Revisited - 2004 - Each episode of this gardening series sees a worthy person getting a garden makeover.

My Dream Farm - 2010 - Monty Don follows first-time farmers as they learn to give up city life and make a living from the land.

Secret Gardens - 2005 - Alan Titchmarsh visits eight lesser-known gardens of England, including Hestercombe House, Brook Cottage, Cobblers on the Kent, and the Kensington Roof Garden.

Travel

Britain's Best Drives - 2009 - Richard Wilson (*One Foot in the Grave*) celebrates the 50th anniversary of Britain's first motorway with a trip around the country in six classic cars.

Chef's Diaries: Scotland - 2019 - Two Spanish restaurateurs decide to explore Scotland and its cuisine.

Daniel & Majella's B&B Road Trip – 2016 - This show offers a delightful journey through some of the loveliest B&Bs in Ireland.

Dan Snow's Norman Walks - 2010 - Presenter Dan Snow walks us through some of the areas of Britain with significant Norman history.

Discover Ireland – 2000 - Once you've watched Discover England and Discover Scotland, why not check out Discover Ireland?

Discover Scotland – 2004 - Heavy on the history, this series offers four 1-hour episodes that take you around Scotland.

Edinburgh: More than Words - 2019 - This brief programme takes you on a quick tour through the streets of Edinburgh.

Flying Across Britain with Arthur Williams - 2018 - Take in the British landscape from above while learning more about the country's aviation history.

Galway, Ireland: Busy Streets and Irish Music in the Pubs – 2018 - This series looks around Galway, Ireland.

Great Irish Journeys with Martha Kearney - 2015 - Martha Kearney follows in the footsteps of George Victor Du Noyer, a famed Irish artist and geologist. In this four-part series, you'll travel the island and get an idea of what it might have looked like in the early 19th century.

Grand Tours of Scotland - 2011 - Historian Paul Murton uses *Black's Picturesque Guide* as he tours his home country of Scotland.

Grand Tours of Scotland's Lochs – 2017 - Historian Paul Murton takes us on an incredibly scenic journey around some of Scotland's most beautiful lochs.

The Great Antiques Map of Britain - 2015 - Tom Wonnacott travels around Great Britain seeking out antiques that tell stories about their regions.

Great Lighthouses of Ireland - 2019 - With gorgeous coastal footage, this series gives you a mix of history, science, and scenery - along with plenty of stories from lighthouse keepers of today and yesterday.

Great Scottish Singalong - 2003 - This musical travelogue features 16 traditional Scottish songs and loads of great scenery.

Guardians of the Night - 2007 - This series offers a look at the history of lighthouses, with on-location footage from lighthouses around the world.

Highlands and Islands: Where Scotland's Heart Beats Loudest - 2016 - Travel journalist Erik Peters visits the Scottish Highlands and islands.

Icelandic Tails - 2020 - Robson Green (*Grantchester*) hosts this series about fishing in Iceland.

Ireland with Ardal O'Hanlon – 2017 - This three-part series is a quick romp around Ireland with famed comedian Ardal O'Hanlon.

Ireland's Wild River - 2014 - Follow the River Shannon as it passes through the beautiful rural landscapes of Ireland.

Isle of Man: From the Air - 2014 - Between Great Britain and Ireland, you'll find the Isle of Man. This series take a look at the lovely island from above.

James May: Our Man in Japan - 2020 - James May embarks on a journey across the island nation of Japan, travelling from the icy north to the balmy south.

London: A City in Time - 2015 - This programme mixes live footage with historical documents and photos to tell the story of London.

London: A Tale of Two Cities – 2015 - This hour-long documentary looks at the highs and lows London has faced over the years.

Love London - 2015 - A London taxi driver and a young Londoner travel the city to learn its secrets.

Memories of Scotland – Date Unknown - This 48-minute program focuses on the major tourist attractions in Scotland.

On the Ballykissangel Trail – 2007 - This short programme discusses the making of *Ballykissangel*, along with a tour of the area.

On the Whisky Trail: The History of Scotland's Famous Drink - 2003 - Learn more about the history of whisky and how it's made.

Penelope Keith's Hidden Villages - 2014 to 2016 - Penelope Keith takes us on a tour of the UK's loveliest villages and quirkiest characters.

Richard Wilson On the Road - 2014 - Richard Wilson (*One Foot in the Grave*) takes a trip around Britain with only his antique Shell travel guides to help him.

Rick Steves' Europe – 2000 to 2019 - Seasons 7 to 10 of this popular series are offered on Amazon. Of interest to Anglophiles will be: 7-8, London, 7-9 Northern England, 9-8 Western England, 9-9 Southeast England, 9-10 Cornwall, 10-1 Heart of England, 10-10 Scotland's Highlands, 10-11 Scotland's Islands, and 10-12 Glasgow.

Robson Green's Wild Swimming Adventure - 2009 - Over the course of two episodes, Robson Green (*Grantchester*) swims his way through some of Britain's wild waters.

The Seasoned Traveler: Scottish Castles - 2005 - This brief film takes a look at a handful of castles around Scotland.

Skye's the Limit - 2017 - Follow one woman as she circumnavigates the Isle of Skye on a stand-up paddleboard.

Stephen Tompkinson's Australian Balloon Adventure – 2010 - Stephen Tompkinson (*Ballykissangel, DCI Banks*) stars in this three-part travel series checking out Australia by balloon.

The Story of London - 2014 - Six episodes walk us through different sites in London.

Travel Man – 2015 to present - Richard Ayoade (*The IT Crowd*) takes 48 hour trips to various destinations, always bringing along a celebrity guest.

Travel Scotland with James McCreadie: Trossachs Trip – 2018 to 2019 - This half-hour special has James McCreadie taking you on a journey through the Trossachs. See also: *Travel Scotland with James McCreadie: Tourist Towns*

Walks Around Britain – 2016 to 2019 - Britain is one of the greatest places in the

PRIME VIDEO

world to go walking, and Amazon Prime lets you enjoy two series of short scenic walks around the countryside.

Walks Around Britain: The Great Glen Way – 2016 - This 48-minute programme shows rambler Andrew White walking The Great Glen Way from Fort William to Inverness. If you enjoy this one, also check out *Footloose in Scotland: The West Highland Way*. Together, the two journeys represent a walk all the way from Glasgow to Inverness.

My Welsh Sheepdog - 2016 - BBC presenter Kate Humble travels around Wales with her dog Teg to learn more about the rare Welsh sheepdog breed.

Whistlestop Edinburgh: Scotland's Beautiful Capital - 2014 - Tour guide Liam Dale leads us around some of Edinburgh's most interesting sites.

York, UK - 2016 - Tour guide Dennis Callan offers bite-sized videos taken around the city of York.

The Footloose Series

This series of travel videos features a British couple as they travel around Europe. We've only listed the episodes pertaining to the British Isles, but there are others set in mainland Europe if you search for them. They're great because instead of rushing through each bit and showing only the highlights, their videos are long and in-depth. Filming dates range from 1998 to present.

A Classic Tour of Scotland: Footloose Special – UK filmmakers Debra and David Rixon travel Scotland in an Airstream trailer, stopping off to visit locations like the Isle of Skye, Glasgow, Stirling Castle, Edinburgh, and Inverness.

Footloose in the Cotswolds, Part 1 – UK filmmakers Debra and David Rixon visit Stow, Chipping Camden, Broadway, and the gardens of Kiftsgate and Hidcote.

Footloose in the Cotswolds, Part 2 – UK filmmakers Debra and David Rixon visit Cheltenham, Painswick, Tetbury, and the City of Bath.

Footloose in England: Along the Ridgeway - This two-hour walking film takes you along southern England's oldest green road. The 85-mile walk includes stone circles, hill forts, villages, and more.

Footloose in London: All the Best Sights of our Capital – UK filmmakers Debra and David Rixon offer budget-minded tips for visiting London and viewing its best sites.

Footloose in Oxford & York - Filmed in between lockdowns in 2020, this video takes us on a tour of the Roman city of York, the famed university city of Oxford, and some of the surrounding areas.

Footloose in Ireland – This nearly two-hour programme sees David and Debra travelling both Dublin and the Dingle Way.

PRIME VIDEO

Narrowboats & Canals

100 Years of British Ships - 2007 - Though slightly broader than just narrowboats and canals, this series looks at all manner of British boats over the past 100 years.

Britain by Narrowboat - 2020 - Colin and his partner Shaun quit their jobs, sell their home, and start up life aboard a narrowboat.

Britain's Best Canals - 2015 to 2016 - BBC presenter John Sergeant takes us on a different British canal journey with each episode.

British Inland Waterways – Date Unknown - If you've ever dreamed of lazily floating along the beautiful canals of England and Scotland, this series will be sure to delight.

Cruising the Cut – 2019 to present - This is another series about a different British man who quit his job to go live on the canals and travel. See also: *Cruising the Cut: Special Editions*

Narrowboat Houseboating Through the English Countryside – 2001 - This instruction-oriented programme shows you what it takes to make the most of your houseboating adventure.

Travels by Narrowboat – 2018 to presents - Newer than many of the other narrowboating shows on Amazon, this one follows Kevin as he quits his job and embarks on a new life on the canals.

British Railway Journeys

100 Years of British Trains - 2016 - Follow along as this series traces the evolution of British trains throughout the 20th century.

100 Years of British Trams - 2007 - This documentary offers a history of trams and their use around Britain.

The Barry Scrapyard Story - 1994 - In 1959, the Barry scrapyard received a number of locomotives for breaking up, followed by more than 300 over the next 10 years. Luckily, not all were scrapped - and 213 were eventually purchased by railway enthusiasts and preservationists.

Best of British Heritage Railways - 2016 - Four episodes take us along some of Britain's rarest heritage railways. Look for episode 2 as a separate "Volume 2" listing.

Britain's Railways: Then & Now - 2010 - Using archival footage, this series takes a look at today's railways compared with those of the past.

Britain's Railways Then & Now: LNER - 2010 - This review begins at King's Cross Station and takes a look at the trains that travel her rails.

British Railway Journeys – 2012 - Each of these episodes is roughly an hour long, and they take you through interesting railway journeys around Britain. There is some commentary, and plenty of scenery around the rails (you're not just looking out a train window).

The journeys included are: The Severn Valley and the Cotswolds, Southwest Scotland, East Anglia, The Lake District, The Peak District, The North East, North Wales, The South West, Northern England, and South Wales.

British Railways - 2016 - This series includes eight episodes about different trains around Great Britain. They are: Waterloo Sunset, Rails in the Isle of Wight, Vintage Southern, From Bewdley to Blaenau, British Narrow Gauge Miscellany, Steam in the Midlands, Channel Tunnel Trains, and English Branch Lines and Byways.

Classic British Steam Engines – 2015 - This series devotes nearly an hour each to several of Britain's most famous trains.

Classic Steam Train Collection - 2009 - This programme takes a look at the Taw Valley engine's journey through England.

Driving & Firing: The Art of Driving - 2007 - Experienced engineer Clive Groome shows you what it takes to drive a steam locomotive.

Driving & Firing: The Art of Firing - 2007 - Follow experienced British engineman Clive Groome as he demonstrates how to fire four different steam locomotives.

The Fall & Rise of Britain's Railways - 2008 - This docu-series follows the history of Britain's railways - from the early days through WWII, to the years of neglect after the war, to the disastrous Beeching-era cuts. It also looks ahead to the future and the possibility of a renewal.

The Flying Scotsman: A Rail Romance - 2013 - Barbara Flynn narrates this hour-long story of the world's love affair with the Flying Scotsman.

The Flying Scotsman Steam Train Comes Home - 2018 - After years away, the world's most famous locomotive train returns to its homeland.

Flying Scotsman: The Ultimate Profile - 2005 - This programme tells the story of Britain's most beloved steam locomotive.

The Magical World of Trains - 2007 - This hour-long feature celebrates all that is wonderful about trains - including train travel, the future of trains, and trainspotting.

Preserved Lines - 2009 - This series takes a look at a variety of heritage steam and diesel rail adventures to be had around Britain. Episodes include: Bluebell Railway, Avon Valley, Swanage, Gloucestershire Warwickshire Railway, and Didcot.

Smoke and Steam - 2007 - This series celebrates steam railways around Britain.

Vintage Steam Trains: Great British Steam – 2015 - This hour-long feature focuses exclusively on the British steam train and its history.

IMDB TV

Website: https://www.imdb.com/tv/

Description: IMDb TV is a free, ad-supported streaming service that offers a variety of programming from the US and abroad. Though most of their shows are older, they will be premiering the new *Alex Rider* series later this year.

Available On: Roku, Amazon Fire TV, Apple TV, Apple iPhone & iPad, Android TV, Android phones and tablets, Google Chromecast, computer (via web browser). You can also watch via Amazon Prime Video.

Cost: Free with ads

Now Streaming

Scripted Shows

A Family At War - 1970 - In this classic family saga, we follow the daily life of the Ashtons, a working-class family in Liverpool during the time of WWII.

Alex Rider - 2020 - Midsomer Murders and Foyle's War writer Anthony Horowitz is behind this teenage spy series based on his popular young adult novels. Unbeknownst to Alex, his uncle and reluctant guardian has been training him as a spy. When he's suddenly forced to go on an undercover mission at Point Blanc academy, he begins to realise he has skills he wasn't even aware of.

Apparitions - 2008 - Martin Shaw stars in this supernatural drama about a priest drawn into the world of demons and exorcism.

Appropriate Adult – 2011 - A woman finds herself involved in a serial killer case as the "appropriate adult" who helps vulnerable adults facing criminal charges.

At Home With the Braithwaites – 2000 to 2003 - With an all-star cast that includes Amanda Redman, Peter Davison, and Julia Graham, this drama follows the life of Aliston Braithwaite and her family. She wins 38 million pounds in the lottery, only to hide it from her family in favour of setting up a secret charity to do good things with the money.

Atlantis High – *New Zealand* – 2001 - This teen show is set in a school believed to be build atop the Lost City of Atlantis.

Band of Gold – 1995 to 1997 - Geraldine James stars in this Bradford-based series about desperate streetwalkers trying to make their way through hard times in Northern England.

Beaver Falls – 2011 to 2012 - Three British friends decide to have one last crazy summer working in an American summer camp.

Being Human – 2008 to 2013 - A vampire, werewolf, and ghost try to coexist as roommates.

Black Books – 2000 to 2004 - Bernard Black runs a bookshop, but he's not particularly good at dealing with customers.

Black Harbour - *Canada* - 1997 to 1998- When her mother gets ill, Katherine and her husband Nick give up their prestigious careers in Los Angeles to move back home to Nova Scotia.

Blandings – 2013 to 2014 - This fun period comedy follows an eccentric aristocratic family and their crumbling ancestral home. It's based on the writings of PG Wodehouse, and stars Timothy Spall and Jennifer Saunders.

Blue Murder - 2003 to 2009 - DCI Janine Lewis struggles with the challenge of being a single mom to four kids while leading a team of detectives through homicide investigations. Caroline Quentin (*Jonathan Creek*) stars.

The Blue Rose - *New Zealand* - 2013 - This investigative drama sees a group of law firm employees joining together to figure out what happened in the mysterious death of a co-worker.

Body and Soul - 1993 - Kristin Scott Thomas stars as Sister Gabriel, a nun forced to leave the convent when her brother dies and her family needs her help to save their mill. This miniseries is based on Marcell Bernstein's novel.

Bonekickers – 2008 - Archaeologists piece together mysteries and find themselves in dangerous situations.

Boy Meets Girl - 2009 - After a freak accident, a man and woman find themselves trapped in each other's bodies. Martin Freeman (*Sherlock*) and Rachael Stirling (*Detectorists*) star in this ITV dramedy. This is not to be confused with the other *Boy Meets Girl* on BritBox.

Bridget & Eamon – 2016 to 2019 - Bridget and Eamon are an Irish couple living with an unknown number of children in the Midlands in the 1980s.

The Brief – 2004 to 2005 - This legal series comes from the creators of *Inspector Morse* and *Kavanagh QC*, and it stars Alan Davies (*Jonathan Creek*) as a criminal lawyer with a penchant for gambling.

The Broker's Man – 1997 to 1998 - A former detective investigates insurance claims while trying to hold his family life together. Features Kevin Whately (*Inspector Morse*) in the lead.

Cadfael - 1994 to 1998 - In 12th century Shrewsbury, a monk solves mysteries. Derek Jacobi (*Last Tango in Halifax*) stars.

Captain Scarlet & the Mysterons – 1967 - This 1960s series followed an unkillable

agent in charge of the fight against extraterrestrial terrorists.

Case Histories - 2011 to 2013 - Based on the *Jackson Brodie* novels by Kate Atkinson, this Edinburgh-based series features a tough guy PI with a heart of gold.

Chancer – 1990 to 1991 - Clive Owen plays Stephen Crane, a schemer with a talent for misdirection. As a young business analyst/con man in London, he's called in to help save a struggling motor company.

Chiller – 1995 - Martin Clunes and Nigel Havers star in this horror series about a group of friends who receive prophecies during a seance in the basement of a London cafe.

The City & the City – 2018 - David Morrissey stars in this BBC sci-fi/mystery production about an inspector in the Extreme Crime Squad of the fictional European city-state of Beszel. When a student is murdered in Beszel's twin city of Ul Qoman, he investigates.

City Homicide – *Australia* – 2007 to 2011 - In Melbourne, Australia, a group of homicide detectives work to find justice for victims of murder.

City of Vice – 2008 - This historical crime drama is set in Georgian London, and it follows the creation of the city's first modern police force.

Cold Feet - 1998 to 2003 - This long-running dramedy follows the lives of six thirtysomething friends living in Manchester, England as they do their best to get their lives sorted.

Cold Squad – *Canada* – 1998 to 2005 - This long-running Canadian series follows a team that works on cold cases ranging from 5 to 50 or more years old.

Colonel March of Scotland Yard – 1956 - This vintage detective series offers 26 episodes of classic 1950s British mystery.

The Colour of Magic - 2009 - This series is based on the *Discworld* series of novels by Terry Pratchett, and features Sean Astin as tourist Twoflower alongside Sir David Jason as wizard Rincewind. When a fire breaks out during Twoflower's holiday, the two flee the city together, beginning an interesting magical journey.

Crims – 2015 - Two teenage boys with no street smarts end up together in a young offender's institute in the UK.

Danger Man, aka Secret Agent – 1961 to 1968 - Patrick McGoohan (*The Prisoner*) stars as John Drake, a special operative for NATO specialising in security assignments involving threats to world peace.

The Darling Buds of May - 1991 to 1993 - Based on the 1958 H.E. Bates novel of the same name, this series is set in rural 1950s Kent and follows the Larkin family as they go about their daily lives. This early 90s dramedy was a breakout role for Welsh actress Catherine Zeta-Jones.

The Delivery Man – 2015 - Former police officer Matthew begins work as a midwife. He's the first male midwife to hit the unit, and he hopes his new career will give him more satisfaction than his previous work.

Desi Rascals – 2015 - This series follows young adult members of the British-Asian community.

Detectorists - 2014 to 2017 - Two quirky friends scan the fields of England with metal detectors, hoping for the big find that will finally let them do the gold dance.

The Devil's Mistress – 2008 - During the English Civil War, a young woman exploits a country in crisis for her own self-preservation. The follow-up to this series is called *New Worlds*.

Drifters – 2013 to 2016 - Meg, Bunny, and Laura share a flat in Leeds and face the ups and downs of post-university life.

Durham County – *Canada* – 2007 to 2010 - A man moves his family in hopes of a new start, then a local serial killer throws a wrench in that peaceful new beginning.

Emmerdale - 1972 to present - Originally known as Emmerdale Farm, this series was originally set in a village called Beckindale. In the 90s, the show rebranded and began to focus on the entire village of Emmerdale. Now, storylines are bigger, sexier, and more dramatic than ever.

Enemy at the Door – 1978 - This drama focuses on life in the British Channel Islands during the German occupation in WWII.

Enid Blyton Adventure Series – *UK/New Zealand* – 1996 - This series sees a group of kids on adventures in New Zealand, and it's based on Enid Blyton's novels.

Enid Blyton Secret Series – *UK/New Zealand* – 1997 - This fanciful young adult series is based on author Enid Blyton's much-loved *Secret* novels, and it s a follow-up to the Adventure Series.

Eternal Law - 2012 - In *Eternal Law*, angels live among us and help humans when they're at their most desperate – in this case, the angels are lawyers in the lovely and historic city of York.

Father Ted – 1995 to 1998 - This classic Britcom follows a group of zany priests on the fictional Craggy Island in Ireland.

The Fenn Street Gang – 1971 to 1973 - This spin-off of *Please Sir!* follows the students after they leave school.

The Field of Blood - 2011 to 2013 - Set in early 1980s Glasgow, a young woman skillfully solves murders on a police force full of men. Unfortunately, her dedication to the truth also puts her in danger. The series stars BAFTA winner Jayd Johnson (*River City*) as Paddy Meehan, working alongside Peter Capaldi (*Doctor Who*) and David Morrissey (*The Missing*).

Flickers – 1980 - During the early days of silent film, a lovable Cockney tries to make his fortune in the industry.

Flood – 2008 - An engineer must rush to save millions of Londoners when floods threaten the city.

The Gentle Touch - 1980 - Jill Gascoine stars as Britain's first female police detective. Within hours of her promotion to Detective Inspector, she learns her husband has been gunned down.

Go Girls – *New Zealand* – 2009 to 2013 - Three twentysomething women realize they've made little progress towards their life goals, and vow to achieve their respective goals of being married, rich, and famous within a year.

Grafters - 1998 to 1999 - Robson Green (*Grantchester*) and Stephen Tompkinson (*DCI Banks*) star in this series about two brothers who work together as builders and have terribly dysfunctional family lives.

The Grand - 1997 to 1998 - This period drama was written by Russell T Davies (*Doctor Who*) and takes place in 1920s Manchester. It follows the Bannerman family as they re-open The Grand after WWI.

Green Wing – 2004 to 2007 - This zany medical comedy features a largely incompetent staff that does very little actual medical work. Among the stars are

Tamsin Greig (*Friday Night Dinner*), Mark Heap (*Friday Night Dinner*), Olivia Colman (*Broadchurch*), and Stephen Mangan (*Hang-Ups, Episodes*).

The Guilty – 1992 - Michael Kitchen (*Foyle's War*) and Caroline Catz (*Doc Martin*) star in this miniseries in which a young man gets in over his head searching for his father.

Hammer House of Horror – 1980 - This classic anthology series tells tales of mystery, suspense, and horror.

Hearts & Bones – 2000 to 2001 - This drama follows a group of 20 and 30-something friends who move to London and transition into proper adult lives.

Heartbeat - 1992 to 2010 - This Yorkshire-based period crime drama ran for 18 seasons and 372 episodes, focusing on the lives of characters in a small village. Initially, it focused on a central couple, PC Nick Rowan and Dr. Kate Rowan, but as time went on, it branched out to include storylines all over the village. The series is based on the "*Constable*" novels written by Peter N. Walker under the pseudonym Nicholas Rhea.

Heat of the Sun – 1998 - This series was filmed on location in Africa, and set in 1930s high society Kenya. It follows a policeman working within the close-knit community of expats – many of whom harbour dark secrets.

He Kills Coppers - 2008 - This three-part miniseries follows the death of three police officers during the 1966 World Cup celebrations, looking closely at the three men most connected to the unfortunate deaths.

The Incredible Journey of Mary Bryant - 2007 - After stealing a woman's picnic, starving Mary Broad is convicted to death. Before realizing that fate, however, she's granted mercy and allowed to live out her life on a penal colony in New South Wales, Australia.

Island at War – 2004 - This miniseries depicts life under Nazi occupation on St. Gregory Island (a fictionalized version of the Channel Islands – see *The Guernsey Literary and Potato Peel Pie Society* on Netflix for something similar).

Jackson's Wharf – *New Zealand* – 1999 to 2000 - Set in a fictional coastal town, this series revolves around the rivalry between two brothers: cop Frank and lawyer Ben.

Jessica – *Australia* – 2003 - In Australia, a young girl is placed in an asylum on false pretenses, and her only hope is a less-than-promising lawyer.

Joe 90 – 1968 - Another marionette-based programme, this one follows the adventures of a pre-teen secret agent who can almost instantly have any skills loaded into his brain.

The Jury – 2002 to 2011 - This series follows the men and women brought together to act as jurors in a high-profile case involving a young Sikh student.

Kavanagh QC - 1995 to 2001 - John Thaw (*Inspector Morse*) stars as James Kavanagh QC, a barrister with a working-class background and a strong sense of right and wrong. It was one of Thaw's final roles before he died of cancer at the age of 60. Pay close attention to the guest stars in this one, as it's full of actors who went on to well-known roles, including Lesley Manville (*Mum*), Larry Lamb (*Gavin & Stacey*), Barry Jackson (*Midsomer Murders*), Phyllis Logan (*Downton Abbey*), Bill Night (*Love Actually*), and Julian Fellowes (*Downton Abbey*).

Laid – *Australia* – 2011 to 2012 - When she realizes all her former lovers are dying in unusual ways, a young woman tries to save the remaining men.

Legends - *United States* - 2014 to 2015 - Brit Sean Bean stars as deep cover operative Martin Odum, a man with an abnormally strong ability to change his identity as needed for the job at hand.

Lillie - 1978 - This period drama tells the story of Lillie Langtry, a beautiful woman who managed to woo tons of wealthy men and become a well-known actress. Francesca Annis (*Reckless*) and Peter Egan (*Downton Abbey*) star.

London Irish – 2013 - This occasionally off-colour comedy focuses on a group of Northern Irish ex-pats in the city of London. The series was written by Lisa McGee, best known as the writer and creator of *Derry Girls*.

London's Burning - 1988 to 2002 - This series about a London fire brigade began as a TV movie and evolved into a long-running drama series.

Love/Hate – 2010 to 2014 - When a young man returns to Dublin after a year away, he wants to stay clean, but circumstances drag him into the world of Irish gangs.

Love Lies Bleeding – 2006 - A self-made millionaire finds himself caught up in a strange and deadly conspiracy after an old friend shows up.

Lunch Monkeys – 2009 to 2011 - This comedy focuses on the administrative staff at a British law firm.

Market Forces – *New Zealand* – 1998 - This satirical comedy revolves around a group of government employees in New Zealand.

Married Single Other - 2010 - Set in Leeds, this series follows a group of young friends trying to figure out their love lives.

Men Behaving Badly – 1992 to 2014 - Two young male flatmates act like...a couple of young male flatmates. The two explore adult life and love, frequently acting like cads. Stars Martin Clunes (*Doc Martin*), Neil Morrisey (*Line of Duty*), and Caroline Quentin (*Jonathan Creek*).

Midsomer Murders - 1998 to present - In Midsomer County, the landscapes are beautiful, the villagers all have secrets, and murder is rampant. This British mystery classic features John Nettles as DCI Tom Barnaby through the first 13 seasons, with Neil Dudgeon as DCI John Barnaby for the later seasons.

Mind Your Language – 1977 to 1979 - This series follows Jerry Brown, an eager young teacher who takes a job teaching English to students from all over the world.

Miranda – 2009 to 2013 - Miranda Hart stars as a lovably awkward woman who runs a joke shop with her best friend and seems to specialize in getting herself into pickles.

Mobile – 2007 - Michael Kitchen (*Foyle's War*) appears in this miniseries about a fictional mobile phone conglomerate and a conspiracy tied into a gangland shooting.

Monroe - 2011 to 2012 - James Nesbitt (*Cold Feet*) stars in this medical drama about a brilliant but quirky neurosurgeon and the talented doctors who work with him.

Mount Royal – *Canada* – 1988 - This drama brings to mind shows like Dallas or Dynasty, but it's set against the cosmopolitan backdrop of 1980s Montreal.

McLeod's Daughters - 2002 to 2009 - Two sisters separated as children are reunited when they jointly inherit a ranch in the Australian bush: the independent Claire McLeod (Lisa Chappell, *Gloss*) and her estranged half-sister, Tess (Bridie Carter, *800 Words*), a stubborn city girl with a drive to change the world. Together, they build an all-female workforce and commit to life at Drovers Run. Nearby, the men of the Ryan family help keep things interesting.

The Mixer – 1992 - Though technically a French and German production, this series is set in 1930s London. It focuses on a penniless nobleman who robs thieves of their stolen property with the help of his trusty valet.

Mom P.I. – *Canada* – 1990 to 1991 - Rosemary Dunsmore stars as Sally Sullivan, a widowed mother who teams up with PI Bernie Fox (Stuart Margolin) to solve mysteries and bring down criminals.

My Uncle Silas – 2001 to 2003 - Based on stories by H.E. Bates, this series follows a boisterous Bedfordshire uncle as he cares for his nephew over the summer in turn-of-the-century England. Stars Sue Johnston and Albert Finney.

The New Tomorrow - *New Zealand* - 2005 - After a virus kills all the adults, kids are left to take care of themselves.

The Nightmare Worlds of HG Wells – 2016 - This four-part series dramatizes several of Wells' short stories.

Nothing Trivial – *New Zealand* – 2011 to 2014 - For one group of thirtysomething friends, a weekly trivia night is the only thing that's constant in their lives.

Only When I Laugh – 1979 to 1982 - A group of patients constantly attempt to one-up each other, driving hospital staff crazy.

Outrageous Fortune – *New Zealand* – 2005 to 2010 - A colourful family of criminals tries to clean up their act.

The Palace – 2008 - A fictional British royal family deals with all manner of upper class problems.

Parents - 2012 - A businesswoman finds out her husband has lost their life savings on the day she loses her job, and they have to go live with her parents.

Party Tricks - *Australia* - 2014 - This Australian series follows Kate Ballard (Asher Keddie, *X-Men Origins: Wolverine*), a woman facing her first election for State Premier. Victory seems guaranteed until the opposition brings in a new shock candidate – David McLeod (Rodger Corser, *The Heart Guy*). McLeod is a popular media figure, but more concerning is the fact that she had a secret affair with him years earlier.

Peak Practice - 1993 to 2002 - This drama takes place in and around a GP surgery in the fictional town of Cardale in Derbyshire's Peak District (mostly filmed in the real-life village of Crich, also in Derbyshire). The series was popular during its run, lasting for 12 series and 147 episodes. Fair warning, though: it ends on a cliffhanger. Cast members over the years included Kevin Whately (*Lewis*), Amanda Burton (*Silent Witness*), Clive Swift (*Keeping Up Appearances*), and Sarah Parish (*Bancroft*).

Pete vs. Life - 2010 to 2011 - Journalist Pete is a pretty normal guy, except that he's constantly observed and analysed by a couple of sports commentators.

The Protectors – 1972 to 1974 - Robert Vaughn stars in this 1970s series about a London-based crime-fighting team that strives to protect the innocent and apprehend the guilty.

Rescue Me - 2002 - This short-lived rom-com focuses on a newly-divorced couple trying to move on with their lives, but not entirely sure they should be apart. Sally Phillips (*Miranda*) stars. As a note of warning, the series was cancelled due to low numbers, so it ends on a cliffhanger.

Rocket's Island – 2012 to 2015 - Filmed on location on the Isle of Man, this young adult fantasy drama follows foster children who go on magical adventures.

Roman Mysteries – 2007 to 2008 - This young adult series follows four kids in Ancient Rome as they go on quests and solve mysteries.

Rovers – 2016 - This working-class comedy centers around the people who spend time at the Redbridge Rovers Football Club

The Royal – 2003 to 2011 - This *Heartbeat* spinoff is set in the 1960s and focuses on an NHS hospital serving the seaside Yorkshire town of Elsinby.

The Ruth Rendell Mysteries - 1994 to 2000 - This collection includes a variety of suspenseful tales adapted from the novels of author Ruth Rendell.

The Saint - 1962 to 1969 - Roger Moore stars as Simon Templar, a wealthy adventurer who travels the world solving crimes and engaging in all manner of secret agent hijinks. Though the settings are occasionally exotic, nearly every episode was filmed at a studio in Hertfordshire using "blue-screen" technology. The series was based on the Simon Templar novels by Leslie Charteris.

Sam's Game - 2001 - This short-lived comedy starred TV presenter Davina McCall as Sam, a single woman living in a London flat over a High Street shop. To help pay the rent, she illegally sublets to Alex (comedian Ed Byrne), an Irishman who seems to find no end of troubles.

Sapphire and Steel – 1979 to 1982 - Interdimensional operatives save the world from evil forces on a regular basis. Stars Joanna Lumley and David McCallum.

Sara Dane - *Australia* - 1982 - This miniseries follows a young woman banished from England to Australia for a crime she didn't commit.

Secrets and Lies – *Australia* – 2015 to 2016 - A regular suburban family guy finds the body of a young child and promptly becomes the leading suspect.

Secret Smile – 2005 - David Tennant stars as a smooth and manipulative spurned lover seeking revenge.

See No Evil: The Moors Murders - 2006 - Joanne Froggatt (*Downton Abbey*), Sean Harris (*Prometheus*), and Maxine Peake (*Shameless*) star in this true crime drama about notorious child killers Ian Brady and Myra Hindley.

The Silence – 2010 - While struggling to integrate into the hearing world, a young girl with a new cochlear implant witnesses the murder of a police officer. Douglas Henshall (*Shetland*) is among the stars of this miniseries.

Single-Handed - 2007 to 2010 - *Ireland* - Jack Driscoll is transferred back to his hometown to take over the Garda Sergeant role his father left.

Soldier Soldier – 1991 to 1997 - Robson Green and Jerome Flynn star in this military drama about soldiers in the King's Own Fusiliers regiment.

Spaced – 1999 to 2001 - To get an affordable flat in North London, two young people pretend to be a couple. Simon Pegg (*Shaun of the Dead*) and Jessica Hynes (*There She Goes*) star.

IMDB TV

Step Dave – *New Zealand* – 2014 to 2015 - A young slacker in New Zealand meets the woman of his dreams, only to realize she's 15 years older than him and comes with major baggage.

Stingray – 1964 - This 1960s marionette-based series focused on the missions of the World Aquanaut Security Patrol.

Stranded – 2002 - Roger Allam (*Endeavour*) stars in this retelling of the classic Swiss Family Robinson.

The Street – 2009 - This drama features a number of familiar faces as they go on about their lives in a rough-around-the-edges Northern English town.

Switch – 2012 - In this short-lived supernatural comedy, a group of young witches lives it up in the big city.

The Syndicate – 2013 - Each season of this series looks at what happens after a group of people wins the lottery. IMDb TV offers Season 2 only (the one that takes place among hospital workers).

The Take - 2009 - Shaun Evans (*Endeavour*) and Tom Hardy (*Peaky Blinders*) star in this four-part 2009 miniseries about a man newly released from prison (Hardy) who learns his cousin (Evans) is trying to build a criminal reputation on the back of his reputation. Fun fact: Tom Hardy met Charlotte Riley (*Press*) while filming this series, and the two later married.

Then There Were Giants - 1994 - John Lithgow, Michael Caine, and Bob Hoskins star in this miniseries about how Roosevelt, Churchill, and Stalin navigated the events of World War II.

Tales of the Unexpected – 1979 to 1985 - Though not a traditional mystery series, this Roald Dahl-created anthology series features a variety of unusual and bizarre stories.

Terry Pratchett's Hogfather – 2006 - The Hogfather has gone missing on Hogswatch, and Death must take his place.

That's My Boy – 1981 to 1986 - Mollie Sugden (*Are You Being Served?*) visits an employment agency and quickly finds herself under the employ of the son she gave up for adoption years earlier.

Thunderbirds – 1966 - This 1960s TV series used marionettes to tell the story of the 21st century Tracy family, who operated a private emergency response service.

To the Ends of the Earth – 2005 - This BBC series is based on William Golding's novels of a sea journey to Australia from England in 1812-13. Benedict Cumberbatch (*Sherlock*) stars.

Touching Evil – 1997 to 1999 - Robson Green (*Grantchester*) and Nicola Walker (*River*) star in this series about a police officer with a special ability to detect criminals.

The Tribe – *New Zealand* – 1999 - In a world where all the adults were killed off by a virus, a group of young people try to stay alive.

Truckers - 2013 - Stephen Tompkinson (*DCI Banks*) stars in this drama about a group of truck drivers in Nottinghamshire.

Two's Company – 1975 to 1979 - This sitcom follows the relationship between an American woman and a British gentleman.

Two Thousand Acres of Sky - 2001 - Michelle Collins (*EastEnders*) and Paul Kaye (*After Life*) star in this series about two young Londoners who pretend to be married so they can relocate to a Scottish island in need of a young family to keep the local school open.

Ultimate Force - 2002 to 2007 - Ross Kemp (*EastEnders*) stars in this action series about a Special Air Service team that stops things like anthrax poisonings, assassinations, and bank sieges.

Underbelly – *Australia* – 2011 to 2013 - Each season of this Australian series focuses on a different underworld figure. While not all seasons are available on Prime, you can enjoy Series 6, about Leslie Squizzy Taylor, and Series 4, about two Australian crime queens.

Vexed – 2010 to 2012 - A young male and female detective team frustrate each other with their different attitudes and complicated personal lives.

The Vice – 1999 to 2003 - Inspector Chappel leads the Metropolitan Vice Squad, investigating cases of prostitution and pornography in London.

Vincent - 2005 to 2006 - Vincent is an ex-cop who becomes a private investigator and takes on the tough cases. Ray Winstone (*The Trials of Jimmy Rose*) and Suranne Jones (*Doctor Foster*) star.

We'll Meet Again – 1982 - Set in 1943, this series shows us what happens in a small

East Anglian town when war-weary Brits play host to American troops.

Where the Heart Is – 1997 to 2004 - Pam Ferris and Sarah Lancashire star in this Yorkshire-based UK drama. It follows a group of dedicated nurses and their community.

White Van Man - 2011 - Will Mellor (*No Offence*) and Georgia Moffett (*The Bill*) are among the stars of this sitcom about a terribly incompetent handyman and his assistant.

Wild at Heart - 2006 to 2013 - Stephen Tompkinson (*DCI Banks*, *Ballykissangel*) stars in this series about a British veterinarian who takes his family along to South Africa to release an animal back into the wild. When he sees the area and meets pretty game reserve owner Caroline (Hayley Mills), he ultimately decides to stay.

The Wild Roses – *Canada* – 2009 - In Alberta, a woman and her daughters own the land an oil firm sits on.

William & Mary – 2003 to 2005 - Martin Clunes and Julie Graham star in this dramedy about an odd couple – a woman who welcomes people into the world, and a man who guides them out of it.

Wired – 2008 - Jodie Whittaker stars alongside Riz Ahmed, Laurence Fox, Charlie Brooks, and Toby Stephens in this suspenseful London-based thriller about a young woman whose high-profile promotion carries unexpected costs. She's quickly pushed into a criminal underworld she had no desire to be a part of.

Wolcott – 1981 - Warren Clarke (*Dalziel & Pascoe*) and George Harris (*Casualty*) star in this miniseries about a black policeman promoted to the CID in London's East End.

Wolfblood - 2013 - Wolfblood teenagers have a number of heightened abilities, but their powers also bring danger and a need for secrecy.

Wonderland – *Australia* – 2014 to 2015 - This relationship drama takes place in a Sydney apartment building where most of the characters live.

Wycliffe - 1993 to 1998 - Based on W.J. Burley's novels, this Cornwall-based series features DS Charles Wycliffe, a man who investigates murders with a unique level of determination and accuracy.

Young Dracula - 2006 to 2014 - Count Dracula is a single father, and he's moved his kids Vlad and Ingrid to modern-day Britain. Now, little Vlad wants nothing more than to be a normal British kid and fit in with his friends.

Documentary & Lifestyle

Air Ambulance ER - 2014 - When terrain and road access make it hard for regular ambulances to reach an area quickly, air ambulance teams step in.

A is for Acid – 2002 - Though technically a movie, this one sees Martin Clunes playing John George Haigh, the "Acid Bath Murderer" who killed at least 6 people in 1940s England. Also stars Keeley Hawes.

Animal A&E – *Ireland* – 2010 - This series follows a team of emergency veterinary specialists who help animals in need of urgent care.

Animal Park - 2000 to 2018 - Presenters Ben Fogle and Kate Humble go behind the scenes at Longleat Estate and Safari Park in Wiltshire, telling the stories of the people and animals of the park.

Animal Rescue Squad – 2007 - This series takes us along as professionals work tirelessly to rescue animals from dangerous situations.

Anna's Wild Life – 2011 to 2012 - After buying a wildlife park with no experience in caring for wild animals, Anna and Colin are somehow surprised to find it's hard to care for 100+ exotic creatures.

The Ballymurphy Precedent - 2018 - In August 1971, 10 apparently innocent Catholics were killed in Northern Ireland by an elite British Parachute Regiment. Officially, the British army claims they were armed terrorists.

Banged Up - 2008 - This docuseries follows a unique experiment fronted by British Home Secretary the Rt. Hon David

Blunkett. For 10 days, the empty Scarborough Prison is re-opened to take in a group of out of control teenagers.

Battle of Kings: Bannockburn - 2014 - King Robert the Bruce's campaign against King Edward II of England culminated in the Battle of Bannockburn in 1314. This docudrama tells the story.

Bear Grylls: Survival School - 2016 - Adventurer Bear Grylls takes a group of kids out to test their outdoor skills and teach them more about survival.

The Big House Reborn – 2015 - This series follows National Trust conservators as they restore the Mount Stewart House.

Bridges that Built London – 2012 - This hour-long special examines London's great bridges.

Britain's Best Bakery - 2012 to 2014 - Experts travel Great Britain in search of the best independent bakeries.

Brushstrokes: Every Picture Tells a Story – 2013 - British art critic Waldemar Januszczak dives into the stories behind four works from Gauguin, Van Gogh, Cezanne, and Dobson.

Celtic Britain - 2000 - This docuseries takes a look at Celtic history in Scotland, Wales, Ireland, and elsewhere in the British Isles.

The Celts – 2013 - This series takes a look at who the Celts were, where they came from, and how they influenced history and modern times.

The Celts: Blood, Iron, and Sacrifice with Alice Roberts and Neil Oliver – 2015 - Alice Roberts and Neil Oliver examine the origins of the Celts in this three-part documentary.

Classic Mary Berry - 2018 - In this series, famed chef Mary Berry travels around England, cooking dishes inspired by the locations she visits. This includes ethnically-diverse South London, the classic British countryside, and even Port Isaac on the Cornish coast (aka Portwenn of *Doc Martin* fame).

Comfort Eating - 2017 - Comedian Nick Helm goes on the road seeking out Britain's best comfort foods in places like Islington, Camden, Leeds, Brighton, Berlin, St. Albans, Paris, Little Europe, Peckham, Essex, Soho, Wales, Notting Hill, Glasgow, and Borough Market.

The Crest - 2019 - Two cousins meet for the first time in Ireland to celebrate their shared heritage and love of surfing.

Crime Secrets - 2013 - This fascinating series takes a look at the tricks criminals use to separate victims from their money and possessions.

Derek Acorah's Ghost Towns – 2013 - This paranormal investigation show takes you around England with host Derek Acorah.

Design Doctors – Ireland – 2018 - This series helps Irish homeowners make their homes more attractive.

The Detectives –2015 to 2017 - More true crime than mystery, this documentary series follows a special sex crimes unit in the Greater Manchester Police.

Diana: The New Evidence - 2017 - This documentary takes a look at new evidence in the case of Lady Diana's death.

Donal MacIntyre: Breaking Crime – Ireland – 2015 - In this series, Donal MacIntyre takes a look at youth crime and what causes it.

England's Forgotten Queen: The Life and Death of Lady Jane Grey - 2018 - Historian Helen Castor guides us through this documentary series about Lady Jane Grey, the young woman who served as first reigning queen of England. Though she had a reputation as one of the most learned young women of her time, her reign would last just nine days and end in tragedy.

Escape to the Country – 2002 to present - Each episode follows a different set of homebuyers looking to leave crowded areas and find new homes in the British countryside.

The Farm Fixer – Ireland – 2012 - This show visits struggling small farms around Ireland and attempts to help them improve their situations.

Gangs of Britain - 2013 - Martin and Gary Kemp visit a number of cities around Great Britain to investigate their histories with organised crime.

George III: The Genius of the Mad King - 2017 - This documentary takes a look at the newly-unlocked personal papers and documents of King George III.

Grand Designs – 1999 to present - Kevin McCloud follows people as they attempt to build their dream homes.

Grand Tours of the Scottish Islands – 2013 to 2016 - Paul Murton guides us around some of Scotland's most beautiful islands.

Greatest Gardens - 2015 - This series seeks out the best private gardens in Northern Ireland.

The Great Hip Hop Hoax - 2013 - This documentary tells the story of two Scottish students who faked American accents and identities in pursuit of rap careers in California.

Grow, Cook, Eat - *Ireland* - 2019 to present - This Irish series is designed for people who don't know much about gardening, but want to try growing something they can eat.

Harrow: A Very British School – 2013 - A reality program set in a posh boarding school.

History Cold Case - 2010 to 2011 - Professor Sue Black and her team use modern forensic techniques to examine the remains of the past.

The Hollies: Look Through Any Window - 2011 - This documentary takes a look back at one of the most successful British bands of the 1960s and 70s.

Home of Fabulous Cakes - 2013 - In this brief series, Leicestershire baker Fiona Cairns shares some of her top cake baking secrets. Royal fans will likely remember Ms. Cairns as the creator of the lovely eight-tiered cake for the wedding of the Duke and Duchess of Cambridge back in 2011. She offers practical tips any baker can put to use in their own confections.

The House that 100k Built: Tricks of the Trade – 2015 - This series takes a look at some of the low-cost building and renovation methods used to create really amazing spaces on a budget.

Idris Elba: King of Speed - 2013 - Idris Elba explores the world's greatest raceways, contemplating the question of why we're so obsessed with speed. In his quest, he travels from London to America to Finland.

The Impressionists – 2015 - British art critic Waldemar Januszczak travels around the world investigating the great Impressionists.

Inside the Ambulance – 2016 to 2018 - In this series, an ambulance is rigged with cameras to offer a new perspective on the lives of paramedics in the West Midlands region of the UK.

Inside the Tower of London: Crimes, Conspiracies, Confessions – 2017 - This four-part series goes into the gruesome history of the Tower of London.

Ireland's Greatest Robberies - Jim McCabe presents this look at some of the most ambitious robberies to occur on Irish soil.

The Irish Pub – 2013 - This documentary explores the history and culture of pubs in Ireland.

It Came From Connemara - 2017 - In the mid-1990s, legendary Hollywood producer Roger Corman decided to open a production studio in Ireland. This documentary takes a look at his work there.

The Joy of Techs - 2017 - A technophobe and a technophile join forces to test some of the world's top gadgets. Rather than simply grabbing an iPhone and reviewing it, they put the products into taxing real world situations. They attempt to destroy indestructible gadgets, navigate the French Alps, survive off the grid, and romance women, among other things.

Julius Caesar with Mary Beard - 2018 - Historian Mary Beard reveals new insights on Julius Caesar and how he rose to power.

Kitchen Nightmares - 2007 to 2014 - British chef Gordon Ramsay hosts this series in which he visits struggling American restaurants and spends a week trying to help them succeed.

The Last Days of Anne Boleyn - 2013 - This documentary takes a look at who Anne Boleyn really was, and why her life had to end in such a tragic, violent way.

Legends of King Arthur – 2001 - This series takes a look at the enduring appeal of Arthurian legend.

Len and Ainsley's Big Food Adventure – 2015 - Two celebrities go on a culinary road trip of Britain.

The Life & Crimes of William Palmer – 1998 - Based on a true story, this miniseries tells the story of Victorian doctor and murderer William Palmer.

Lily Allen: From Riches to Rags - 2011 - This documentary series follows early-2000s pop singer Lily Allen as she and her sister launch a fashion line in London.

Living the Tradition: An Enchanting Journey into Old Irish Airs - 2017 - This documentary takes the viewer on a journey into the world of traditional Irish music.

Manet & the Birth of Impressionism - 2009 - British art critic Waldemar Januszczak takes a look at the difficult artist who is often cited as the father of Impressionism, even though he distanced himself from the movement.

The Man Who Cracked the Nazi Code - 2018 - This documentary celebrates the awkward but brilliant man, Alan Turing, whose work helped to make the D-Day landings possible.

The Man Who Killed Richard III – 2015 - This documentary attempts to prove that King Richard III was killed by Welshman Sir Rhys ap Thomas of Carew Castle in Pembrokeshire. Richard III's death paved the way for the Tudor monarchy, thus giving Britain its current queen. Many believe we owe ap Thomas a debt of gratitude for that reason, and though a strong case can be made, it's impossible to be 100% certain he was the one who committed the act of regicide.

Martin Clunes: A Man and His Dogs - 2010 - Martin Clunes takes a closer look at how and why we've decided to share our lives and homes with dogs.

Martin Clunes & a Lion Called Mugie – 2014 - Martin Clunes travels to Kenya to meet an orphaned lion cub brought to the Kora National Reserve.

Martin Clunes: Heavy Horsepower – 2010 - *Doc Martin* star Martin Clunes investigates man's relationship with horses.

Martin Clunes: Last Lemur Standing – 2012 - Martin Clunes travels to the Indian Ocean to find out about the challenges facing lemurs.

Meet the Romans - 2012 - British historian Mary Beard takes us along on a deep dive into what life was like during the Roman Empire.

Missing Persons Unit - *Australia* - 2006 to 2009 - This series uses footage captured over months of investigative work to show what happens when someone goes missing.

Most Haunted - 2002 to present - Yvette Fielding leads this paranormal investigation series that primarily focuses on the UK and Ireland.

Mummy's Little Murderer - 2013 - This true crime documentary tells the story of Elliot Turner, a boy whose mother helped him cover it up when he murdered his girlfriend.

Nature's Treasure Islands - 2014 - Stewart McPherson attempts to become the first person to visit all 14 British Overseas Territories. Along the way, he shares loads of beautiful flora and fauna.

Older Than Ireland – 2015 - This series interviews 30 Irish centenarians to build a living history of modern-day Ireland.

One Born Every Minute - 2010 to 2018 - This popular documentary series highlights the drama of one of the most ordinary things people do – giving birth. Focusing on the human stories behind each situation, you'll see both the highs and lows of what happens in a maternity hospital.

One Night Stand with Anne Sibonney - *Canada* - 2014 - This Canadian food and travel series includes an episode in Glasgow.

On the Yorkshire Buses - 2014 - Buses make up roughly two-thirds of all public transport usage in the UK today, but what's it like to be one of the bus drivers who keep Britain moving? This series follows a number of bus drivers over the course of the summer holiday season in Yorkshire. This is not to be confused with *All Aboard!*, the series that takes you through scenic journeys.

The Real Middle Earth - 2007 - Sir Ian Holm narrates this look at the buildings and places that helped shape J.R.R. Tolkien's Middle Earth.

Renaissance Unchained – 2015 - British art critic Waldemar Januszczak explores the history of the Renaissance throughout Europe.

Restoration Home – 2010 - Actress Caroline Quentin (*Jonathan Creek, Blue Murder*) hosts this series about restoring neglected historic homes around Britain.

Restoration Man – 2014 - Architect George Clarke helps people all over the UK as they take on ambitious renovations and transformations of unique and historic spaces.

Rococo Before Bedtime – 2014 - British art historian Waldemar Januszczak examines the history and grandeur of the Rococo period.

IMDB TV

Room to Improve – 2013 to 2019 - Irish architect Dermot Bannan travels Ireland helping people create their dream homes.

Ross Kemp: Back on the Frontline - 2011 - Actor Ross Kemp returns to Afghanistan in 2011 to find out how things have changed since 2001 and 9/11

Ross Kemp: Return to Afghanistan - 2009 - Ross Kemp and his team visit Britain's frontline in Helman province, Afghanistan, offering a view of what it's really like to fight the Taliban.

Rubens: An Extra Large Story - 2015 - British host Waldemar Januszczak takes a look at the world of Sir Peter Paul Rubens.

Scapegoat – 2017 - This story is the dramatisation of the real story of one of Ireland's most famous unsolved murders, which resulted in an innocent man being found guilty but insane. Not to be confused with *Scapegoat*, a 2012 film starring Matthew Rhys and Eileen Atkins.

Secret Nature - 2004 - This series opens up Oxford Scientific Films' archives to take a look at some of the most difficult animals to capture on film.

Secrets of the Irish Landscape - *Ireland* - 2018 - Presenter Derek Mooney travels around Ireland and Europe to piece together the history of Ireland's landscape and how it came to be.

The Shelbourne Hotel – *Ireland* - 2016 to 2017 - This reality show takes us behind the scenes at one of Dublin's poshest hotels.

Shoreline Detectives - 2017 to 2019 - Dr. Tori Herridge and her team of historians and archaeologists explore seabeds and sand banks to find remnants of Britain's history.

Smart Travels with Rudy Maxa – 2002 to 2006 - Although not exclusively about Great Britain, this series includes episodes in London, the London countryside, Dublin, Ireland's West Coast, Bath, South Wales, Edinburgh, and St. Andrews (not to mention a lot of other lovely cities around the world).

Snowdonia 1890 - 2010 - Two families live as though they were 19th century farmers on Mount Snowdonia in Wales.

The Special Needs Hotel – 2015 - On the Somerset coast, a grand Victorian hotel trains special needs individuals for careers in hospitality.

Surgery School - 2010 - Follow the lives of 10 junior doctors setting out as surgical trainees.

Terry Jones' Great Map Mystery – 2008 - *Monty Python* star Terry Jones travels around Britain to see if it's still possible to follow the earliest roadmaps of Wales.

This is Personal: The Hunt for the Yorkshire Ripper – 2000 - This short series is a dramatisation of the investigation into the Yorkshire Ripper murders of the 1970s, and the effect it had on the man who led the enquiry.

The Toilet: An Unspoken History - 2012 - This quirky programme takes a look at toilets throughout the ages.

Tony Robinson's Gods and Monsters – 2011 - Tony Robinson explores the dark corners of Britain's history, including witches, human sacrifice, demons, and sprites.

Trolley Dollies – 2002 - This docu-soap features the lives of a charter flight crew that travels to some of the most popular vacation destinations in the world.

The Tube: Going Underground – 2016 - This documentary gives you a behind-the-scenes look at what it takes to keep the Tube functioning.

Very British Problems – 2015 to 2016 - This hilarious program interviews celebrities about the cultural quirks of being British.

Walking Through History With Tony Robinson – 2013 to 2015 - Tony Robinson selects long walks around Britain for their combined scenery and historic merits.

Whisky: The Islay Edition - 2010 - This special takes a look at what goes on at Islay, the Scottish capital of whisky.

The Witness - 2016 - This suspenseful documentary takes a look at the Kitty Genovese murder - the shocking case where 38 witnesses watched a woman get stabbed to death during an hour-long attack.

IMDB TV

NETFLIX

Website: http://netflix.com

Description: One of the biggest and oldest streaming services, Netflix offers a wide variety of content from all over the world - along with quite a bit of their own original content.

Available On: Roku, Fire TV, Apple TV, Apple iPhone & iPad, Chromecast, Fire tablets, select Smart TVs, Android phones and tablets, and computer (via web browser).

Cost: $8.99/month (1 screen), $13.99 HD (2 screens same time), $17.99 UHD (4 screens same time)

Now Streaming
Mysteries & Crime Dramas

Behind Her Eyes - 2021 - This thriller blends supernatural elements into the story of Louise, a single woman whose world changes when she starts having an affair with her boss and simultaneously becomes friends with his wife.

Broadchurch – 2013 to 2017 - When an 11-year-old boy is murdered in a quiet coastal community, town secrets are exposed. David Tennant (*Deadwater Fell*) and Olivia Colman (*Rev*) star.

Collateral – 2018 - When a pizza delivery man is gunned down in London, DI Kip Glaspie refuses to accept that it's just a random act of violence. Her investigation drags her into a dark underworld she never could have predicted. The series stars John Simm of *Life on Mars*, along with Nicola Walker (*River*), Billie Piper (*Doctor Who*), and Carey Mulligan (*Never Let Me Go*).

Criminal: United Kingdom – 2019 - This three-episode series takes a look at the intense interrogation of three different suspects in London. David Tennant makes an appearance in one episode.

Deadwind – *Finland* – 2018 to present - Detective Sofia Karppi investigates a murder with ties to a construction firm.

Fallet - *Sweden* - 2017 - Two detectives, one Swedish and one British, attempt to solve a murder together.

The Five – 2016 - Years after a young boy disappears, his DNA turns up at a crime scene. Based on the novel by Harlen Coben.

The Frankenstein Chronicles – 2015 to 2017 - In 1827 London, a detective hunts a killer with an appetite for dismemberment.

Giri/Haji - 2019 - Japanese detective Kenzo Mori travels to London to figure out whether his brother Yuto, presumed dead, is actually dead. Yuto is believed to have killed the nephew of a Yakuza member, and the search draws Kenzo into the criminal underworld of London.

Hinterland – 2013 to 2016 - This Welsh crime drama takes place in the coastal town of Aberystwyth, where DCI Tom Mathias is just getting started in a new position.

The Indian Detective – *Canada* – 2017 - A suspended Canadian police officer returns home to Mumbai and helps out with an investigation.

Intelligence – *Canada* – 2005 to 2007 - The female head of an organized crime unit faces off against the confident male leader of a drug-smuggling ring.

Kiss Me First – 2018 - Two girls become friends in the virtual world of an online game, and one is pulled into something much darker than she had imagined.

Lucifer - *United States* - 2016 to present - Though American, this Los Angeles-based procedural stars British actor Tom Ellis (*Miranda*). He plays Lucifer, the naughty son of God who's decided he's sick of Hell and wants to spend some time on Earth.

Lupin - *France* - 2021 - Inspired by the classic tales of gentleman thief Arsène Lupin, this modern series follows a Senegalese immigrant named Assane Diop. He's seeking revenge for his father's false imprisonment and suicide, and he draws inspiration from the gentleman thief.

Marcella – 2016 to present - After her divorce, Marcella returns to work as a detective in London. A serial killer she once pursued may have done the same.

Paranoid – 2016 - What begins as a cozy British mystery quickly evolves into a massive European conspiracy.

Quicksand - *Sweden* - 2019 - After a school tragedy, a teenager finds herself on trial for murder.

Requiem – 2018 - After her mother commits suicide, a young woman finds evidence that might tie her to an abduction in Wales more than 20 years prior.

Retribution – 2016 - When a newlywed couple is killed, police question their feuding families and uncover more than they expected.

Ripper Street – 2012 to 2017 - This detective series is set in 1889 London in the aftermath of the Jack the Ripper killings.

Safe – 2018 - Michael C. Hall (*Dexter*) tries on a British accent for his role in this series about a widowed surgeon whose teenage daughter goes missing.

Sherlock – 2010 to 2017 - Benedict Cumberbatch stars in this modern-day version of Sir Arthur Conan Doyle's *Sherlock Holmes* tales.

The Stranger - 2020 - Based on the Harlan Coben novel of the same title, this series sees a mysterious stranger tell a man a secret that destroys his otherwise nice life.

Tidelands – *Australia* – 2018 - When an ex-con returns to her hometown, it brings long-hidden truths to the surface.

Traitors – 2019 - Near the end of World War II, a young English woman assists a mysterious American agent as he tries to root out Russian infiltration in the British government.

Vexed – 2010 to 2012 - A young male and female detective team frustrate each other with their different attitudes and complicated personal lives.

Wanted – *Australia* – 2016 to 2018 - Two strangers become involuntary partners when they witness a murder and get framed for the crime.

Young Wallander – 2020 - Though the Kenneth Branagh adaptation of Wallander left Netflix this year, Netflix made this new series, an adaptation that imagines Kurt Wallander as a police officer in his early 20s in 2020 Sweden.

Dramas

Alias Grace – *Canada* – 2017 - In 19th-century Canada, a murderess might be deemed not guilty by reason of insanity. This limited series is based on Margaret Atwood's novel.

Anne With An "E" – *Canada* – 2017 to 2019 - Based on Anne of Green Gables, this series follows a spirited young orphan who goes to live with a spinster.

Between – *Canada* – 2016 - When a strange disease kills every town resident over the age of 21, the youthful inhabitants of the town are quarantined.

Black Earth Rising – 2018 - Investigator Kate Ashby is forced to investigate her own past when she takes on war crimes cases.

Black Mirror – 2007 to 2019 - This ominous modern thriller anthology gives us glimpses into some very dark possibilities for the future.

Black Mirror: Bandersnatch – 2018 - In 1984, a programmer adapts a novel into a video game, growing less connected to reality as the project moves along. This is an interactive story with multiple endings.

Bodyguard – 2018 - Keeley Hawes and Richard Madden star in this hit drama about a veteran who helps thwart a terrorist attack and gets assigned to protect a prominent politician.

The Borgias – *Canada* – 2011 to 2013 - This period drama follows the notorious and frequently unethical Borgia family.

Bridgerton - 2020 - Based on Julia Quinn's best-selling historical romance series, *The Bridgertons*, this period drama will mark one of Shonda Rhimes' first projects with streaming giant Netflix. The eight-episode, hour-long series is set in Regency London's high society, but with a healthy dose of ethnic diversity.

Call the Midwife – 2012 to present - This drama looks into the lives of dedicated midwives in impoverished East London of the 1950s and 60s.

Can't Cope, Won't Cope – *Ireland* – 2016 to 2018 - In Dublin, two young women realize their childish ways are wearing thin.

Cleverman – *Australia* – 2016 to 2017 - In a future world, powerful humanoid creatures try to survive in a world dominated by humans.

The Code - *Australia* - 2014 to 2016 - When two brothers, a hacker and a journalist, are facing the possibility of extradition to the US, the Australian National Security offers them a way out. They're taken to a government facility and told that if they help out, the slate will be wiped clean.

The Crown – 2016 to present - This Netflix original follows some particularly dramatic times in Queen Elizabeth's reign during the last half of the 20th century. Claire Foy and Olivia Colman portray Queen Elizabeth II.

Dark Matter – *Canada* – Waking up on a spaceship with no memories, a crew must attempt to figure out who they are and how they got there.

Dead Set – 2008 - Housemates in a reality show are clueless as the undead attack the compound.

Doctor Foster – 2015 to 2017 - When a woman suspects her husband of having an affair, her investigations lead her down a dark path.

Dracula - 2020 - Mark Gatiss and Steven Moffat have paired up for this new take on Dracula. Danish actor Claes Bang has been cast as Count Dracula, but the biggest treat might be Joanna Scanlan (*No Offence*) as Mother Superior. The new series has been described as a tale in which Dracula is "the hero of his own story".

The End of the F***ing World – 2017 to present - A rebel and a psychopath embark on a teenage road trip.

The English Game – 2020 - This sports-themed period drama was developed by Julian Fellowes (*Downton Abbey*) for Netflix, and it follows the origins of modern football in England. Set in the 1870s, it brings us to a time when football was considered a sport for the wealthy – until two players from opposite ends of the social spectrum come together to change the game forever.

Freud - *Austria* - 2020 - In 1886 Vienna, a young Sigmund Freud hasn't yet risen to prominence. When a series of murders happens within Vienna high society, he teams up with a medium and a policeman to get to the bottom of things.

Frontier – *Canada* – 2016 to 2018 - In 18th-century North America, trappers and traders try to gain control in the fur trade.

Get Even - 2020 - At the elite Bannerman Independent School, a group of teenage girls band together to expose bullies and fight for justice. It's all going rather well until one of their targets is murdered and found holding a note pointing the finger at their group.

Glitch – *Australia* – 2015 to 2019 - In a small Australian town, seven local residents return from the dead in perfect condition.

Heartland – *Canada* – 2007 to present - A young woman deals with the stress of potentially losing the family ranch after the sudden death of her mother.

The Innocents – 2018 - Two teenage lovers find themselves in a world of trouble when one begins to show unexplainable abilities.

Land Girls - 2009 to 2011 - Land Girls follows four women in the Women's Land Army during WW2.

The Last Kingdom – 2020 - Set in the days of Alfred the Great, this Netflix Original takes us on one man's quest to reclaim his birthright.

Last Tango in Halifax – 2012 to present - Once upon a time, they were in love. Now, decades later, they meet again for a second chance. This time, there's more baggage.

The Letter for the King - 2020 - Based on the 1962 Dutch novel *De brief voor de Koning* by Tonke Dragt, this series follows an aspiring knight as he attempts to deliver a secret letter to the king.

London Spy – 2015 - After his lover disappears, a fun-loving young man dives into the dangerous world of espionage.

Merlin - 2009 to 2013 - Colin Morgan (*The Fall*) stars as a young Merlin in his days as a mere servant to Prince Arthur of Camelot. In this version of Camelot, magic is banned and Merlin is forced to keep his talent hidden away.

Nightflyers - *United States* - 2018 - Though it's an American series, much of the cast for this horror-sci fi series is English or Irish. Based on George R.R. Martin's novella and short story series of the same name, the show is set in 2093, and it sees a group of scientists venturing into space to make contact with alien life forms.

Outlander - 2014 to present - In 1945, an English nurse is mysteriously transported back in time to Scotland in 1743. The massively-popular series is based on the novels of Diana Gabaldon.

Peaky Blinders – 2014 to present - Set in early 20th century Birmingham, this series focuses on gang boss Tommy Shelby and his family.

Pine Gap – *Australia* – 2018 - At a top-secret US and Australian defense facility, the alliance begins to show strain.

The Queen's Gambit - *United States* - Though not technically British, this critically-acclaimed chess drama features a number of British actors. Lead Anya Taylor-Joy was raised in England and appeared on shows like *Endeavour* and *Peaky Blinders*. The series follows a young, orphaned chess prodigy from childhood to adulthood.

Rake - *Australia* - 2011 to 2018 - Defense lawyer Cleaver Greene makes a career out of hopeless cases, perhaps because his own personal life is troubled enough to help him relate.

The Rain - *Denmark* - 2018 to 2020 - After a virus wipes out most of the world's population, two siblings battle to survive their new reality.

Rebellion – 2016 - During WWI, three Irish women must choose sides in the revolt against English rule.

Republic of Doyle – *Canada* – 2010 to 2014 - Jake and Malachy Doyle are a father and son PI team in Newfoundland.

Secret City – *Australia* – 2016 - One student's protest leads to government scandal.

Shameless (US) - *United States* - 2011 to present - This American series is an adaptation of Paul Abbott's British series of the same name and features an ensemble cast led by William H. Macy and Emmy Rossum.

Skins – 2007 to 2013 - This racy classic offers a look into modern teenage life in England.

Top Boy – 2019 to present - This gritty drama focuses on drug dealers in London public housing. See also: Top Boy – Summerhouse.

Travelers – *Canada* – 2016 to 2018 - In the far future, special agents are tasked with traveling back in time to prevent the collapse of society.

Troy: Fall of a City – 2018 - This miniseries is a retelling of the siege of Troy, loosely based on the Iliad.

Van Helsing – *Canada* – 2016 to present - After waking up from a coma, a young woman finds the world ravaged by vampires.

Wanderlust – 2018 - A middle-aged couple decides the answer to their marital doldrums is to see other people. Toni Collette and Steven Mackintosh star.

Watership Down – 2018 - This modern-day retelling of the British classic features a warren of rabbits on a daring journey to find a new place to call home.

Wentworth – *Australia* – 2013 to present - An innocent woman has to figure out how to survive in prison while awaiting trial for the murder of her husband.

White Lines - 2020 - When a popular Manchester DJ's body turns up twenty years after his disappearance from Ibiza, his sister makes a trip to the island in hopes of finding out what really happened. Her quest leads her through shady nightclubs, super yachts, and a multitude of lies and coverups. The series is headed up by Alex Pina, writer of *La Casa de Papel*, one of Netflix's most popular non-English series.

The Witcher - 2019 - Henry Cavill stars in this upcoming series about a solitary monster hunter in a world full of wicked people. It's been billed as Netflix's attempt at a Game of Thrones-style series, and it's already been renewed for a second season. The series is based on the book series of the same name by Andrzej Sapkowski. See also: *Making the Witcher* and *Inside the Episodes: The Witcher*.

Wyonna Earp – *Canada* – 2016 to present - A descendant of Wyatt Earp teams up with an immortal Doc Holiday in this supernatural comic-inspired Wild West tale.

Comedies

After Life – 2019 to present - After losing his wife to cancer, a suicidal widower struggles to come to terms with his new life. Starring Ricky Gervais (in a series that will surprise many, especially those who aren't normally fans of Gervais).

Borderline – 2016 to 2018 - This comedy follows an inept team of border patrol agents at a fictitious airport.

Crashing – 2016 - A group of young people live as property guardians in an unused hospital in London. Phoebe Waller-Bridge (*Fleabag*) stars.

Crazyhead – 2016 - 20-somethings work on becoming adults while also battling demons in this comedy.

Cuckoo – 2012 to 2019 - When a British woman brings an American hippie back home as her husband, it sets off turmoil in her polite and proper family.

David Brent: Life on the Road - 2016 - Ricky Gervais returns to the role of David Brent in this spin-off film that sees him attempting to become a rock star.

Derek – 2012 to 2014 - Ricky Gervais stars in this comedy about a good-hearted but slow nursing home care assistant.

Derry Girls – 2018 to present - This Northern Irish sitcom takes place in 1990s Derry, where a group of young women grow up during the Troubles.

The Duchess - 2020 - Canadian comedienne Katherine Ryan stars in this comedy about a chaotic single mum who enjoys offending the people around her. When she's not telling off fellow mums or sending nudes to their husbands, she's trying to decide if she should have another child with her ex or accept a "second-hand crack baby" via adoption.

Extras – 2005 to 2007 - Ricky Gervais (*The Office*) stars as an actor reduced to working as an extra, forever making himself look bad as he attempts to get ahead.

Feel Good - 2020 - This comedy series follows two young women who fall in love in London. Mae is a Canadian comedian, while George is a typical middle-class English woman who struggles to tell others about their relationship. Mae Martin and Charlotte Richie star as Mae and George, while Lisa Kudrow plays Mae's mother.

Flowers – 2016 to 2018 - Olivia Colman and Julian Barratt star in this dark comedy about a very troubled English family.

Greg Davies: You Magnificent Beast - 2018 - British comedian Greg Davies talks manscaping, family pranks, and more.

Hoff the Record – 2015 to 2016 - This David Hasselhoff mockumentary sees him attempting to make a comeback in the UK.

The IT Crowd – 2006 to 2013 - Banished to the basement, two nerds and their clueless leader service the IT needs of a strange and generic corporation.

Jack Whitehall at Large – 2017 - This hour-long comedy special features the standup work of comedian Jack Whitehall.

Jack Whitehall: Christmas With My Father – 2019 - This Christmas special sees Jack Whitehall NOT travelling with his father – instead, taking the stage in London's West End with a host of celebrity guests.

Jack Whitehall: I'm Only Joking - 2020 - Comedian Jack Whitehall talks about life in hotels, human stupidity, and of course, his father.

Jack Whitehall: Travels with My Father – 2017 to present - A man and his father have little in common, but they come together as they travel around the world.

James Acaster: Repertoire – 2018 - This collection features four performances from quirky comedian James Acaster.

Jimmy Carr: Funny Business - 2016 - British comedian Jimmy Carr delivers a set to the UK's Hammersmith Apollo.

Jimmy Carr: The Best of Ultimate Gold Greatest Hits - 2019 - This collection gathers up some of the most outrageous and entertaining jokes from Jimmy Carr's stand-up career.

Kath & Kim – *Australia* – 2002 to 2007 - A quirky mother and daughter pair lead an interesting life in the suburbs of Melbourne. See also: *Da Kath & Kim Code* and *Kath & Kimderella*.

Kim's Convenience – *Canada* – 2016 to present - This sitcom focuses on a Korean family that runs a small convenience store in Toronto.

The Letdown – *Australia* – 2019 - A new mum meets strange friends in a new parent support group.

Loaded – 2017 - After four friends sell their startup for $300 million, life gets a bit more difficult. This series is based on the popular Israeli series Mesudarim (which is often described as an Israeli version of Silicon Valley meets Entourage).

Lovesick (aka Scrotal Recall) – 2014 to 2018 - After finding out he has an STD, a young man must attempt to contact former lovers.

Man Down – 2013 to 2017 - Dan is a child trapped in a man's body, and he's not loving adulthood.

Man Like Mobeen – 2017 to present - In Small Heath, Birmingham, ex-drug dealer Mobeen tries to be a good Muslim and make sure his sister grows up properly.

Meet the Adebanjos – 2012 to present - In South London, a Nigerian father tries to teach traditional African values to his modern British family – with entertaining results.

Michael McIntyre: Showman - 2020 - Comedian Michael McIntyre talks about family, tech, accents, and sharks in this hour-long stand-up set.

Monty Python's Almost the Truth – 2009 - Though this is technically a documentary, it made sense to include it here alongside the other Monty Python titles.

Monty Python and the Holy Grail – 1975 - King Arthur and his knights seek the Holy Grail, but they're not very well-suited to the task.

Monty Python Before the Flying Circus – 2000 - This documentary takes a look at how six talented men became the groundbreaking troupe, Monty Python.

Monty Python Best Bits – 2014 - This series compiles clips + opinions from prominent comedians, many of whom considered Monty Python to be influential on their careers.

Monty Python Conquers America – 2008 - This documentary takes a look at how Monty Python shaped a number of American comedians.

Monty Python's Fliegender Zircus – 1972 - This collection of sketches was created for German television. A must-watch for serious Monty Python fans.

Monty Python's Flying Circus – 1969 to 1974 - The classic British sketch comedy is now streaming on Netflix.

Monty Python's Life of Brian – 1979 - More Monty Python fun revolving around a man who deals with a particularly nasty case of mistaken identity.

Monty Python Live at Aspen – 1998 - The men of Monty Python reunite to discuss the making of their iconic show.

Monty Python Live at the Hollywood Bowl – 1982 - Clips and animations feature in this live-to-tape performance of Monty Python's greatest hits.

Monty Python Live (Mostly): One Down, Five to Go – 2014 - Live from London in a sold-out final show, the remaining members of Monty Python reunited to reprise their old roles.

Monty Python's Personal Best – 2005 - Members of the Monty Python troupe select their favorite sketches.

Monty Python: The Meaning of Live – 2014 - After a lengthy hiatus, the Monty Python crew reunited for this live performance.

Offspring - *Australia* - 2010 to 2017 - This dramedy follows a thirtysomething obstetrician and her circle of friends in Melbourne.

NETFLIX

115

People Just Do Nothing – 2014 to 2018 - This mockumentary follows some very bad wannabe MCs from West London.

Ricky Gervais: Humanity - 2018 - Ricky Gervais performs a standup routine on celebrity, mortality, and the way modern society is offended by everything.

Rita - *Denmark* - 2017 to present - Danish schoolteacher Rita may be popular with her students, but she struggles with adults. See also: *Hjørdis*

Russell Howard: Recalibrate - 2017 - Comedian Russell Howard talks about everything from politics to porn in this hour-long set.

Schitt's Creek – *Canada* – 2015 to 2020 - After a wealthy family loses everything, they attempt to rebuild in the small town they once bought their son as a birthday gift gag.

Sex Education – 2019 to present - Though technically British, there's something VERY American-feeling about this series. It's a series about a socially awkward teen whose mother is a sex therapist.

Sick Note – 2018 - When an aimless young man is misdiagnosed with cancer, his life starts to get exciting.

Simon Amstell: Set Free – 2019 - If you enjoyed *Grandma's House*, you might like this standup set from comedian Simon Amstell (star and co-writer of the British comedy). He's an introspective comic, and this set dives into love, ego, intimacy, and ayahuasca.

Sisters – *Australia* – 2018 - A young woman suddenly finds out she has two sisters and more than 100 brothers.

Some Assembly Required – *Canada* – 2015 - A teenager takes over control of a toy company.

Still Game – 2002 to 2019 - Scottish comedy about three old men in a Glasgow highrise.

Toast of London – 2013 to 2015 - A classically trained British actor struggles with both his personal and professional lives.

Trailer Park Boys – Canada – 2001 to present - This trailer park comedy follows a group of men in constant pursuit of a big score and an easier life. See also: *The Movie, Trailer Park Boys: Xmas Special, Trailer Park Boys: Live at the North Pole, The Animated Series, Countdown to Liquor Day, Out of the Park: USA, Out of the Park: Europe, Say Goodnight to the Bad Guys, SwearNet, SwearNet Live, Trailer Park Boys: Drunk, High, & Unemployed: Live in Austin*, and *Live in F**kin Dublin*.

Turn Up Charlie - 2019 - Idris Elba (*Luther*) stars as Charlie, a struggling DJ and confirmed bachelor. When he sees a possible upside for his career, he reluctantly agrees to play nanny to a good friend's dreadful young daughter. Piper Perabo (*Coyote Ugly*) stars as his famous friend Sara.

The Very Best of Monty Python's Flying Circus - 1989 - In celebration of the 20th anniversary of the TV series, Steve Martin presents this anthology of Monty Python's best sketches.

W1A – 2014 to 2017 - This mockumentary-style show follows the new head of values at the BBC. Hugh Bonneville (*Downton Abbey*) stars, and the series features numerous cameos.

White Gold – 2017 to 2019 - This period comedy takes place in 1980s Essex, where obnoxious salesman Vincent Swan and his team do whatever it takes to sell double-glazed windows.

The Windsors – 2016 to present - This mockumentary parodies the current British royal family.

Workin' Moms – Canada – 2017 to present - When their (remarkably long Canadian) maternity leaves are over, a group of moms return to work.

Documentary & Lifestyle

21 Again - 2019 - A group of young women disguise their mothers as 21-year-olds and send them out into the wild.

3 Wives, One Husband – 2018 - Originally created for British audiences, this series takes a look at modern polygamist families.

Above Us Only Sky - 2018 - Using interviews and behind the scenes footage, this documentary tells the real story behind John Lennon and Yoko Ono's 1971 album, "Imagine".

A Grand Night In: The Story of Aardman - 2015 - This documentary celebrates the animation studio that gave the world *Wallace & Gromit*.

Alien Worlds - 2020 - This docu-series mixes fantasy and science to imagine what life might be like on other planets.

Amazing Interiors – 2018 - This British show travels the world to visit eccentric homeowners and their eccentric homes.

Attacking the Devil - 2014 - This documentary takes a look at Sir Harold Evans' investigations into thalidomide, a drug that left 10,000 babies with deformities.

Baby Ballroom – 2018 - This series goes deep into the cutthroat world of children's ballroom dancing (which we didn't realise existed).

Bad Boy Billionaires: India - 2020 - This docuseries examines the dizzying success and mind-blowing greed of some of India's most infamous tycoons.

Behind Enemy Lines – 2001 - This series takes a look at some of the changes Winston Churchill instituted after WWII setbacks in 1940. He set out to create a force powered by intelligence, stealth, and cunning more than ruthless brute force, and it paid off.

The Big Family Cooking Showdown – 2017 to present - This unscripted reality show brings us some of Britain's most passionate amateur cooks.

The Big Flower Fight – 2020 - This one is best described as "the Great British Bake Off meets the RHS Chelsea Flower Show".

Cabins in the Wild with Dick Strawbridge – 2017 - An engineer and craftsman tour a set of unique cabins in Wales, then build their own.

Caught on Camera – 2015 - This series shows crimes caught on CCTV and cell phones, and how technology is used to solve otherwise unsolvable cases.

Churchill's Secret Agents: The New Recruits - 2018 - This reality series takes 14 modern contestants through the same selection process used for World War II spies.

Click for Murder – 2017 - This docuseries takes a look at the deadly dangers that lurk within the bowels of the internet.

Cocaine – 2005 - This series takes a look at the cocaine industry and its impact on people of all walks of life.

The Code – 2011 - Not to be confused with the fictional TV series, this three-part documentary looks at the mathematics behind all of life.

Conspiracies – 2015 - This series dives into a number of potential coverups and secrets.

Crazy Delicious - 2020 - This food competition show rewards talented home chefs with a golden apple.

Edge of the Universe – 2008 - Astronomers reveal the latest discoveries about the world beyond Earth.

Everyday Miracles – 2014 - Scientist Mark Miodownik highlights the everyday miracles that make modern life so much better than the not-so-distant past.

The Fix - 2018 - Jimmy Carr and a rotating set of comedians sit down and try to solve major world problems with the help of an actual expert.

Genius of the Ancient World – 2015 - Historian Bettany Hughes travels the world to study the lives of great philosophers like Socrates, Confucius, and Buddha.

Genius of the Modern World – 2016 - Historian Bettany Hughes looks at the world that helped shape intellectual greats like Friedrich Nietzsche, Sigmund Freud, and Karl Marx.

Glow Up – 2020 - This series aims to see who can take the sexiest selfie – and the loser gets a makeover.

Grand Designs – 1999 to present- This British reality show that follows people as they attempt to build or massively overhaul homes.

The Great British Baking Show – 2010 to present - This popular British baking show sees amateurs facing off and trying to avoid the dreaded soggy bottom.

The Great British Baking Show: Holidays - 2019 - This series gathers up festive holiday episodes of the popular baking competition.

The Great British Baking Show: Masterclass - 2018 - Mary Berry and Paul Hollywood offer tips on many of the baking techniques used in the popular competition show.

The Great British Baking Show: The Beginnings - 2012 - A dozen amateur bakers compete on this early edition of the Great British Baking Show.

Greatest Events of WWII in Colour – 2019 - This series also takes a look at WWII footage that's been restored with colour.

History 101 – 2020 - This educational series offers short history lessons for those challenged in the "attention span" department – everything from fast food to plastics to the space race and the rise of China.

Hitler's Circle of Evil – 2017 - This docuseries takes a look at the power struggles, plots, and betrayals that took place behind the scenes within Nazi leadership.

How to Live Mortgage Free with Sarah Beeny – 2018 - Sarah Beeny talks to people who've managed to free themselves of a mortgage or monthly rental payment.

I Am a Killer – 2020 - This show goes to America, where capital punishment is still legal, and listen to the stories of Death Row inmates.

I Am a Killer: Released - 2020 - 30 years after being sentenced to death for a murder, a convict is paroled and begins a new life.

Inside the Freemasons – 2017 - This brief series takes a look inside the free and often controversial Freemasons.

Inside the Real Narcos – 2018 - Ex-Special Forces commando Jason Fox takes us inside the world of drug traffickers and cartel members.

Inside the World's Toughest Prisons – 2016 to present - Journalists put themselves inside – behind bars – in some of the world's roughest prisons.

Interior Design Masters – 2019 - Aspiring interior designers transform a variety of spaces in a competition to win a contract with a fashionable London hotel.

The Investigator: A British Crime Story – 2018 - This British true crime series features renowned criminologist Mark Williams-Thomas as he examines unsolved murders.

Keith Richards: Under the Influence - 2015 - This documentary takes a look at the people and music that influenced Keith Richards.

Killer Women with Piers Morgan – 2017 - Women commit just a tiny fraction of all murders, making female murderers a particularly interesting group for study. Who are they? Why do they do it? Piers Morgan takes a closer look.

The Meaning of Monty Python - 2013 - Five Pythons take a look back at their decades of comedic success, along with reflections on process, politics, and change.

Million Pound Menu – 2019 - Young restaurateurs open pop-up restaurants in hopes of attracting and impressing investors.

The Mitfords: A Tale of Two Sisters - 2017 - In the aristocratic Mitford family of Northumberland, sisters Jessica and Diana couldn't have been more different in their political beliefs. Jessica would go on to become a communist, while Diana would ultimately become a fascist.

Murder Maps – 2017 - Dramatic reenactments of famous British murders.

My Beautiful Broken Brain - 2016 - After having a devastating stroke at just 34, a woman documents her rehabilitation efforts.

My Hotter Half – 2017 - Couples compete to see which member of the pair can take the better selfie.

Myths and Monsters - 2017 - This docuseries investigates legends set within the ancient landscapes of Europe.

Nadiya Bakes - 2021 - This series sees chef Nadiya Hussain return to baking, offering recipes from sweet to savoury.

Nadiya's Time to Eat – 2020 - Nadiya Hussain shows how modern families can make great food with limited time.

Nurses Who Kill – 2016 - While nurses are mostly good and compassionate people, a handful use their positions to hurt, rather than heal. This series takes a look at what motivates them.

Our Godfather - 2019 - This documentary takes a look at the life of Tommaso Buscetta, the first high-ranking mafia figure ever to testify against the Cosa Nostra. Though he helped convict more than 400 members, 11 members of his family were killed for his efforts.

Paul Hollywood's Big Continental Road Trip - 2017 - Celebrity chef and car enthusiast Paul Hollywood explores the food and car cultures of France, Germany, and Italy.

Real Crime: Diamond Geezers - 2008 - This docu-film sees a group of old thieves trying - and nearly succeeding - to steal the world's largest perfect diamond.

Real Crime: Supermarket Heist - 2009 - This documentary follows the search for the Tesco bomber, a man who demanded money from the supermarket chain whilst calling himself "Sally".

The Repair Shop – 2017 to present - This delightfully calm series follows a group of craftspeople who help restore objects of importance, many of them antique.

The Ripper - 2020 - This limited series follows the 1970s search for the Yorkshire Ripper.

Rolling Stones: Olé Olé Olé! - 2016 - This feature-length documentary follows the Rolling Stones as they tour Latin America and Cuba.

Roman Empire - 2019 - This docu-drama follows the reigns of three of the Roman Empire's best-known and most interesting leaders: Commodus, Julius Caesar, and Caligula. Sean Bean (*Game of Thrones*) is among the narrators.

The Royal House of Windsor – 2017 - This docuseries analyzes the British royal family's ability to hold onto power over the last century of struggles and changes.

Secrets of Great British Castles – 2016 - Documentary-style program highlighting some of the largest and most historically-important castles around Great Britain (including Stirling, York, and Edinburgh, among others).

Serial Killer with Piers Morgan – 2018 - Piers Morgan takes a closer look at three convicted serial killers and their crimes.

Stunt Science – 2018 - This series looks at the science behind daredevil stunts.

Sunderland 'Til I Die – 2020 - This docuseries follows the Sunderland Association Football Club through the 2017-2018 season as they try to make a big comeback.

They've Gotta Have Us – 2018 - This series interviews black entertainers to trace the history of black cinema.

Win the Wilderness – 2020 - This reality show pits six couples against each other to see who has the best survival skills. The winning couple gets the deed to a home in the wilds of Alaska.

Witches: A Century of Murder – 2015 - Historian Suzannah Lipscomb takes a look at the British witch hunts of the 17th century.

The World's Most Extraordinary Homes – 2017 to present - Caroline Quentin (*Jonathan Creek*) and architect Piers Taylor travel the world to view extraordinary and unusual homes.

World War II in Colour – 2009 - In this 13-episode series, WWII footage is restored and given new life – in colour.

Kids & Young Adults

The A List - 2018 - This series blends romance, drama, suspense, and mystery when a group of young women go to a remote camp with a supernatural presence.

Bottersnikes and Gumbles - 2015 to present - Set in and near a junkyard, this animated programme sees the fun-loving Gumbles attempting to steer clear of the smelly Bottersnikes. Unfortunately, Netflix decided to re-dub the series with American accents.

Creeped Out – 2017 to present - A masked figure known only as "The Curious" collects dark tales in this dramatic young adult anthology series.

Danger Mouse - 2015 to present - These modern episodes see Danger Mouse and hamster Penfold returning for more jet-setting spy adventures.

Danger Mouse: Classic Collection - 1981 to 1992 - This collection of classic episodes features the spy Danger Mouse and his sidekick Penfold as they foil evil plots around the world.

Degrassi : Next Class – *Canada* – 2016 to 2017 - This follow-up to the classic Canadian teen drama features a new generation of teenagers.

Dennis and Gnasher Unleashed - 2017 - This cartoon follows fearless Dennis, his dog Gnasher, and his friends as they seek out fun and adventure around their town.

Free Rein – 2017 to present - A teenager from LA spends the summer in England and bonds with a mysterious horse. See also: *Free Rein: The 12 Neighs of Christmas* and *Free Rein: Valentine's Day*

H2O: Just Add Water – 2009 - A group of young girls deal with turning into mermaids.

Horrid Henry - 2006 to 2019 - Based on Francesca Simon's *Horrid Henry* book series, this show follows the adventures of a very naughty young boy. See also: *Horrid Henry's Gross Day Out*

The Inbestigators - *Australia* - 2019 to present - This light-hearted kids' series follows a group of children who start a detective agency to solve crimes at school and around the neighbourhood.

Little Baby Bum - 2019 - Animated nursery rhyme friends sing fun songs for the little ones. See also: *Learning Songs by Little Baby Bum* and *Little Baby Bum's Go Buster*.

Morphle - 2020 - Little Mila goes on fun and educational adventures with her magical morphing pet called Morphle.

The Octonauts - 2010 to present - This cartoon follows an underwater exploring crew of animals who live in an undersea base called the Octopod.

Operation Ouch - 2012 - This entertaining series takes a lighthearted approach to educating children about doctor visits and medical procedures.

Pablo - 2017 - Using only crayons and creativity, a young boy with autism draws an imaginary world where animal friends help him with real life difficulties.

Robozuna - 2018 to present - A young orphan boy builds a homemade robot to help free his country from an evil empire.

Shaun the Sheep - 2007 to present - This *Wallace & Gromit* spin-off follows the adventures of an unusually clever sheep named Shaun. See also: *Shaun the Sheep: Adventures from Mossy Bottom* and *Shaun the Sheep: The Farmer's Llamas*

Sunny Bunnies - 2015 to present - These furry, colourful bunnies seek fun and mischief wherever they go in this children's series.

Thomas & Friends - 1984 to present - This animated series follows the friendly blue tank engine who lives on the Island of Sodor. See also: *Thomas & Friends: Digs & Discoveries: All Tracks Lead to Rome, Thomas & Friends: Steam Team to the Rescue, Thomas & Friends: Royal Engine, Thomas & Friends: Digs & Discoveries: Mines of Mystery, Thomas & Friends: Marvelous Machinery: A New Arrival*, and *Thomas & Friends: Marvelous Machinery: World of Tomorrow*.

Timmy Time - 2009 to 2012 - This claymation series is a spin-off of *Shaun the Sheep*, and follows little Timmy the lamb as he enters nursery school. See also: *Learning Time Timmy*

The Unlisted - *Australia* - 2019 - This thriller sees a pair of identical twins uncovering a secret conspiracy to track and control kids. Together, they team up with a band of rebels to help stop the plot and take back their world.

The Worst Witch – 2017 to present - This young adult comedy follows a bumbling young witch who accidentally stumbles into witching school.

HULU

Website: http://hulu.com

Description: Hulu is a hybrid service that can offer both streamed television and live TV with the addition of a more expensive plan.

Available On: Roku, Fire TV, Apple TV, Apple iPhone & iPad, Chromecast, Fire Tablets, Playstation 3 & 4, Nintendo Switch, Samsung TV (select models), LG TVs (Select models) Android phones and tablets, and computer (via web browser).

Cost: $5.99/month or $59.99/year, No Ads - $11.99/month, + live TV $54.99/month

Now Streaming

Dramas

The Accident - 2019 - Sarah Lancashire (*Happy Valley*) stars as a hairdresser named Polly in this series about a small Welsh community torn apart by a terrible accident. The series takes us through the aftermath - families waiting for news, lives changed forever, and the search for someone to blame.

Apple Tree Yard - 2017 – This miniseries is based on Louise Doughty's novel by the same name, and it's a suspenseful combination of sex and murder. When a woman gets an intriguing proposition, it excites her – until she realizes it may not be quite what it seemed. Emily Watson and Ben Chaplin star.

Atlantis – 2013 - A young man washes up on the shores of ancient Atlantis.

Baghdad Central - 2020 - This six-part "period drama" is set in US-occupied Iraq in October 2003. In the aftermath of the invasion, the Iraqi army, police forces, and civil leadership have all been disbanded. To reclaim his identity after losing everything, one Iraqi ex-policeman (played by Waleed Zuaiter of *The Spy*) works as a detective to help solve a murder for the coalition forces. Together with British ex-cop Frank Temple (Bertie Carvel, *Doctor Foster*), he works the case while the Iraqi Police Force is being re-built.

Banished – 2015 - British convicts are sent to Australian to pay for their crimes, and both they and the soldiers have a great deal of adapting to do.

Bedlam – 2011 to 2012 - When a haunted former asylum is turned into a high-end apartment building, it has unexpected consequences for the building's new tenants.

Being Erica – *Canada* – 2009 to 2011 - A young woman participates in a strange form of therapy that involves time travel.

The Bisexual - 2018 - This dramedy follows a London-based American woman who breaks up with her girlfriend and decides to give heterosexual relations a try. American Desiree Akhavan (*Flowers*) plays Leila alongside Irish actor Brian Gleeson (*Peaky Blinders*) and English actress Maxine Peake (*Silk*).

Black Narcissus - 2020 - Based on Rumer Godden's 1939 book, *Black Narcissus* tells the story of Sister Clodagh as she leads the nuns of St. Faith's to set up a brand of their order in the Himalayas. They make their home in the remote palace of Mopu, a former home for concubines known as the "House of Women". As time goes on, Sister Clodagh finds herself increasingly tempted by an arrogant land agent, Mr. Dean. She's not the only one, though. The fragile and unstable Sister Ruth is similarly attracted, and both women find themselves struggling with forbidden feelings and unsatisfied desires.

This production includes one of Dame Diana Rigg's final performances.

Bleak House – 2005 - This classic BBC Dickens adaptation is based on the legal drama of the same name. The central story surrounds a person who left several versions of his will when he died.

Butterfly – 2018 - When a young boy named Max decides he would prefer to live as a girl named Maxine, his parents have to decide how to handle it.

City Homicide – *Australia* – 2007 to 2011 - In Melbourne, Australia, a group of homicide detectives work to find justice for victims of murder.

Clique - 2017 to 2019 - When two best friends go off to university in Edinburgh, it seems like everything will be amazing. When one of them is pulled into a clique of popular, powerful women, however, their university lives take a dark turn.

Coronation Street - 1960 to present - Running since 1960, and there are more than 9400 episodes of this daytime drama classic. The show is set in the fictional area of Wetherfield, where residents walk cobbled streets among terraced houses and the ever-present Rovers Return pub.

Daniel Deronda – 2002 - This adaptation of George Eliot's final novel focuses on a Victorian man torn between the love of two women.

David Copperfield – 1999 - Daniel Radcliffe (*Harry Potter*) stars as young David in this adaptation of the Dickens novel.

DCI Banks – 2010 to 2016 - Stephen Tomkinson (Ballykissangel, Wild at Heart) stars as DCI Alan Banks, a skilled but stubborn Yorkshire-based investigator.

The Fades – 2011 - A young man is haunted by dreams he can't explain, and he begins to see spirits around him – some of them malicious.

The Great - *United States* - 2020 - Though this dramedy is an American production, much of the cast is British. It's loosely based on the rise of Catherine the Great.

Hard Sun – 2018 - Two detectives work together to fight crime in a world that may be doomed anyway.

Harlots – 2007 to 2019 - In 18th century London, a brothel owner struggles to raise her daughters. The series was inspired by historian Hallie Rubenhold's book, *The Covent Garden Ladies*.

Harrow - *Australia* - 2018 to present - Welshman Ioan Gruffudd stars as Dr. Daniel Harrow, a forensic pathologist with authority issues. Still, his empathy for the dead makes him brilliant at what he does.

Hollyoaks - 1995 to present - This young adult soap opera is set in the fictional village of Hollyoaks, a suburb of Chester. As a youth-oriented programme, it frequently covers topics considered taboo.

In My Skin - 2020 - 16-year-old Bethan is doing her best to grow up and get along at school, but she has a turbulent home life she hides from friends.

In the Flesh – 2013 - After the government gets a handle on the recent zombie epidemic, they begin to rehabilitate zombies for re-entry into society. They aren't always warmly received.

Intruders – 2014 - John Simm (*Life on Mars*) stars as an ex-cop whose wife goes missing. The ensuing investigation leads him to Seattle, and a secret society dedicated to chasing immortality by hiding in the bodies of others. Based on Michael Marshall Smith's novel.

Jane Eyre – 2006 - This two-part adaptation of the classic Charlotte Bronte novel tells the story of a young woman who falls in love with the dark and brooding Mr. Rochester. Ruth Wilson (*Luther*) stars.

Killing Eve – 2018 to present - A bored but highly competent MI5 officer trades her life behind a desk to pursue an elusive and particularly aggressive female serial killer.

Lark Rise to Candleford - 2008 to 2011 - Set in the late 19th century in the small Oxfordshire hamlet of Lark Rise and the nearby market town of Candleford, this period drama follows a young woman who moves towns to work in a post office. It's based on Flora Thompson's semi-autobiographical novels.

Legends - *United States* - 2014 to 2015 - Brit Sean Bean stars as deep cover operative Martin Odum, a man with an abnormally strong ability to change his identity as needed for the job at hand.

Line of Duty – 2012 to present - This suspenseful British police series is set in the fictional "anti-corruption unit" AC-12, where the police police the police. Yes, we know that sounds a bit odd. Lennie James, Vicky McClure, Martin Compston, and Adrian Dunbar all feature.

Luther – 2010 to 2019 - Idris Elba stars as a brilliant London detective who frequently gets into trouble because of his passion for the job.

Merlin - 2009 to 2013 - Colin Morgan (*The Fall*) stars as a young Merlin in his days as a mere servant to Prince Arthur of Camelot. In this version of Camelot, magic is banned and Merlin is forced to keep his talent hidden away.

Murdoch Mysteries - *Canada* - 2008 to present - Set in the 1890s, Murdoch uses early forensics to solve murders. Yannick Bisson stars as Detective William Murdoch, Helene Joy plays Dr. Julia Ogden, and Thomas Craig and Jonny Harris fill the roles of Inspector Thomas Brackenreid and Constable George Crabtree, respectively. Hulu has the first 10 seasons.

The Musketeers – 2014 to 2016 - This modern retelling of the classic Dumas novel includes appearances by Peter Capaldi, Tom Burke, and Rupert Everett.

My Mad Fat Diary – 2013 to 2015 - In 1990s Lincolnshire, a young woman grapples with depression and body image issues.

National Treasure - 2016 - Robbie Coltrane (*Cracker*) stars as Paul Finchley, a once-popular comedian accused of raping several young women earlier in his career. The miniseries follows his downward spiral and the impact the accusations have on his family. Julie Walters (*Harry Potter*) plays his wife.

New Tricks – 2003 to 2015 - This long-running series focuses on a group of police who come out of retirement to work unsolved cases.

Normal People – *Ireland* – 2020 – This series follows a couple navigating their relationship after secondary school. Though they're from the same small Irish town, their different social classes cause friction.

Oliver Twist – 2007 - In this adaptation of the Dickens classic, we see appearances from Morven Christie, Tom Hardy, and Sarah Lancashire, among others. The story focuses on the difficult life of a young orphan after he's sold into an apprenticeship with an undertaker.

Paradox – 2009 - This sci-fi police drama focuses on a group of investigators who seek out evidence for crimes that haven't yet occurred.

Prey – 2014 to 2015 - Manchester detective Marcus Farrow (played by John Simm) is on the run, accused of a crime and desperate to prove his innocence. All the while, his former friends and colleagues do their best to hunt him down. This series reunites Philip Glenister and John Simm, who also appeared together in *Life on Mars*.

Pride & Prejudice – 1995 - Colin Firth and Jennifer Ehle star in this adaptation of the classic tale of Elizabeth Bennet and the snobbish but enticing Mr. Darcy.

Prime Suspect - 1991 to 2006 - Helen Mirren stars as Detective Jane Tennison, battling crime as well as sexism on the job.

Primeval – 2008 to 2011 - When strange things start happening around England, a professor and his team are forced to capture a variety of unusual creatures from other time periods. Includes Ben Miller (of *Death in Paradise*).

Scott & Bailey - 2011 to 2016 - Two very different female police detectives enjoy a close friendship and productive partnership.

The Secret of Crickley Hall – 2012 - Suranne Jones and Tom Ellis star in this supernatural miniseries about a family that relocates to a grand old estate up north after the disappearance of their young son.

Sense & Sensibility – 2008 - When a woman finds herself newly widowed and destitute with three unmarried daughters, she downsizes and attempts to find good husbands for them.

Silk – 2011 to 2014 - This series focuses on the challenges modern-day barristers face in their careers.

The Sister - 2020 - *Luther* creator and screenwriter Neil Cross brings us this upcoming four-part story "of murder – and perhaps ghosts – which exposes the quiet terror of a man trying to escape his past." It's inspired by Cross's novel *Burial*, released in 2009.

Russell Tovey (*Years and Years*) will play Nathan, a man trying to hide a terrible secret. His world is rocked when Bob (Bertie Carvel, *Doctor Foster*) spears on his doorstep with shocking news. Amrita Acharia (*The Good Karma Hospital)* also appears. This series was previously titled "*Because the Night*".

Skins – 2007 to 2013 - This racy classic offers a look into modern teenage life in England.

The Split – 2018 to 2020 - After a 30-year absence, a family of female lawyers has enough trouble dealing with their personal lives...and then their long-absent father returns.

Top of the Lake - 2013 to 2017 - This UK/New Zealand co-production follows the investigation into the disappearance of a drug lord's pregnant 12-year-old daughter. In the second series, the story moves to Sydney as the same detective investigates a body found at Bondi Beach.

Upstairs Downstairs - 2010 to 2012 - This series picks up the *Upstairs Downstairs* saga shortly after the period covered by the original series. Covering 1936 to 1939, it tells the story of the new owners of 165 Eaton Place, ending with the outbreak of World War II. Ed Stoppard (*Home Fires*) and Keeley Hawes (*Bodyguard*) play new owners Sir Hallam Holland and Lady Agnes Holland.

Whitechapel - 2009 to 2013 - An inspector, a detective sergeant, and a historical homicide expert look at crimes that may have connections to the Whitechapel district.

Comedies

Absolutely Fabulous - 1992 to 2012 - In this groundbreaking classic, two wild women do everything but act their age. The series was based on a sketch comedy called "Modern Mother and Daughter" by Dawn French (*Vicar of Dibley*) and Jennifer Saunders (Edina Monsoon in *Absolutely Fabulous*). Joanna Lumley stars alongside Saunders as Patsy Stone, and Julia Sawalha plays Edina's daughter Saffron.

The Aliens – 2016 - After aliens crash-land in the Irish Sea, they're allowed onto British soil but forced to live in a ghetto called Troy. Border guard Lewis helps to maintain the separation, but it becomes a tough position to hold when he learns he's half-alien.

Blackadder - 1983 to 1989 - Rowan Atkinson stars as antihero Edmund Blackadder, accompanied by Sir Tony Robinson as his sidekick Baldrick. Each series of this quirky comedy is set in a different period within British history, and Edmund carries different titles throughout. The "essence" of each character remains largely the same in each series, though.

Brassic - 2019 to present - This working-class comedy follows a young man named Vinnie (Joe Gilgun) and his occasionally criminal friends as they go about their lives in the northern English town of Hawley. It's a lively, rough-around-the-edges comedy about desperate small-town life and the ever-present question of whether there might be something better elsewhere. *Brassic* gets its name from Cockney rhyming slang. It's a shortening of "boracic lint", slang for "skint".

Breeders - 2020 - Martin Freeman (*Sherlock*) and Daisy Haggard (*Black Mirror*) star in this sitcom about modern parenting and the inevitable discovery that you're not quite the person you thought you were before you had kids. Freeman was quoted saying it explores "some of the less-discussed truths and challenges of being a parent."

Coupling – 2000 to 2004 - Six young adults in London navigate the work, love, and the transition into responsible adulthood. Many have called this "the British Friends".

Dead Boss – 2012 - Helen Stephens has been wrongly convicted of killing her boss, and while she hopes she'll be cleared soon, everyone she knows seems to want her in prison.

Dirk Gently's Holistic Detective Agency – 2016 to 2017 - While this reinterpretation of the famous Douglas Adams detective is technically American, it's based on Douglas Adams' work. In this one, a holistic detective investigates cases involving the supernatural.

Doc Martin - 2004 to present - Martin Clunes (*Men Behaving Badly*) stars in this comedy about a brilliant but grumpy London surgeon who suddenly develops a fear of blood. He leaves his high-flying career and takes a post in a Cornish fishing village where he spent holidays as a child with his Aunt Joan. His bad attitude and lack of social skills makes it a challenge to adapt to his new life.

Dream Corp LLC – 2016 to present - Though this animated series is not strictly British, Brit Stephen Merchant plays a lead role as T.E.R.R.Y., and the series includes guest appearances from Liam Neeson, Toby Kebbell, and Rupert Friend. It's a workplace comedy that takes place in a dilapidated dream therapy centre in a strip mall. Patients come to have their dreams recorded, studied, and occasionally, adjusted. Darren Boyd (*The Salisbury Poisonings*) stars.

Gameface – 2014 to 2019 - A young woman navigates her 30s with the help of her friends, a questionable life coach, and her eternally patient driving instructor.

Getting On – 2009 to 2012 - This dark comedy follows the staff and residents in a geriatric ward.

Hang-Ups - 2018 - Stephen Mangan (*Dirk Gently*) stars as a therapist whose practice has collapsed, leaving him to conduct therapy sessions via webcam. Katherine Parkinson (*The IT Crowd*) also stars.

The Hitchhiker's Guide to the Galaxy - 1981 - Arthur Dent is one of the last surviving members of the human race. Still in his dressing gown, he's dragged through an intergalactic portal and sent on an adventure through the universe. The series is based on Douglas Adams' novel of the same name, and he also wrote the TV adaptation.

Horrible Histories – 2009 to present - While designed for children, this amusing educational program is every bit as entertaining for adults. The sketches cover different parts of history, but always with a dramatic or funny take on the event.

Hunderby – 2012 to 2015 - Julia Davis stars in this dark period comedy about a woman who washes ashore after a shipwreck off the English coast.

Inside No. 9 - 2014 to 2020 - Dark humor, crime, drama, and horror are showcased in this anthology series. Every episode incorporates the number nine in some way, so keep an eye out as you watch.

The Kennedys – 2015 - Katherine Parkinson (*The IT Crowd*) stars in this comedy about a family moving from a housing estate to a home, eager to move up the social ladder.

Ladhood - 2019 to present - This coming-of-age sitcom takes a look at mischief and modern masculinity.

Maxxx – 2020 – Maxx is a has-been boy band star working on a comeback, but between the distractions in his life and his massive ego, he'll have some challenges.

The Mighty Boosh – 2003 to 2007 - Two young musicians work for a madman at a zoo.

Miranda – 2009 to 2013 - Miranda Hart stars as a lovably awkward woman who runs a joke shop with her best friend and seems to specialize in getting herself into pickles.

Misfits – 2009 to 2013 - A group of young offenders develops superpowers when they're struck by lightning.

Moone Boy – 2012 to 2014 - A young boy copes with life in a small Irish town, thanks to his imaginary friend.

Mr. Bean - 1992 to 1995 - Bumbling Mr. Bean rarely speaks and has some very peculiar ways of doing things, but it usually works out for him. Rowan Atkinson (*Maigret*) stars as the British icon.

The Office - 2001 to 2003 - Before there was Michael Scott in the US, there was David Brent in Slough, England. Written by Ricky Gervais (*After Life*) and Stephen Merchant (*Hello Ladies*), this mockumentary-style programme takes place in the office of the fictional Wernham Hogg paper company. Mackenzie Crook (*Detectorists*) and Martin Freeman (*Sherlock*) are also among the stars.

Peep Show – 2003 to 2015 - Two dysfunctional and very different friends share a flat in London and attempt (rather poorly) to grow up.

Shameless - 2004 to 2013 - Before he created *No Offence*, Paul Abbott created Shameless - the story of a rough-around-the-edges family living in a Manchester housing estate. It was later adapted into an American series starring William H. Macy. This one contains some strong language and sexual content, so it's not for everyone.

Spaced – 1999 to 2001 - To get an affordable flat in North London, two young people pretend to be a couple. Simon Pegg (*Shaun of the Dead*) and Jessica Hynes (*There She Goes*) star.

Staged - 2020 - This comedy series, set during the COVID-19 pandemic, was filmed using video-conferencing technology. David Tennant (*Doctor Who*) and Michael Sheen (*Frost/Nixon*) play fictionalized versions of themselves attempting to rehearse Luigi Pirandello's play, *Six Characters in Search of an Author*, during the lockdown.

The Thick of It – 2005 to 2012 - This political satire takes place among the team at the Department of Social Affairs and Citizenship, where everything seems to be one giant farce.

This Way Up - 2019 - Aisling Bea (*Trollied, Finding Joy*) stars as Aine, a single Irish Catholic woman who has a nervous breakdown while living in London and teaching English as a second language. Sharon Horgan (*Catastophe*) co-produces and co-stars as Shona, her older sister.

Uncle - 2014 to 2017 - Nick Helm stars as Andy, a 30-something slacker who's left to care for his nephew in spite of the fact that he's utterly unsuited to the task.

Wasted – 2016 - In the fictional West Country village of Neston Berry, young slackers spend their days getting drunk and smoking marijuana at "Stoned Henge", a souvenir shop and tattoo parlour.

Whose Line Is It Anyway? – 1988 to 1999 - While the US has since made its own version, this is the original *Whose Line*, the show where four performers create characters, songs, and scenes on the spot based on prompts they receive from the host or audience.

The Wrong Mans – 2013 to 2014 - After a council worker answers a ringing phone at the site of a crash, he and an acquaintance in the same building become entangled in a web of crime and corruption. James Corden (*Gavin & Stacey*) and Mathew Baynton (*Horrible Histories*) star.

Zomboat! - 2019 - This apocalypse comedy sees zombies unleashed in Birmingham, England. Two sisters join up with a couple of guys and flee by narrowboat. For those not familiar with narrowboats and British canals, it's worth noting that canal speed limits are generally 3-4 mph, and the boats themselves can't go much faster unless there's a strong current pushing them along.

Documentary & Lifestyle

Absolutely Ascot - 2018 to present - This reality show follows a group of fame-hungry individuals in the Ascot area.

Dress to Impress - 2017 to present - This British dating show sees competitors choosing attire for a fashion-conscious singleton, with the winner getting the date.

Gordon Ramsay's American Road Trip - 2021 - This special sees chef Gordon Ramsay on a roadtrip through the United States, with a variety of excursions like cattle wrangling and spearfishing.

Gordon Ramsay's 24 Hours to Hell & Back – 2018 to present - In this series, Gordon Ramsay attempts to help failing restaurants in just 24 hours.

Gordon Ramsay's The F Word – 2005 to 2010 - Each episode of this cooking series sees Gordon Ramsay preparing a meal for 50 guests at The F Word restaurant. In between, there are bits about cooking and farming, plus guest challenges.

Gordon Ramsey's Ultimate Home Cooking – 2013 - This series helps people learn to cook simple, healthy, practical meals in their own home kitchens.

Hell's Kitchen – 2004 to 2009 - This series pits prospective chefs against one another, with the winner getting a head chef position.

Jamie: Keep Cooking and Carry On – 2020 – Jamie Oliver shows recipes, tips, and tricks aimed at the unique times we live in. The recipes are prepared with limited ingredients and substitutions.

Jamie's Quick and Easy Food – 2017 to present - Chef Jamie Oliver shows off quick and easy recipes using just five ingredients.

Kitchen Nightmares - 2007 to 2014 - Acclaimed British chef Gordon Ramsay hosts this series in which he visits struggling American restaurants and spends a week trying to help them be more successful.

Love Island – 2015 to present - This reality series places singles on an island and eliminates contestants based on audience voting.

The Only Way is Essex – 2010 to present - This reality series follows a group of young and "socially ambitious" individuals living in Essex.

Shipwrecked - 2019 - This British competition series sees contestants sent to islands to compete against one another.

Tea with the Dames - 2018 - Dames Maggie Smith, Judi Dench, Eileen Atkins, and Joan Plowright come together to share stories of their lives and careers.

> **Website:** http://sundancenow.com
>
> **Description:** Sundance Now is a cousin to Acorn TV, and it has a broader focus. Their offerings include a good mix of international titles and indie productions. A number of the titles on Sundance Now are also on Acorn TV.
>
> **Available On:** Roku, Amazon Fire TV, Apple TV, Apple iPhone & iPad, Android TV, Android phones and tablets, Google Chromecast, computer (via web browser). You can also subscribe via Amazon Prime Video.
>
> **Cost:** $6.99/month, $59.99 billed yearly

Now Streaming

A Discovery of Witches – 2018 to present – When an Oxford historian and reluctant witch is able to access a book no one else can, it sets off a chain of events involving an eternal feud between witches and vampires.

Away - 2016 - This British film follows two people, Ria and Joseph, as they try to find a way out of their current life situations.

Back - 2017 to present - After the death of his father, 42-year-old Stephen returns home to take over the family pub in Stroud, Gloucestershire. At the same time, Andrew, a former foster child briefly raised by his parents, returns to renew his own relationship with the family. What happens next is a serious case of sibling rivalry. The series sees David Mitchell and Robert Webb (both of *Peep Show* fame) together again.

Bad Mothers - *Australia* - 2019 - This juicy Australian drama sees a group of misfit women coming together to help each other out with parenting, work challenges, relationships, and murder.

The Bad Seed - *New Zealand* - 2019 - Successful obstetrician Simon Lampton thinks he's left his dysfunctional past behind him, but when a neighbour and former patient is brutally murdered,

everything he's built comes crumbling down. **Premieres April 29th.**

Bang - 2017 to present - In this bilingual Welsh crime drama, a man comes into possession of a gun and his life is forever changed.

Being Human - *Canada* - 2011 to 2014 - This is the North American adaptation of the British series about a set of supernatural roommates trying to keep their secrets and live normal lives.

Blinded - *Sweden* - 2019 - When a young financial journalist has a secret affair with a bank director, it complicates both her personal life and her career.

Britain's Bloodiest Dynasty - 2014 - Historian Dan Jones tells the story of the Plantagenets, one of Britain's darkest and most brutal dynasties.

Britain's Bloody Crown - 2016 - Dan Jones presents this four-part documentary about the War of the Roses.

The Bureau - *France* - 2020 - This French spy series has taken inspiration from the real accounts of former spies, weaving their experiences into new stories inspired by current events. It takes place within the "Bureau of Legends", an agency responsible for training and handling deep cover agents as they complete long-term missions in areas with French interests. Fans of the charming French film *Amélie* may recognise Mathieu Kassovitz as intelligence officer Guillaume Debailly.

Cheat - 2019 - When university lecturer Dr. Leah Dale confronts a student about suspected cheating, the student takes it as a personal attack. A simple academic issue soon spirals out of control, putting both women at risk. Katherine Kelly (*Happy Valley*) and Molly Windsor (*Three Girls*) star in this chilling psychological drama.

Cleaning Up - 2019 - Sheridan Smith (*Gavin & Stacey*) stars as Sam, a debt-ridden mum trying to get by on a zero-hour contract cleaning job while her husband attempts to gain full custody of their children. While on the job, she overhears information that leads her into the world of insider trading.

Cold Call - 2019 - When a single mum gets caught up in a cold call phone scam, her entire life is turned upside down.

The Commons - *Australia* - 2019 to 2020 - This series sees Joanne Froggatt (*Downton Abbey*) starring as Eadie, a 38-year-old woman who just wants to have a child. Unfortunately, IVF treatments have failed and the world around her is in a chaotic state of global warming, parasitic disease, and increasing gaps between the rich and poor.

Couple Trouble - *Denmark* - 2018 - Anders and Lise are a generally happy thirtysomething couple with a daughter, but after seven years of marriage, the dull routine of marriage and parenthood has begun to get them. This series follows them as they seek counseling to save their relationship.

The Crimson Petal and the White – 2011 – In late 1800s London, a prostitute finds her position greatly improved after becoming the mistress to a powerful man.

The Cry - *Australia* – 2018 – Jenna Coleman stars in this miniseries about a young couple dealing with the abduction of their baby.

Dead Lucky - *Australian* - 2018 – When a dangerous armed robber resurfaces in Sydney, two very different detectives are forced to work together to catch him.

Des - 2020 - David Tennant (*Doctor Who*) stars as Dennis Nilsen, a Scottish serial killer and necrophile arrested in 1983 after murdering at least a dozen young men and boys. He was caught when human remains were discovered to be the cause of a drain blockage near his home.

Deutschland 83 / Deutschland 86 – *Germany* – 2015 to 2018 – This coming of age spy series is set in 1980s Germany.

The Fall - 2013 to 2016 - Gillian Anderson (*The X-Files*) and Jamie Dornan (*50 Shades of Grey*) star in this series about a senior investigator who goes head-to-head with a serial killer who's attacking young professional women in Belfast.

Fingersmith – 2005 – In Victorian England, a young female thief hatches a plan to get close to an heiress and scam her. It doesn't go as planned.

Gold Digger - 2019 - Julia Ormond (*Sabrina*) stars as Julia Day, a wealthy 60-year-old woman who falls in love with a handsome man 26 years her junior. As secrets come to light, no one can be sure what's real and what's merely convenient.

The Gulf – *New Zealand* - 2019 – This series follows a detective who's been in a fatal car accident that causes her to lose her memory.

Idiomatic - *Finland* - 2018 - This modern-day Scandinavian rom-com follows an educated left-wing couple after they move to an apartment owned by Micke's wealthy parents.

Innocent – 2018 – Innocent is set around the beautiful southern coast of England, and it tells the story of a man rebuilding his life after his conviction for the murder of his wife is overturned.

Interview with a Murderer - 2016 - Criminologist and professor David Wilson conducts a series of interviews with convicted murderer Bert Spencer. Bert was convicted for the murder of farmer Hubert Wilkes, but he's always been suspected of the brutal killing of a young newspaper delivery boy, Carl Bridgewater.

Law & Order: UK - 2009 to 2014 - This adaptation of the successful American courtroom drama sees the format carried over to the British legal system. It's one-part law (investigative work) and one-part order (the court proceedings).

Leverage - *United States* - 2008 to 2012 - This series follows a group of high-tech criminals who attempt to steal from wealthy people who don't deserve their money. Though it's American, it stars British actress Gina Bellman (*Coupling*). For a British series that's somewhat similar in tone, check out *Hustle*.

Liar – 2017 to 2020 – After a seemingly pleasant date, a schoolteacher accuses a prominent local surgeon of rape. The situation continues to spiral out of control as more information comes to light. The second series takes a different angle, but there's little we can say without it being a spoiler.

The Little Drummer Girl – 2018 – An English actress is recruited by the Israelis to help infiltrate a Palestinian assassin's terrorist cell.

Madame Bovary - 2014 - This film adaptation of the classic novel sees Mia Wasikowska (*In Treatment*) as the bored country wife Emma Bovary.

McMafia – 2018 to present - James Norton (*Grantchester*) stars as the English-raised son of a Russian mafia figure who was exiled from his country. Though his family tried to correct course, a murder draws them back in. A second series is on the way, though we've yet to see a date for it.

Motherland – 2016 to present – Mums take on the challenges of middle-class motherhood, and it's not always pretty. This 30-minute comedy aims to show real motherhood, not the pretty and acceptable public idea of what motherhood should be.

Murder Trial: The Disappearance of Margaret Fleming - 2020 - Two carers were accused of murdering a 35-year-old woman and claiming benefits in her name for 16 years. This series takes a look at their trial.

The Name of the Rose - 2019 - In 1327, a friar and his apprentice investigate deaths at a nearby abbey. They soon find themselves mixed up in something much bigger than they might have imagined. Rupert Everett (*My Best Friend's Wedding*) and John Turturro (*Barton Fink*) star.

Next of Kin – 2018 – A GP is devastated after hearing her brother was kidnapped on his way home to the UK.

The Night Caller - *Australia* - 2020 - This four-part true crime drama follows the investigation into a serial killer who terrorised Perth, Australia between 1959 and 1963. In their determination to stop the killings, police arrested two different men, both of whom would be convicted and serve time in spite of their innocence.

One Lane Bridge - *New Zealand* - 2020 - While working a murder investigation, a young Maori detective accidentally awakens a spiritual gift that may harm the case.

Penance - 2020 - After her son's death in Thailand, a woman begins having lusty thoughts about a young man she met in grief counseling (who just happens to look a lot like her dead son). Julie Graham (*Queens of Mystery*), Neil Morrissey (*Men Behaving Badly*), and Nico Mirallegro (*Hollyoaks*).

Playing for Keeps - *Australia* - 2018 to 2019 - This soapy drama dives into the world of footballer's wives in Australia.

The Real Des - 2020 - If you watched the David Tennant series *Des*, you may also want to watch this documentary about professor David Wilson, a criminologist who spend decades interviewing and corresponding with serial killer Dennis Nilsen (the subject of *Des*).

The Red Shadows - *France* – 2019 – In 1993, a five-year-old girl was kidnapped. 25 years later, her sister uncovers clues that suggest she may still be alive.

The Restaurant - *Sweden* – 2017 to 2018 – At the end of WWII, two strangers cross social classes with a kiss that has lasting repercussions. This series has been called a Swedish *Downton Abbey*.

The Returned - *France* - 2013 - In a peaceful French village, people begin returning home. Unfortunately, the people returning have all been dead for years, so nobody was actually expecting them to return home. At the same time, there's a series of gruesome murders that looks suspiciously like those of a serial killer from the past.

Rillington Place – 2016 – This three-part miniseries is a dramatization of the murders at 10 Rillington Place in the 1940s and 50s.

River - 2015 - Stellan Skarsgård, Nicola Walker, and Lesley Manville star in this series about a brilliant police officer haunted by guilt.

Riviera – 2017 to present – Riviera is a UK production set in France. When a newlywed's wealthy husband is killed in an explosion, she's stunned to learn what lurked behind the facade of their upper-class lifestyle.

Safe House – 2015 to 2017 – Christopher Eccleston (*Doctor Who*) stars in this series about a married couple asked to turn their guest house into a safe house.

Sanctuary - *Sweden* - 2019 - This psychological thriller sees a woman lured to the Alps to visit her twin sister, only to find herself trapped in her sister's life and imprisoned in a sanatorium where no one believes her.

Secrets of a Psychopath - *Ireland* - 2019 - This three-part true crime series takes a look back at one of Ireland's most complicated murder cases. It looks at the events surrounding the murder of Elaine O'Hara, a Dublin woman whose murderer engaged in extreme BDSM practices and nearly committed the perfect crime.

The Secrets She Keeps - *Australia* - 2020 - When two heavily pregnant women from different worlds meet in an upmarket Sydney supermarket, they have no idea their lives are about to come together in a very dramatic way.

Secret State – 2012 – In a miniseries that will reassure you that the US isn't the only place where government and big business are way too close, Secret State shows a Deputy Prime Minister entangled in an international conspiracy.

Shadow Lines - *Finland* - 2019 - In the 1950s, the Cold War raged in the small nation of Finland. This espionage thriller focuses on a secret intelligence team who sought to maintain Finland's independence at any cost.

Slings & Arrows - *Canada* - 2003 to 2006 - This Canadian dark comedy is set at a fictitious Shakespeare festival in Canada as they embark on a production of Hamlet. Paul Gross (*Due South*) stars as washed-up actor Geoffrey Tennant, along with Rachel McAdams (*Wedding Crashers, The Notebook*), Luke Kirby (*The Marvelous Ms. Maisel*), Stephen Ouimette (*Mentors*), and Mark McKinney (*Kids in the Hall, Superstore*), who is also the co-creator/co-writer.

The Split – 2018 to 2020 - After a 30-year absence, a family of female lawyers has enough trouble dealing with their personal lives...and then their long-absent father returns.

State of the Union - 2019 - Chris O'Dowd (*The IT Crowd*) and Rosamund Pike (*Pride & Prejudice*) star in this short-form comedy about a couple that visits a pub each week before their marriage counseling session.

Stella Blomkvist - *Icelandic* – 2017 – A young and morally dubious lawyer takes on dangerous murder cases.

Straight Forward - *Denmark / New Zealand* - 2019 - After attempting to get revenge for her father's death, a Danish conwoman is forced to flee to New Zealand.

Striking Out - *Ireland* - 2017 - Amy Huberman (*Finding Joy*) stars as Tara Rafferty, a successful Dublin lawyer who abandons her safe life after discovering that her fiancé is cheating on her. She cancels the wedding, quits her job, and begins a new and unconventional private practice. Neil Morrissey (*Men Behaving Badly*) and Rory Keenan (*War & Peace*) also star.

The Suspect - *Canada* - 2020 - This true-crime series takes a look at the murder of Richard Oland, the prosecution of his son Dennis, and the fight for a retrial.

Thin Ice - *Sweden* - 2020 - When a research vessel disappears off the coast of Greenland, it's hard to be sure whether it's coincidence or something much more sinister. **Premieres April 22nd.**

Total Control - *Australia* - 2019 - Deborah Mailman (*Offspring*) and Rachel Griffiths (*Dead Lucky*) star in this political drama about a charismatic indigenous woman recruited by the prime minister to help further her own agenda.

Upright - *Australia* - 2020 - Comedian Tim Minchin stars in this series about two people trying to get an upright piano from one side of Australia to the other.

Wisting - *Norway* - 2019 – Norwegian detective William Wisting discovers a corpse at a Christmas tree farm that may be connected to an American serial killer. He may be living among them.

Witches: A Century of Murder – 2015 - Historian Suzannah Lipscomb takes a look at the British witch hunts of the 17th century.

AMC+

Now Streaming

Everything on Sundance Now + the titles below...

Almost Royal - 2014 to 2016 - This BBC America faux-reality series follows a couple of extremely minor British royals as they visit the US for the first time.

Attenborough and the Giant Elephant - 2019 - Sir David Attenborough takes a look back at the life of the world's most famous elephant, "Jumbo the Circus Elephant".

A Wild Year on Earth - 2021 - This series follows some of the world's most interesting seasonal animal behaviour over the course of a year.

Cold Courage - *Finland* - 2020 - This international crime drama follows a couple of Finnish women who become involved with a secret organisation while living in London.

CripTales - 2020 - This BBC America series sees a variety of differently-abled adults performing dramatic monologues about life-changing moments. Liz Carr (Silent Witness) is among them.

Doctor Who: The Faceless Ones - 1967 - This animated special features original audio from the "mostly lost" eighth serial of the fourth season of the original *Doctor Who*. Patrick Troughton is the Doctor.

Exit Through the Gift Shop - 2010 - When shop owner Thierry Guetta attempts to document the world of street art, he inadvertently meets Banksy, who then films the shop owners attempts at street art.

Gangs of London – 2020 to present – This drama takes a look at the struggles of rival gang families in modern-day London. The series begins after the murder of Finn Wallace, the most powerful criminal in London. Nobody knows who did it or why, and his absence has created a dangerous power vacuum.

The Graham Norton Show - 2021 - Presenter Graham Norton chats with some of the world's biggest celebrities.

Meerkat Manor - 2005 to 2008 - This British series follows a family of meerkats in the Kalahari Desert. Though commercially successful, it's worth mentioning that the producers did not intervene when animals were sick or injured, as it was filmed in conjunction with a research project. If you can't watch that sort of thing, skip this series.

Orphan Black - *Canada* - 2013 to 2017 - A young woman's life is changed when she learns she's been part of a clone experiment, and she has a number of sister clones around North America and Europe.

Princess Diana: A Life After Death - 2019 - On the 20th anniversary of her death, this documentary looks at Diana's legacy.

Queers - 2017 - This series features stories about homosexual men in Britain, told in celebration of the 50th anniversary of The Sexual Offenses Act. The historic act partially decriminalised homosexual activities between men in the UK.

Quiz - 2020 - Matthew Macfadyen (*Pride & Prejudice*) stars as Charles Ingram in this drama based on the real-life story of a man accused of cheating his way to the top prize on *Who Wants To Be A Millionaire?*.

Rebellion – 2016 - During WWI, three Irish women must choose sides in the revolt against English rule.

The Salisbury Poisonings - This factual drama miniseries takes a look at the 2018 Novichok poisonings in Salisbury, England. Mark Addy (*Game of Thrones*), Anne-Marie Duff (*Shameless*), Amber Aga (*Shakespeare & Hathaway*), and Rafe Spall (*Hot Fuzz*) are among the cast members.

Snatches - 2018 - This series features monologues inspired by women who have spoken out or changed the status quo.

Snow Animals - 2021 - Liz Bonnin introduces us to a variety of animals and the tactics they use to survive and thrive in cold climates.

Tea with the Dames - 2018 - Dames Maggie Smith, Judi Dench, Eileen Atkins, and Joan Plowright come together to share stories of their lives and careers.

The War of the Worlds - 2020 - After a meteor touches down in Surrey, humans face a battle for survival against an alien race. The classic HG Wells tale is told through the lens of Amy and George, two people who are in love and ready to embark on a new (though forbidden) life together.

The Watch - 2021 - This comedy-fantasy police procedural was inspired by Sir Terry Pratchett's *Discworld* series. It's set in the world's principal city of Ankh-Morpork, and Sir Pratchett himself described it as a "Pratchett-style CSI".

Wild City - 2019 - This nature series looks at the animals living in Singapore's hidden wilderness.

Wild India - 2020 - Sir David Attenborough narrates this documentary about the lives of creatures in India's Karnataka.

AMC+

133

TUBI TV

Website: http://tubi.tv

Description: Tubi is a free, ad-supported streaming service with a wide variety of programming from all over the world. They typically have around 100 British TV titles, and they're especially strong on unscripted programming.

Available On: Roku, Fire TV, Apple TV, Apple iPhone & iPad, Chromecast, Android TV, Android phones and tablets, Cox Contour, Xfinity x1, TiVO, Xbox One, PS3 & 4, computer (via web browser).

Cost: Free with ads

Now Streaming
Mysteries & Crime Dramas

The Bench – 2001 to 2002 - This legal drama takes place in a busy magistrates court in Wales. It follows the challenges they face in court, along with the pressures of working on a high-profile legal team.

Blue Murder - 2003 to 2009 - Caroline Quentin (*Jonathan Creek*) stars in this series about a single mom struggling to raise four kids while also heading up a team of homicide detectives.

The Broker's Man - 1997 to 1998 - An ex-cop now puts his detective skills to work for insurance companies. Kevin Whately (*Lewis*) stars.

Cadfael - 1994 to 1998 - In 12th century Shrewsbury, a monk solves mysteries. Derek Jacobi (*Last Tango in Halifax*) stars.

Case Histories - 2011 to 2013 - Based on the Jackson Brodie novels by Kate Atkinson, this Edinburgh-based series features a tough guy PI with a heart of gold.

City Homicide – *Australia* – 2007 to 2011 - In Melbourne, Australia, a group of homicide detectives work to find justice for victims of murder.

Cracker – *United States* - 1997 to 1998 - While this is the US version, we're including it here because it's inspired by the original British show, *Cracker*. It's the story of an unlikeable, anti-social criminal psychologist who proves brilliant in assisting on tough cases.

Cuffs – 2015 - In quirky coastal Brighton, police officers are over-stretched and under-resourced, but they do the best they can with what they've got.

Eternal Law – 2012 - In the lovely, historic city of York, a group of angels find themselves assisting in court cases. Though the premise is a bit silly, remarkably few British television shows are set in the city of York, making it a

Exile – 2011 - John Simm (*Life on Mars*) stars in this mystery-thriller about a man who returns home after his life falls apart – only to find different troubles there.

The Fall - 2013 to 2016 - Gillian Anderson (*The X-Files*) and Jamie Dornan (*50 Shades of Grey*) star in this series about a senior investigator who goes head-to-head with a serial killer who's attacking young professional women in Belfast.

The Ghost Squad - 2005 - Similar to *Line of Duty*, this series follows an Internal Affairs division designed to help find and fix corruption within the police. Elaine Cassidy (*No Offence*) stars.

Gracepoint - *United States* - 2014 - This American *Broadchurch* adaptation sees David Tennant put on an American accent and return to the central role, this time as Detective Emmett Carver. It tells the story of a coastal California town turned upside-down when a young boy is found dead on the beach.

Hamish Macbeth - 1995 to 1997 - Hamish Macbeth (Robert Carlyle, *The Full Monty*) is a talented but unambitious Highlands constable who doesn't always follow the rules. The series was filmed in the lovely Highland village of Plockton on the shores of Loch Carron, and it's a great watch for those who enjoy good scenery.

Hustle - 2004 to 2012 - Adrian Lester (*Bonekickers*), Robert Vaughn (*The Man from U.N.C.L.E.*), and Robert Glenister (*Paranoid*) star in this series about grifters who live by the motto, "you can't cheat an honest man". The specialise in long cons on the undeserving wealthy.

Kavanagh QC - 1995 to 2001 - John Thaw (Inspector Morse) stars as James Kavanagh QC, a barrister with a working-class background and a strong sense of right and wrong. It was one of Thaw's final roles before he died of cancer at the age of 60. Pay close attention to the guest stars in this one, as it's loaded with actors who went on to well-known roles, including Lesley Manville (*Mum*), Larry Lamb (*Gavin & Stacey*), Barry Jackson (*Midsomer Murders*), Phyllis Logan (*Downton Abbey*), Bill Night (*Love Actually*), and Julian Fellowes (*Downton Abbey*).

Law & Order: UK – 2009 to 2014 – This popular procedural is adapted from the American series *Law & Order*. Though set within a different legal system, the basic formula is the same. In the first half of an episode, police investigate a crime. In the second half, prosecutors take the case to court.

Midsomer Murders - 1998 to present - In Midsomer County, the landscapes are beautiful, the villagers all have secrets, and murder is rampant. This British mystery classic features John Nettles as DCI Tom Barnaby through the first 13 seasons, with Neil Dudgeon as DCI John Barnaby for the later seasons.

The Saint - 1962 to 1969 - Roger Moore stars as Simon Templar, a wealthy adventurer who travels the world solving crimes and engaging in all manner of secret agent hijinks. Though the settings are occasionally exotic, nearly every episode was filmed at a studio in Hertfordshire using "blue-screen" technology. The series was based on the Simon Templar novels by Leslie Charteris.

The Sandbaggers - 1978 to 1980 - This spy drama follows the men and woman on the front lines of the Cold War. Based in Leeds and produced by Yorkshire Television, it starred Roy Marsden (Adam Dalgliesh in the P.D. James adaptations), Director of Operations in Britain's Secret Intelligence Service.

Sherlock Holmes: The Classic Collection - 1942 to 1946 - This "series" is actually a collection of four performances by Basil Rathbone. Though the movies are old, many consider him to be the definitive Sherlock Holmes. Frequently typecast as a villain, Rathbone was excited to play Holmes, stating, "For once, I got to beat the bad guy instead of play him." Though this guide is primarily for TV series, we do recommend searching "Sherlock Holmes" on Tubi because there are quite a few other films available on the platform.

Ultimate Force - 2002 to 2007 - Ross Kemp (*EastEnders*) stars in this action series about a Special Air Service team that stops things like anthrax poisonings, assassinations, and bank sieges.

Vincent – 2005 to 2006 - Suranne Jones and Ray Winstone star in this series about an ex-cop turned PI who brings incredible skill and determination to his cases.

Wycliffe - 1993 to 1998 - Based on W.J. Burley's novels, this Cornwall-based series features DS Charles Wycliffe, a man who investigates murders with a unique level of determination and accuracy.

Trinity – 2009 - Convinced her father's death is somehow linked to prestigious Trinity College, Charlotte enrolls there to get to the bottom of the mystery. Charles Dance stars as Dr. Edmund Maltravers, and Antonia Bernath plays Charlotte.

TUBI

Dramas

The Ambassador - 1998 - Pauline Collins stars as Ambassador Harriet Smith, British ambassador to Ireland. She's a woman under constant pressure from all angles, and she still struggles with guilt about her husband's death from a car bomb meant for her.

Anzac Girls - *Australia* - 2014 - Heroic women rise to the occasion during the war.

Being Human - 2008 to 2013 - Aidan Turner (*Poldark*) stars in this series about a werewolf, vampire, and ghost attempting to live together.

Bramwell – 1995 to 1998 - In 1895, Dr. Eleanor Bramwell does her best to improve public health in Victorian London.

Brideshead Revisited - 1981 - Jeremy Irons and Anthony Andrews star in this adaptation of Evelyn Waugh's novel by the same name. *The Telegraph* awarded it the top position in its list of greatest television adaptations of all time.

Camelot - 2011 - This short-lived adventure series was created by Michael Hirst (*The Tudors*) and Chris Chibnall (*Broadchurch*), and it focuses on the period of time after King Uther's death when Merlin puts forth Arthur as the new king.

Camomile Lawn – 1991 - Felicity Kendal (*The Good Life*) and Jennifer Ehle (*Pride & Prejudice* '95) star in this series about a family spending the summer of 1939 together, just as World War II begins.

Cold Feet - 1998 to 2003 - This long-running dramedy follows the lives of six thirtysomething friends living in Manchester, England as they do their best to get their lives sorted.

The Colour of Magic - 2009 - This series is based on the *Discworld* series of novels by Terry Pratchett, and features Sean Astin as tourist Twoflower alongside Sir David Jason as wizard Rincewind. When a fire breaks out during Twoflower's holiday, the two flee the city together, beginning an interesting magical journey.

The Darling Buds of May - 1991 to 1993 - Based on the 1958 H.E. Bates novel of the same name, this series is set in rural 1950s Kent and follows the Larkin family as they go about their daily lives. This early 90s dramedy was a breakout role for Welsh actress Catherine Zeta-Jones.

The Devil's Mistress – This two-part series takes place against the backdrop of the English Civil War, following a young woman as she moves between poverty and power.

Emmerdale - 1972 to present - Originally known as *Emmerdale Farm*, this series was originally set in a village called Beckindale. In the 90s, the show rebranded and began to focus on the entire village of Emmerdale. Now, storylines are bigger, sexier, and more dramatic than ever.

A Family At War - 1970 - In this classic family saga, we follow the daily life of the Ashtons, a working-class family in Liverpool during the time of WWII.

The Fragile Heart - 1996 - Nigel Hawthorne (*Yes Minister*) stars as a brilliant and successful surgeon whose work heading a medical delegation in China forces him into a serious ethical dilemma.

The Great Fire - 2015 - This four-part series is a dramatisation of 1666's Great Fire of London. The fire went on for four days, leaving nearly 90% of the city's population homeless.

Heartbeat - 1992 to 2010 - This Yorkshire-based period crime drama ran for 18 seasons and 372 episodes, focusing on the lives of characters in a small village. Initially, it focused on a central couple, PC Nick Rowan and Dr. Kate Rowan, but it ultimately branched out to include storylines all over the village. The series is based on the "Constable" novels written by Peter N. Walker under the pseudonym Nicholas Rhea.

Hearts & Bones – 2000 to 2001 - This drama follows a group of 20 and 30-something friends who move to London and transition into proper adult lives.

Hollyoaks - 1995 to present - This young adult soap opera is set in the fictional village of Hollyoaks, a suburb of Chester. As a youth-oriented programme, it frequently covers topics considered taboo.

Homefront - 2012 - This dramatic miniseries follows the lives of the wives and girlfriends of soldiers serving in Afghanistan.

TUBI

Jason and the Argonauts - *United States* - 2000 - Though this was a Turkish-American co-production, you'll likely spot a number of familiar British faces in this adaptation of the classic mythological story of Jason and the Argonauts. Derek Jacobi (Cadfael, Last Tango in Halifax) stars alongside Angus Macfadyen (Braveheart), Ciarán Hinds (Above Suspicion), Adrian Lester (*Hustle*), and Olivia Williams (*Emma*).

Jekyll & Hyde - 2015 - Set in 1930s London, this variation of the classic story sees Robert Jekyll living in London, a sensitive young man trying to find his way independent of his foster family. Unfortunately, be begins to feel the influence of a powerful darkness that's outside his control – and he realises his parents had been trying to protect him all along. Young Robert has inherited his grandfather's curse, and he's soon drawn into Hyde's dark and unsavoury world.

Labyrinth - *Germany/South Africa* - 2012 - This international co-production jumps between modern and medieval France, and includes a cast of mostly British and Irish actors. It follows two women across time in their searches for the Holy Grail.

Lip Service - 2010 to 2012 - This serial drama takes a look at the lives of a group of lesbian women living in Glasgow, Scotland.

Liverpool 1 - 1998 to 1999 - This gritty, Liverpool-based police drama dives into the city's underworld. We follow the vice squad at Bridewell as they fight drug dealers, paeodophiles, pimps, and porn peddlers in this rough-around-the-edges port city. Samantha Womack stars as DC Isobel de Pauli.

Lost in Austen – 2008 - A bored young Pride and Prejudice fan is changed forever when Elizabeth Bennet stumbles into her modern bathroom. This miniseries includes Hugh Bonneville (*Downton Abbey*) as Mr. Bennet, Morven Christie (*Grantchester*) as Jane Bennet, and Jemima Rooper (*Gold Digger*) as lead Amanda Price.

Love My Way - 2004 to 2007 - This Australian drama follows a thirtysomething woman as she attempts to juggle her desires for a rewarding career, a good relationship, and a healthy family life. Claudia Karvan (*Newton's Law*) stars.

McLeod's Daughters - 2002 to 2009 - Two sisters separated as children are reunited when they jointly inherit a ranch in the Australian bush: the independent Claire McLeod (Lisa Chappell, Gloss) and her estranged half-sister, Tess (Bridie Carter, 800 Words), a stubborn city girl with a drive to change the world. Together, they build an all-female workforce and commit to life at Drovers Run. Nearby, the men of the Ryan family help keep things interesting.

Merlin's Apprentice - *United States/Canada* - 2005 - This miniseries is a follow-up to the 1998 NBC miniseries called *Merlin*, not the longer-running British TV show *Merlin*. The series features British actress Miranda Richardson (*Blackadder*) as The Lady of the Lake, and much of the rest of the cast is from the Commonwealth.

The Mill - 2013 to 2014 - This period drama is based on the real stories of textile mill workers in 1830s England. Set in Cheshire, it depicts the harsh realities of the Industrial Revolution.

Moll Flanders – Daniel Craig stars in this miniseries adaptation of the classic Daniel Defoe novel.

Murphy's Law – 2003 to 2007 - James Nesbitt stars as DS Tommy Murphy, a maverick cop with a dark personal history. When given a final chance to prove his suitability for duty, he takes on a dangerous undercover assignment.

Nero: The Obscure Face of Power - 2004 - John Simm (*Life on Mars*), Liz Smith (*Lark Rise to Candleford*), and Ian Richardson (*House of Cards*) are among the British actors that appear in this epic British-Italian miniseries about the Roman empire.

The New Tomorrow - *New Zealand* - 2005 - After a virus kills all the adults, kids are left to take care of themselves.

The Other Wife - 2012 - This two-part drama tells the story of a woman who finds out about her husband's secret life after he dies in a plane crash. Rupert Everett (*Parade's End*), John Hannah (*McCallum*), Natalia Wörner (*Berlin Station*), and Phyllida Law (*Kingdom*) star.

Our Girl - 2014 to present - This series follows a young woman from East London as she embarks on her career as an army medic. Lacey Turner (*EastEnders*) stars as Molly Dawes, with Michelle Keegan (*Brassic*) entering later as Georgie Lane.

Peak Practice - 1993 to 2002 - This drama takes place in and around a GP surgery in the fictional town of Cardale in Derbyshire's Peak District (mostly filmed in the real-life village of Crich, also in Derbyshire). The series was popular during its run, lasting for 12 series and 147 episodes. Fair warning, though: it ends on a cliffhanger. Cast members over the years included Kevin Whately (*Lewis*), Amanda Burton (*Silent Witness*), Clive Swift (*Keeping Up Appearances*), and Sarah Parish (*Bancroft*).

Porterhouse Blue - 1987 - This British comedy classic takes place at the fictional Porterhouse College at Cambridge, where everyone is rich and male and stuck in the past. When the old headmaster dies and a new one comes to power, he attempts to make changes.

Prisoners' Wives - 2012 to 2013 - In South Yorkshire, four different women struggle to deal with life after men in their lives go to prison. Iain Glen (*Jack Taylor*) fans will be delighted to see him opposite Polly Walker (*Age Before Beauty*).

Queens: The Virgin & the Martyr - 2017 - This costume drama explores the rivalry between Queens Mary Stuart of Scotland and Elizabeth I of England.

Queer as Folk - 1999 to 2000 - This groundbreaking drama followed the lives and loves of a group of young gay men in Manchester.

Rosamund Pilcher's September - 1996 - In a Highland village, a young woman causes a stir when she returns after once leaving under a cloud of suspicion.

The Royal – 2003 to 2011 - This *Heartbeat* spinoff is set in the 1960s and focuses on an NHS hospital serving the seaside Yorkshire town of Elsinby.

Secret Diary of a Call Girl - 2007 to 2011 - Billie Piper (*Doctor Who*) stars as a high-end London call girl.

Secret State – 2012 – In a miniseries that will reassure you that the US isn't the only place where government and big business are way too close, Secret State shows a Deputy Prime Minister entangled in an international conspiracy.

Space: 1999 - 1975 to 1977 - This British-Italian sci-fi series begins when nuclear waste on the far side of the moon explodes, sending both it and its inhabitants out of orbit and into space. At the time it was produced, *Space: 1999* was the most expensive British television series ever produced. Married American actors Martin Landau and Barbara Bain starred.

The Tribe – *New Zealand* – 1999 - In a world where all the adults were killed off by a virus, a group of young people try to stay alive.

Truckers - 2013 - Stephen Tompkinson (*DCI Banks*) stars in this drama about a group of truck drivers in Nottinghamshire.

A Very British Coup - 1988 - When a radical Labour Party politician becomes Prime Minister, he quickly finds he has a lot of enemies.

The Village - 2013 to 2014 - Written by Peter Moffat (*Cambridge Spies*), this series is set in a Derbyshire village between 1914 and the mid-1920s. Though originally envisioned as a 42-hour epic, it lasted just two seasons. It tells the story of life and history through the eyes of Bert Middleton and his fellow villagers.

Wild at Heart - 2006 to 2013 - Stephen Tompkinson (*DCI Banks*, *Ballykissangel*) stars in this series about a British veterinarian who takes his family along to South Africa to release an animal back into the wild. When he sees the area and meets pretty game reserve owner Caroline (Hayley Mills), he ultimately decides to stay.

Wolfblood - 2012 to 2017 - This British-German young adult series revolves around the lives of teenage "wolfbloods", creatures that look like humans but have the ability to transform into wolves at will - and with the full moon.

Comedies

At Home with the Braithwaites - Amanda Redman (*Good Karma Hospital*) and Peter Davison (*Doctor Who*) star in this dramedy about a woman who wins the lottery and starts a charity with the winnings instead of telling her family.

At Last the 1948 Show – This sketch series preceded Monty Python's Flying Circus, and included several cast members.

Beaver Falls – 2011 to 2012 - Three friends decide to have one last crazy summer working in an American summer camp.

Black Books – 2000 to 2004 - Bernard Black runs a bookshop, but he's not really cut out for customer service. He spends most of his time having adventures with his employee and a nearby shopkeeper.

Blandings – 2013 to 2014 - This fun period comedy follows an eccentric aristocratic family and their crumbling ancestral home. It's based on the writings of PG Wodehouse, and stars Timothy Spall and Jennifer Saunders.

The Book Group - 2002 to 2003 - When an American woman moves to Glasgow, she starts a book group to make friends.

Bounty Hunters - 2017 - Rosie Perez and Jack Whitehall star in this comedy about an oddball partnership between a British man and a New York City bounty hunter.

Boy Meets Girl - 2009 - After a freak accident, a man and woman find themselves trapped in each other's bodies. Martin Freeman (*Sherlock*) and Rachael Stirling (*Detectorists*) star in this ITV dramedy.

Bridget & Eamon – 2016 to 2019 - Bridget and Eamon are an Irish couple living with an unknown number of children in the Midlands in the 1980s.

Budgie - 1971 to 1972 - Pop star Adam Faith (*Love Hurts*) starred in this series about a recently released prisoner who always manages to find trouble. The first four episodes were filmed in black and white due to the ITV Colour Strike of late 1970 to early 1971.

Carters Get Rich - 2017 - This British sitcom follows a family after their child develops an app and sells it for £10 million. James van der Beek (*Dawson's Creek*) appears as the wealthy CEO who buys the app and later tries to mentor the young programmer.

Crims - 2015 - This sitcom follows two young men sent to a young offenders' institution after one got the other involved in a bank robbery without his knowledge.

Detectorists - 2014 to 2017 - Two quirky friends scan the fields of England with metal detectors, hoping for the big find that will finally let them do the gold dance.

Doc Martin - 2004 to present - Martin Clunes (*Men Behaving Badly*) stars in this comedy about a brilliant but grumpy London surgeon who suddenly develops a fear of blood. He leaves his high-flying career and takes a post in a Cornish fishing village where he spent holidays as a child with his Aunt Joan. His bad attitude and lack of social skills makes it a challenge to adapt to his new life.

Doctor at Large - 1971 - Bill Oddie, John Cleese, Graham Clapham, and a number of other British comedy greats were involved in the script for this short-lived series about a group of newly-qualified doctors heading to work. The first six episodes were filmed in black and white due to the ITV Colour Strike of late 1970 to early 1971.

Drifters – 2013 to 2016 - Meg, Bunny, and Laura share a flat in Leeds and face the ups and downs of post-university life.

The Goes Wrong Show - 2019 - This sitcom follows an amateur dramatic society as they perform a variety of short plays in which everything that can go wrong, does go wrong.

Grafters - 1998 to 1999 - Robson Green (*Grantchester*) and Stephen Tompkinson (*Ballykissangel*) starred in this dramedy about two brothers who run a building company together and move to London to renovate a house.

The Inbetweeners – 2008 to 2010 - This raunchy teen comedy focuses on a group of young men who aren't quite as cool as they'd like to be.

The Inbetweeners Movie - 2012 - Though not a TV series, this Is the natural sequel to the series, and it sees the gang together again on holiday.

London Irish – 2013 - This occasionally off-colour comedy focuses on a group of Northern Irish ex-pats in the city of London. The series was written by Lisa McGee, best known as the writer and creator of *Derry Girls*.

Lunch Monkeys – This workplace comedy focuses on the administrative support staff at a busy law firm.

Outnumbered - 2007 to 2014 - Hugh Dennis and Claire Skinner star in this sitcom about a couple who are outnumbered by their three children.

Outrageous Fortune – *New Zealand* – 2005 to 2010 - A trashy family of criminals tries to clean up their act.

Parents - 2012 - Sally Phillips (*Miranda*) starred in this sitcom about a middle-class fortysomething woman who moves her family out of London to live with her parents in Kettering. Though well-reviewed, a second series was never made.

Peep Show – 2003 to 2015 - Two dysfunctional and very different friends share a flat in London and attempt (rather poorly) to grow up.

Plebs - 2013 to present - Three young men make their way in Ancient Rome. Tom Rosenthal (*Friday Night Dinner*) stars.

Plus One – 2009 - A man attempts to find a date to an ex's wedding.

The Royal Bodyguard - 2011 to 2012 - Follow the exploits of Captain Guy Hubble, a fictional ex-guardsman who now works as a Royal Bodyguard after saving the queen's life on the day of the State Opening of Parliament. Sir David Jason stars.

Smack the Pony – 2003 - This British sketch comedy features an all-female cast, including Fiona Allen, Doon Mackichan, and Sally Phillips.

Some Girls - 2012 to 2014 - This sitcom follows a group of teenage girls who live in the same South London housing estate.

Spaced – When a young man and woman struggle to find affordable housing, they're tempted into a lie.

Spy – 2011 to 2012 - When a man loses his self-esteem and the respect of his loved son, he has to take drastic action to get it back. He applies for a job as a civil servant, but accidentally applies to become a spy.

Teachers - 2001 to 2004 - This dramedy follows the teachers and students in one British school. Andrew Lincoln (*The Walking Dead*) stars, but it's also one of James Corden's earliest appearances. You'll also spot a young Shaun Evans (*Endeavour*) and Mathew Horne (*Gavin & Stacey*) in this series.

Vexed – 2010 to 2012 - A young male and female detective team frustrate each other with their different attitudes and complicated personal lives.

Vicious - 2013 to 2016 - Sir Ian McKellen and Sir Derek Jacobi star as an aging gay couple with a hilariously snarky love/hate relationship. The two live together in a Covent Garden flat, entertaining frequent guests, hoping for Freddie's big acting break, and checking to make sure their elderly dog is still alive.

Warren – 2019 - In this offbeat Lancashire-based comedy, Martin Clunes (*Doc Martin*) stars as an impatient and unsuccessful driving instructor who has recently moved in with his partner and her teenage sons. Unfortunately, it wasn't renewed for a second series.

Westside – *New Zealand* – 2015 to 2017 - This prequel to Outrageous Fortune is set between 1974 and 1979, and it recounts stories of crime and passion in Auckland.

Whites - 2010 - Alan Davies (*Jonathan Creek*) stars as a chef in a posh country hotel.

White Van Man - 2011 - Will Mellor (*No Offence*) and Georgia Moffett (*The Bill*) are among the stars of this sitcom about a terribly incompetent handyman and his assistant.

You, Me, & Them - 2013 to 2015 - Anthony Head and Eve Myles star in this sitcom about an age gap romance.

The Young Person's Guide to Becoming a Rock Star - 1998 - A young Gerard Butler (*P.S. I Love You*) stars in this series about a young Glasgow band trying to get their big break.

Thriller & Horror

Hammer House of Horror – 1980 - This classic anthology series tells tales of mystery, suspense, and horror.

Thriller – 1973 to 1976 - This long-running 1970s anthology series includes a few supernatural tales, but mostly a lot of suspense and mystery. It also includes a surprising number of American guest stars.

Tales of the Unexpected – 1979 to 1988 - This anthology series features terrifying tales and a variety of well-known Brits, including Roald Dahl and Timothy West (Great Canal Journeys).

The House that Dripped Blood – This anthology series tells four stories about a haunted home in the UK. Christopher Lee,

Jon Pertwee, and Peter Cushing are featured.

The Prisoner – 1967 to 1968 - After his resignation, a secret agent wakes up to find himself stuck in a strange coastal prison known as The Village. They want information he's not prepared to share, and he makes numerous attempts to escape. The series is set in the Welsh village of Portmeirion, the lovely but unusual creation of Sir Clough Williams-Ellis.

Secret Agent – Patrick McGoohan stars as John Drake, an M9 agent who specialises in handling subversive elements that threaten world peace. Though he travels the world on his adventures, the first episode takes him to the Welsh seaside resort village of Portmeirion.

Ultraviolet - 1998 - Jack Davenport (*Coupling*) and Idris Elba (*Luther*) are among the stars of this series about a detective who discovers a secret government unit dedicated to hunting vampires.

Undeniable - 2014 - This two-part thriller follows the story of a murderer brought to justice by the woman who saw him killing her mother many years earlier.

Documentary & Lifestyle

16 Kids & Counting - 2012 - Though the number of kids has increased in recent years (22 as of 2021), this series follows England's fast-breeding Radford family. See also: *17 Kids & Counting*, *18 Kids & Counting*, and *19 Kids & Counting*

Aerial Britain - 2019 - Enjoy aerial scenery from England, Scotland, and Wales. Each episode has a theme - stately homes, work and industry, and spiritual locations.

Animal Madhouse - 2010 - In the Warwickshire countryside, there's a clinic that helps animals of all types and sizes. This series is similar to Yorkshire Vet, but a bit wilder.

Animal Rescue School - 2018 - Follow Royal Society for the Prevention of Cruelty to Animals candidates as they progress through the grueling 10-month training process.

At Your Service – 2016 - This documentary series takes a look at people who specialise in the lost art of service and hospitality. Though it's set in Ireland, it's part of the British Isles – so we're including it.

Auction - 2015 - This series travels the world, looking at some of the most impressive items up for auction. Episodes feature everything from pop art in New York to the letters of Winston Churchill and a clear-out at Chatsworth.

The Auction House - 2014 - This series goes behind the scenes at Lots Road Auctions in London, where the hardworking staff does their best to find unusual items for wealthy clients.

Endeavour fans will recognise Roger Allam's voice doing the narration.

Baby Beauty Queens - 2009 - This series follows three young girls, aged seven through nine, as they enter Britain's very first pre-teen beauty pageant.

Booze Britain – 2004 - In this series, the cameras follow hard-drinking Brits in a variety of locations, including Newcastle and Isle of Man.

Boozed Up Brits Abroad – In mainland Europe, British tourists have something of a reputation for being drunk and disorderly. This series follows a number of British tourists as they set out on vacations and stag parties.

The Bridal Coach – A former model and current bridal coach helps a number of British brides-to-be as they prepare for the big day.

Darcey Bussell: Looking for Margot - 2016 - Famed ballerina Darcey Bussell looks back at the life of Margot Fonteyn.

David Suchet: In the Footsteps of St. Peter - 2014 - David Suchet (Poirot) hosts this series in which he attempts to learn more about the life of St. Peter.

Designer Darlings – This series follows the Bassi family as they run a business selling expensive clothing to parents who don't mind spending a fortune to keep their kids looking fashionable.

Discovering the World - 2019 - London-based Belgian journalist Pierre Brouwers travels the world, going beyond the typical tourist attractions. Though the British Isles don't factor in too heavily, one episode does visit Scotland.

The Dog Rescuers – 2017 - Alan Davies (*Jonathan Creek, QI*) appears in this series about dog rescues around the UK.

Edwardian Farm - 2010 - In this series, the creators of *Victorian Farm* turn their attention to the Edwardian period, looking at the way farming life looked a little more than 100 years ago.

Emergency Firefighters – 2005 - This series takes a look at the intense, demanding situations encountered by the Avon Fire and Rescue Service.

Fake or Fortune? - 2011 to present - Philip Mould and Fiona Bruce present this series in which they attempt to authenticate potentially significant works of art.

Fat Men Can't Hunt - 2008 - Four overweight British men and women are taken to the African desert to try out the hunter-gatherer diet.

The Farmer's Country Showdown - 2016 - This celebration of rural Britain shows off farming families and the events that show off their hard work.

The French Collection - 2016 - British bargain hunters cross the channel to scour French antique markets for bargains.

Get a Life – This series aims to help people with basic life skills like confidence, flirting, style, and courage.

Hidden Europe - 2002 - British zoologist Bobbie Fletcher travels Europe in search of overlooked places and rare animals.

The Hotel - 2011 - This hilarious docu-series follows overconfident hotelier Mark Jenkins as he attempts to work in a variety of hotel settings. Hugh Bonneville (*Downtown Abbey*) narrates series two through four.

Husbands from Hell - 2019 - Marrying a British man isn't all charming accents and afternoon teas. This series takes a look at some of the worst husbands in the nation.

The Irish Pub – 2013 - This documentary explores the history and culture of pubs in Ireland.

The Island with Bear Grylls - 2014 - Adventurer Bear Grylls puts 13 British men and women on an island to see if they can survive for 6 weeks.

James May's Man Lab – 2010 to 2013 - James May sets out to teach modern men a few useful skills.

James May's Toy Stories – 2009 to 2014 - James May sets out on a mission to get kids away from screens and back to classic toys.

Ladette to Lady – 2008 - This series follows a group of young women as they attend a finishing school to teach them proper etiquette, deportment, and elocution.

Laura McKenzie's Traveler - *United States* - 2002 - Though not a British series, this one features three episodes set in the British Isles - London, Dublin, and Edinburgh.

Lily Allen: From Riches to Rags - 2011 - This documentary series follows early-2000s pop singer Lily Allen as she and her sister launch a fashion line in London

Killer Roads - 2011 - The UK has a number of dangerous roads that host more than their fair share of devastating accidents.

Made Over By - 2016 - This series sees experts transforming the looks of some of the UK's most fashion-challenged residents.

Make Me Perfect - 2006 - This series uses major cosmetic intervention (including surgery) to help people feel better about their appearances and get over past traumas.

Married to a Celebrity – 2017 - This series takes a look at the worst things about being married to a celebrity.

Masterpiece - 2018 - Alan Titchmarsh stars in this series about antiques enthusiasts attempting to separate trash from treasure.

My Pet Shame - 2010 - Joanna Page of Gavin & Stacey presents this series about Britain's most embarrassing pet problems.

No Ordinary Party – 2011 - This series takes a look at incredible and extreme parties in the UK – including a puppy party, a naturist party, and a fetish party in Edinburgh.

Older Than Ireland – 2015 - This series interviews 30 Irish centenarians to build a living history of modern-day Ireland.

The Only Way is Essex - 2010 to present - Proof that British TV isn't all thoughtful dramas and intelligent mysteries, this reality series follows a group of wild young people living in Essex.

Oxford Street Revealed - 2017 - This series takes a closer look at one of the UK's most famous streets.

Oz & James's Big Wine Adventure - 2007 - Wine expert Oz Clarke takes a wine-tasting trip to France with James May.

Park Life: London – 2016 - This program takes a look at London's Hyde Park through the seasons.

Personal Services Required – 2007 - Two well-off families seek someone to manage their households.

Quizeum - 2018 - Griff Rhys Jones stars in this quiz show set at some of the most remarkable museums in Britain.

Retail Therapy – 2011 - This series follows Brits who need serious help as they embark on a shopping excursion.

Salt Beef and Rye – 2016 - This fun documentary looks at the characters who frequent London's Brick Lane.

Secrets of the Stones – 2018 - This two-part series dives into the history and archaeology of Ireland.

The Shelbourne Hotel – 2017 - This reality series takes a look at what goes on behind the scenes of an upscale hotel.

Small Animal Hospital - 2014 - This series follows the action at the Small Animal Hospital at the University of Glasgow.

Smart Travels with Rudy Maxa – 2002 to 2006 - Although not exclusively about Great Britain, this series includes episodes in London, the London countryside, Dublin, Ireland's West Coast, Bath, South Wales, Edinburgh, and St. Andrews (not to mention a lot of other lovely cities around the world).

Snowdonia 1890 - 2010 - Two families live as though they were 19th century farmers on Mount Snowdonia in Wales.

Spendaholics – 2005 - This show follows a variety of Brits with major spending problems and the debt to match.

Streetmate - 2017 - Scarlett Moffatt hits the streets to help singles find matches based on first impressions.

Thelma's Big Irish Communions – 2015 - A dressmaker explores the world of Irish Catholic Holy Communion celebrations – and the dresses that go along with it.

Time Team – 1994 to 2014 - A group of archaeologists visits different excavation sites. Amazon currently offers Set 20 of this long-running British series. If you like that one, you can go here for more.

Total Wipeout - 2011 - This British game show sees guests attempting to complete obstacle courses to win cash prizes.

Tower Block Kids – 2017 - In an attempt to house their poor, the UK built more than 4000 bleak tower blocks. This is the two-part story of kids growing up in those buildings.

Trouble in Poundland – 2017 - The modern economy challenges businesses of all types, and this series looks at what Poundland is doing to survive.

Very British Problems – 2016 - This hilarious series takes a look at what it means to be British.

Victorian Farm - 2009 - On the Acton Scott Estate in rural Shropshire, things continue as they might have been more than 100 years ago.

Victorian Farm: Christmas Special - 2009 - This series shows us how the Victorians changed the way we celebrate Christmas.

Walks With My Dog - 2017 - British celebrities like John Nettles and Robert Lindsay explore the countryside with their dogs.

Wedding SOS - 2008 - A top British wedding planner helps couples whose weddings seem doomed.

Wild Animal Rescue - 2016 - This series follows animal rescue missions to some of the wildest places on the planet.

The Yorkshire Vet - 2015 to present - This engaging series follows the staff of Skeldale Veterinary Centre as they work with the animals.

Medical, Police, & Rescue

24 Hours in Police Custody - 2014 - This long-running docuseries goes behind the scenes at the Luton Police Station.

999 What's Your Emergency? - 2012 - Take a look at what goes on behind the scenes when you dial 999 (the British equivalent of 911).

Air Ambulance ER - 2014 - When terrain and road access make it hard for regular ambulances to reach an area quickly, air ambulance teams step in.

Ambulance – 2016 - This series follows the London Ambulance Service as they struggle to prioritize resources for those who need them most.

Baby Baby – 1997 - This documentary series follows couples as they bring multiples into the world.

Baby Hospital – 2005 - This British reality series takes a look at growing families in a variety of different situations.

Cars, Cops, & Criminals - 2008 - The Association of Vehicle Crime Intelligence Service fights vehicle-related crimes in Great Britain.

Children's Hospital - 1993 - The Royal Manchester Children's Hospital opens its doors to let viewers see the challenging work they do.

Extreme A&E – 2012 - This graphic series follows top paramedics as they deal with major emergencies around the world - including an episode in London.

Helicopter ER - 2017 - This series follows the doctors and paramedics of the Yorkshire Air Ambulance.

Helicopter Search & Rescue - *Ireland* - 2018 - If you've ever wondered what goes on behind the scenes of Ireland's key rescue agencies, you'll want to check out this series that takes a peek at the work being done by the Irish Coast Guard, Cork Fire Brigade, the RNLI, the Irish Naval Services, and mountain rescue teams.

Inside the Ambulance - 2016 - This series goes behind the scenes with a West Midlands ambulance crew.

Kids on the Edge – 2015 - This three-part series takes a look at families involved with the Tavistock Gender Identity Development Service, the NHS's gender identity clinic for children with gender dysphoria.

Nursing the Nation – 2013 - This series follows district nurses around the UK, taking a look at their day-to-day working lives.

One Born Every Minute UK – 2010 to present - This series follows families as their children are born.

One Born Every Minute UK: What Happened Next? – 2011 - This series follows up with families from *One Born Every Minute*, seeing how life is going for them after the birth of their children.

Secret Eaters - 2012 - Anna Richardson visits households around the UK to help people figure out why they're gaining weight.

Street Hospital – 2013 - This series follows paramedics as they deal with some of the wildest emergencies the UK has to offer – stag parties gone wrong, births in nightclub basements, and so, so many drunks.

Supersized Hospitals – 2010 - This two-part series takes a look at the opening of the New South Glasgow Hospital, the largest medical campus in Western Europe.

Supersize vs. Superskinny - 2008 - This docu-series takes a look at extreme eaters on both ends of the spectrum.

Trauma Rescue Squad - 2017 - Britain's toughest medics are ready to go when the worst disasters strike.

Food & Cookery Shows

Catherine's Family Kitchen - 2018 - Chef Catherine Fulvio celebrates traditional Irish cooking.

Celebrity Restaurant in Our Living Room - 2010 - This version of *Restaurant in Our Living Room* features celebrities to make things a little more interesting.

Chef's Protégé - 2014 - This BBC Two series follows Michelin star chefs as they return to school and choose protégés.

Cook Yourself Thin UK - 2007 - This series focuses on helping Brits lose weight by transforming unhealthy dishes into healthier choices.

Choccywoccydoodah - 2011 - This now-defunct Brighton bakery was once famous for its quirky cakes, attracting a slew of celebrity clients.

Comfort Eating - 2017 - Comedian Nick Helm goes on the road seeking out Britain's best comfort foods in Islington, Camden, Leeds, Brighton, Berlin, St. Albans, Paris, Little Europe, Peckham, Essex, Soho, Wales, Notting Hill, Glasgow, and Borough Market.

The F Word - 2007 - This reality series sees Gordon Ramsay preparing a three-course meal at the F Word Restaurant while interacting with guests and celebrities.

Gordon Behind Bars, aka Ramsay Behind Bars - 2012 - Gordon Ramsay goes behind bars to help a group of prisoners start a bakery.

Hell's Kitchen – 2004 to 2009 - This series pits prospective chefs against one another, with the winner getting a head chef position.

James & Thom's Pizza Pilgrimage – 2017 - James and Thom travel around Italy to learn about pizza, and even sell a bit of it on the street in London.

James Martin's United Cakes of America – 2012 - British chef James Martin travels the United States in search of cake.

James Martin's Mediterranean – 2011 - James Martin shows off what might be the best job in the world as he sails around the Mediterranean and eats...a lot.

James Martin Home Comforts – 2015 - James Martin tackles cool weather comfort foods – including jacket potatoes and Toad in the Hole. See also: *James Martin Home Comforts at Christmas*

Kitchen Nightmares - 2007 to 2014 - Acclaimed British chef Gordon Ramsay hosts this series in which he visits struggling American restaurants and spends a week trying to help them be more successful.

Marco's Great British Feast - 2008 - Chef Marco Pierre White travels around Britain sourcing some of the best and most unique local ingredients (including gull eggs).

Mary Berry's Absolute Favourites - 2014 to 2015 - Britain's favourite home cook shares some of her absolute favourite recipes from a lifetime of cooking.

Mary Berry's Foolproof Cooking – 2015 - Mary Berry offers tips and demonstrations for simple, foolproof recipes anyone can attempt.

My Life on a Plate – 2014 - A variety of notable Brits like Mary Berry and Nigel Havers take a look back at their lives and the foods that accompanied them.

Modern Irish Food: Kevin Dundon – *Ireland* - 2013 - While there's just one episode of this one, it's great if you want to learn how to tackle baked lobster with mustard sauce, seared fillet beef and blue cheese salad, apple tart, or potato pie.

Nigel Slater Eating Together – 2014 - Nigel Slater explores modern British home cooking with basics like noodles, soup, custard, and hotpots.

Rachel Allen Home Cooking - *Ireland* - Irish chef Rachel Allen goes into the home kitchens of well-known chefs to see how they operate when they're at home.

Rachel Allen's Dinner Parties - *Ireland* - 2010 - Irish chef Rachel Allen shows viewers how to throw the perfect dinner party.

Remarkable Places to Eat - 2018 - Top chefs in England walk us through incredible meals in Venice, Edinburgh, Paris, and San Sebastian.

Restaurant in Our Living Room – 2010 - In each episode, two couples turn their homes into restaurants and compete for the best takings.

Scotch: A Golden Dream - 2019 - Jim McEwan takes us on a journey through Scotland to learn more about whisky.

Scotch! The Story of Whisky – 2015 - This short series takes a look at the history and science of the Scottish whisky industry.

The Story of Tea: The History of Tea & How to Make the Perfect Cup – 2007 - This documentary takes a look at the history of tea and tea culture.

Home & Garden

Art Deco Icons: Britain's Bling and Glamour – 2009 - David Heathcote visits four Art Deco icons around Britain.

Best Laid Plans – 2017 - Charlie helps couples tackle major home renovations around the UK.

Brand New House on a Budget - 2014 - This show features home makeovers on a budget.

Brick by Brick: Rebuilding Our Past – 2011 - Dan Cruickshank and Charlie Luxton follow along with the reconstruction of historic British buildings.

Build a New Life in the Country – 2005 to 2010 - This series follows families as they relocate to the countryside. See also: *Build a New Life in the Country Revisits*

Dermot Bannon's Incredible Homes - *Ireland* - 2018 - Irish architect Dermot Bannon explores gorgeous homes in Sydney, Melbourne, Sweden, London, New York, and Los Angeles.

Design Doctors – 2018 - British couples get design help in this reality series.

Double Your House for Half the Money - 2012 - British families see their homes transformed.

First Homes – This series focuses on first-time homebuyers around the UK, with locations including Glasgow, Chester, and Northampton.

Getting the Builders In – 2017 - In this series, teams of builders pitch to win a variety of construction and renovation jobs.

Greatest Gardens - 2017 - Diarmuid Gavin and Helen Dillonare look for the best private gardens in Northern Ireland.

Honey, I Bought the House – 2014 - Couples hunting for a home allow one member of the couple to make the final property decision.

The House that 100k (GBP) Built – 2016 - Homes are expensive in the UK, but this series looks at people building homes from scratch – and on a budget. See also: *The House that 100k Built: Tricks of the Trade*

Location, Location, Location - 2000 to present - This long-running British house-hunting show has hosts Kirstie Allsopp and Phil Spencer helping guests find the right house in the right location.

Make My Home Bigger – 2015 - Jonnie Irwin follows along as people seek to enlarge their homes.

Millionaire Basement Wars – 2015 - In the increasingly crowded and expensive City of London, many homeowners are building large and elaborate basements.

My Flat Pack Home – 2010 to 2012 - This British series takes a look at unusual prefab homes and their owners.

Nick Knowles: Original Home Restoration – 2014 - This series follows families as they renovate their historic homes.

Restoration Home – 2010 - Actress Caroline Quentin (*Jonathan Creek, Blue Murder*) hosts this series about restoring neglected historic homes around Britain.

Project Restoration – 2016 - Historical building surveyor Marianne Suhr travels the UK helping out on challenging restoration projects.

Restoration Man – 2014 - Architect George Clarke helps people all over the UK as they take on ambitious renovations and transformations of unique and historic spaces. See also: *Restoration Man Best Builds*

Room to Improve – *Ireland* - 2007 to present - This Ireland-based series follows a variety of housing situations, including people seeking to downsize, upsize, and renovate.

To Build or Not to Build - 2013 - This series follows people who've decided to build their own homes, watching as they learn the necessary skills and battle with their local councils to get the proper permissions.

Unreal Estate - *Australia* - 2015 - This series takes a look at some of the most incredible and over-the-top homes in Australia.

What the Neighbours Did – This show follows Brits as they renovate spaces in their homes.

Young, Rich, and Househunting – 2010 - This house hunting show focuses exclusively on young buyers at the upper end of the British home market.

Website: http://pluto.tv	

Description: Pluto is another ad-supported streaming service, but they also offer the option to watch some shows through their "live" streaming. The major downside to Pluto is that they don't have a search function.

Available On: Roku, Fire TV, Apple TV, Apple iPhone & iPad, Chromecast, Android phones and tablets, and computer (via web browser).

Cost: Free with ads

Now Streaming

999 What's Your Emergency? - 2012 - See what goes on behind the scenes when you dial 999 (the British equivalent of 911).

Ambassadors - 2013 - David Mitchell and Robert Webb (both of *Peep Show*) star in this series about employees at the British embassy in the fictional Asian country of Tazbekistan.

Anna Karenina - 1978 - Nicola Pagett (*Upstairs Downstairs*) stars as Anna Karenina in this retelling of Tolstoy's classic tale of family passions in 1870s Russia.

Antiques Roadshow - 1979 to present - Filmed at a variety of stately homes around the country, this series allows members of the public to bring in cherished items for expert appraisal.

Archangel - 2006 - Daniel Craig stars as a middle-aged former Oxford historian whose studies in a Moscow Library lead him into the middle of a dark and dramatic plot. This series was produced by the BBC and also includes Gabriel Macht of *Suits* fame.

At Home With the Braithwaites - 2000 to 2003 - Amanda Redman (*Good Karma Hospital*) and Peter Davison (*Doctor Who*) star in this dramedy about a woman who wins the lottery and starts a charity with the winnings instead of telling her family.

Ballykissangel - *Ireland* - 1996 to 2001 - A young English priest adjusts to the pace of life in a small Irish village. Stephen Tompkinson (*DCI Banks*) stars as Father Peter Clifford.

Being Human - 2008 to 2013 - Aidan Turner (*Poldark*) stars in this series about a werewolf, vampire, and ghost attempting to live together. This is not to be confused with the American version of the series that was made a few years later.

Big Bad Battles: Weekend Warriors - 2015 - This quirky reality series catches up with battle reenactors to see what life might have been like for soldiers in various conflicts.

Big School - 2013 to 2014 - A new French teacher arrives at Greybridge School and gives the long-time Deputy Head of Science second thoughts about resigning.

Blackpool - 2004 - Shortly after Ripley Holden opens his arcade, a man is murdered. The investigation jeopardizes all his big plans.

Blandings - 2013 to 2014 - A nobleman struggles to keep his stately home and strange family in line so he can spend more time with his beloved pig. The series was based on P.G. Wodehouse's *Blandings Castle* stories, and it's one of a relatively small number of scripted programmes filmed on location in Northern Ireland (mostly at Crom Castle in County Fermanagh).

Blood Ties - *Canada* - 2007 - When a Toronto detective begins losing her eyesight, she becomes a PI and teams up with a 470-year-old vampire (who is also the illegitimate son of Henry VIII). The series is an adaptation of author Tanya Huff's *Blood* novels.

Bluestone 42 - 2013 to 2015 - This dark comedy follows the lives of British soldiers working in a bomb disposal detachment in Afghanistan.

Bomb Girls - *Canada* - 2012 to 2013 - Set during World War II, BOMB GIRLS tells the stories of women who risked their lives in a munitions factory to make bombs for the Allied Forces. The series stars Meg Tilly (*The Big Chill*), Jodi Balfour (*Quarry*), Charlotte Hegele (*When Calls the Heart*) and Ali Liebert (*Ten Days in the Valley*).

Britain's Best Bakery - 2012 to 2014 - Experts travel Great Britain in search of the best independent bakeries.

Bromwell High - 2005 - This animated comedy follows a group of naughty schoolgirls at an under-funded South London secondary school.

Build a New Life in the Country – 2005 to 2010 - This series follows families as they relocate to the countryside and build new lives.

Cadfael - 1994 to 1998 - In 12th century Shrewsbury, a monk solves mysteries. Derek Jacobi (*Last Tango in Halifax*) stars.

The Case - 2011 - This legal drama tells the story of a man put on trial for the murder of his terminally ill partner after he helped her commit suicide.

Case Histories - 2011 to 2013 - Based on the Jackson Brodie novels by Kate Atkinson, this Edinburgh-based series features a tough guy PI with a heart of gold.

Celtic Britain - 2000 - This docuseries takes a look at Celtic history in Scotland, Wales, and elsewhere in the British Isles.

The Detectives: Murder on the Streets - 2017 - With unprecedented levels of access, this series takes a look at the activities of Manchester's homicide detectives as they work complex cases over the course of a year.

The Devil's Mistress, aka The Devil's Whore – 2008 - This two-part series takes place against the backdrop of the English Civil War, following a young woman as she moves between poverty and power.

Dickensian - 2015 to 2016 - This ambitious miniseries is set in the world of Charles Dickens's novels, bringing together a variety of characters in 19th century London.

The Diplomat - 2009 - This two-part television miniseries follows a British diplomat who's been arrested on charges of working with the Russian mafia. Richard Roxburgh (*Rake*) and Claire Forlani (*Meet Joe Black*) are among the stars.

Doc Martin - 2004 to present - Martin Clunes (*Men Behaving Badly*) stars in this comedy about a brilliant but grumpy London surgeon who suddenly develops a fear of blood. He leaves his high-flying career and takes a post in a Cornish fishing village where he spent holidays as a child with his Aunt Joan.

Doctor at Large - 1971 - In this follow-up to *Doctor in the House*, Michael Upton (Barry Evans) heads out on a solo career.

Drifters – 2013 to 2016 - Meg, Bunny, and Laura share a flat in Leeds and face the ups and downs of post-university life.

Father Ted - 1995 to 1998 - Father Ted lives with two other very strange priests on the not-so-quiet Craggy Island in Ireland.

The Field of Blood - 2011 to 2013 - Set in early 1980s Glasgow, a young woman skillfully solves murders on a police force full of men. Unfortunately, her dedication to the truth also puts her in danger. The series stars BAFTA winner Jayd Johnson (*River City*) as Paddy Meehan, working alongside Peter Capaldi (*Doctor Who*) and David Morrissey (*The Missing*).

Fifth Gear - 2002 to present - This series talks cars, offering reviews, close-up looks, and industry information.

Fresh Meat – 2011 to 2016 - Six young friends go off to university.

Gangsters: Faces of the Underworld - 2009 - This true-crime series takes a look at some of the world's most notorious gangsters.

Getting On - 2009 to 2012 - This dark comedy follows the residents and staff in a geriatric ward.

The Ghost Squad - 2005 - Similar to *Line of Duty*, this series follows an Internal Affairs division designed to help find and fix corruption within the police. Elaine Cassidy (*No Offence*) stars.

The Grand - 1997 to 1998 - Written by Russell T Davies (*Doctor Who*), this 1920s-era period drama follows the Bannerman family as they re-open The Grand after WWI.

Guy Martin: Industrial Wonders - 2011 - Guy Martin celebrates the best of the Industrial Revolution by getting involved with six large restoration projects.

Guy Martin: Spitfire Restoration - 2014 - Guy Martin helps restore one of the world's most iconic planes.

Hammer House of Horror – 1980 - This classic anthology series tells tales of mystery, suspense, and horror.

Hearts and Bones - 2000 to 2001 - Damian Lewis (*Band of Brothers*), Dervla Kirwan (*Ballykissangel*), Hugo Speer (*London Kills*) and Sarah Parish (*Bancroft*) star in this drama about a group of young adults who move from Coventry to London together.

<u>Henry and Anne: The Lovers Who Changed History</u> - 2014 - Historian Dr. Suzannah Lipscomb tells the story of the love affair between Henry VIII and Anne Boleyn.

Him & Her - 2010 to 2013 - This sitcom follows a twenty-something working-class couple. The series portrays the couple with a brutal honesty that can make it a bit uncomfortable to watch, particularly if you don't like swearing or adult situations.

History Cold Case - 2010 to 2011 - Professor Sue Black and her team use modern forensic techniques to examine the remains of the past.

The Hollies: Look Through Any Window - 2011 - This documentary takes a look back at one of the most successful British bands of the 1960s and 70s.

The Hour - 2011 - This period drama takes us behind the scenes during the launch of a new London news programme during the mid-1950s. Ben Whishaw (*Spectre*), Romola Garai (*Emma*), Dominic West (*The Affair*), and Peter Capaldi (*Doctor Who*) are among the cast members.

Hustle - 2004 to 2012 - This series follows a group of talented con artists who prefer to operate long cons on the greedy and corrupt of London.

Imagine a School: Summerhill - 2008 - Summerhill is a "free school" in England where students do as they please so long as they aren't hurting anyone else. Not surprisingly, the school has had some issues with the government. This documentary takes a look at their battle.

The Incredible Journey of Mary Bryant - 2007 - After stealing a woman's picnic, starving Mary Broad is convicted to death. Before realizing that fate, however, she's granted mercy and allowed to live out her life on a penal colony in Australia.

Inside Men - 2012 - This miniseries tells the story of three employees who plan and execute a major heist.

Ireland's Greatest Robberies - Jim McCabe presents this look at some of the most ambitious robberies to occur on Irish soil.

K-9 - 2009 - This *Doctor Who* spin-off follows the robot dog companion K-9.

<u>Kavanagh QC</u> - 1995 to 2001 - John Thaw (*Inspector Morse*) stars as James Kavanagh QC, a barrister with a working-class background and a strong sense of right and wrong. It was one of Thaw's final roles before he died of cancer at the age of 60.

Little Dorrit – 2008 - Claire Foy and Matthew Macfayden star in this adaptation of Dickens' story of struggle in 1820s London.

Love London - 2015 - Guided by a London taxi driver, you'll follow a young Londoner trying to learn more about her city.

<u>Man Stroke Woman</u> – 2005 to 2007 - This British sketch comedy includes appearances by Nick Frost, Daisy Haggard, Nick Burns, and Amanda Abbington.

<u>*McLeod's Daughters*</u> - *Australia* - 2002 to 2009 - Two sisters are reunited when they jointly inherit a ranch in the Australian bush: the independent Claire McLeod (Lisa Chappell, Gloss) and her estranged half-sister, Tess (Bridie Carter, 800 Words), a stubborn city girl with a drive to change the world. Together, they build an all-female workforce and commit to Drovers Run.

<u>Merlin</u> - 2009 to 2013 - Colin Morgan (*The Fall*) stars as a young Merlin in his days as a mere servant to Prince Arthur of Camelot. In this version of Camelot, magic is banned and Merlin is forced to keep his talent hidden away.

Midsomer Murders - 1998 to present - In Midsomer County, the landscapes are beautiful, the villagers all have secrets, and murder is rampant.

Monarch of the Glen - 2000 to 2005 - Young Archie MacDonald returns home to the Scottish Highlands to take his place as laird and save the family estate.

Mr. Bean - 1992 to 1995 - Bumbling Mr. Bean rarely speaks and has some very peculiar ways of doing things, but it usually works out for him. Rowan Atkinson (*Maigret*) stars.

The Musketeers – 2014 to 2016 - This modern retelling of the classic Dumas novel includes appearances by Peter Capaldi, Tom Burke, and Rupert Everett.

My Family - 2000 to 2011 - Set in Chiswick, this family sitcom was conceived as a British version of the classic American sitcom. It follows the fictional Harper family, and the central cast includes Robert Lindsay, Zoe Wanamaker, and Kris Marshall.

My Kitchen Rules - 2017 - This British cookery show looks for the UK's top home cooks.

Nature's Treasure Islands - 2014 - Stewart McPherson attempts to become the first person to visit all 14 British Overseas Territories. Along the way, he shares loads of beautiful flora and fauna.

Neil Gaiman's Neverwhere - 1996 - Based on Neil Gaiman's fantasy novel, this miniseries follows Scotsman Richard Mayhew after he encounters an injured girl named Door on the streets of London. Against his fiancee's wishes, he decides to help the girl, following her into "London Below" and ceasing to exist on the surface.

The New Tomorrow - *New Zealand* - 2005 - After a virus kills all the adults, kids are left to take care of themselves.

Ultimate Force - 2002 to 2007 - Ross Kemp (*EastEnders*) stars in this action series about a Special Air Service team that stops things like anthrax poisonings, assassinations, and bank sieges.

The Only Way is Essex - 2010 to present - Proof that British TV isn't all thoughtful dramas and intelligent mysteries, this reality series follows a group of wild young people living in Essex.

The Palace – 2008 - A fictional British royal family deals with all manner of upper-class problems.

Peak Practice - 1993 to 2002 - This drama takes place in and around a GP surgery in the fictional town of Cardale in Derbyshire's Peak District. The series was popular during its run, lasting for 12 series and 147 episodes. Fair warning, though: it ends on a cliffhanger.

Pete vs. Life - 2010 to 2011 - Journalist Pete is a pretty normal guy, except that he's constantly observed and analysed by a couple of sports commentators.

Primeval – 2008 to 2011 - When strange things start happening around England, a professor and his team are forced to capture a variety of unusual creatures from other time periods. Includes Ben Miller (of *Death in Paradise*).

Prison: First and Last 24 Hours - This docuseries follows convicted criminals on their first and last days in Scottish prisons.

QB VII - *United States* - 1974 - Welshman Sir Anthony Hopkins stars in this miniseries about a Polish doctor who escapes from a concentration camp, only to later face accusations of war crimes.

Rachel Allen: All Things Sweet - *Ireland* - 2017 - Irish celebrity chef conquers the perfect desserts for everyday occasions.

Rachel Allen: Easy Meals - *Ireland* - 2011 - Irish chef Rachel Allen focuses on meals anyone can replicate in their homes.

Rachel Allen's Cake Diaries - *Ireland* - 2012 - Chef Rachel Allen offers tips for cakes of all types.

Rachel Khoo's Cosmopolitan Cook - 2014 - British chef Rachel Khoo travels the world in search of inspiration for new dishes.

Richard Wilson On the Road - 2014 - Richard Wilson (*One Foot in the Grave*) takes a trip around Britain with only his antique Shell travel guides to help him.

Robin Hood – 2006 - After fighting in the Crusades, Robin Hood returns home to find a corrupt, changed Nottingham.

Rovers – 2016 - This working-class comedy centers around the people who spend time at the Redbridge Rovers Football Club.

Rugged Wales - 2014 - Iolo Williams (*Winterwatch*) takes us on an interesting tour of Wales and its landscape.

The Shadow Line - 2011 - DI Jonah Gabriel returns to work after a near fatal return, quickly finding himself going deep into the dangerous world of drug dealing. The miniseries includes performances from Christopher Eccleston, Tobias Menzies, Lesley Sharp, and Rafe Spall.

The Silence – 2010 - While struggling to integrate into the hearing world, a young girl with a new cochlear implant witnesses the murder of a police officer. Douglas Henshall (*Shetland*) is among the stars of this miniseries.

Shameless - 2004 to 2013 - Before *No Offence*, Paul Abbott created *Shameless* - the story of a rough-around-the-edges family living in a Manchester housing estate. It was later adapted into an American series starring William H. Macy. This one contains some strong language and sexual content, so it's not for everyone.

Speed with Guy Martin - 2013 to 2016 - Motorcycle racer Guy Martin performs a variety of speed challenges.

Super Sleuths: Midsomer Murders - 2006 - With interviews from investigative writers, fellow members of the cast and crew, crime writers, and criminologists, this documentary takes a look at how Inspector Barnaby solves crimes.

Surgeons: At the Edge of Life - 2018 to 2020 - Using behind-the-scenes access at the Queen Elizabeth Hospital Birmingham, this series takes a look at the incredible work being done by some of the UK's finest surgeons.

Terry Jones' Great Map Mystery – 2008 - *Monty Python* star Terry Jones travels around Britain to see if it's still possible to follow the earliest roadmaps of Wales.

Terry Pratchett's Going Postal - 2010 - This adaptation of Pratchett's novel sees con man Moist von Lipwig (Richard Coyle, *Chilling Adventures of Sabrina*) caught by the law and given two choices: suffer a painful death, or take over a derelict post office.

Threesome - 2011 - A straight couple and their gay friend live together happily until one sordid night changes their lives forever.

To the Ends of the Earth – 2005 - This BBC series is based on William Golding's novels of a sea journey to Australia from England in 1812-13. Benedict Cumberbatch (*Sherlock*) stars.

Treasure Island - 2012 - Eddie Izzard stars as Long John Silver in this retelling of the classic Robert Louis Stevenson story.

Truckers - 2013 - Stephen Tompkinson (*DCI Banks*) stars in this drama about a group of truck drivers in Nottinghamshire.

Truckers: Eddie Stobart - 2010 to 2014 - Excerpted from *Eddie Stobert: Trucks & Trailers*, this observational series explores the world of Eddie Stobart's UK-based logistics company as they tackle tough and interesting journeys.

Valentine Warner's Coast to Coast - 2011 - Valentine Warner takes a trip around the UK to help transform the way we think about fish.

William & Kate: A Royal Love Story - 2010 - This documentary follows the courtship and engagement of Will and Kate.

Wired – 2008 - Jodie Whittaker stars alongside Riz Ahmed, Laurence Fox, Charlie Brooks, and Toby Stephens in this suspenseful London-based thriller about a young woman whose high-profile promotion carries unexpected costs. She's quickly pushed into a criminal underworld she had no desire to be a part of.

Wolfblood - 2013 - Wolfblood teenagers have a number of heightened abilities, but their powers also bring danger and a need for secrecy.

Wycliffe - 1993 to 1998 - Based on W.J. Burley's novels, this Cornwall-based series features DS Charles Wycliffe, a man who investigates murders with a unique level of determination and accuracy.

Young Dracula - 2006 to 2014 - Count Dracula is a single father, and he's moved his kids Vlad and Ingrid to modern-day Britain. Now, little Vlad wants nothing more than to be a normal British kid and fit in with his friends.

TOPIC

Website: http://topic.com

Description: This new service focuses on international programming, and it includes a number of countries often overlooked (including the Middle East and African countries). Their British library is relatively small but there are some good titles.

Available On: Roku, Fire TV, Apple TV, Apple iPhone & iPad, Android phones and tablets, and computer (via web browser). You can also subscribe via Amazon Prime Video.

Cost: $5.99/month, $59.99/year

Now Streaming

Against the Law - 2017 - When Peter Wildeblood and Edward McNally fell in love in 1952, it was still a crime in Britain. This film takes a look at the devastating consequences for each of the two men.

Aileen: Life and Death of a Serial Killer - 2003 - This feature-length documentary looks at the Florida case of Aileen Wuornos, a woman executed in spite of her lack of sound mind.

B.B. King: The Life of Riley - 2012 - This documentary takes a look at the life and career trajectory of famed musician B.B. King.

Babs - 2018 - This short film sees a young man make a shocking discovery about how his father lived and loved.

Biggie & Tupac - 2002 - English documentarian Nick Broomfield conducts an intense investigation into the unsolved murders of two rap musicians called Biggie Smalls and Tupac Shakur, and his evidence points to involvement of the LAPD and an imprisoned recording executive, Marion Knight.

Bringing Babs Home - 2018 - In this short film, a young man brings his dead father's lover home.

Capital - 2015 - When property values soar on a once middle-class London street, residents receive mysterious postcards saying, "We want what you have."

Chimerica - 2019 - Based on real events, this series follows a photojournalist attempting to uncover the identity of the protester who stood in front of the tanks in Tiananmen Square.

Cla'am - 2019 - In this short comedy, a man becomes convinced that a large-scale conspiracy is driving the rapid gentrification of his London neighbourhood.

Come Home - 2018 - After nineteen years of marriage, a woman suddenly walks out on her family.

Death Over Dinner - 2019 - This series invites strangers to dine together and talk about death.

Down from London - 2019 - This British comedy follows a couple that attempts to ignore their relationship troubles by taking trips away from London.

The Drummer & the Keeper - *Ireland* - 2017 - This Irish film sees a bipolar drummer in Dublin forming a unique friendship with an institutionalised teen with Asperger's syndrome.

Enterprice - 2019 - In this BBC Three sitcom, a couple of young entrepreneurs in

South London attempt to launch their new delivery service, Speedi-Kazz.

Exile – 2011 - John Simm (*Life on Mars*) stars in this mystery-thriller about a man who returns home after his life falls apart – only to find a different kind of trouble there.

Fry Up - 2018 - This film short takes a look at what could be a family's last day together before their son goes to prison.

Getting High for God? - 2016 - This hour-long documentary follows Mawaan Rizwan as he explores whether drugs can bring you closer to your maker.

Head Over Heels - 2012 - This Oscar-nominated animated short follows a married couple who've grown apart. Husband Walter lives on the floor and wife Madge lives on the ceiling.

How Gay is Pakistan? - 2015 - Though it's illegal to be homosexual in Pakistan, the country has a growing gay community. Mawaan Rizwan takes a look at what life is like for gay Pakistanis.

Hugh the Hunter - 2019 - This short film sees a man wandering the Scottish moors in search of prey.

The Image You Missed - 2018 - This experimental documentary takes a look at the Northern Irish Troubles through the lens of one filmmaker's personal story.

Intruders – 2014 - John Simm (*Life on Mars*) stars as an ex-cop whose wife goes missing. The ensuing investigation leads him to Seattle, where a secret society chases immortality by hiding in the bodies of others.

Jamie's American Road Trip - 2009 - In this series, Jamie Oliver travels around the US to discover its food - including stops in Wyoming, New York, Louisiana, LA, Georgia, Florida, and Arizona.

Jamie's Food Escapes - 2010 - Jamie Oliver visits Marrakesh, Andalucia, Stockholm, Venice, the French Pyrenees, and Athens to experience their unique foods and cultures.

Jamie's Super Food - 2015 - Jamie Oliver travels the world in search of super foods in their native homelands.

Lost in France - 2016 - This documentary takes a look at the rise of the Glaswegian music scene.

Louis Theroux's Altered States: Choosing Death - 2018 - In this hour-long documentary, Louis spends time with individuals facing the decision to end their own lives.

Louis Theroux's Altered States: Take My Baby - 2018 - In this hour-long documentary, Louis heads to the open adoption state of California, where he talks with women handing over their babies to families paying tens of thousands of dollars.

Miriam's Big American Adventure - 2018 - Miriam Margolyes (*Call the Midwife, Bucket*) sets off on a fun and entertaining road trip around the United States. She begins in Chicago before moving on to an Indiana summer camp and a prison in Ohio. In the final entry, she ponders whether the United States is actually "the Divided States".

Monkman & Seagull's Genius Guide to Britain - 2018 - This fun travel series originally aired on BBC Two in the UK, and it follows a couple of quiz show champions as they visit some of the country's greatest triumphs of science and engineering. If you enjoy great scenery and more insight into the way things work, you'll love this one. One episode is dedicated to each of the four countries of the UK.

Moses Jones - 2009 - After a body is discovered in the Thames, DI Moses Jones investigates possibilities of witchcraft in London's Ugandan exile community. Shaun Parkes (*Line of Duty, Hooten & the Lady*) stars as DI Moses Jones, with Matt Smith (*Doctor Who*) and Dennis Waterman (*New Tricks*) in supporting roles.

Not Safe for Work - 2015 - When budget cuts move Katherine's civil servant job to Northampton, she reluctantly goes along with the relocation.

The Office - 2001 to 2003 - Before there was Michael Scott in the US, there was David Brent in Slough, England. Written by Ricky Gervais (*After Life*) and Stephen Merchant (*Hello Ladies*), this mockumentary-style programme takes place in the office of the fictional Wernham Hogg paper company. Mackenzie Crook (*Detectorists*) and Martin Freeman (*Sherlock*) are also among the stars.

Penny Slinger: Out of the Shadows - 2017 - This documentary tells the story of 1960s British erotic artist Penny Slinger and the traumatic life events that inspired her to create her 1977 masterpiece, *An Exorcism*.

Pulp: A Film About Life, Death and Supermarkets - 2014 - This rock documentary follows the Britpop band Pulp as they head back to Sheffield for one last concert.

Run - 2013 - Olivia Colman and Lennie James star in this four-part miniseries about four seemingly unconnected people whose lives intersect after a random act of violence.

Shut Up & Play the Hits - 2012 - This music documentary takes a look at the last days of LCD Soundsystem.

Song of Granite - 2017 - This documentary takes a closer look at Joe Heaney, a shy boy born in a remote Irish village who would later grow up to become one of the country's most loved traditional vocalists.

Still Life - 2013 - Eddie Marsan and Joanne Froggatt star in this film about a council case worker trying to find the relatives of those who've died alone.

The Sunshine Makers - 2017 - This documentary shares the untold story of Nicholas Sand and Tim Scully, a duo at the heart of the 1960s LSD/counterculture movement in America.

Transsiberian - 2008 - Woody Harrelson, Kate Mara, Emily Mortimer, and Ben Kingsley star in this dramatic film about an American couple who encounter a pair of mysterious travelers on a train journey from China to Moscow.

The Virtues - 2019 - When his personal life falls apart, Joseph travels to Ireland in hopes of making amends with his estranged sister Anna. In doing so, he unearths the horrors of his past while also finding a path to move forward. Stephen Graham (*Snatch*) stars.

Weapons of Mass Production - 2019 - This docuseries takes a look at the price people in Britain are paying for the country's arms business.

White Morning - 2015 - This animated film short offers a dreamy look at childhood pranks turned sinister.

The Witness - 2016 - This suspenseful documentary takes a look at the Kitty Genovese murder - the shocking case where 38 witnesses watched a woman get stabbed to death during an hour-long attack.

Wuthering Heights - 2012 - This artsy adaptation of Brontë's classic stars James Howson and Kaya Scodelario as an older Heathcliff and Cathy, with Solomon Glave and Shannon Beer as younger version of themselves. Reviews of this nontraditional retelling were mixed, but it's a must-watch for anyone who enjoys Brontë.

Year of the Rabbit - 2019 - Matt Berry (*The IT Crowd*) stars in this period comedy about an eclectic group of Victorian detectives who fight crime whilst mingling with street gangs, spiritualists, politicians, Bulgarian princes, and even the Elephant Man.

STARZ

Now Streaming

American Gods - *United States* - 2017 to present - Though it's American, American Gods is based on the novel of the same name by British-born author Neil Gaiman, and the series stars Ian McShane (*Lovejoy*). It tells the story of a prisoner who's just days away from release when he finds out his wife has been killed in an accident. After his early release, he encounters a strange man, Mr. Wednesday (McShane), who offers him a job that ultimately brings him into a world of magic and old gods.

Da Vinci's Demons - 2013 to 2015 - This historical fantasy offers a fictional retelling of Leonardo da Vinci's early life.

Dublin Murders - 2019 - Based on the Dublin Murder Squad book series by Tana French, the first season of this British-American-Irish co-production features eight episodes adapted from In the Woods and The Likeness. Killian Scott (*C.B. Strike*) stars as Rob Reilly, and English detective dispatched to investigate the murder of a young girl just outside Dublin. The case forces Reilly to confront his own dark past, and it puts his relationship with partner Cassie Maddox (Sarah Greene, *Penny Dreadful*) to the test.

Howards End – 2017 - This miniseries is based on the E.M. Forster novel, and it examines class differences in 1900s England through the lens of three families.

In the Long Run - 2017 to present - This period comedy is set in 1980s London, where the Easmon family sees their lives disrupted when a relative from Sierra Leone moves in. Created by Idris Elba (*Luther*), this series stars Jimmy Akingbola (*Rev*) and Madeline Appiah (*Partners in Crime*).

Little Dorrit - 1987 - Sir Derek Jacobi (*Cadfael*) stars in this classic Dickens tale of a young girl, her indebted father, and the benefactor who helps her.

The Luminaries - *New Zealand* - 2020 - This British-New Zealand co-production is based on Eleanor Catton's Booker Prize-winning novel of the same name, and it follows a young adventurer named Anna Wetherell as she travels from the UK to New Zealand during the 1860s West Coast Gold Rush.

Luther – 2010 to 2019 - Idris Elba stars as a brilliant London detective who frequently gets into trouble because of his passion for the job.

Men in Kilts - 2021 - Sam Heughan and Graham McTavish (both of *Outlander*) host this travel series in which they escort viewers around Scotland.

The Missing – 2014 to 2017 - James Nesbitt (*Cold Feet*) stars in this drama about the disappearance of a 5-year-old and the manhunt that follows.

MotherFatherSon - 2019 - Richard Gere stars in his first major television role as Max Finch, American newspaper owner. The 8-part series is a psycho thriller about power, politics, and the media. Helen McCrory (*Peaky Blinders*), Sarah Lancashire (*Happy Valley*), Sinéad Cusack (*Marcella*), and Ciarán Hinds (*Above Suspicion*) are among the other cast members.

Outlander - 2014 to present - In 1945, an English nurse is mysteriously transported back in time to Scotland in 1743. The massively-popular series is based on the novels of Diana Gabaldon.

The Pillars of the Earth - 2010 - This miniseries is based on the 1989 Ken Follett novel of the same name, and it follows the construction of a cathedral during the 12th century.

The Rook - 2019 - Emma Greenwell stars as Myfanwy Thomas, a young woman who finds herself at the Millennium Bridge in London surrounded by corpses and no memory of how she ended up there. While the series is American, it features a largely British cast, and it takes place in London. It was based on the novel of the same name by Daniel O'Malley, originally adapted by Stephenie Meyer of *Twilight* fame.

The Spanish Princess - 2019 - This period drama is based on the novels *The Constant Princess* and *The King's Curse* by Philippa Gregory, and it's a sequel to the previous miniseries *The White Queen* and *The White Princess*. The series follows teenage princess Catherine of Aragon as she travels to England to meet her husband by proxy.

The White Princess - 2017 - Based on the Philippa Gregory book of the same name, this miniseries tells the story of Elizabeth of York and her marriage to Henry VII. It's the sequel to *The White Queen*.

The White Queen - 2013 - This miniseries is based on Philippa Gregory's historical series, *The Cousins' War*, and it tells the story of the women involved in the conflict for England's throne during the War of Roses.

World Without End - 2012 - This miniseries is a sequel to *The Pillars of the Earth*, and it's set 150 years later in the same English town of Knightsbridge. This time, they're facing the outbreak of the Black Death and the Hundred Years' War. It's based on the Ken Follett novel of the same name.

CINEMAX

> **Website:** http://cinemax.com
>
> **Description:** Cinemax is an older premium cable service, and they're owned by HBO. Programming mostly consists of older movies, original action series, and documentaries, but they do have a handful of British shows.
>
> **Available On:** Roku, Amazon Fire TV, Apple TV, Apple iPhone & iPad, Android TV, Android phones and tablets, computer (via web browser). You can also subscribe via Amazon Prime Video or Hulu.
>
> **Cost:** $9.99/month

Now Streaming

Cinemax will no longer be producing original shows, and it will focus primarily on movies going forward. While most shows will not be moved over to HBO Max (HBO owns Cinemax), CB Strike has been pushed over to HBO Max.

C.B. Strike (aka Strike) - 2017 to present - Based on the *Cormoran Strike* novels written by JK Rowling under the Robert Galbraith pseudonym, this series sees war veteran Cormoran Strike team up with a highly-competent assistant who helps him solve cases and transform his ailing business.

Hunted - 2012 - After an attempt on her life, a spy goes back undercover as a nanny, unsure of who she can trust.

Rellik - 2017 - DCI Markham and his team hunt down a killer in this mystery told in reverse. The serial killer is a man who attacks his victims with acid, and the investigating officer becomes a surviving victim of the killer.

Strike Back- 2010 to 2020 - This British/American spy series is based on the 2007 novel of the same name by former SAS soldier Chris Ryan. It follows the goings on of Section 20, a secret branch of the British Defence Intelligence service who conduct high-risk, high-priority missions around the world. Jed Mercurio (*Line of Duty*) was among the writers, and stars have included Richard Armitage (*North & South*), Andrew Lincoln (*The Walking Dead*), and Robson Green (*Grantchester*).

HBO

Now Streaming

Adult Material - 2020 - Hayley Squires stars as Jolene Dollar, a mother of three and proud breadwinner in spite of her unusual career as a famous porn star. Her life is basically good, and she's come to act as a mother figure for other young women in the industry - until she meets 19-year-old Amy. Though she tries to look after Amy like the others, the relationship soon causes all sorts of problems in both her work and home life.

The Alienist - *United States* - 2018 - Though American, this series stars Welshman Luke Evans. It's a period crime drama set in late 1800s New York City, with the first season focusing on finding someone who's killing boy prostitutes. The second season sees some of the characters working as private detectives to find a kidnapped infant.

Almost Royal - 2014 to 2016 - This BBC America faux-reality series follows a couple of extremely minor British royals as they visit the US for the first time.

Avenue 5 - *United States* - 2020 - Hugh Laurie and Josh Gad star in this science fiction comedy about a space cruise ship. They've been thrown off course, and it's estimated that it will take them three years to get back to Earth - but they only have enough supplies for eight weeks. Along with Hugh Laurie, you'll spot a number of popular British actors including Daisy May Cooper (*This Country*) and Matthew Beard (*Vienna Blood*).

The Casual Vacancy - 2015 - This miniseries is based on JK Rowling's novel of the same name, and it tells the story of a town resident's sudden death and how it impacts the local community.

Catherine the Great - 2019 - Helen Mirren stars as Catherine the Great in this four-part miniseries. The series covers the later portion of her life, from 1764 until her death in 1796. Jason Clarke (*Zero Dark Thirty*), Rory Kinnear (*Penny Dreadful*), Richard Roxburgh (*Rake*), and Paul Ritter (*No Offence*) also appear.

C.B. Strike (aka Strike) - 2017 to present - Based on the *Cormoran Strike* novels written by JK Rowling under the Robert Galbraith pseudonym, this series sees war veteran Cormoran Strike team up with a highly-competent assistant who helps him solve cases and transform the business.

Chernobyl - 2019 - Screenwriter Craig Mazin created this moving five-part historical adaptation of the Chernobyl nuclear disaster. It includes a number of actors familiar to British TV fans, including Jared Harris (*The Crown*), Stellan Skarsgård (*Pirates of the Caribbean*), Paul Ritter (*No Offence*), and Emily Watson (*Miss Potter*).

Cowboy Builders - 2009 to present - Cowboy builders are tradesmen who do rubbish work at inflated prices - often not even finishing the job. This series aims to help the affected homeowners.

DCI Banks – 2010 to 2016 - Stephen Tomkinson (*Ballykissangel, Wild at Heart*) stars as DCI Alan Banks, a skilled but stubborn Yorkshire-based investigator.

Doctor Who - 1963 to present - A mysterious Time Lord travels through time and space, exploring and saving the world in equal measure. HBO Max has all the modern *Doctor Who* episodes.

The Dog House UK - 2019 - This series follows the dedicated animal heroes at Wood Green animal charity in Godmanchester as they help homeless dogs find new humans.

Elizabeth I - 2006 - Helen Mirren, Jeremy Irons, and Hugh Dancy star in this two-part miniseries about the second half of Queen Elizabeth I's reign.

Family Tree – 2013 - This hilarious series follows one man's efforts to track down long-lost members of his family tree.

First Dates Hotel - 2017 to present - This spin-off of *First Dates* sees two strangers meeting on a date, but with the option to check into a boutique hotel together.

First Dates Ireland - 2016 to present - This reality series looks at what happens when two strangers meet on a first date.

First Dates UK - 2013 to present - This long-running dating show follows new potential couples as they meet for a date.

Five Days - 2007 to 2010 - Each series covers five non-consecutive days in a major police investigation.

Food CIA - 2012 to 2014 - This docu-series sends its hosts all over the world to find out more about what goes into our food.

Frayed - 2019 - In this period comedy-drama, a wealthy London housewife faces serious chances of circumstance after her husband dies. It's 1988, and she's forced to move herself and her two children back to her hometown in Australia, only to find that no one there likes her. Star Sarah Kendall was also the creator and writer.

Game of Thrones - 2011 to 2019 - In a mythical world, families fight for control of the Iron Throne. The series is based on the novels of George R.R. Martin, and the show is estimated to have had the largest cast on television.

Gentleman Jack - 2019 to present - The incomparable Sally Wainwright (*Happy Valley, Last Tango in Halifax*) ventures into historical drama, bringing us the story of 19th century English industrialist, landowner, and lesbian Anne Lister. Suranne Jones (*Doctor Foster*) stars as Lister, a Yorkshire woman who was very much ahead of her time. Other cast members include Sophie Rundle as Ann Walker, Timothy West as Jeremy Lister, and Stephanie Cole as Aunt Ann Walker.

Ghosts - 2019 to present - This series focuses on a group of ghosts who have accumulated over the course of centuries in a country house. When a young couple inherits the grand but crumbling pile, they have to learn to co-exist. The series was written and performed by a number of cast members from the BBC children's series *Horrible Histories*.

The Great Pottery Throwdown - 2015 to present - This competition series follows a group of amateur potters as they compete to see who's best.

Gunpowder - 2017 - Kit Harington (*Game of Thrones*) stars in this three-part period drama about the Gunpowder Plot of 1605.

His Dark Materials - 2019 - Based on the trilogy by Oxford novelist Philip Pullman, this eight-episode fantasy series takes place in an alternate world where each human has an animal companion called a daemon. A young orphan living at Jordan College, Oxford, is drawn into a dangerous puzzle when her friend, a fellow orphan, is kidnapped.

Home - 2019 to present - After a holiday to France, a middle-class British family finds a Syrian man, Sami, hiding in their boot. This comedy-drama follows Sami as he builds a new life in the UK.

I Hate Suzie - 2020 - Billie Piper (*Doctor Who*) stars in this eight-part original drama about a young woman whose life is upended when her phone is hacked and a compromising photo of her goes public. Lucy Prebble (*Secret Diary of a Call Girl*) was Piper's co-creator on the series.

I May Destroy You - 2020 - This sexual consent drama sees Michaela Coel (*Chewing Gum*) playing a care-free Londoner whose existence is turned upside-down after her drink is spiked.

HBO

Industry - 2020 - Lena Dunham (*Girls*) will direct and executive produce this eight-part series about a group of young people trying to break into the world of high-finance in London around the 2008 market collapse. As a note, this series has some fairly extreme adult content involving sex and drug use.

Inside No. 9 - 2014 to 2020 - Dark humor, crime, drama, and horror are showcased in this anthology series. Every episode incorporates the number nine in some way, so keep an eye out as you watch.

It's a Sin - 2021 - This Russell T Davies series follows a group of gay men in London during the HIV/AIDS crisis of the 1980s. Olly Alexander stars as Ritchie Tozer, and the cast includes a number of well-known actors including Keeley Hawes, Neil Patrick Harris, and Stephen Fry.

Jane Eyre – 2006 - This two-part adaptation of the classic Charlotte Bronte novel tells the story of a young woman who falls in love with the dark and brooding Mr. Rochester. Ruth Wilson (*Luther*) stars.

Life's Too Short - 2011 to 2012 - Warwick Davis stars as a scheming actor aiming to be nothing less than Britain's number one little person.

Hello Ladies – *United States* - 2013 - While not technically British, this series comes from Stephen Merchant, a British actor and writer who has partnered with Ricky Gervais. See also - *Hello Ladies: The Movie*

Little Britain USA – 2008 - British tourists Lou and Andy travel around the United States.

Louis Theroux Collection - This collection gathers up a number of British-American documentarian Louis Theroux's works, with many of them exploring themes of poverty and social justice.

Luther – 2010 to 2019 - Idris Elba stars as a brilliant London detective who frequently gets into trouble because of his passion for the job.

The Misadventures of Romesh Ranganathan - 2019 to 2020 - This reality series follows British comedian Romesh Ranganathan as he travels to some of the world's least popular tourist destinations.

Miss Sherlock - *Japan* - 2018 - This Japanese adaptation of the Sherlock Holmes story sees a young "Miss Sherlock" working alongside the Tokyo police.

Motorheads - 2016 - In this BBC series, hosts Tom Ford and Jonny Smith seek out the funniest, strangest, and most interesting motor vehicles.

The Murders at White House Farm - 2020 - This crime drama series is an adaptation of real-life events that took place in August 1985, when Jeremy Bamber murdered his entire family. Freddie Fox (*Cucumber*) plays Jeremy Bamber, Mark Addy (*Game of Thrones*) plays Stan Jones, a detective convinced of his guilt, and Cressida Bonas (Prince Harry's ex) fills the role of Bamber's sister Sheila.

The Nevers - 2021 - Joss Whedon (*Buffy the Vampire Slayer*) is the creator for this Victorian sci-fi drama about a group of Victorian women with unusual abilities. The cast includes Laura Donnelly, Olivia Williams, Eleanor Tomlinson, and James Norton, and the series will premiere on April 11th.

The No. 1 Ladies' Detective Agency - 2009 - Based on the novels of Scottish author Alexander McCall Smith, this series follows a young woman in Botswana as she opens her country's first female-owned detective agency.

The Office - 2001 to 2003 - Before there was Michael Scott in the US, there was David Brent in Slough, England. Written by Ricky Gervais (*After Life*) and Stephen Merchant (*Hello Ladies*), this mockumentary-style programme takes place in the office of the fictional Wernham Hogg paper company.

The Outsider - *United States* - 2020 - Based on the Stephen King novel of the same name, this miniseries includes British stars Paddy Considine (*Peaky Blinders*) and Cynthia Erivo (*Mr. Selfridge*). The series follows a particularly confounding investigation into the murder of a young boy.

Parade's End - 2013 - Benedict Cumberbatch (*Sherlock*) stars in this series adapted from Ford Madox Ford's tetralogy of novels. It focuses on the lives and relations of three Brits just before and at the outset of World War I.

Perry Mason - *United States* - 2020 - Welshman Matthew Rhys stars in this prequel to the original *Perry Mason*. It's set in 1932 Los Angeles, when Mason is struggling to get back on track after a divorce and his war trauma.

HBO

Pure - 2019 - This quirky sitcom focuses on a young woman who is plagued by constant, irrepressible sexual thoughts. As she attempts to get a handle on her problem, she's also embarking on a journey of personal growth and exploration in the city of London. The series is an adaptation of Rose Cartwright's book.

Run - *United States* - 2020 - This comedy-thriller begins with two people who once made a promise that if either ever texted the word "RUN" to the other, they'd drop everything and meet in Grand Central Terminal and travel the country together. Though American, Brit Phoebe Waller-Bridge is both executive producer and a recurring character.

Sally4Ever - 2018 - A woman decides to leave a boring man to have an affair with a woman instead.

Sarah Jane Adventures - 2007 to 2011 - This children's show is a *Doctor Who* spin-off that follows former companion Sarah Jane Smith, now an investigative journalist.

Scott & Bailey - 2011 to 2016 - Two very different female police detectives enjoy a close friendship and productive partnership.

Singletown - 2019 - This British reality series follows a group of young people who've agreed to pause their current relationships and spend a month going on dates with other people.

Stacey Dooley Investigates Collection - 2009 to present - Amateur British journalist Stacey Dooley travels the world to uncover and expose injustice.

Supernanny - 2004 to 2008 - This reality series follows professional nanny Jo Frost as she helps parents facing tough parenting challenges.

The Third Day - 2020 - This drama follows the individual journeys of a man (Jude Law, *Sherlock Holmes*) and woman (Naomie Harris, *Skyfall*) who are drawn to a mysterious island off the British coast.

Top Gear - 2002 to present - This long-running remake of the classic 1970s series sees Jeremy Clarkson and a variety of other presenters checking out some of the world's finest cars.

Torchwood - 2006 to 2011 - A secret agency called Torchwood fights off threats from aliens and the supernatural. The series is a spin-off of *Doctor Who*.

The Trial of Christine Keeler - 2019 - This miniseries is based on the events surrounding the Profumo affair of the 1960s, when Secretary of State for War John Profumo was found to be having a sexual relationship with Christine Keeler, a 19-year-old aspiring model. Sophie Cookson (*Red Joan*), James Norton (*Grantchester*), and Emilia Fox (*Silent Witness*) star.

Trigonometry - 2020 - This eight-part rom-com tells the story of a cash-strapped London couple (played by Thalissa Teixeira and Gary Carr) who open their cramped apartment to a third person (Ariane Labed). Life gets easier with an extra set of hands around, but the emotional side of things gets infinitely more complicated.

Two Weeks to Live - 2020 - A relatively dark comedy, *Two Weeks to Live* follows Kim, a young misfit whose mother dragged her off to the country for a survivalist lifestyle after her father died. The series picks up as she sets off on her own, but things go pear-shaped quickly when an awkward young man's prank puts all their lives in danger.

The Undoing - 2020 - A successful New York therapist sees her life start falling apart when she publishes her first book. Though American, Hugh Grant stars.

Wallander - 2008 to 2016 - This English-language, Sweden-based mystery series is an adaptation of Henning Mankell's novels about detective Kurt Wallander.

Whitechapel - 2009 to 2013 - An inspector, a detective sergeant, and a historical homicide expert look at crimes that may have connections to the Whitechapel district.

Years and Years - 2019 - This series follows the Manchester-based Lyons family as they their lives progress through 15 years of politics, technology, and human events. Emma Thompson, Rory Kinnear, and Anne Reid are among the cast.

Zapped - 2016 to 2018 - When Brian, a temporary office worker in West London, opens a package containing a mysterious amulet, he decides to put it on. The amulet transports him to a medieval place called Munty, where he'll have to figure out how to fit in or get back to his modern life.

HBO

EPIX

Website: https://www.epix.com/

Description: Epix is a subsidiary of Metro-Goldwyn-Mayer. Their content is a mix of older motvies, original TV shows, documentaries, and music/comedy specials.

Available On: The EPIX NOW app is available for download on iPhones and iPads, Apple TV, Android phones, tablets and TVs, Roku and Fire TV.

Cost: $5.99/month

Now Streaming

Belgravia - 2020 - Belgravia's story opens on the eve of Napoleon's battle against the Duke of Wellington at Waterloo, taking place at a high society ball attended by a number of people who will go on to die in the conflict. It then picks up decades later when a newly emerging upper class begins to butt heads with the established upper classes. Even then, the events of 25 years prior continue to resonate. Julian Fellowes (*Downton Abbey*) is the creator of this period drama.

Berlin Station - *United States* - 2016 to 2019 - Though American, this series stars Englishman Richard Armitage and Welshman Rhys Ifans. It follows Daniel Miller (Armitage), a man with a clandestine mission to uncover the source of a CIA leak at a station in Berlin, Germany.

Brittania - 2017 to present - This US-UK co-production shows the Roman invasion in 43AD Britannia.

Deep State - 2018 to present - Mark Strong (*The Imitation Game*) stars as Mark Easton, a former MI6 agent who returns to the field to avenge the death of his son.

Pennyworth - *United States* - 2019 to present - Jack Bannon (*Endeavour*) stars as Alfred Pennyworth, a former British SAS soldier who will ultimately become Batman's butler.

Perpetual Grace, LTD - *United States* - 2019 - Sir Ben Kingsley stars as Pastor Byron Brown in this series about a young grifter who attempts to prey on a pastor who's more dangerous than he initially appears.

War of the Worlds - *United States* - 2020 - Not to be confused with the 2019 British production, this adaptation of the H.G. Wells classic is worthy of mention here for a few reasons. Aside from Wells himself being English, stars Gabriel Byrne, Natasha Little, Stephen Campbell Moore, Aaron Heffernan, and Daisy Edgar-Jones all hail from the British Isles. American Elizabeth McGovern (Cora Crawley in *Downton Abbey*) also appears.

SHOWTIME

Now Streaming

The Affair - 2014 to 2019 - A man (Dominic West) and woman (Ruth Wilson) have an affair that gets complicated.

Back to Life - 2019 to Present - Following an 18-year prison sentence, Miri Matteson (*Daisy Haggard*) returns home to Hythe, Kent, and attempts to rebuild her life.

The Borgias - *Canada/Hungary* - 2011 to 2013 - Jeremy Irons (*Brideshead Revisited*) and Holliday Grainger (*CB Strike*) star in this series about the rise of Italy's Borgia family during the Renaissance.

Brotherhood - *United States* - 2006-2008 - Irish-American brothers' lives intertwine as they go their own way.

The End - *Australia* - 2020 - Frances O'Connor (*Mansfield Park*) stars as a palliative care specialist who's passionate about her opposition to euthanasia. Her mother Edie (played by Dame Harriet Walter) believes she has a right to die on her own terms.

Episodes - *United States* - 2011 to 2017 - Two married British TV producers are offered a deal in the US, then everything goes wrong. Stephen Mangan (*Hang-Ups*) and Tamsin Greig (*Friday Night Dinner*) star.

Guerrilla - 2017 - Set in early 1970s London, Guerrilla tells the story of a couple whose relationship is tested when they free a political prisoner.

Happyish - *United States* - 2015 - Brit Steve Coogan (*The Trip*) stars as a depressed middle-aged man who contents himself with feeling merely "happy-ish".

Just Another Immigrant - 2018 - Comedian Romesh Ranganathan uproots his entire family and moves to the United States.

Patrick Melrose - 2018 - Based on the semi-autobiographical Patrick Melrose novels by Edward St. Aubyn, this miniseries tells the story of an upper class man's addictions and family troubles.

Penny Dreadful - 2014 to 2016 - A group of adventurers team up to fight supernatural threats in Victorian England. See also: *Penny Dreadful: City of Angels*

Shameless (US) - *United States* - 2011 to present - This American series is an adaptation of Paul Abbott's British series of the same name.

The Tudors - 2007 to 2010 - The Tudors is a drama about Henry VIII and his extensive love life.

We Hunt Together - 2020 - This drama sees two conflicted detectives tracking down a pair of deadly killers. Starring Eve Myles (*Torchwood*).

PEACOCK

Website: http://peacocktv.com

Description: This NBC-owned subscription service is the major online home of NBCUniversal content. British programming is limited.

Available On: Roku, Amazon Fire TV, Apple TV, Apple iPhone & iPad, Android TV, Android phones and tablets, most recent game consoles, Google Chromecast, computer (via web browser).

Cost: Limited Free Membership, Peacock Premium - $4.99/month or $49.99/year, go ad-free for an extra $5/month to watch without ads.

Now Streaming

The Affair - *United States* - 2014 to 2019 - A man (Dominic West) and woman (Ruth Wilson, *Luther*) have an affair that leads to a complex series of events.

The Alfred Hitchcock Hour - *United States* - 1962 to 1965 - Alfred Hitchcock hosts this classic mystery and thriller anthology series.

Alfred Hitchcock Presents - *United States* - 1955 to 1962 - The English master of suspense hosts this anthology series full of mystery and murder.

Brave New World - *United States* - 2020 - The dystopian series takes place in a futuristic World State where citizens are genetically modified and the social hierarchy is determined by intelligence. Harry Lloyd stars as Bernard Marx (*Game of Thrones*), and Jessica Brown-Findlay (*Downton Abbey*) plays Lenina Crowne.

The Capture - 2019 - Holiday Grainger (*C.B. Strike*) stars in this series about a detective who uncovers a massive conspiracy while investigating the charges against a British soldier.

Case Histories - 2011 to 2013 - Based on the Jackson Brodie novels by Kate Atkinson, this Edinburgh-based series features a tough guy PI with a heart of gold.

Chancer – 1990 to 1991 - Clive Owen plays Stephen Crane, a schemer who takes advantage of opportunities using manipulation and misdirection. As a young business analyst/con man in London, he's called in to help save a struggling motor company.

Code 404 - 2020 - When the talented detective John Major (Daniel Mays, *Good Omens*) is killed during a sting operation, he's brought back as part of an experimental project. Understandably, the newly-revived detective is intent on finding his killer.

Departure - 2019 - This series follows the mystery of the disappearing passenger flight 716.

Downton Abbey - 2010 to 2015 - This popular period drama follows the lives of the Crawley family and their servants during the early 1900s.

Escape to the Chateau - 2016 to 2019 - This British reality series follows Dick Strawbridge and Angela Adoree as they buy and renovate the 19th-century Château de la Motte-Husson in Martigné-sur-Mayenne, France.

Escape to the Chateau DIY - 2018 to present - This *Escape to the Chateau* spinoff follows a variety of British families who are renovating French chateaux. Dick Strawbridge narrates, and he and his wife offer up advice to others doing the same.

The Fall - 2013 to 2016 - Gillian Anderson (*The X-Files*) and Jamie Dornan (*50 Shades of Grey*) star in this series about a senior investigator who goes head-to-head with a serial killer who's attacking young professional women in Belfast.

Hell's Kitchen – 2004 to 2009 - This series pits prospective chefs against one another, with the winner getting a head chef position.

Hitmen - 2020 - This comedy follows two best friends who have fallen into a career in contract killing. Mel Giedroyc (*Spies of Warsaw*) and Sue Perkins (*The Great British Baking Show*) star.

Homefront - 2012 - This dramatic miniseries follows the lives of the wives and girlfriends of soldiers serving in Afghanistan.

Intelligence - 2020 - An NSA agent joins forces with a computer analyst to establish a new cyber crimes department in the UK. American David Schwimmer (*Friends*) stars.

More Manners of Downton Abbey - 2016 - Alastair Bruce interviews *Downton Abbey* cast members and looks at the social rules of early 1900s Britain.

Murder, She Wrote - *United States* - 1984 to 1996 - British-born Angela Lansbury stars in this classic series about a novelist who seems to encounter murder everywhere she goes.

Noughts & Crosses - 2020 - Based on the Malorie Blackman novel of the same name, this series is set in an alternate reality where black "Cross" people rule over white "Noughts". Jack Rowan (*Peaky Blinders*) and Masali Baduza (*Trackers*) star as Callum and Sephy, an interracial couple whose romance leads them into danger.

Save Me - 2018 - Lennie James and Suranne Jones star in this series about a man who will do anything to find his missing daughter.

RENEWALS & CANCELLATIONS

This list is based on the best information available at print time (March 2021). Last-minute changes can always occur, and that's doubly true in pandemic times.

For returning shows, we've not added dates because very few are able to make accurate predictions given the constant changes in pandemic restrictions.

Shows Not Expected to Return

No Offence
Scarborough
Wild Bill
Warren
Age Before Beauty

Giri/Haji
Turn Up Charlie
Harlots
Hard Sun
Mum

Still Game
Black Mirror

Returning for Another Season

Shakespeare & Hathaway
Shetland
Vienna Blood
Agatha Raisin
Finding Joy
Ms. Fisher's Modern
Murder Mysteries
Father Brown
Manhunt
Death in Paradise
Call the Midwife
Vera
Life on Mars
Endeavour
The Bletchley Circle: San
Francisco
Miss Scarlet and the Duke
Grantchester

Sex Education
Top Boy
After Life
My Life is Murder
Balthazar
Killing Eve
Avenue 5
American Gods
Flack
Doc Martin
McDonald & Dodds
Queens of Mystery
The Split
Sanditon **
The Crown
Industry
The Irregulars
Horrible Histories

We Hunt Together
The Bay
Two Doors Down
His Dark Materials
Bridgerton
Gangs of London
Ghosts
All Creatures Great & Small
Brassic
Killing Eve
Ackley Bridge
Alex Rider
Ted Lasso
Don't Forget the Driver
The Capture

Not Yet Announced

Good Karma Hospital
Friday Night Dinner

Dead Still
Cold Feet: The New Years

**A casting call went out, but we've not seen official confirmation.

MOVIE NIGHT

While this streaming guide primarily covers television, there are loads of British movies across different streaming services. The main reason we don't issue a guide just for movies is that there are quite a lot of them, and they tend to rotate between services much faster than TV shows.

This "Movie Night" section is a new feature in this edition of the guide, and we hope you find it useful. If we get good feedback, we'll continue to offer a couple pages of film suggestions in each quarterly streaming guide.

This section will likely become inaccurate a bit faster than the rest of the guide, but we hope you'll be able to find some movies you may not have otherwise discovered. We've left out any movies on Acorn TV and BritBox since those are mentioned in their relevant sections.

One further note: Every movie included below will be included through at least one subscription service, but most will also be available via "streaming rental".

Apple TV+, iTunes, Amazon Prime Video, Vudu, and YouTube all offer streaming rentals and purchases, so if you don't wish to subscribe to a service but you still want to watch something, that's when the "streaming rental" comes into play. Most cost between $2.99-$5.99 for a rental (less than Blockbuster charged near the end, and no need to return the DVD or rewind the VHS).

Emma - 2020 - Anna Taylor-Joy (*The Queen's Gambit*) and Miranda Hart appear in this recent adaptation of the Jane Austen classic. For those not familiar with the story, it follows the misadventures of a young woman named Emma who enjoys meddling in the love lives of those around her. **HBO Max or streaming rental.**

A Month in the Country - 1987 - Five hundred years ago, a mural was painted in an old country church in Yorkshire, only to be hidden away under layers of paint. The film is set during the summer of 1920 when the mural is discovered and restored. It's based on the 1980 novel of the same name by JL Carr, and Colin Firth, Kenneth Branagh, Natasha Richardson, and Patrick Malahide star. **Amazon Prime Video, Tubi, or streaming purchase.**

The Dig - 2021 - This drama re-imagines the 1939 excavation of Sutton Hoo, and it's already received five nominations for the British Academy Film Awards. Carey Mulligan (*Never Let Me Go*) stars as Edith Pretty, a Suffolk landowner who hires the self-taught archaeologist Basil Brown (Ralph Fiennes, The English Patient) to handle the burial mounds at her rural estate. Before too long, it becomes clear that it's a site of significant archaeological importance, and the situation gets complicated. **Netflix.**

The Lady in the Van - 2015 - This uplifting film is based on the true story of a woman who temporarily parked her van in a man's drive, then proceeded to live outside his house for the next 15 years. Dame Maggie Smith stars. **Starz or streaming rental.**

The Quartet - 2012 - This delightful dramedy is one no British TV and film fan should miss. It includes performances from British acting greats like Dame Maggie Smith, Sir William Connolly, Sir Tom Courtenay, and Sir Michael Gambon. The action takes place in Beecham House, a retirement home for former professional musicians, and it sees our main characters attempting to raise funds to save the home. There's music, drama, romance, and a number of appearances from British TV favourites like Sheridan Smith and the late Trevor Peacock. **Netflix or streaming rental.**

Ammonite - 2020 - Loosely inspired by the true story of palaeontologist Mary Anning, this film stars Kate Winslet as Anning and Saoirse Ronan as Charlotte Murchison, a woman rumoured to be her romantic partner. James McArdle, Gemma Jones, and Fiona Shaw also star. **Hulu or streaming rental.**

Fisherman's Friends - 2019 - This feel-good dramedy is set in Cornwall, and it's going to look very familiar to many of our readers. That's because it's filmed in the very same village as TV series *Doc Martin* - Port Isaac. The series follows a London music executive who visits Cornwall for a colleague's stag do, only to have his boss trick him into trying to sign a group of sea shanty-singing fishermen. He struggles to gain the respect of the community, but they'll teach him a thing or two before it's all over. The film is based on a true story. **Netflix or streaming rental.**

Downton Abbey - 2019 - This 2019 film is a must-watch for any Downton Abbey fan, and it sees the Crawley family and their staff preparing for a royal visit. **HBO Max and streaming rental.**

The Adventures of Greyfriars Bobby - 2007 - This fun and family-friendly film is based on the famed Edinburgh Skye Terrier, Greyfriars Bobby, who is said to have spent 14 years guarding the grave of his beloved human. In this particular adaptation, a new dog licensing law puts Bobby's life in danger, leading a local lad to fight for him. **Amazon Prime Video, Tubi, or streaming rental.**

Summerland - 2020 - While WWII rages on around them, a reclusive writer in Kent takes in a young evacuee from London. Gemma Arterton and Dame Penelope Wilton play younger Alice and older Alice, while Lucas Bond (*The Miniaturist*) plays Frank. **Showtime or streaming rental.**

Saving Grace - 2000 - Brenda Blethyn (*Vera*) stars in this film about an English widow who's been left destitute after her husband's suicide. She decides to take drastic measures to survive. Craig Ferguson, Martin Clunes, and Phyllida Law are also in the cast. Interestingly, this film featured Clunes as a doctor, and that role was later spun off into two films before the character was changed quite drastically to create the *Doc Martin* television series. If you watch the end credits on *Doc Martin*, you'll see a nod to *Saving Grace* as the origin of the series. **Starz or streaming purchase.**

The Limehouse Golem - 2016 - Bill Nighy and Olivia Cooke star in this mystery-horror film about a serial murderer in Victorian London. The film is based on Peter Ackroyd's 1994 mystery novel, *Dan Leno and the Limehouse Golem*. **Hulu or streaming rental.**

Enola Holmes - 2020 - This playful mystery is based on Nancy Springer's young adult mystery novels, and both follow the adventures of Sherlock Holmes' younger sister Enola. Millie Bobbie Brown stars alongside Henry Cavill, Sam Claflin, and Helene Bonham Carter. There's been no word on whether there will be a sequel, but the film was popular and there are more books available to adapt, so it seems like a solid possibility. **Netflix.**

Love & Friendship - 2016 - Based on Jane Austen's epistolary novel *Lady Susan*, this film is set in 1790s London and follows the scheming, recently widowed Lady Susan Vernon and she aims to secure husbands for both her daughter and herself. Kate Beckinsale stars, but British TV fans will also spot Stephen Fry in the cast. **Amazon Prime Video or streaming rental.**

Hysteria - 2011 - Hugh Dancy and Maggie Gyllenhaal star in this Victorian era film about a young doctor who joins a medical practice where they specialise in treating "hysteria". It's a delightfully funny film, but not for the those who are easily offended by sexual topics. **Starz or streaming rental.**

Juliet Naked - 2018 - This fun film offers a twist on the rom-com genre, telling the story of an unlikely friendship and romance between a British woman and a washed up singer from the United States (who happens to be her boyfriend's obsession). Rose Byrne (*Bridesmaids*), Chris O'Dowd (*The IT Crowd*), and Ethan Hawke (*Before Sunset*) star. **Pluto TV, Tubi, or streaming rental.**

Harry Potter & the Sorcerer's Stone - 2001 - Though many have written the series off as "kid stuff", the entire Harry Potter series is imaginative, beautifully filmed, and well-acted. If you're looking for something you can watch with the kids or grandkids, you could do far worse than to start with Harry Potter & the Sorcerer's Stone and continue on through the series. **All are available on Peacock or streaming rental.**

Daphne - 2017 - An unhappy young Londoner is forced to confront the need for change after she sees a shopkeeper get stabbed during an unsuccessful robbery attempt. Though it might not sound like it, there's an element of comedy to this drama, along with performances from Emily Beecham (*Into the Badlands*) and Geraldine James (*Kavanagh QC*). Those who prefer to avoid profanity and sexual situations will want to avoid this one. **Hulu, Tubi, Peacock, or streaming rental.**

The Little Stranger - 2018 - This gothic drama is set in 1948 and it follows a doctor who visits an old house where his mother used to work, only to find the house may be hiding a secret. Domhnall Gleeson and Ruth Wilson star. **Peacock or streaming rental.**

Clockwise - 1986 - Though dated, *Monty Python*/John Cleese fans will enjoy this light 80s comedy in which John Cleese plays Brian Stimpson, a headmaster with an obsession for punctuality. The film includes quite a few familiar favourites, including Dame Penelope Wilton (*After Life*), Alison Steadman (*Hold the Sunset*), and Geoffrey Palmer (*As Time Goes By*). **Amazon Prime Video or streaming rental.**

The Bookshop - 2017 - Emily Mortimer stars in this film about a widow who moves to a small coastal town to follow her dream of opening a bookshop. Set in the 1950s, the film also includes performances from Patricia Clarkson and Bill Nighy. It's adapted from Penelope Fitzgerald's 1978 novel of the same name. **Epix, Amazon Prime Video, or streaming rental.**

Swimming With Men - 2018 - This light-hearted film sees a group of middle-aged men come together on a synchonised swimming team. British TV fans will likely recognise Jim Carter (*Downton Abbey*), Rob Brydon (*Gavin & Stacey*), Nathaniel Parker (*Inspector Lynley Mysteries*), Rupert Graves (*The Forsyte Saga*), Jane Horrocks (*Absolutely Fabulous*) and Charlotte Riley (*Press*). **Hulu or streaming rental.**

Cry of the Penguins - 1971 - This British classic stars Sir John Hurt and Hayley Mills. The story follows a young London biologist who's more interested in penguins than women. **Amazon Prime Video.**

Black Narcissus - 1947 - If you watched the recent adaptation of Black Narcissus starring the late Dame Diana Rigg (Hulu), you may also want to go back and watch the original film adaptation of Rumer Godden's 1939 novel. Both adaptations revolve around sexual tension and nuns at a small convent in the Himalayas. **HBO Max or streaming rental.**

Molly Moon and the Incredible Book of Hypnotism - 2015 - Young Molly Moon (Raffey Cassidy) lives in an orphanage until she finds a book on hypnotism and uses it to earn herself a starring role in a West End play. Unfortunately, she'll soon learn that grass isn't always greener on the other side. This fun, family-friendly film features performances from British TV favourites like Dominic Monaghan (*Hetty Wainthropp Investigates*), Lesley Manville (*Mum*), Emily Watson (*Chernobyl*), Celia Imrie (*Kingdom*), and Ben Miller (*Death in Paradise*). **Amazon Prime Video or streaming rental.**

AUTISM IN BRITISH TV

April is **World Autism Month**, so we thought it only fitting that our spring edition should do its part to raise awareness and offer up some shows that might be of interest to those who have autism, know someone with autism, or wish to know more about autism.

In particular, we'd like to draw attention to the plight of autistic women, as it's only in recent years that psychologists have begun to realise just how many women have been overlooked and mis-diagnosed due to gender-biased diagnostic criteria.

Many women - especially those of average or above average intelligence - can be autistic without realising it. Often, they've spent their entire lives feeling different from everyone around them. Many have been misdiagnosed and medicated to within an inch of their lives, all because doctors and therapists have long considered autism to be almost exclusively a male condition.

Since more than 80% of our readers are women, we felt this was worthy of mention.

Some may wonder why anyone would need to know they were autistic if no doctor or family member had ever noticed it, but there are a few very good reasons:

- A lot of autistic women have spent a lifetime beating themselves up for being weird or abnormal or socially inept. When they're diagnosed (or when they read descriptions that resonate), it can lead to a new level of self-understanding and forgiveness.

- Many women who don't know they're autistic have problems with depression or mental illness (often from the stress of living in a world not well-suited to their needs). By knowing what's wrong, they can make better decisions about how to adapt.

- Autistic people are prone to being abused and manipulated. By knowing they're autistic, friends and family can help them avoid many dangerous situations (particularly things like date rape and abusive relationships).

- Knowing you're autistic can make it easier to find and befriend people who are like you.

It's mostly about the autistic person being able to improve his or her life, but if he or she chooses to be open about it, it can also mean that those around him or her can be more understanding.

If you'd like to learn more about women and autism, you can Google the resources below:

- **BBC**: It All Made Sense When We Found Out We Were Autistic

- **The Conversation**: The Women Who Don't Know They're Autistic

- **Washington Post**: "You Don't Look Autistic" - The Reality of High-Functioning Autism

- **YouTube**: Tony Attwood - Aspergers in Girls

If you wish to donate to an organisation that supports autistic people and their families, we recommend ASAN (Autistic Self Advocacy Network). Visit their website at AutisticAdvocacy.org.

British TV Shows About Autism

Girls with Autism - 2015 - Because autistic girls and women are often better at masking their unique traits, they've gone largely overlooked in studies of autism. At the Limpsfield Grange boarding school, they're doing their best to change perceptions and help autistic girls lead better lives. **BritBox.**

Pablo - 2017 - Using only crayons and creativity, a young boy with autism draws an imaginary world where animal friends help him with real life difficulties. **Netflix.**

Louis Theroux: Extreme Love - Autism - 2012 - British filmmaker Louis Theroux looks at how autistic children perceive the world around them, and the impact it can have on their families. **BBC Select.**

The Autistic Gardener - 2015 to 2017 - This fun series sees a team of autistic gardeners - led by an award-winning autistic gardener - as they remodel garden spaces for a variety of individuals around the UK. Aside from gardening knowledge, you'll also learn a thing or two about the unique skills and challenges of people on the autism spectrum. **Inside Outside.**

One Deadly Weekend in America: A Killing at the Carwash - 2017 - In May 2015, an autistic teenager was murdered for wearing the wrong colour of shoes. Through his story, we get a look at what life is like in LA's gangland. **BBC Select.**

British TV Shows With Autistic Characters or Presenters

The A Word - 2016 to present - This drama follows the Hughes family through their son's autism diagnosis and the events that follow it. Christopher Ecclestone (*Doctor Who*) and Morven Christie (*Grantchester*) star alongside child actor Max Vento. **Amazon Prime Video.**

Doc Martin - 2004 to present - Martin Clunes (*Men Behaving Badly*) stars in this comedy about a brilliant but grumpy London surgeon who suddenly develops a fear of blood. He leaves his high-flying career and takes a post in a Cornish fishing village where he spent holidays as a child with his Aunt Joan. Many believe Martin's social troubles stem from Asperger's (an outdated term now bundled under Autism Spectrum Disorder). There's one episode where it's actually suggested by a professional, but the producers haven't confirmed or denied the diagnosis. **Acorn TV, Hulu, Tubi, Pluto.**

The IT Crowd – 2006 to 2013 - Banished to the basement, two nerds and their clueless leader service the IT needs of a strange and generic corporation. The character Maurice Moss is frequently cited as a textbook example of an autistic male. **Netflix.**

Springwatch, Autumnwatch, and Winterwatch - Annual - Presenter Chris Packham was diagnosed with Asperger's before they stopped using the term, and he's a fantastic example of a successful adult on the spectrum who's managed to adapt his life to his needs. His enthusiasm for nature is infectious, and his knowledge is deep. **BritBox.**

The Good Doctor - *United States* - 2017 to present - While the series is American, lead actor Freddie Highmore is English. He plays Dr. Shaun Murphy, an autistic young man who's going through his surgical residency. **Hulu.**

The Tunnel - 2016 to 2018 - This British and French co-production is based on the Danish-Swedish series *The Bridge*. Both feature a female detective with Asperger's, which is rather unusual since very few autistic women are shown in TV and film. In *The Tunnel*, the character is named Capitaine Elise Wassermann, and in *The Bridge*, it's Saga Norén. ***The Tunnel* is available on Amazon Prime Video, while *The Bridge* is on Sundance Now/AMC+.**

It's also worth mentioning that Paddy Considine (*Peaky Blinders, Informer, The Suspicions of Mr. Whicher*) has recently opened up about his own Asperger's diagnosis and how it was a great relief to him.

INDEX

Animal Madhouse - Tubi
Animal Park - IMDb
Animal Rescue School - Tubi
Animal Rescue Squad - IMDb
Animal Squad - AMZ
Anna's Wild Life - IMDb
Anna Karenina - Acorn TV, Pluto
Anner House - Acorn TV
Anne With An "E" - Netflix
Anthem for Doomed Youth: The War Poets - BritBox
Antiques Roadshow - BritBox, Pluto
Antony and Cleopatra (1981) - BritBox
Anzac Girls - Acorn TV, AMZ, Tubi
Apparitions - IMDb
Apple Tree Yard - Hulu
Appropriate Adult - IMDb
Archaeology: A Secret History - BBC
Archangel - Pluto
Are You Being Served? (16) - BritBox
Are You Being Served? (72) - BritBox
Are You Being Served? Again! - BritBox
Ariana Grande: Live in London - BBC
Aristocrats - BritBox
The Aristocrats - BritBox, AMZ
Armadillo - BritBox
Around the World in 80 Faiths - BritBox
Art Deco Icons: Britain's Bling and Glamour - Tubi
The Art Detectives - Acorn TV
Art of China - BBC
Art of France - BBC
Art of Russia - BBC
Art of Scandinavia - BBC
Art of Spain - BBC
Some Assembly Required - Netflix
As Time Goes By - BritBox
As You Like It (78) - BritBox
At Home With the Braithwaites - IMDb, Tubi,

Pluto
At Home with the Georgians - Acorn TV
Atlantis - Hulu
Atlantis High - IMDb
At Last the 1948 Show - Tubi, BritBox
The Attaché - Acorn TV
Attacking the Devil - Netflix
Attenborough and the Giant Elephant - AMC+
At Your Service - Tubi
Auction - Tubi
The Auction House - AMZ, Tubi
Aung San Suu Kyi: The Fall of an Icon - BBC
Auschwitz: The Nazis and the Final Solution - BBC
The Autistic Gardener - I/O
Autumnwatch - BritBox
Avenue 5 - HBO
Away - Sundance
B.B. King: The Life of Riley - Topic
Babs - Topic
Baby Baby - Tubi
Baby Ballroom - Netflix
Baby Beauty Queens - Tubi
Baby Hospital - Tubi
Back - Sundance
Back Home - Acorn TV
Back to Life - Showtime
Bad Boy Billionaires: India - Netflix
Bad Mothers - Sundance
The Badness of King George IV - Acorn TV
The Bad Seed - Sundance
Baghdad Central - Hulu
The Ballroom Boys - Acorn TV
Ballykissangel - BritBox, Pluto
The Ballymurphy Precedent - IMDb
Balthazar - Acorn TV
Banana - AMZ
Bancroft - BritBox
Band of Gold - IMDb
Bang - Acorn TV, Sundance
Banged Up - IMDb
Banished - BritBox, AMZ, Hulu

The Baron - BritBox
Baroque - Acorn TV
Barristers - Acorn TV
The Barry Scrapyard Story - AMZ
Battle Castle - AMZ
Battle of Kings: Bannockburn - IMDb
The Bay - BritBox
The BBC at War - BritBox
BBC's Lost Sitcoms - BritBox
Bear Grylls: Survival School - AMZ, IMDb
Beau Geste - AMZ
The Beauty of Anatomy - BBC
Beaver Falls - IMDb, Tubi
Bedlam - AMZ, Hulu
Bed of Roses - Acorn TV, AMZ
Beechgrove Garden - BritBox
Behind Enemy Lines - Netflix
Behind Her Eyes - Netflix
Being Erica - AMZ, Hulu
Being Human - IMDb, Sundance, Tubi, Pluto
Belonging - Acorn TV
The Bench - AMZ, Tubi
Benidorm - BritBox
Best in Paradise - BritBox
Best Laid Plans - Tubi
Best of British Heritage Railways - AMZ
Between - Netflix
Big Bad Battles: Weekend Warriors - Pluto
Big Dreams Small Spaces - I/O, AMZ
The Big Family Cooking Showdown - Netflix
The Big Flower Fight - Netflix
Biggie & Tupac - Topic
The Big House Reborn - Acorn TV, IMDb
Big School - Pluto
Big Sky - AMZ
Bill - BritBox
Billionaire Boy - BritBox
The Birth of Empire: The East India Company - BBC
The Bisexual - Hulu
A Bit of Fry & Laurie -

BritBox, AMZ
Blackadder - BritBox, AMZ, Hulu
A Black and White Killing - BBC
Black Books - IMDb, Tubi
Black Earth Rising - Netflix
Black Harbour - IMDb
Black Mirror - Netflix
Black Mirror: Bandersnatch - Netflix
Black Narcissus - Hulu
Blackpool - Pluto
The Black Velvet Gown - Acorn TV
Black Widows - Acorn TV, AMZ
The Blake Mysteries: Ghost Stories - BritBox
Blandings - BritBox, IMDb, Tubi, Pluto
Bleak House (05) - Hulu
Bleak House (85) - BritBox, AMZ
The Bleak Old Shop of Stuff - AMZ
The Bletchley Circle: San Francisco - BritBox
Blinded - Sundance
Bliss - BritBox
Blitzed: Nazis on Drugs - Acorn TV
Blood - Acorn TV
Bloodlands - Acorn TV
Blood Ties - AMZ, Pluto
Blue Murder - BritBox, IMDb, Tubi
The Blue Rose - Acorn TV, IMDb
Bluestone 42 - Pluto
Bodies - AMZ
Bodily Harm - Acorn TV
Body and Soul - IMDb
The Body Farm - BritBox
Bodyguard - Netflix
Bollywood: The World's Biggest Film Industry - Acorn TV
Bomber Boys - AMZ
Bomb Girls - Acorn TV, Pluto
The Bone Detectives - Acorn TV
Bonekickers - IMDb
The Book Group - AMZ, Tubi

Boomers - Acorn TV
Boon - BritBox
Booze Britain - Tubi
Boozed Up Brits Abroad - Tubi
Borderlands: Life on the Line - BBC
Borderline - Netflix
The Borgias - Netflix, Showtime
Bottersnikes and Gumbles - Netflix
Bottom - AMZ
Bounty Hunters - AMZ, Tubi
Boy Meets Girl (09) - IMDb, Tubi
Boy Meets Girl (15) - BritBox
The Boy with the Topknot - Acorn TV
Brainwashing Stacey - BBC
Bramwell - BritBox, AMZ, Tubi
Brand New House on a Budget - Tubi
Brassic - Hulu
Brave New World - Peacock
Brazil with Michael Palin - BBC
Breeders - Hulu
Brick by Brick: Rebuilding Our Past - Tubi
The Bridal Coach - Tubi
Brideshead Revisited - BritBox, Tubi
Bridgerton - Netflix
Bridges that Built London - IMDb
Bridget & Eamon - IMDb, Tubi
The Brief - IMDb
Brief Encounters - Acorn TV
Bright Lights Brilliant Minds: A Tale of Three Cities - BBC
The Brilliant Brontë Sisters - Acorn TV
Brilliant Gardens - AMZ
Bringing Babs Home - Topic
Britain's Outlaws: Highwaymen, Pirates, and Rogues - AMZ
Britain AD: King Arthur's Britain - AMZ
Britain by Narrowboat -

AMZ
Britain's Best Bakery - IMDb, Pluto
Britain's Best Canals - AMZ
Britain's Best Drives - AMZ
Britain's Biggest Adventures with Bear Grylls - BritBox
Britain's Bloodiest Dynasty - Acorn TV, Sundance
Britain's Bloody Crown - Acorn TV, Sundance
Britain's Forgotten Slave Owners - BBC
Britain's Railways: Then & Now - AMZ
Britain's Railways Then & Now: LNER - AMZ
Britain's Real Monarch - AMZ
Britain's Royal Weddings - BritBox
Britain's Secret Treasures - BritBox
Britain's Tudor Treasure - BritBox
Britannia - AMZ
The Britannia Awards - BritBox
British Bouncers - AMZ
British Inland Waterways - AMZ
British Railway Journeys - AMZ
British Railways - AMZ
British Royal Heritage: The Royal Kingdom - AMZ
Broadchurch - Netflix
Broadmoor: A History of the Criminally Insane - AMZ
Broken - BritBox
The Brokenwood Mysteries - Acorn TV
The Broker's Man - Acorn TV, Tubi, IMDb
Bromwell High - Pluto
Brontë Country: The Life and Times of Three Famous Sisters - AMZ
The Brontë Sisters - AMZ
Brotherhood - Showtime
Brushstrokes: Every Picture Tells a Story - IMDb
The Buccaneers - AMZ
Bucket - BritBox

Budgie - Tubi
Build a New Life in the Country - Tubi, Pluto
Build a New Life in the Country Revisits - Tubi
Building Dream Homes - AMZ
The Bureau - Sundance
Butterfly - Hulu
Byron - AMZ
Bäckström - Acorn TV
C.B. Strike (aka Strike) - Cinemax, HBO
Cabins in the Wild with Dick Strawbridge - Netflix
Cadfael - BritBox, IMDb, Tubi, Pluto
Caligula with Mary Beard - Acorn TV
Call the Midwife - Netflix
Camelot - Tubi
Cameraman to the Queen - BritBox
Camomile Lawn - Tubi
Campion - BritBox
Can't Cope, Won't Cope - Netflix
Can a Computer Write a Hit Musical - Acorn TV
Capital - Topic
Captain Scarlet & the Mysterons - IMDb
The Capture - Peacock
Care - Acorn TV, AMZ
Caroline Quentin's National Parks - BritBox
Cars, Cops, & Criminals - Tubi
Carters Get Rich - Tubi
The Case - Acorn TV, Pluto
Case Histories - IMDb, Tubi, Pluto, Peacock
Castle Builders - AMZ
Castles and Palaces of Europe - AMZ
Casualty - BritBox
Casualty 1900s: London Hospital - BritBox, AMZ
The Casual Vacancy - HBO
Catastophe - AMZ
Catherine the Great - HBO
Catherine's Family Kitchen - Tubi
Cat Hospital - Acorn TV

Caught on Camera - Netflix
Celebrity Restaurant in Our Living Room - Tubi
Celebs, Brands, and Fake Fans - BBC
Celtic Britain - IMDb, Pluto
The Celts - IMDb
The Celts: Blood, Iron, and Sacrifice with Alice Roberts and Neil

Oliver - IMDb
The Champions - BritBox
Chancer - IMDb, Peacock
Charles & Diana: Wedding of the Century - BritBox
Charles and Di: The Truth Behind Their Wedding - BBC
Charles Dickens: The Man That Asked for More - AMZ
Charles I: Downfall of a King - AMZ
Charles II: The Power and the Passion - BritBox
Chatsworth - AMZ
Cheat - Sundance
Chef's Diaries: Scotland - AMZ
Chef's Protégé - Tubi
Chernobyl - HBO
Children's Hospital - Tubi
A Child's Christmases in Wales - BritBox
Chiller - IMDb
Chimerica - Topic
China: A New World Order - BBC
China: Triumph and Turmoil - BBC
China on Four Wheels - BBC
Choccywoccydoodah - Tubi
Chopin Saved My Life - BBC
A Christmas Carol - BritBox
Christopher and His Kind - BritBox
Churchill: Blood Sweat, & Oil Paint - Acorn TV, AMZ
Churchill: The Darkest Hour - BritBox
The Churchills - Acorn TV
Churchill's Secret Agents: The New Recruits - Netflix

Cilla - Acorn TV
The Circuit - Acorn TV
The City & The City - BritBox, IMDb
City Homicide - IMDb, Hulu, Tubi
City of Vice - IMDb
Civilisation - BritBox
Civilization: Is the West History? - BBC
Civil War - Acorn TV, AMZ
Civil War: The Untold Story - Acorn TV
Cla'am - Topic
Clarissa & the King's Cookbook - I/O
Clash of the Santas - BritBox
Classic British Steam Engines - AMZ
Classic Doctor Who - BritBox
Classic Doctor Who Comic Con Panel - BritBox
Classic Mary Berry - IMDb
Classic Steam Train Collection - AMZ
A Classic Tour of Scotland: Footloose Special - AMZ
Clean Break - Acorn TV
Cleaning Up - Sundance
Cleverman - Netflix
Click and Collect - BritBox
Click for Murder - Netflix
Click to Change Your Life: Secrets of a Global Craze - BBC
Clink - AMZ
Clique - Hulu
Close to the Enemy - Acorn TV
Cloudstreet - Acorn TV
Coalition - BritBox
Coast - BritBox
Coastal Railways with Julie Walters - Acorn TV
Coast and Country Walks - Acorn TV
Cobra - PBS
Cocaine - Netflix
The Code (11) - Netflix
The Code (14) - Netflix, Acorn TV
Code 404 - Peacock
Code Blue: Murder - BritBox
Codebreakers: The Secret

Geniuses of World War II - BritBox
Code of a Killer - Acorn TV
Cold Blood - BritBox
Cold Call - Acorn TV, Sundance
Cold Courage - AMC+
Cold Feet - BritBox, IMDb, Tubi
Cold Feet: The New Years - BritBox
Cold Squad - IMDb
Collateral - Netflix
Colonel March of Scotland Yard - IMDb
The Colour of Magic - IMDb, Tubi
The Comedy of Errors (1983) - BritBox
Come Home - Topic
Comfort Eating - IMDb, Tubi
The Commander - Acorn TV
The Commons - Sundance
A Confession - BritBox
Confessions of a Serial Killer - BBC
Conspiracies - Netflix
Conspiracy Files: George Soros - The Billionaire Global Mastermind? -

BBC
Conspiracy Files: Vaccine Wars - BBC
Cook Yourself Thin UK - Tubi
The Cops - AMZ
Coronation Street - BritBox, Hulu
The Coronavirus Newscast - BritBox
The Coroner - BritBox
Count Arthur Strong - Acorn TV
Countryfile - BritBox
Countryfile Autumn Diaries - BritBox
Countryfile Spring Diaries - BritBox
Couples on the Couch - BBC
Couple Trouble - Sundance
Coupling - AMZ, Hulu
Cowboy Builders - HBO
Crackanory - AMZ
Cracker - BritBox, Tubi

Cracking the Shakespeare Code - AMZ
Cradle to Grave - Acorn TV
Cranford - BritBox
Crashing - Netflix
Crazy Delicious - Netflix
Crazyhead - Netflix
Creeped Out - Netflix
The Crest - IMDb
Crime & Violence in England - AMZ
Crime and Punishment - AMZ
Crime Secrets - IMDb
Crime Story - BritBox
Criminal: United Kingdom - Netflix
Crims - IMDb, Tubi
The Crimson Petal & the White - Acorn TV, Sundance
CripTales - AMC+
The Crown - Netflix
Crown and Country - AMZ
Crownies - AMZ
Cruise of the Gods - BritBox
Cruising the Cut - AMZ
The Cry - Acorn TV, Sundance
Cuba with Simon Reeve - BBC
Cuckoo - Netflix
Cucumber - AMZ
Cuffs - AMZ, Tubi
Cut from a Different Cloth - AMZ
Cymbeline (82) - BritBox
Daleks' Invasion Earth 2150 A.D. - BritBox
Dalziel & Pascoe - BritBox
Damned - BritBox
Damned Designs: Don't Demolish My Home - I/O
A Dance to the Music of Time - Acorn TV
Danger Man, aka Secret Agent - IMDb
Danger Mouse - Netflix
Danger Mouse: Classic Collection - Netflix
Dangerous Roads - AMZ
Danger UXB - Acorn TV
Daniel & Majella's B&B Road Trip - AMZ

Daniel Deronda (02) - Hulu, AMZ, BritBox
Dan Snow's Norman Walks - AMZ
Darcey Bussell: Looking for Margot - Tubi
Dark Ages: An Age of Light - AMZ
Dark Angel - AMZ
The Dark Charisma of Adolf Hitler - BBC
Dark Heart - BritBox
Dark Matter - Netflix
The Darling Buds of May - BritBox, IMDb, Tubi
David Brent: Life on the Road - Netflix
David Copperfield (86) - AMZ, BritBox
David Copperfield (99) - AMZ, Hulu, BritBox
David Jason's Secret Service - Acorn TV, AMZ
David Suchet: In the Footsteps of St. Peter - AMZ, Tubi
David Suchet on the Orient Express - BritBox
David Suchet's Being Poirot - Acorn TV
Da Vinci's Demons - Starz
Days of Majesty - BritBox
DCI Banks - AMZ, Hulu, HBO
Dead Boss - AMZ, Hulu
Dead Good Job - BritBox
Dead Lucky - Acorn TV, AMZ, Sundance
Dead Set - Netflix
Deadwater Fell - Acorn TV
Deadwind - Netflix
Dear Murderer - Acorn TV
Death in Paradise - BritBox
Death Over Dinner - Topic
Decline and Fall - Acorn TV
The Deep - AMZ
Deep Water - Acorn TV
Degrassi : Next Class - Netflix
Delicious - Acorn TV
The Delivery Man - Acorn TV, IMDb
Dennis and Gnasher Unleashed - Netflix
Departure - Peacock

Derek - Netflix
Derek Acorah's Ghost Towns - IMDb
Dermot Bannon's Incredible Homes - Tubi
Derry Girls - Netflix
Des - Sundance
Design Doctors - Tubi
Designer Darlings - Tubi
Design for Life - BBC
Desi Rascals - IMDb
Desperate Romantics - BritBox, AMZ
The Detectives - IMDb, Pluto
Detectorists - Acorn TV, IMDb, Tubi
Deutschland 83 / Deutschland 86 - Sundance
The Devil's Mistress - IMDb, Tubi, Pluto
Diana & Sarah: The Royal Wives of Windsor - AMZ
Diana: 7 Days That Shook the World - BBC
Diana: The Interview that Shook the World - BritBox
Diana: The New Evidence - IMDb
Dickensian - BritBox, AMZ, Pluto
Dictatorland - BBC
Did Darwin Kill God? - BBC
A Difficult Woman - Acorn TV, AMZ
Digging for Britain - Acorn TV
Dinosaur Britain - AMZ
The Diplomat - Pluto
Dirk Gently's Holistic Detective Agency (16) - Hulu
Dirk Gently (10) - BritBox
Discovering Britain - Acorn TV
Discovering Korean Food with Gizzi Erskine - I/O
Discovering the World - Tubi
Discover Ireland - AMZ
Discover Scotland - AMZ
A Discovery of Witches - Sundance
Doc Martin - Acorn TV, Hulu, Tubi, Pluto

Doctor at Large - Tubi, Pluto
The Doctor Blake Mysteries - BritBox
Doctor Finlay - Acorn TV, AMZ
Doctor Foster - Netflix
The Doctors - AMZ
Doctor Thorne - AMZ
Doctor Who - HBO
Doctor Who: Tales Lost in Time - AMZ
Doctor Who: The Doctors Revisited - BritBox
Doctor Who: The Faceless Ones - AMC+
Doctor Who Specials - BritBox
Doctor Zhivago - BritBox
The Dog House UK - HBO
The Dog Rescuers - Tubi
Dombey and Son (15) - AMZ
Dombey and Son (83) - AMZ
Dominion Creek - Acorn TV
Donal MacIntyre: Breaking Crime - IMDb
Donovan - AMZ
Don't Forget the Driver - BritBox
Don't Panic: How to End Poverty in 15 Years - BBC
Don't Panic: The Truth About Population - BBC
Double Your House for Half the Money - AMZ, Tubi
Down from London - Topic
Downton Abbey - AMZ, BritBox, Peacock
Downton Abbey Extras - BritBox
Dr. Who and the Daleks - BritBox
Dracula - Netflix
Dream Corp LLC - Hulu
Dress to Impress - Hulu
Drifters - IMDb, Tubi, Pluto
The Driver - AMZ
Driving & Firing: The Art of Driving - AMZ
Driving & Firing: The Art of Firing - AMZ
Drovers' Gold - AMZ
Drowning in Plastic - BBC
The Drummer & the Keeper - Topic

Dublin Murders - Starz
The Duchess - Netflix
The Duchess of Duke Street - AMZ
Dunkirk - BritBox
Durham County - IMDb
The Durrells in Corfu - AMZ
EastEnders - BritBox
East of Everything - Acorn TV
East West 101 - Acorn TV
Eat to Live Forever with Giles Coren - BBC
Ed Balls: Trump's America - BBC
Edge of Heaven - BritBox
Edge of the Universe - Netflix
Edible Gardens - BritBox
Edinburgh: More than Words - AMZ
Edward & Mary: The Unknown Tudors - Acorn TV, AMZ
Edwardian Farm - Tubi
Edward VIII: The King Who Threw Away His Crown - AMZ
Elizabeth I & Her Enemies - Acorn TV
Elizabeth I (06) - HBO
Elizabeth I (14) - AMZ
Elizabeth I: Killer Queen - AMZ
Elizabeth I: War on Terror - AMZ
Elizabeth is Missing - PBS
Elizabeth R - BritBox
Emerald Falls - BritBox
Emergency Firefighters - AMZ, Tubi
Emma - BritBox
Emmerdale - BritBox, IMDb, Tubi
Empire: The Soul of Britannia - AMZ
The End - Showtime
Endeavour - AMZ
The End of the F***ing World - Netflix
Enemy at the Door - IMDb
England's Forgotten Queen: The Life and Death of Lady Jane Grey -

IMDb
The English Game - Netflix
Enid Blyton Adventure Series - IMDb
Enid Blyton Secret Series - IMDb
Enterprice - Topic
Episodes - Showtime
Escape to the Chateau - Peacock
Escape to the Chateau DIY - Peacock
Escape to the Country - BritBox, IMDb
Eternal Law - IMDb, Tubi
Everyday Miracles - Netflix
Executive Stress - Acorn TV
Exhibition on Screen: History's Greatest Painters - AMZ
Exile - Tubi, Topic
Exit Through the Gift Shop - AMC+
Extraordinary Places to Eat - BBC
Extras - Netflix
Extreme A&E - Tubi
Extreme Combat: The Dancer and the Fighter - BBC
Extremely Dangerous - BritBox
The Fades - AMZ, Hulu
Fake News: A True History - BBC
Fake or Fortune? - Tubi
The Fall & Rise of Britain's Railways - AMZ
The Fall - BritBox, AMZ. Sundance, Tubi, Peacock
Fallet - Netflix
A Family At War - IMDb, Tubi
Family Business - Acorn TV
The Family Farm - Acorn TV
Family Tree - HBO
Fanny by Gaslight - AMZ
Fanny Hill - Acorn TV
The Farmer's Country Showdown - Tubi
The Farm Fixer - IMDb
Father and Son - BritBox
Father Brown (13) - BritBox
Father Brown (74) - BritBox

Father Ted - IMDb, Pluto
Fat Men Can't Hunt - Tubi
Fawlty Towers - BritBox
Feasts - BBC
Feathers & Toast - AMZ
Feel Good - Netflix
The Fenn Street Gang - IMDb
The Field of Blood - Acorn TV, IMDb, Pluto
Fields of Gold - BritBox
Fifth Gear - Pluto
Finding Joy - Acorn TV
Fingersmith - Acorn TV, Sundance
First Dates Hotel - HBO
First Dates Ireland - HBO
First Dates UK - HBO
First Homes - Tubi
The First Silent Night - AMZ
The Five - Netflix
Five by Five - BritBox
Five Days - HBO
The Fix - Netflix
Fix Her Up - AMZ
Flack - AMZ
Flame Trees of Thika - Acorn TV
Fleabag - AMZ
Flesh & Blood - PBS
Flickers - IMDb
Flood - IMDb
Florence Nightingale - BritBox
Flowers - Netflix
The Flu That Killed 50 Million - BBC
Flying Across Britain with Arthur Williams - AMZ
The Flying Scotsman: A Rail Romance - AMZ
Flying Scotsman: The Ultimate Profile - AMZ
The Flying Scotsman Steam Train Comes Home - AMZ
Food CIA - HBO
Food Glorious Food - I/O
Footloose in England: Along the Ridgeway - AMZ
Footloose in Ireland - AMZ
Footloose in London: All the Best Sights of our Capital - AMZ
Footloose in Oxford & York -

AMZ
Footloose in the Cotswolds - AMZ
The Force: Manchester - AMZ
Foreign Exchange - AMZ
Fortitude - AMZ
Foyle's War - Acorn TV
The Fragile Heart - Acorn TV, AMZ, Tubi
Frankenstein and the Vampire: A Dark and Stormy Night - BBC
The Frankenstein Chronicles - Netflix
Frankie - BritBox
Frat Boys - BBC
Frayed - HBO
Fred Dinenage Murder Casebook - AMZ
Free Rein - Netflix
The French Collection - Tubi
French Fields - Acorn TV
Fresh Fields - Acorn TV
Fresh Meat - AMZ, Pluto
Freud - Netflix
Friday Night Dinner - AMZ
From Darkness - BritBox
From Father to Daughter - Acorn TV
From There to Here - AMZ
Frontier - Netflix
Fry Up - Topic
Fungus the Bogeyman - AMZ
Funny is Funny: A Conversation with Normal Lear - BritBox
The F Word - Tubi
Gadget Man - AMZ
Galway, Ireland: Busy Streets and Irish Music in the Pubs - AMZ
Gameface - Hulu
Game of Thrones - HBO
Gandhi - BBC
Gangs of Britain - IMDb
Gangs of London - AMC+
Gangsters: Faces of the Underworld - Pluto
Gardeners' World - I/O, AMZ, BritBox
The Garden Pantry - I/O
Garden Rescue - I/O

Gardens of the National Trust - AMZ

Gauguin: The Full Story - AMZ

Gavin & Stacey - BritBox, AMZ

Genderquake - BBC

The Genius of Carl Faberge - BBC

The Genius of Roald Dahl - Acorn TV

Genius of the Ancient World - Acorn TV, BBC, Netflix

Genius of the Modern World - BBC, Netflix

Gentleman Jack - HBO

Gentlemen, The Queen - BritBox

The Gentle Touch - IMDb

George Gently - Acorn TV

George III: The Genius of the Mad King - IMDb

Germany's New Nazis - BBC

Get a Life - Tubi

Get Even - Netflix

Get Growing - I/O, AMZ

Getting High for God? - Topic

Getting On - AMZ, Pluto, Hulu

Getting the Builders In - Tubi

Ghosts - HBO

The Ghost Squad - AMZ, Tubi, Pluto

Gideon's Daughter - BritBox

The Gil Mayo Mysteries - BritBox

Giri/Haji - Netflix

Girlfriends - Acorn TV

Some Girls - AMZ, Tubi

Girls with Autism - BritBox

Glitch - Netflix

Glorious Gardens from Above - AMZ

Glow Up - Netflix

The Gods of Wheat Street - Acorn TV

The Goes Wrong Show - AMZ, Tubi

Go Girls - IMDb

Gold Digger - Acorn TV, Sundance

Golden Years - Acorn TV

Good Cop - BritBox

The Good Karma Hospital - Acorn TV

Good Morning Britain - BritBox

Good Omens - AMZ

Gorbachev: The Man Who Changed the World - BBC

Gordon Behind Bars, aka Ramsay Behind Bars - Tubi

Gordon Ramsay's 24 Hours to Hell & Back - Hulu

Gordon Ramsay's The F Word - Hulu

Gordon Ramsay's American Road Trip - Hulu

Gordon Ramsey's Ultimate Home Cooking - Hulu

Grace - BritBox

Gracepoint - AMZ, Tubi

Grafters - IMDb, Tubi

The Graham Norton Show - AMC+

The Grand - IMDb, Pluto

Grand Designs - BritBox, IMDb, Netflix

A Grand Night In: The Story of Aardman - Netflix

The Grand Tour - AMZ

Grand Tours of Scotland's Lochs - AMZ

Grand Tours of Scotland - AMZ

Grand Tours of the Scottish Islands - IMDb

Grantchester - AMZ

Grayson Perry: All Man - BBC

Grayson Perry: Big American Road Trip - BBC

Grayson Perry: Who Are You? - BBC

Grayson Perry's Art Club - BBC

The Great - Hulu

The Great Antiques Map of Britain - AMZ

Great Artists with Tim Marlow - AMZ

The Great British Baking Show - Netflix

The Great British Baking Show: Holidays - Netflix

The Great British Baking

Show: Masterclass - Netflix

The Great British Baking Show: The Beginnings - Netflix

The Great British Benefits Handout - AMZ

The Great British Countryside - BritBox

Great Cars: British Elegance - AMZ

The Great Chelsea Garden Challenge - BritBox

Great Escape: The Untold Story - BritBox

Greatest Events of WWII in Colour - Netflix

Greatest Gardens - I/O, IMDb, Tubi

Great Expectations (11) - BritBox

Great Expectations (81) - AMZ, BritBox

Great Expectations (99) - AMZ, BritBox

The Great Gardens of England - AMZ

The Great Hip Hop Hoax - IMDb

Great Interior Design Challenge - I/O

Great Irish Journeys with Martha Kearney - AMZ

Great Lighthouses of Ireland - AMZ

The Great Pottery Throwdown - HBO

Great Scottish Singalong - AMZ

The Great Train Robbery - Acorn TV, AMZ

Greek Myths: True Stories - BBC

The Green Park - AMZ

Green Wing - IMDb

Greg Davies: You Magnificent Beast - Netflix

Ground Force - AMZ

Ground Force Revisited - AMZ

Grow, Cook, Eat - IMDb

Guardians of the Night - AMZ

Guerrilla - Showtime

The Guilty - IMDb
The Gulf - Sundance
Gunpowder - HBO
Guy Martin: Industrial Wonders - Pluto
Guy Martin: Spitfire Restoration - Pluto
The Gypsy Matchmaker - AMZ
H2O: Just Add Water - Netflix
Hadrian's Wall: Antonine Wall - AMZ
Hairy Bikers' Bakeation - BritBox
Hairy Bikers' Christmas Party - BritBox
Hairy Bikers' Everyday Gourmets - BritBox
Half-Built House - AMZ
Half Moon Investigations - AMZ
Halloween: Feast of the Dying Sun - AMZ
Hamish Macbeth - Acorn TV, AMZ, Tubi
Hamlet, Prince of Denmark (1980) - BritBox
Hammer House of Horror - IMDb, Tubi, Pluto
Hang-Ups - Hulu
Happyish - Showtime
The Harbour: Aberdeen - AMZ
Hard Sun - Hulu
Hard Times - AMZ
Harlots - Hulu
Harrow - Hulu
Harrow: A Very British School - IMDb
Harry - Acorn TV
Harry Potter: A History of Magic - BBC
Harry Styles Live in Manchester - BBC
Head Over Heels - Topic
Heartbeat - BritBox, IMDb, Tubi
The Heart Guy - Acorn TV
Heartland - Netflix
Hearts & Bones - IMDb, Tubi
Hearts and Bones - Pluto
Heat of the Sun - IMDb
The Heist at Hatton Garden - BritBox

He Kills Coppers - IMDb
The Helen West Casebook - Acorn TV
Helicopter ER - AMZ, Tubi
Helicopter Search & Rescue - AMZ, Tubi
Hell's Kitchen - Hulu, Peacock
Hello Ladies - HBO
Henry IV: Parts 1 and 2 (1979) - BritBox
Henry IX - Acorn TV
Henry V (1979) - BritBox
Henry VI: Parts 1-3 (1983) - BritBox
Henry VII: Winter King - AMZ
Henry VIII (1979) - BritBox
Her Story: The Female Revolution - BBC
Hetty Wainthropp Investigates - BritBox
Hidden (11) - Acorn TV
Hidden (18) - Acorn TV
Hidden: World's Best Monster Mystery - Loch Ness - BritBox
Hidden Britain by Drone - Acorn TV
Hidden Europe - Tubi
The High Art of the Low Countries - BBC
Highlands and Islands: Where Scotland's Heart Beats Loudest - AMZ
High Times - AMZ
Him & Her - Pluto
Him - BritBox
Hinterland - Netflix
Hiroshima: The Real History - BBC
His Dark Materials - HBO
Historic Hauntings (aka Castle Ghosts of England) - AMZ
History 101 - Netflix
History Cold Case - IMDb, Pluto
A History of Ancient Britain - BritBox
The Hitchhiker's Guide to the Galaxy - BritBox, AMZ, Hulu
Hitler's Circle of Evil - Netflix

Hitmen - Peacock
Hoarders, Get Your House in Order - I/O
Hoarder SOS - I/O
Hoff the Record - Netflix
Holbein: Eye of the Tudors - AMZ
Holby City - BritBox
Hold the Dream - AMZ
Hold the Sunset - BritBox
The Hollies: Look Through Any Window - IMDb, Pluto
Hollyoaks - Hulu, Tubi
Home & Away - AMZ
Home - HBO
Home Away from Home - BritBox
Home Fires - AMZ
Homefront - BritBox, Tubi, Peacock
Home of Fabulous Cakes - IMDb
Homes By Design - Tubi
The Home Show - AMZ
Homes Under the Hammer - I/O
Honest - AMZ
Honey, I Bought the House - Tubi
Honour - BritBox
Horrible Histories - AMZ, Hulu
Horrible Histories: Formidable Florence Nightingale - BritBox
Horrid Henry - Netflix
The Hotel - Tubi
The Hotel Fixers - AMZ
Hotel Secrets with Richard E. Grant - BBC
Hound of the Baskervilles - BritBox
The Hour - Acorn TV, Pluto
The House of Cards Trilogy - AMZ
House of Saud - BBC
House Swap - I/O
The House that 100k (GBP) Built - AMZ, Tubi
The House that 100k Built: Tricks of the Trade - IMDb, Tubi
The House that Dripped Blood - Tubi

Howards End - AMZ, Starz
How Gay is Pakistan? - Topic
How to Get Ahead - AMZ
How to Go Viral - BBC
How to Haggle for a House - I/O
How to Live Mortgage Free with Sarah Beeny - Netflix
Huge Moves - AMZ
Hugh the Hunter - Topic
Humans - AMZ
Hunderby - AMZ, Hulu
Hunted - Cinemax
Husbands from Hell - Tubi
Hustle - AMZ, Tubi, Pluto
Hyperdrive - AMZ
I, Claudius - Acorn TV
I Am a Killer - Netflix
I Am a Killer: Released - Netflix
The Ice House - BritBox
Icelandic Tails - AMZ
Idiomatic - Sundance
Idris Elba: King of Speed - IMDb
I Hate Suzie - HBO
The Image You Missed - Topic
Imagine a School: Summerhill - Pluto
I May Destroy You - HBO
The Impressionists - AMZ, IMDb
The Impressionists with Tim Marlow - AMZ
In and Out of Hell: The Meat Loaf Story - BBC
The Inbestigators - Netflix
The Inbetweeners - AMZ, Tubi
The Inbetweeners Movie - Tubi
The Incredible Journey of Mary Bryant - IMDb, Pluto
In Deep - Acorn TV
The Indian Detective - Netflix
The Indian Doctor - Acorn TV, AMZ
Industry - HBO
Injustice - Acorn TV, AMZ
In Louboutin's Shoes - BBC
In My Skin - Hulu

Innocent - Sundance
The Innocents - Netflix
In Plain Sight - BritBox
In Search of Frida Kahlo - BBC
Insert Name Here - BritBox
Inside Broadmoor - AMZ
Inside Claridge's - BritBox
Inside Men - Pluto
Inside No. 9 - BritBox, Hulu, HBO
Inside the Ambulance - IMDb, Tubi
Inside the Billionaire's Wardrobe - BBC
Inside the Freemasons - Netflix
Inside the Merchant - AMZ
Inside the Real Narcos - Netflix
Inside the Tower of London: Crimes, Conspiracies, Confessions - IMDb
Inside the World's Toughest Prisons - Netflix
An Inspector Calls - BritBox
The Inspector Lynley Mysteries - BritBox
Inspector Morse - BritBox
The Instant Gardener - BritBox
Intelligence (05) - Netflix
Intelligence (20) - Peacock
Interior Design Masters - Netflix
Interview with a Murderer - Sundance
In the Dark - BritBox
In the Flesh - AMZ, Hulu
In the Long Run - Starz
In Toni's Footsteps: The Channel Islands Occupation - AMZ
Intruders - AMZ, Hulu, Topic
The Investigator: A British Crime Story - Netflix
The Invisibles - Acorn TV, AMZ
Ireland with Ardal O'Hanlon - AMZ
Ireland's Greatest Robberies - IMDb, Pluto
Ireland's Wild River - AMZ
The Irish Pub - IMDb, Tubi

The Irish R.M. - Acorn TV
Iron Men - AMZ
A is for Acid - IMDb
Isis: The Origins of Violence - BBC
Island at War - IMDb
The Island with Bear Grylls - AMZ, Tubi
Isle of Man: From the Air - AMZ
Isolation Stories - BritBox
It Came From Connemara - IMDb
The IT Crowd - Netflix
It Was 50 Years Ago Today - BBC
It's a Sin - HBO
Ivanhoe - AMZ
I Was Once a Beauty Queen - BBC
I've Got a Job for You Gav - AMZ
Jack Irish - Acorn TV
Jackson's Wharf - IMDb
Jack Taylor - Acorn TV
Jack the Ripper - AMZ
Jack the Ripper: The Definitive Story - AMZ
Jack Whitehall: Christmas With My Father - Netflix
Jack Whitehall: I'm Only Joking - Netflix
Jack Whitehall: Travels with My Father - Netflix
Jack Whitehall at Large - Netflix
James & Thom's Pizza Pilgrimage - Tubi
James Acaster: Repertoire - Netflix
James Martin's Mediterranean - Tubi
James Martin's United Cakes of America - Tubi
James Martin Home Comforts - Tubi
James Martin Home Comforts at Christmas - Tubi
James May's Man Lab - AMZ, Tubi
James May's Toy Stories - AMZ, Tubi
James May: Oh Cook - AMZ

James May: Our Man in Japan - AMZ

James May's Cars of the People - AMZ

Jamie's American Road Trip - Topic

Jamie's Food Escapes - Topic

Jamie's Super Food - Topic

Jamie: Keep Cooking and Carry On - Hulu

Jamie's Quick and Easy Food - Hulu

Jane Austen: Life - AMZ

Jane Austen Country: The Life and Times of Jane Austen - AMZ

Jane Eyre (06) - AMZ, HBO, BritBox, Hulu

Jane Eyre (83) - AMZ, BritBox

Janet King - Acorn TV

Japan with Sue Perkins - BBC

Jason and the Argonauts - Tubi

Jekyll & Hyde - BritBox

Jennie: Lady Randolph Churchill - Acorn TV

Jericho - Acorn TV

Jericho of Scotland Yard - Acorn TV

Jessica - IMDb

Jim Henson's The Storyteller - AMZ

Jimmy Carr: Funny Business - Netflix

Jimmy Carr: The Best of Ultimate Gold Greatest Hits - Netflix

Jimmy Doherty's Escape to the Wild - I/O

Joanna Lumley's Japan - BBC

Joanna Lumley's Trans-Siberian Adventure - BBC

The Job Lot - BritBox

Joe 90 - IMDb

Jonathan Creek - BritBox

Joseph Campbell: Mythos 1 - Acorn TV

The Joy of Techs - IMDb

The Joy of Winning - BBC

Julius Caesar (1979) - BritBox

Julius Caesar with Mary Beard - IMDb

The Jury - BritBox, IMDb

Just Another Immigrant - Showtime

Justice - BritBox

Just William - Acorn TV

K9 & Company: A Girl's Best Friend - BritBox, Pluto

Kat & Alfie: Redwater - BritBox

Kate & Koji - BritBox

Kate: The Making of a Modern Queen - AMZ

Kath & Kim - Netflix

Kavanagh QC - BritBox, IMDb, Tubi, Pluto

Keeping Faith - Acorn TV

Keeping the Castle - Acorn TV

Keeping Up Appearances - BritBox

Keith Richards: Under the Influence - Netflix

The Kennedys - AMZ, Hulu

Kevin McCloud's Escape to the Wild - I/O

Keys to the Castle - AMZ

Kids on the Edge - Tubi

Killed By My Debt - BritBox

Killer Net - Acorn TV

Killer Roads - Tubi

Killer Women with Piers Morgan - Netflix

The Killer Years - BBC

Killing Eve - Hulu

Kim's Convenience - Netflix

King Arthur's Lost Kingdom - AMZ

Kingdom - Acorn TV, AMZ

King Gary - AMZ

King Lear (18) - AMZ

King Lear (82) - BritBox

King of Scots - AMZ

Kirstie's Vintage Home - BritBox

Kiss Me First - Netflix

Kitchen Criminals - I/O

Kitchen Nightmares - IMDb, Hulu

Know the British - AMZ

Kolkata with Sue Perkins - BBC

Kylie's Secret Night - BBC

Labyrinth - AMZ, Tubi

Ladette to Lady - Tubi

Ladhood - Hulu

Ladies of Letters - Acorn TV

Lady Chatterley - Acorn TV

Laid - IMDb

Land Girls - Acorn TV, Netflix

Lanester - AMZ

Lark Rise to Candleford - BritBox, Hulu

Last Contact - AMZ

The Last Days of Anne Boleyn - IMDb

The Last Detective - BritBox

The Last Kingdom - Netflix

Last of the Summer Wine - BritBox

The Last Post - AMZ

Last Tango in Halifax - Netflix

Laura McKenzie's Traveler - Tubi

Law & Order: UK - Sundance, Tubi

The League of Gentlemen - BritBox

Leaving Amish Paradise - BBC

Legends - IMDb, Hulu

Legends of King Arthur - IMDb

Legends of Power with Tony Robinson - AMZ

Len and Ainsley's Big Food Adventure - IMDb

The Letdown - Netflix

The Letter for the King - Netflix

The Level - Acorn TV

Leverage - Sundance

Liar - Sundance

Licence to Thrill: Paul Hollywood Meets Aston Martin - BritBox

The Life & Crimes of William Palmer - IMDb

The Life and Death of King John (1984) - BritBox

Life in a Cottage Garden - BritBox

Life in Squares - AMZ

Life of Crime - BritBox

The Life of Verdi - Acorn TV

Life on Mars - BritBox

Life's Too Short - HBO

The Lights Before Christmas

- BritBox
The Lights Before Christmas: Luminous London - BritBox
The Lilac Bus - Acorn TV
Lillie - IMDb
Lily Allen: From Riches to Rags - IMDb
Line of Duty - Acorn TV, BritBox, AMZ, Hulu
Lip Service - Tubi
Little Baby Bum - Netflix
Little Boy Blue - BritBox
Little Britain USA - HBO
Little Devil - AMZ
Little Dorrit (08) - AMZ, Pluto
Little Dorrit (87) - Starz
The Little Drummer Girl - Sundance
Liverpool 1 - Acorn TV, AMZ, Tubi
Lives in the House of Windsor - AMZ
The Living & the Dead - AMZ
Living in the Shadow of World War II - Acorn TV, AMZ
Living the Dream - BritBox
Living the Tradition: An Enchanting Journey into Old Irish Airs -

IMDb
Loaded - Netflix
Location, Location, Location - Tubi
Loch Ness - Acorn TV
London: A City in Time - AMZ
London: A Tale of Two Cities - AMZ
London Irish - IMDb, Tubi
London Kills - Acorn TV
London Road - BritBox
London Spy - Netflix
London's Burning - IMDb
Looking for Victoria - BritBox
Lord Montagu - AMZ
Lorna Doone (00) - AMZ
Lorna Doone (76) - Acorn TV
Lost in Austen - Tubi, BritBox
Lost in France - Topic

The Lost Village - AMZ
Louis Theroux - BritBox
Louis Theroux: A Different Brain - BBC
Louis Theroux: Altered States - Choosing Death - BBC, Topic
Louis Theroux: Altered States - Love Without Limits - BBC
Louis Theroux: Altered States - Take My Baby - BBC, Topic
Louis Theroux: Beware of the Tiger - BBC
Louis Theroux: Drinking to Oblivion - BBC
Louis Theroux: Extreme Love - Autism - BBC
Louis Theroux: Extreme Love - Dementia - BBC
Louis Theroux: LA Stories - City of Dogs - BBC
Louis Theroux: LA Stories - Edge of Life - BBC
Louis Theroux: Law and Disorder in Johannesburg - BBC
Louis Theroux: Law and Disorder in Lagos - BBC
Louis Theroux: Miami Mega Jail - BBC
Louis Theroux: Most Hated Family in America - BBC
Louis Theroux: Mothers on the Edge - BBC
Louis Theroux: Selling Sex - BBC
Louis Theroux: Surviving America's Most Hated Family - BBC
Louis Theroux: Talking to Anorexia - BBC
Louis Theroux: The Night in Question - BBC
Louis Theroux: The Return of America's Most Hated Family - BBC
Louis Theroux: The Ultra Zionists - BBC
Louis Theroux: Under the Knife - BBC
Louis Theroux Collection - HBO

Love & Marriage - AMZ
Love, Lies, & Records - Acorn TV
Love/Hate - IMDb
Love Hurts - Acorn TV
Love in a Cold Climate - AMZ
Love Island - Hulu
Lovejoy - Acorn TV, PBS
Love Lies Bleeding - IMDb
Love London - AMZ, Pluto
Love My Way - Acorn TV, Tubi
Lovesick (aka Scrotal Recall) - Netflix
Love Your Garden - I/O
Love's Labour's Lost (85) - BritBox
Lucifer - Netflix
Lucy Worsley's 12 Days of Tudor Christmas - PBS
Lucy Worsley's Royal Myths and Secrets - PBS
The Luminaries - Starz
Lunch Monkeys - IMDb, Tubi
Lupin - Netflix
Luther - Hulu, Starz, HBO
L'Accident - Acorn TV
Macbeth (83) - BritBox
The Machine That Made Us - AMZ
Madame Bovary (00) - AMZ
Madame Bovary (14) - Sundance
Mad Dog: Inside the Secret World of Muammar Gaddafi - BBC
Made Over By - Tubi
The Magical World of Trains - AMZ
Magic Numbers: Hannah Fry's Mysterious World of Maths - Acorn TV, AMZ
Maigret (16) - BritBox
Maigret (92) - BritBox
Make Me Perfect - Tubi
Make My Home Bigger - AMZ, Tubi
The Making of Merkel - BBC
The Mallorca Files - BritBox
Man & Beast with Martin Clunes - AMZ
Man Down - Netflix
Manet & the Birth of Impressionism - IMDb

Manhunt - Acorn TV
Man in an Orange Shirt - PBS
Man Like Mobeen - Netflix
Mansfield Park (07) - PBS
Mansfield Park (83) - AMZ
Man Stroke Woman - Pluto
The Man Who Cracked the Nazi Code - IMDb
The Man Who Killed Richard III - IMDb
The Man Who Lost His Head - Acorn TV
The Man Who Shot Vietnam - BBC
Mapp and Lucia (14) - BritBox
Mapp and Lucia (85) - BritBox
Marcella - Netflix
Marco's Great British Feast - BritBox, Tubi
Margaret - BritBox
Margaret: The Rebel Princess - PBS
Market Forces - IMDb
Market Kitchen - I/O
Mark Zuckerberg: Inside Facebook - BBC
Marley's Ghosts - BritBox
Married Single Other - IMDb
Married to a Celebrity - Tubi
Martin Chuzzlewit - AMZ
Martin Clunes & a Lion Called Mugie - IMDb
Martin Clunes: A Man and His Dogs - IMDb
Martin Clunes: Heavy Horsepower - IMDb
Martin Clunes: Islands of America - Acorn TV
Martin Clunes: Islands of Australia - Acorn TV
Martin Clunes: Last Lemur Standing - IMDb
Martin Clunes: Man to Manta - AMZ
Marvellous - Acorn TV
Mary Berry's Foolproof Cooking - Tubi
Mary Berry's Absolute Favourites - BritBox
Mary Berry's Country House Secrets - BritBox

Masterpiece - Tubi
Masterpiece: Indian Summers - AMZ
Masterpiece: The Chaperone - PBS
Masterpiece: Wind in the Willows - PBS
Maxxx - Hulu
Mayday - Acorn TV, AMZ
The Mayor of Casterbridge - Acorn TV
McCallum - Acorn TV, AMZ
McDonald & Dodds - BritBox
McLeod's Daughters - Acorn TV, IMDb, Tubi
McMafia - Sundance
Me, My Selfie, and I - BBC
Me and My Penis - BBC
The Meaning of Monty Python - Netflix
Measure for Measure (1979) - BritBox
Medieval Lives - Acorn TV
Medieval Paranormal Activity - AMZ
Meerkat Manor - AMC+
Meet the Adebanjos - Netflix
Meet the Romans - IMDb
Meet the Trumps: From Immigrant to President - BBC
Meet the Young Americans - BBC
The Mekong River with Sue Perkins - BBC
Memories of Scotland - AMZ
Men Behaving Badly - IMDb
Men in Kilts - Starz
The Merchant of Venice (1980) - BritBox
Merlin - AMZ, Netflix, Hulu, Pluto
Merlin's Apprentice - Tubi
The Merry Wives of Windsor (1982) - BritBox
MI-5 - BritBox
Michael McIntyre: Showman - Netflix
Middlemarch - AMZ
Midsomer Murders - Acorn TV, BritBox, IMDb, Tubi, Pluto
Midsomer Murders: 20th

Anniversary Documentary - BritBox
Midsomer Murders: 20th Anniversary Special - Acorn TV
Midsomer Murders: Neil Dudgeon's Top 10 - Acorn TV
Midsomer Murders Favourites - BritBox
A Midsummer Night's Dream (16) - BritBox
A Midsummer Night's Dream (81) - BritBox
The Mighty Boosh - AMZ, Hulu
The Mill - AMZ, Tubi
Millionaire Basement Wars - Tubi
Million Dollar Wedding Planner - BBC
Million Pound Menu - Netflix
Mind Games - Acorn TV
Minding Our Manors - AMZ
Mind Your Language - IMDb
The Miniaturist - PBS
Miranda - IMDb, Hulu
Miriam's Big American Adventure - Topic
The Misadventures of Romesh Ranganathan - HBO
Misfits - Hulu
Miss Austen Regrets - BritBox, AMZ
Miss Fisher & The Crypt of Tears - Acorn TV
Miss Fisher's Murder Mysteries - Acorn TV
Missing - Acorn TV
The Missing - AMZ, Starz
Missing Persons Unit - IMDb
Miss Marple - BritBox
Miss Scarlet and the Duke - PBS
Miss Sherlock - HBO
The Mitfords: A Tale of Two Sisters - Netflix
The Mixer - IMDb
Mo - BritBox
Mobile - IMDb
Moby Dick (11) - AMZ
Moby Dick (98) - AMZ

Mock the Week - BritBox
Modern Irish Food - Tubi
Moll Flanders - Tubi
Mom P.I. - IMDb
Monarch of the Glen - Pluto
The Monarchy - BritBox
Monday, Monday - Acorn TV
Monkman & Seagull's Genius Guide to Britain - Topic
Monroe - IMDb
Monty Don's Paradise Gardens - Acorn TV
Monty Python's Almost the Truth - Netflix
Monty Python's Fliegender Zircus - Netflix
Monty Python's Flying Circus - Netflix
Monty Python's Life of Brian - Netflix
Monty Python's Personal Best - Netflix
Monty Python: The Meaning of Live - Netflix
Monty Python and the Holy Grail - Netflix
Monty Python Before the Flying Circus - Netflix
Monty Python Best Bits - Netflix
Monty Python Conquers America - Netflix
Monty Python Live (Mostly): One Down, Five to Go - Netflix
Monty Python Live at Aspen - Netflix
Monty Python Live at the Hollywood Bowl - Netflix
Monumental Challenge - BritBox
The Moodys - Acorn TV
Moone Boy - AMZ, Hulu
The Moonstone (16) - BritBox, AMZ
The Moonstone (72) - BritBox
The Moorside - BritBox
The Moors Murders - AMZ
More Manners of Downton Abbey - Peacock
Morphle - Netflix
Moses Jones - Topic

Most Haunted - AMZ, IMDb
MotherFatherSon - Starz
Motherland - Sundance
Mother's Day - BritBox
Motorheads - HBO
Mount Pleasant - Acorn TV
Mount Royal - IMDb
Moving On - BritBox
Mr. and Mrs. Murder - Acorn TV
Mr. Bean - BritBox, AMZ. Hulu, Pluto
Mr. Selfridge - PBS
Mr. Stink - BritBox
Mrs. Biggs - Acorn TV
The Mrs. Bradley Mysteries - BritBox
Mrs. Brown - BritBox
Mrs. Brown's Boys - BritBox
Ms. Fisher's Modern Murder Mysteries - Acorn TV
Much Ado About Nothing (1984) - BritBox
Mum - BritBox
Mummy's Little Murderer - IMDb
Murder, Mystery, and My Family - BritBox
Murder, She Wrote - Peacock
Murder 24/7: True Crime/Real Time - BBC
Murder Call - AMZ
Murder City - AMZ
The Murder Detectives - BBC
Murdered by My Boyfriend - BritBox
Murdered by My Father - BritBox
Murdered for Being Different - BritBox
Murderers & Their Mothers - AMZ
Murder Investigation Team - Acorn TV
Murderland - Acorn TV
Murder Maps - Netflix
The Murders at White House Farm - HBO
Murdertown - AMZ
Murder Trial: The Disappearance of Margaret Fleming -

Sundance
Murdoch Mysteries - Acorn TV, Hulu
Murdoch Mysteries: The Movies - Acorn TV
Murphy's Law - AMZ, Tubi, Acorn TV
Muse of Fire: A Shakespearean Road Movie - Acorn TV
A Music Lover's Guide to Murdoch Mysteries - Acorn TV
The Musketeers - Hulu, Pluto
Muslim Beauty Pageants and Me - BBC
My Beautiful Broken Brain - Netflix
My Boy Jack - BritBox
My Dream Derelict Home - AMZ
My Dream Farm - AMZ
My Family - Pluto
My Flat Pack Home - Tubi
My Hotter Half - Netflix
My Kitchen Rules - Pluto
My Life is Murder - Acorn TV
My Life on a Plate - Tubi
My Mad Fat Diary - Hulu
My Mother & Other Strangers - AMZ
My Pet Shame - Tubi
Mysteries of Stonehenge - AMZ
The Mystery of Agatha Christie with David Suchet - AMZ
The Mystery of a Hansom Cab - Acorn TV
The Mystery of Mary Magdalene - BritBox
Mystery of the Missing Princess - BBC
Mystery Road - Acorn TV
Myths and Monsters - Netflix
My Uncle Silas - IMDb
My Welsh Sheepdog - Acorn TV, AMZ
Nadiya's Time to Eat - Netflix
Nadiya Bakes - Netflix
The Name of the Rose -

Sundance
Narnia's Lost Poet: The Secret Lives and Loves of C.S. Lewis - Acorn TV, AMZ
Narrowboat Houseboating Through the English Countryside - AMZ
National Treasure - Hulu
A Nation Divided: The Charlie Hebdo Aftermath - BBC
The Nativity - AMZ
Nature's Treasure Islands - IMDb, Pluto
Neighbourhood Blues - AMZ
Neil Gaiman's Neverwhere - Pluto
Nero: The Obscure Face of Power - Tubi
The Nest - Acorn TV
Neverland - AMZ
The Nevers - HBO
New Blood - BritBox
The New Tomorrow - IMDb, Tubi, Pluto
Newton's Law - Acorn TV
New Tricks - AMZ, Hulu
New Worlds - Acorn TV
Newzoids - BritBox
Next of Kin - Sundance
Nick Knowles: Original Home Restoration - Tubi
Nigellissima - BritBox
Nigel Slater Eating Together - Tubi
The Night Caller - Sundance
Nightflyers - Netflix
The Night Manager - AMZ
The Nightmare Worlds of HG Wells - IMDb
The Nile: 5000 Years of History - Acorn TV, AMZ
The No. 1 Ladies' Detective Agency - HBO
No Offence - Acorn TV
No Ordinary Party - Tubi
Normal People - Hulu
The Norman Conquests - Acorn TV
Northern Lights - BritBox
No Tears - Acorn TV
Nothing Trivial - IMDb

Not Safe for Work - BritBox, Topic
Not the Nine O'Clock News - BritBox
Noughts & Crosses - Peacock
The Nude in Art - AMZ
The Nurse - AMZ
Nurses Who Kill - Netflix
Nursing the Nation - Tubi
NW - BritBox
NY-LON - AMZ
Obsessed with My Body - BBC
The Octonauts - Netflix
The Office - BritBox, AMZ, Hulu, Topic, HBO
Offspring - Netflix
Off the Beaten Track - Acorn TV
The Oldenheim 12 - Acorn TV
Older Than Ireland - IMDb, Tubi
Oliver Twist (07) - AMZ, Hulu
Oliver Twist (85) - AMZ, BritBox
One Born Every Minute - IMDb, Tubi
One Born Every Minute UK: What Happened Next? - Tubi
One Deadly Weekend in America: A Killing at the Carwash - BBC
One Foot in the Grave - BritBox
One Lane Bridge - Acorn TV, Sundance
One Night - BritBox
One Night Stand with Anne Sibonney - IMDb
Only Foals & Horses - Acorn TV
Only Fools and Horses - BritBox
The Only Way is Essex - AMZ, Hulu, Tubi, Pluto
Only When I Laugh - IMDb
On the Ballykissangel Trail - AMZ
On the Whisky Trail: The History of Scotland's Famous Drink - AMZ

On the Yorkshire Buses - IMDb
Open All Hours - BritBox
Operation Homefront - I/O
Operation Ouch - Netflix
Ordinary Lies - BritBox
Orphan Black - AMC+
Othello (81) - BritBox
The Other One - Acorn TV
The Other Wife - Tubi
Our Cops in the North - BritBox
Our Friends in the North - BritBox
Our Girl - BritBox, AMZ, Tubi
Our Godfather - Netflix
Our Mutual Friend - AMZ
Outlander - Netflix, Starz
Outnumbered - AMZ, Tubi
Outrageous Fortune - IMDb, Tubi
The Outsider - HBO
Over the Rainbow - Acorn TV
Oxford Street Revealed - Tubi
Oz & James's Big Wine Adventure - Tubi
Pablo - Netflix
The Palace - IMDb, Pluto
The Pale Horse - AMZ
Panorama: Fighting Coronavirus - The Scientific Battle - BritBox
Parade's End - HBO
The Paradise - AMZ
Paradox - AMZ, Hulu
Paranoid - Netflix
Parents - Acorn TV, IMDb, Tubi
Park Life: London - Tubi
Party Tricks - Acorn TV, IMDb
The Passing Bells - AMZ, BritBox
Patrick Melrose - Showtime
Paul Gauguin: Paradise Beyond the Horizon - AMZ
Paul Hollywood's Big Continental Road Trip - Netflix
Paul Hollywood's Pies & Puds - I/O
Paul O'Grady: For the Love

of Dogs - BritBox

Pawnbrokers - AMZ

Peak Practice - IMDb, Tubi, Pluto

Peaky Blinders - Netflix

Peep Show - AMZ, Hulu, Tubi

Penance - Sundance

Penelope Keith's Hidden Coastal Villages - Acorn TV

Penelope Keith's Hidden Villages - Acorn TV, AMZ

Penelope Keith's Village of the Year - Acorn TV

Penny Dreadful - Showtime

Penny Dreadful: City of Angels - Showtime

Penny Slinger: Out of the Shadows - Topic

People Just Do Nothing - Netflix

People Like Us - AMZ

Pericles, Prince of Tyre (84) - BritBox

Perry Mason - HBO

Personal Services Required - Tubi

Pete vs. Life - IMDb, Pluto

The Petrol Age - AMZ

Pet School - AMZ

The Pickwick Papers - AMZ

Picnic at Hanging Rock - AMZ

Pie in the Sky - Acorn TV

The Pillars of the Earth - Starz

Pine Gap - Netflix

Pinocchio - AMZ

Pitching In - Acorn TV

Place of Execution - Acorn TV

A Place to Call Home - Acorn TV

The Plastic Surgery Capital of the World - BBC

Playing for Keeps - Sundance

Plebs - Tubi

Plus One - AMZ, Tubi

Pointless - BritBox

Poirot: Super Sleuths - Acorn TV

The Poison Tree - Acorn TV

Poldark (15) - AMZ

Poldark (75) - Acorn TV

Poldark (96) - AMZ

Pompeii: The Last Day - BritBox

Pompidou - AMZ

Porridge (16) - BritBox

Porridge (74) - BritBox

Porterhouse Blue - AMZ, Tubi

Posh Neighbours at War - AMZ

Power and the World's Women - BBC

Pramface - AMZ

The Pregnant Man - BBC

Preserved Lines - AMZ

Prey - AMZ, Hulu

Pride & Prejudice (95) - Hulu, BritBox

Pride and Prejudice (80) - AMZ, BritBox

Prime Minister's Questions - BritBox

Prime Suspect - BritBox, Hulu

Prime Suspect: Tennison - AMZ

Primeval - Hulu, Pluto

Prince Charles: The Royal Restoration - AMZ

Princess Diana: A Life After Death - AMC+

Princess Margaret: Her Real Life Story - AMZ

Prison: First and Last 24 Hours - Pluto

The Prisoner - AMZ, Tubi

The Prisoner of Zenda - AMZ

Prisoners' Wives - Acorn TV, AMZ, Tubi

The Private Lives of the Tudors - AMZ

Project Restoration - AMZ, Tubi

The Promised Life - Acorn TV

Proof - AMZ

The Protectors - IMDb

Psychoville - BritBox

Public Enemies - Acorn TV, AMZ

Pulp: A Film About Life, Death and Supermarkets - Topic

Puppy Love - BritBox

Pure - HBO

Putin: A Russian Spy Story - BBC

Putin's Russia - BBC

QB VII - AMZ, Pluto

QI - BritBox

The Quatermass Experiment - BritBox

A Queen is Crowned - BritBox

Queens: The Virgin & the Martyr - Tubi

Queens of Mystery - Acorn TV

Queen Victoria's Letters: A Monarch Unveiled - AMZ

The Queen's Gambit - Netflix

Queer as Folk - AMZ, Tubi

Queers - AMC+

Question Time - BritBox

Quicksand - Netflix

Quirke - BritBox

Quiz - AMC+

Quizeum - Tubi

Rachel Allen: All Things Sweet - AMZ, Pluto

Rachel Allen: Easy Meals - Pluto, AMZ

Rachel Allen Home Cooking - Tubi

Rachel Allen's Cake Diaries - AMZ, Pluto

Rachel Allen's Dinner Parties - Tubi

Rachel Allen's Everyday Kitchen - AMZ

Rachel Khoo's Cosmopolitan Cook - Pluto

Rachel Khoo's Kitchen Notebook: London - BritBox

Rachel's Coastal Cooking - BritBox

The Rain - Netflix

The Rainbow - AMZ

Raised by Wolves - Acorn TV

Rake - Acorn TV, AMZ, Netflix

Rallying: The Killer Years - BBC

Rat Pack: A Conference of

Cool - BBC
Reagan - BBC
Real Crime: Diamond Geezers - Netflix
Real Crime: Supermarket Heist - Netflix
The Real Des - Sundance
The Real Middle Earth - IMDb
The Real Prince Philip - Acorn TV
Rebecca - PBS
Rebecka Martinsson - Acorn TV
The Rebel - Acorn TV
Rebellion - Netflix, AMC+
Rebus - Acorn TV, BritBox
Red Dwarf - BritBox
Red Rock - AMZ
The Red Shadows - Sundance
Reg - BritBox
Reggie Perrin - Acorn TV, AMZ
Reggie Yates in China - BBC
Reilly, Ace of Spies - PBS
Relative Strangers - Acorn TV
Rellik - Cinemax
Remarkable Places to Eat - Tubi
Remastered - BritBox
Rembrandt - BBC
Remember Me - PBS
Renaissance Unchained - IMDb
The Repair Shop - Netflix
Republic of Doyle - AMZ, Netflix
Requiem - Netflix
Rescue Me - IMDb
The Restaurant - Sundance
Restaurant in Our Living Room - Tubi
Restless - Acorn TV
Restoration Home - IMDb, Tubi
Restoration Man - IMDb, Tubi
Restoration Man Best Builds - Tubi
Retail Therapy - Tubi
Retribution - Netflix
The Return - Acorn TV

The Returned - Sundance
Return of the Black Death - AMZ
Rev. - BritBox
Richard II (1979) - BritBox
Richard Wilson On the Road - AMZ, Pluto
Rick Steves' Europe - AMZ
Ricky Gervais: Humanity - Netflix
Rillington Place - Sundance
The Ripper - Netflix
Ripper Street - Netflix
Ripping Yarns - BritBox
The Rise of Female Violence - BBC
The Rise of the Murdoch Dynasty - BBC
The Rise of the Nazi Party - Acorn TV
Rita - Netflix
The Rivals of Sherlock Holmes - Acorn TV
River - AMZ
Riviera - Sundance
Roadkill - PBS
Robin Hood - AMZ, Pluto
Robin of Sherwood - AMZ
Robozuna - Netflix
Robson Green's Wild Swimming Adventure - AMZ
Rocket's Island - IMDb
Rock 'n' Roll Guns for Hire: The Story of the Sidemen - BBC
Rococo Before Bedtime - Acorn TV, IMDb
Rolling Stones: Olé Olé Olé! - Netflix
Roman Britain: From the Air - AMZ
Roman Empire - Netflix
Roman Mysteries - IMDb
Rome: Empire Without Limit - Acorn TV, AMZ
Romeo and Juliet (1978) - BritBox
The Rook - Starz
Room at the Top - AMZ
Room to Improve - IMDb, Tubi
Rosamund Pilcher's September - Tubi

Rose & Maloney - AMZ
Rosemary & Thyme - BritBox
Ross Kemp: Back on the Frontline - IMDb
Ross Kemp: Return to Afghanistan - IMDb
Rovers - IMDb, Pluto
Rowan Atkinson Presents: Canned Laughter - BritBox
The Royal - BritBox, IMDb, Tubi
The Royal Bodyguard - Tubi
Royal Britain: An Aerial History of the Monarchy - AMZ
Royal Celebration - BritBox
Royal Cousins at War - BBC
A Royal Hangover - AMZ
The Royal House of Windsor - Netflix
Royal Paintbox - PBS
Royals & Animals: 'Til Death Do Us Part - AMZ
The Royals - AMZ
The Royal Today - BritBox
A Royal Tour of the 20th Century - Acorn TV
Royal Upstairs Downstairs - I/O
Royal Wives at War - PBS
The Royle Family - AMZ
Rubens: An Extra Large Story - IMDb
Rugged Wales - Pluto
Rumpole of the Bailey - Acorn TV, PBS
Run (13) - Acorn TV, AMZ, Topic
Run (20) - HBO
Rural Britain: A Novel Approach - AMZ
Russell Howard: Recalibrate - Netflix
Russia 1917: Countdown to Revolution - BBC
The Ruth Rendell Mysteries - IMDb
The Ruth Rendell Mysteries: Next Chapters - BritBox
Safe - Netflix
Safe House - Sundance
The Saint - Acorn TV, IMDb, Tubi

The Salisbury Poisonings - AMC+
Sally4Ever - HBO
Sally Lockhart Mysteries - BritBox
Salt Beef and Rye - AMZ, Tubi
Sam's Game - IMDb
Sanctuary - Sundance
The Sandbaggers - BritBox, Tubi
Sanditon - PBS
Sando - Acorn TV
Sapphire and Steel - IMDb
Sara Dane - IMDb
Sarah Jane Adventures - HBO
Save Me - Peacock
Savile Row - Acorn TV
Saving Britain's Worst Zoo - Acorn TV
The Scapegoat - Acorn TV
Scapegoat - IMDb
Scarborough - BritBox
The Scarlet Pimpernel - Acorn TV
Scarlet Woman: The True Story of Mary Magdalene - AMZ
Schitt's Creek - Netflix
The Schouwendam 12 - Acorn TV
Scotch! The Story of Whisky - AMZ, Tubi
Scotch: A Golden Dream - Tubi
Scott & Bailey - BritBox, AMZ, Hulu, HBO
The Scottish Covenanters - AMZ
Scottish Myths and Legends - AMZ
Seachange - Acorn TV
Seachange: Paradise Reclaimed - Acorn TV
Sean Bean on Waterloo - AMZ
The Seasoned Traveler: Scottish Castles - AMZ
Second Sight - AMZ
The Secret - Acorn TV
Secret Agent - Tubi
Secret City - Netflix
Secret Daughter - Acorn TV

Secret Diary of a Call Girl - Tubi
Secret Eaters - Tubi
Secret Gardens - AMZ
The Secret History of the British Garden - Acorn TV, I/O
The Secret Identity of Jack the Ripper - AMZ
The Secret Life of Michael Fry - AMZ
The Secret Life of Us - AMZ
Secret Nature - IMDb
The Secret of Crickley Hall - AMZ, Hulu
Secret Removers - I/O
Secret Rules of Modern Living: Algorithm - BBC
Secrets and Lies - IMDb
Secrets from the Sky - BritBox
Secret Smile - IMDb
Secrets of a Psychopath - Sundance
Secrets of Britain - PBS
Secrets of Britain's Great Cathedrals - PBS
Secrets of Great British Castles - Netflix
Secrets of Highclere Castle - PBS
Secrets of Iconic British Estates - PBS
Secrets of Silicon Valley - BBC
Secrets of South America - BBC
Secrets of Sugar Baby Dating - BBC
Secrets of the Castle - AMZ
Secrets of the Irish Landscape - IMDb
Secrets of the Magna Carta - AMZ
Secrets of the Manor House - PBS
Secrets of the Six Wives - PBS
Secrets of the Stones - Tubi
The Secrets She Keeps - Sundance
Secret State - AMZ, Sundance, Tubi
See No Evil: The Moors

Murders - IMDb
Seesaw - Acorn TV, AMZ
Sense & Sensibility (08) - Hulu
Sense and Sensibility (08) - AMZ
Sense and Sensibility (81) - AMZ
Sensitive Skin - Acorn TV
Serial Killer with Piers Morgan - Netflix
Serving the Royals: Inside the Firm - AMZ
Seven Wonders of the Commonwealth - BritBox
Sex, Death, and the Meaning of Life - BBC
Sex and the Church - BBC
The Sex Changes That Made History - BBC
Sex Education - Netflix
Sex Pistols: Agents of Anarchy - AMZ
The Shadow Line - Pluto
Shadow Lines - Sundance
Shakespeare & Hathaway - BritBox
The Shakespeare Collection - BritBox
Shakespeare in Italy - BritBox
Shakespeare's Stratford - AMZ
Shameless (US) - Netflix, Showtime
Shameless - Hulu, Pluto
The Shard: Hotel in the Clouds - BritBox
Sharon Horgan's Women - AMZ
Sharpe - BritBox
Shaun the Sheep - Netflix
She-Wolves: England's Early Queens - Acorn TV
The Shelbourne Hotel - IMDb, Tubi
Sherlock - Netflix
Sherlock Holmes & the Case of the Silk Stocking - BritBox
Sherlock Holmes - BritBox
Sherlock Holmes: Incident at Victoria Falls - AMZ
Sherlock Holmes: The

Classic Collection - Tubi
Sherlock Holmes Against Conan Doyle - AMZ
Sherlock Holmes and the Leading Lady - AMZ
Shetland - BritBox
Shipwrecked - Hulu
Shock of the Nude - BBC
Shoreline Detectives - IMDb
Shut Up & Play the Hits - Topic
Sick Note - Netflix
The Silence (06) - Acorn TV
The Silence (10) - Acorn TV, IMDb, Pluto
Silent Witness - BritBox, AMZ, Hulu, HBO
Silk - AMZ, Hulu
Simon Amstell: Set Free - Netflix
Simon Schama's Power of Art - BBC
Simon Schama's Shakespeare and Us - BBC
The Simple Heist - Acorn TV
Sinbad - AMZ
Single-Handed - Acorn TV, IMDb
Single Father - BritBox
Singletown - HBO
Sirens - AMZ
The Sister - Hulu
Sisters, aka Sorelle - Acorn TV
Sisters - Netflix
The Six Wives of Henry VIII - BritBox
Skins - Netflix, Hulu
Skye's the Limit - AMZ
The Slap - Acorn TV
Slings & Arrows - Acorn TV, Sundance
Smack the Pony - Tubi
Small Animal Hospital - AMZ, Tubi
Small Axe - AMZ
Small Island - BritBox
Smartphones: The Dark Side - BBC
Smart Travels with Rudy Maxa - IMDb, Tubi
The Smoke - AMZ
Smoke and Steam - AMZ
Snatches - AMC+

Snow Animals - AMC+
Snowdonia 1890 - IMDb, Tubi
Soldier Soldier - IMDb
The Sommerdahl Murders - Acorn TV
A Song for Jenny - BritBox
Song of Granite - Topic
Soundbreaking: Stories from the Cutting Edge of Recorded Music -

Acorn TV
The Sounds - Acorn TV
Soup Cans and Superstars: How Pop Art Changed the World - BBC
The South Westerlies - Acorn TV
Space: 1999 - Tubi
Spaced - IMDb, Hulu, Tubi
The Spanish Princess - Starz
The Special Needs Hotel - IMDb
Speed with Guy Martin - Pluto
Spendaholics - Tubi
Spies of Warsaw - AMZ
Spirit Breaker - AMZ
Spirited - AMZ
Spitting Image - BritBox, AMZ
The Split - Hulu, Sundance
Springwatch - BritBox
Spy - Tubi
Spying on the Royals - PBS
The Spy Who Went Into the Cold - Acorn TV, AMZ
Stacey Dooley Investigates Collection - HBO
Staged - Hulu
Stalin: Inside the Terror - BBC
State of Mind - AMZ
State of the Union - Sundance
Stella Blomkvist - Sundance
Step Dave - IMDb
Stephen Fry: More Fool Me - AMZ
Stephen Tompkinson's Australian Balloon Adventure - AMZ
Steve Jobs: Billion Dollar

Hippy - BBC
Sticks and Stones - BritBox
Still Game - Netflix
Still Life (film) - Topic
Still Life: A Three Pines Mystery (CAN) - Acorn TV
Still Standing - AMZ
Stingray - IMDb
A Stitch in Time - Acorn TV, AMZ
Stonemouth - BritBox
The Story of Europe - AMZ
The Story of London - AMZ
The Story of Luxury - BritBox
The Story of Tea: The History of Tea & How to Make the Perfect Cup -

Tubi
The Story of the Mini - AMZ
The Story of Women and Art - BBC
The Story of Women and Power - AMZ
Straight Forward - Acorn TV, Sundance
Stranded - IMDb
The Strange Calls - Acorn TV
The Stranger - Netflix
The Street - BritBox, IMDb
Street Hospital - Tubi
Streetmate - Tubi
Strike Back - Cinemax
Striking Out - Acorn TV, Sundance
Stunt Science - Netflix
Suffragettes - BritBox, BBC
The Sum of Us - Acorn TV
Sunderland 'Til I Die - Netflix
Sunny Bunnies - Netflix
The Sunshine Makers - Topic
Supermarket Secrets - BritBox
Supernanny - HBO
Supersized Hospitals - Tubi
Supersize vs. Superskinny - Tubi
Super Sleuths: Midsomer Murders - Pluto
Supply and Demand - Acorn TV
Surgeons: At the Edge of Life - AMZ, Pluto

Surgery School - IMDb
The Suspect - Sundance
Suspects - Acorn TV
The Suspicions of Mr. Whicher: Beyond the Pale - BritBox
The Suspicions of Mr. Whicher: The Murder at Road Hill House - BritBox
The Suspicions of Mr. Whicher: The Murder in Angel Lane - BritBox
The Suspicions of Mr. Whicher: The Ties That Bind - BritBox
The Sweeney - BritBox
Swingin' Christmas - BritBox
Switch - IMDb
The Syndicate - IMDb
The Syndicate: All or Nothing - Acorn TV
Taggart - BritBox
The Take - IMDb
Taken Down - Acorn TV
A Tale of Two Cities - AMZ
Tales from the Coast with Robson Green - BritBox
Tales from the Royal Bedchamber - PBS
Tales from the Royal Wardrobe - PBS
Tales of the City - Acorn TV
Tales of the Unexpected - IMDb, Tubi
The Talisman - AMZ
Talking Heads - PBS
Tamara Rojo's Swan Lake - BBC
The Taming of the Shrew (1980) - BritBox
Teachers - Tubi
Tea with the Dames - Hulu, AMC+
The Tempest (1980) - BritBox
The Tenant of Wildfell Hall - AMZ
Terry Jones' Great Map Mystery - IMDb, Pluto
Terry Pratchett's Hogfather - IMDb
Terry Pratchett's Going

Postal - Acorn TV, AMZ, Pluto
Terry Pratchett's The Colour of Magic - Acorn TV
Tess of the D'Urbervilles - AMZ
That's My Boy - IMDb
That Day We Sang - BritBox
Theatreland - Acorn TV
Thelma's Big Irish Communions - Tubi
Then There Were Giants - IMDb
Therese Raquin - Acorn TV
There She Goes - BritBox
They've Gotta Have Us - Netflix
The Thick of It - BritBox, AMZ, Hulu
The Thin Blue Line - BritBox
Thin Ice - Sundance
The Third Day - HBO
Thirteen - AMZ
This Farming Life - BritBox
This is Personal: The Hunt for the Yorkshire Ripper - IMDb
This Way Up - Hulu
Thomas & Friends - Netflix
Thorne - Acorn TV
Thorne: Scaredy Cat - BritBox
Thorne: Sleepyhead - BritBox
Three Girls - BritBox
Threesome - AMZ, Pluto
Three Sovereigns for Sarah - PBS
Thriller - Tubi
Thunderbirds - IMDb
Tidelands - Netflix
The Tigers of Scotland - AMZ
The Time of Our Lives - Acorn TV, AMZ
Time Team - Acorn TV, AMZ, Tubi
Timmy Time - Netflix
Timon of Athens (1981) - BritBox
Tina & Bobby - BritBox
Tin Star - AMZ
Tipping the Velvet - BritBox
Titus Andronicus (1985) - BritBox

Toast of London - Netflix
To Be the Best - AMZ
To Build or Not to Build - Tubi
The Toilet: An Unspoken History - IMDb
Tom Jones - AMZ
Tony Robinson's Gods and Monsters - IMDb
Top Boy - Netflix
Top Gear - HBO
Top of the Lake - Hulu
Torchwood - HBO
Total Control - Sundance
Total Wipeout - Tubi
To the Ends of the Earth - IMDb, Pluto
Touched by Auschwitz - BBC
Touching Evil - IMDb
A Touch of Cloth - AMZ
A Touch of Frost - BritBox
To Walk Invisible: The Brontë Sisters - AMZ
Tower Block Kids - Tubi
Traces - BritBox
Traffik - Acorn TV
The Tragedy of Coriolanus (1984) - BritBox
The Tragedy of Richard III (1983) - BritBox
Trailer Park Boys - Netflix
Train 48 - AMZ
Traitors - Netflix
Transsiberian - Topic
Trauma - BritBox
Trauma Rescue Squad - Tubi
Travelers - Netflix
Travel Man - AMZ
Travels by Narrowboat - AMZ
Travel Scotland with James McCreadie: Trossachs Trip - AMZ
Treasure Houses of Britain - Acorn TV, AMZ
Treasure Island - Pluto
Trial & Retribution - Acorn TV
The Trial of Christine Keeler - HBO
The Tribe - IMDb, Tubi
Trigonometry - HBO
Trinity - Tubi
Trivia - AMZ

Troilus and Cressida (1981) - BritBox

Trolley Dollies - IMDb

Trouble in Poundland - Tubi

The Trouble with Maggie Cole - PBS

Troy: Fall of a City - Netflix

Truckers - IMDb, Tubi, Pluto

Truckers: Eddie Stobart - Pluto

Trust - Acorn TV

Truth Seekers - AMZ

The Truth Will Out - Acorn TV

The Tube: Going Underground - IMDb

Tudor Monastery Farm at Christmas - AMZ

The Tudors - Showtime

The Tunnel - AMZ

Turning Green - Acorn TV

Turn Up Charlie - Netflix

Tutankhamun - BritBox

TV's Black Renaissance: Reggie Yates in Hollywood - BBC

Twelfth Night (1980) - BritBox

Two's Company - IMDb

The Two Gentlemen of Verona (1983) - BritBox

Two Thousand Acres of Sky - IMDb

Two Weeks to Live - HBO

U2 Live in London - BBC

Ugly Beauty - BBC

Ultimate Force - IMDb, Tubi, Pluto

Ultraviolet - Tubi

Uncle - AMZ, Hulu

Undeniable - AMZ, Tubi

Underbelly - IMDb

Undercover - AMZ

The Undoing - HBO

Unfinished Portrait: The Life of Agatha Christie - BritBox

Unforgiven - BritBox

Unforgotten - PBS , AMZ

United - Acorn TV, AMZ

The Unlisted - Netflix

Unreal Estate - Tubi

Upright - Sundance

The Up Series - BritBox

Upstairs Downstairs (10) - BritBox, Hulu

Upstairs Downstairs (71) - BritBox

Upstart Crow - BritBox

Up the Women - BritBox

Valentine Warner's Coast to Coast - Pluto

Van der Valk - PBS

Van Helsing - Netflix

Vanity Fair (18) - AMZ

Vanity Fair (87) - AMZ

Vanity Fair (98) - AMZ

Vera - Acorn TV, BritBox

Vera Postmortem - BritBox

The Very Best of Monty Python's Flying Circus - Netflix

A Very British Coup - AMZ, Tubi

A Very British Murder with Lucy Worsley - BritBox

Very British Problems - IMDb, Tubi

A Very English Scandal - AMZ

Vexed - Acorn TV, IMDb, Netflix, Tubi

The Vicar of Dibley - BritBox

The Vice - IMDb

Vicious - Tubi

The Victim - BritBox

Victoria - AMZ

Victoria and Albert: The Wedding - PBS

Victorian Farm - Tubi

Victorian Farm: Christmas Special - Tubi

Victorian House of Arts and Crafts - Acorn TV

Victoria Wood's A Nice Cup of Tea - Acorn TV

Vidago Palace - Acorn TV

Vienna: Empire, Dynasty, and Dream - BBC

Vienna Blood - PBS

The Village - BritBox, Tubi

Vincent - IMDb, Tubi

Vincent Van Gogh: Painted with Words - BritBox, BBC

Vintage Roads: Great and Small - Acorn TV

Vintage Steam Trains: Great British Steam - AMZ

Virgin Atlantic: Up in the Air - BritBox

Virtual Adultery and Cyberspace Love - BBC

The Virtues - Topic

A Voyage Round My Father - Acorn TV

W1A - Netflix

Wainwright Walks - Acorn TV

Waiting for God - BritBox

Waking the Dead - BritBox

Walking Through History With Tony Robinson - IMDb

Walks Around Britain - AMZ

Walks Around Britain: The Great Glen Way - AMZ

Walks with My Dog - Acorn TV, AMZ, Tubi

Wallander - BritBox, HBO

Wallis Simpson: The Secret Letters - AMZ

Wanderlust - Netflix

Wanted - Netflix

War & Peace - Acorn TV

The War of the Worlds - AMC+

Warren - AMZ, Tubi

Wartime Farm - Acorn TV

Wasted - Hulu

The Watch - AMC+

Watership Down - Netflix

The Way Back - Acorn TV

The Way We Live Now - AMZ

We'll Meet Again - IMDb

Weapons of Mass Production - Topic

Wedding SOS - Tubi

We Hunt Together - Showtime

Wentworth - Netflix

Westside - AMZ, Tubi

What Remains - BritBox

What the Durrells Did Next - PBS

What the Neighbours Did - Tubi

What to Do When Someone Dies - Acorn TV

When Patrick Met Kylie: A Love of Food Story - I/O

Where the Heart Is - IMDb

Whisky: The Islay Edition - IMDb

Whistlestop Edinburgh: Scotland's Beautiful Capital - AMZ

Whitechapel - AMZ, Hulu, HBO

White Dragon - AMZ

White Gold - Netflix

White Heat - BritBox

White Lines - Netflix

White Morning - Topic

The White Princess - Starz

The White Queen - Starz

Whites - Tubi

White Teeth - Acorn TV

White Van Man - IMDb, Tubi

Whose Line Is It Anyway? - Hulu

Wide Sargasso Sea - Acorn TV

The Widow - AMZ

The Widower - PBS

Wild Animal Rescue - Tubi

Wild at Heart - Acorn TV, IMDb. Tubi

Wild Bill - BritBox

Wild City - AMC+

Wild India - AMC+

The Wild Roses - IMDb

The Wild West - BBC

A Wild Year on Earth - AMC+

William & Kate: A Royal Love Story - Pluto

William & Mary - IMDb

William Dobson: The Lost Genius of Baroque - AMZ

William the Conqueror - AMZ

The Windermere Children - PBS

The Windermere Children: In Their Own Words - PBS

Windsor Castle: After the Fire - AMZ

The Windsors - Netflix

The Windsors: A Royal Family - PBS

Wine Oh TV - I/O

Winter - Acorn TV

Winterwatch - BritBox

A Winter's Tale (81) - BritBox

Win the Wilderness - Netflix

The Wipers Times - Acorn TV

Wired - IMDb, Pluto

Wire in the Blood - Acorn TV

Wisting - Acorn TV, Sundance

The Witcher - Netflix

Witches: A Century of Murder - Netflix, Sundance

The Witches of Essex - AMZ

Without Motive - BritBox

The Witness - IMDb, Topic

Wolcott - IMDb

Wolfblood - IMDb, Tubi, Pluto

Wolf Hall - PBS

The Woman in White - PBS

Women in Love - AMZ

The Women of World War One - BritBox, BBC

Wonderland - IMDb

Workin' Moms - Netflix

The World's Most Extraordinary Homes - Netflix

World on Fire - PBS

World War Three: Inside the War Room - BBC

A World Without Down's Syndrome - AMZ

World Without End - Starz

The World's First Computer - BBC

World's Weirdest Homes - BBC

The Worricker Trilogy - PBS

Worst Week of My Life - Acorn TV

The Worst Witch - Netflix

Would I Lie to You? - BritBox, AMZ

WPC 56 - BritBox, AMZ

Wreckers - Acorn TV

The Wrong Mans - Hulu

Wuthering Heights (09) - PBS

Wuthering Heights (12) - Topic

Wycliffe - BritBox, IMDb, Tubi, Pluto

Wyonna Earp - Netflix

Year of the Hedgehog - AMZ

Year of the Rabbit - Topic

Years and Years - HBO

Yes, Minister - BritBox

Yes, Prime Minister - BritBox

York, UK - AMZ

The Yorkshire Vet - Acorn TV, Tubi

You, Me, & Them - Acorn TV, AMZ, Tubi

You Deserve This House - I/O

Young, Gifted, and Classical: The Making of a Maestro - Acorn TV

Young, Rich, and Househunting - Tubi

Young Dracula - IMDb, Pluto

Young Hyacinth - BritBox

Young Lions - AMZ

The Young Person's Guide to Becoming a Rock Star - Tubi

Young Wallander - Netflix

Zapped - HBO

Zen - BritBox

Zomboat! - Hulu

COMMON QUESTIONS

Why am I seeing ads on Amazon?

There are two reasons you may see ads on Amazon:

- You're watching a "free with Prime Video" show. If a show has the "Prime" banner that tells you it's free with membership, it will frequently show ads for other Amazon shows.

- You're watching a show on IMDb TV. It's a free-with-ads service that integrates with Amazon (since Amazon owns IMDb), and it plays all sorts of different ads (not just Amazon show ads).

Sometimes, a show may be on both IMDb TV *and* a subscription service you use. For example, McLeod's Daughters is on both Acorn TV and IMDb TV. It's very easy to accidentally watch the IMDb TV version and get loads of ads.

Though it varies by device, you can usually fix this by going to your computer, visiting Amazon, and adding the show to your watchlist - making sure you're on the page that mentions your subscription.

If you're on a Roku or similar device, you'll often see two options for viewing, and you can select the subscription rather than IMDb TV.

The Amazon system is a bit wild, so in some cases there's an entirely separate show page for the IMDb TV version and the subscription version - and not in others. If you continue to have trouble with it, contact Amazon's support for help.

In some cases, you may find it beneficial to take your subscription direct to the company in question - but of course, some people find that shows stream more smoothly through Amazon, and others just like having all the billing in one central location.

How do I watch these channels on my TV? I don't have a smart TV and I don't want to watch on my laptop or tablet.

There are a lot of different ways you can do this, but we'll focus on the simplest. For around $30 (base model), you can buy a device called a Roku. They sell them at Walmart, Target, Best Buy, Amazon, and even some pharmacies and convenience stores. It's our top recommendation because they're easy to use and the remote control has big print and few buttons.

A Roku plugs into your television and you can connect it to your internet wirelessly. Then, you can add channels like Acorn TV, BritBox, or Tubi. Some are free (like Tubi), while others require you to set up a monthly subscription with the company in question (like Acorn or BritBox).

You also have the option of subscribing to Amazon's Prime Video service - and then subscribing to your other channels through the Amazon app so all the billing goes through one place.

You only pay for the Roku device one time. There's no monthly cost associated with having a Roku, and if you were so inclined, you could buy one and only use the free channels.

Nearly all channels offer free trials (usually either 7 or 30 days), and the vast majority allow you to log in online and cancel your account without calling anyone on the phone and waiting on hold.

Some cable companies do offer Acorn TV or BritBox, but we generally don't recommend it if you're able to subscribe another way. We see a lot of reader complaints about poor service or inability to cancel without lengthy phone calls to customer service.

Why is Amazon charging me for — show?

This is another area that causes a lot of misunderstanding and frustration. Amazon offers a giant video marketplace, and there are different types of access within the system.

- **IMDb TV Shows** - Shows in this "section" are free to all with ads.
- **Prime Video** - If you're an Amazon Prime member (or purely a Prime Video member), you get access to a larger set of programmes which are included in the price of membership. Sometimes, only the older seasons of a show are included in this membership.
- **Channel Subscriptions** - Dozens of channels make their programming available through Amazon's platform. That includes Acorn TV, BritBox, Sundance Now, and many of the others in this guide. You pay for these channels on top of the basic Amazon Prime or Prime Video fee. An Acorn TV or BritBox subscription won't give you access to all British TV shows on Amazon - only those offered by Acorn TV or BritBox.
- **Rentals & Purchases** - Some shows are not included in any of the plans above (or you may choose to buy/rent them instead of subscribing to a channel). It's a bit like when we all went to the local video store for things not offered on our cable packages. If you really wanted to see it, you could pay a bit extra to get it right away…or wait and hope it showed up on one of your channels eventually.

Where are the rest of the episodes of Season --- of --- show?

If you only see the first couple episodes of a season, don't panic. Many streaming services "drip" episodes - especially if the show is brand new and they're airing it alongside the UK Release dates.

Other times, they do it because they want to give people an incentive to stay subscribed for a longer period of time.

If you don't like it (some people have trouble remembering all the details), there's a very easy solution. Just use Wikipedia or IMDB.com to verify how many episodes are in the season, then you can calculate the ideal time to start watching so you don't forget anything in between episodes.